MESSIER

MES

ALSO BY JEFF Z. KLEIN

The Hockey Compendium
Mario Lemieux
The Coolest Guys on Ice
The Death of Hockey

SIER

JEFF Z. KLEIN

TRIUMPH
BOOKS
CHICAGO

For my mother, my father, and my sister,
with gratitude and, most of all, with love.

————

Library of Congress Control Number: 2003096054

Jacket photograph: © Gregory Heisler / Corbis Outline / Magma
Jacket design: CS Richardson
Text design: Valerie Applebee
Printed and bound in the USA

ISBN 1-57243-591-7

Published in Canada by Doubleday Canada,
a division of Random House of Canada Limited

CONTENTS

MARK MESSIER

CENTER/LEFT WING

BORN JAN. 18, 1961 — EDMONTON, ALTA.

HEIGHT AS PRO 6.00–6.01 — WEIGHT AS PRO 190–213 POUNDS

★   Won Stanley Cup.   ☆   Won international tournament.
*   Led league in category.   a   Schedule shortened by lockout to 48 games.

		REGULAR SEASON						PLAYOFFS					
SEASON	TEAM	GP	G	A	Pts	+/-	PiM	GP	G	A	Pts	+/-	PiM
76–77	Spruce Grove AJHL	57	27	39	55	—	91						
77–78	St. Albert AJHL	54	25	49	74	—	194						
77–78	Portland WHL							7	4	1	5	—	2
78–79	St. Albert AJHL	17	15	18	33	—	64						
78–79	Indianapolis WHA	5	0	0	0	—	0						
78–79	Cincinnati WHA	47	1	10	11	—	58	0	0	0	0	—	0
79–80	Edmonton NHL	75	12	21	33	-10	120	3	1	2	3	+2	2
79–80	Houston CHL	4	0	3	3		4						
80–81	Edmonton NHL	72	23	40	63	-12	102	9	2	5	7	+1	13
81–82	Edmonton NHL	78	50	38	88	+21	119	5	1	2	3	-4	8
82–83	Edmonton NHL	77	48	58	106	+19	72	15	15	6	21	+10	14
83–84★	Edmonton NHL	73	37	64	101	+40	165	19	8	18	26	+9	19
84–85★	Edmonton NHL	55	23	31	54	+8	57	18	12	13	25	+13	12
85–86	Edmonton NHL	63	35	49	84	+36	68	10	4	6	10	even	18
86–87★	Edmonton NHL	77	37	70	107	+21	73	21	12	16	28	+13	16
87–88★	Edmonton NHL	77	37	74	111	+21	103	19	11	23	34	+9	29
88–89	Edmonton NHL	72	33	61	94	-5	130	7	1	11	12	-1	8
89–90★	Edmonton NHL	79	45	84	129	+19	79	22	9	22*	31	+5	20
90–91	Edmonton NHL	53	12	52	64	+15	34	18	4	11	15	+2	16
91–92	NY Rangers NHL	79	35	72	107	+31	76	11	7	7	14	-4	6
92–93	NY Rangers NHL	75	25	66	91	-6	72						
93–94★	NY Rangers NHL	76	26	58	84	+25	76	23	12	18	30	+14	33
1995a	NY Rangers NHL	46	14	39	53	+8	40	10	3	10	13	-11	8
95–96	NY Rangers NHL	74	47	52	99	+29	122	11	4	7	11	-10	16
96–97	NY Rangers NHL	71	36	48	84	+12	88	15	3	9	12	+2	6
97–98	Vancouver NHL	82	22	38	60	-10	58						
98–99	Vancouver NHL	59	13	35	48	-12	33						
99–00	Vancouver NHL	66	17	37	54	-15	30						
00–01	NY Rangers NHL	82	24	43	67	-25	89						
01–02	NY Rangers NHL	41	7	16	23	-1	32						
02–03	NY Rangers NHL	78	18	22	40	-2	30						

INTERNATIONAL

Season	Team Canada	GP	G	A	Pts	+/-	PiM
1984☆	Canada Cup	8	2	4	6	-3	8
1987☆	Canada Cup	9	1	6	7	+2	6
1989	World Championship	6	3	3	6	—	8
1991☆	Canada Cup	8	2	6	8	+7	10
1996	World Cup	7	1	4	5	-5	12

REGULAR SEASON TOTALS

		GP	G	A	Pts	+/-	PiM
24 yrs	NHL	1680	676	1168	1844	+207	1868
12 yrs	Edmonton	851	392	642	1034	+173	1122
9 yrs	NY Rangers	622	232	416	648	+71	625
3 yrs	Vancouver	207	52	110	162	-37	121
1 yr	WHA	52	1	10	11	—	58

PLAYOFF TOTALS

		GP	G	A	Pts	+/-	PiM	
17 yrs	NHL	236	109	186	295	+50	244	
12 yrs	Edmonton	166	80	135	215	+59	175	
5 yrs	NY Rangers	70	29	51	80	-9	69	
3 yrs	Vancouver							
1 yr	WHA	0	0	0	0	—	0	(did not dress)

INTERNATIONAL TOTALS

		GP	G	A	Pts	+/-	PiM
5 yrs	Canada	38	9	23	32	—	44

- NHL career regular-season rankings: No.2 in games played, No.6 in goals, No.2 in assists, No.3 in points.
- NHL career playoff rankings: No.1 in games played, No.2 in goals, No.2 in assists, No.2 in points.
- Winner of Hart Trophy 1990, 92; Lester B. Pearson Award 90, 92; Conn Smythe Trophy 84.
- Named to NHL First All-Star Team at left wing 1982, 83, at center 90, 92; Second All-Star Team at left wing 84. Played in 14 NHL All-Star Games (1982–84, 86, 88–92, 94, 96–98, 00) and both games of Rendez-Vous '87: totals, 16 games, 6 goals, 13 assists, 19 points, 4 penalty minutes.
- Captain, Edmonton 1988–89 through 90–91; New York Rangers 91–92 through 96–97 and 00–01 through 02–03; Vancouver 97–98 through 99–00.

INTRODUCTION

Mark Messier is playing hockey on television as these words are being written, and despite the advancing years his presence on the ice seems entirely appropriate. He has just hit the goalpost with a wrist shot, and now he is a bit late getting to his own end on the backcheck, although the same thing happens all the time to just about every player, including those twenty years younger than he. A few minutes ago he won a face-off and worked over the opponent he had beaten on the draw with a subtle glove to the face and a wicked little slash across the upper arm, the kind of thing he has done forever. But that's the thing about Messier—it feels as if he has always been there, yet he still seems like someone who started in the league just five or ten years ago. Watching Messier in 2003 is not the same thing as watching, say, Gordie Howe in the early '70s, when Howe was getting well into his forties and was still good but clearly old, or watching Stan Mikita at the end of the '70s, when he had ceased to be a factor but was still taking turns more or less for old time's sake. To see Messier play is not to be reminded of how old he is, but rather to think of him as you would any other current player who is a central component on his team. You could certainly argue that he has not done well in that central role for quite a while, given the performance of the Canucks and Rangers under his captaincy the last several years, but that merely proves the point that he still plays a central role: even if Messier is not the player he used to be, he is still very much an active force in 2003, more so even than when he turned pro in 1978.

Consider how vastly different hockey was in 1978, when the seventeen-year-old Messier joined the Indianapolis Racers of the World Hockey Association. The game was only eleven years removed from the ingrown, provincial days of the "Original Six," only six years past Paul Henderson's epochal goal in the Summit Series. Foreign players were still a novelty in the pro leagues, and they were almost exclusively Swedes or Finns. There was one Czechoslovak, no Russians—or more properly, Soviets, because the USSR was still more than a decade from dissolution—and, hardest of all to believe, only a handful of Americans. The game was only starting to open up to influences from outside Canada. Meanwhile, big-league hockey, having burst out of its little six-team cocoon, was still swarming across the continent: of the twenty-four clubs then operating in the NHL and WHA in 1978, thirteen were less than nine years old. There had been overexpansion, too much too fast, to be sure, but the WHA was entering its final season and the sport was beginning to settle into a stronger, more mature position.

The cities that got hockey teams during this supernova-like period of growth weren't the same Sun Belt, suburban-sprawl, Tobacco Road destinations that would mark a later round of NHL overexpansion at the turn of the millennium. True, there were the Atlanta Flames and Birmingham Bulls— but they were more than made up for by young teams in places that had long lived and breathed hockey: Vancouver, Buffalo, Quebec, Winnipeg, New England, and of course, Edmonton. Among fans, there was a feeling of excitement and optimism about the game, a sense that big-time hockey was finally coming home to all the places where it ought to be played. Within a couple of seasons the Atlanta team would move north to Calgary, a transfer that today seems as counter to the natural order as water flowing uphill.

On the ice, the game was rugged, still very much steeped in the wild era of the Broad Street Bullies and the film *Slap Shot*. Many of those who shared the ice with the young Messier wore muttonchops and playoff beards and tended to eschew helmets. The boards and ice were white and pure, uncluttered by advertisements. Cable television was in its infancy, there was no Internet, no all-sports radio or television stations; most fans got their news about the game through the newspapers and from whatever reports aired on conventional radio and TV. The teenaged Messier played in the Winnipeg Arena, beneath a huge portrait of the Queen, and in Le Colisée, where public address announcements were made exclusively in French. The next year, in the NHL, he would skate at the Forum, Maple Leaf Gardens, Boston Garden, Chicago Stadium, Memorial Auditorium, the St. Louis Arena, the Met Center, and a half-dozen other buildings now demolished or devoid of hockey. The tactics of the game were about to change, too, in large part because of Messier and his future teammates; it would be transformed into a wide-open, high-scoring rush to the net in which goalies, clad in skinny pads and some still wearing Jacques Plante–style facemasks, could count themselves lucky to stop nine shots out of ten while their teammates gamboled carefree at the other end of the ice.

This was the now-vanished world that Messier entered when he turned pro. But he was already a different type of player than those alongside whom he began playing. Intelligent, curious, eager for new experiences, he would eventually develop interests far beyond hockey, yet he would direct all of the mental and spiritual proceeds of those interests back into his own total involvement in the game. From his father he learned how to motivate and how to lead, and from his boyhood he thrived in the world of the team. When he began as a pro, he was cocky, raw, an undisciplined hellion eager to challenge the status quo by skipping junior hockey and getting right to the money and excitement of the big leagues, and eager, too, to challenge the players he opposed on the ice, often with his stick and his fists in that anything-goes era. He quickly became something of an adjunct to a young teammate who was already being recognized as the greatest player ever, but in that shadow he thrived and learned so that when the team became his, he was sophisticated, worldly, disciplined, and a strong enough leader to will his teammates to victory. He played for his nation and helped restore its self-respect in the only sport it really cared about, he moved to New York and became the toast of a town notoriously indifferent to hockey, he took a leading role in the struggle between the players' union and management, and he became the paragon of sports leadership. He spent three years on the west coast, where he failed completely, and it seemed as if his legend had gotten too big, too exaggerated; then he returned to New York where, despite his inability to improve the team's miserable fortunes, the level of respect directed toward him remained so high that he retained a central role, probably long after it should have been denied him. Yet at the same time, he was there to help lift the city's spirits after an unspeakable act plunged it into its darkest hour. Where most players, even most great players, have careers traced in one or two arcs, Messier's spans four, five, six.

Many people see Messier as a latter-day Gordie Howe, which arguably makes him this era's Mr. Hockey, and indeed, the game itself has risen and fallen with him. When Messier was a young Edmonton Oiler, a Team Canada mainstay, and then a mature but still youthful New York Ranger, hockey was healthy, its fans were happy, and the future of the game looked bright indeed. It may be only coincidence, but in the years when Messier was no longer called on to play for his country, when he left the Rangers in a swirl of mutual ill will to go to Vancouver and then made misstep after misstep in trying to lead the Canucks, the game's fortunes also seemed to decline. By the time he returned to finish out his career in the city he loved most, hockey was practically invisible in New York and in most of the rest of the United States, where it was a victim of almost universal apathy, while in Canada a huge percentage of fans were alienated from a league grown overlarge, overdiluted, and overpriced.

A quarter-century into Messier's career, hockey may have its problems, but it has the legend of Messier, too. He has been cited as a role model by a generation of players, the number-one hockey hero for a group that ranges across borders and races and genders, from Eric Lindros to Mike Grier to Hayley Wickenheiser. He is unbelievably durable, having undergone surgery only once as one of the toughest players in the toughest sport. The force of his charisma is so undeniably strong that certain moments stand out vividly in the collective memory: skating down the ice with Gretzky and Lemieux in the titanic struggles against the Soviets in the Canada Cup; holding the Stanley Cup high over his head in the corner of the Northlands Coliseum, ecstatically displaying it to family and friends; his guarantee of victory in game six of the Rangers' semifinal series against the Devils. At the same time his forcefulness has left distinctly different impressions wherever his career has taken him: in Edmonton, he's the home-town bad-boy hero; in Vancouver he's a bum; in New York he's a god.

It is probably true that more has been supposed about Messier's personal experiences than about any other player's in the history of the game. He has successfully guarded his eventful private life to a remarkable extent over the course of his long career, and even though he has always given his unflagging cooperation to the press in pregame and postgame situations, dutifully supplying reporters with quotes no matter how well or poorly the team has done, actual one-on-one, in-depth interviews with Messier have been exceedingly rare. While he does nothing to obstruct those who attempt to profile him, neither does he do anything to cooperate with them. Rick Carpiniello, a beat reporter for *The Journal News* in suburban Westchester County, has traveled with and covered the Rangers on a daily basis for every year of Messier's tenure with the team, yet when Carpiniello wrote a biography of him in 1999, Messier politely declined to be interviewed for it. The same is true for this book. Neither Messier nor any members of his family would agree to be interviewed; concerns for Mark's privacy were cited, and I believe it is to his credit that he has preserved that privacy while living what is clearly a very busy, public, and rich life.

At some point, perhaps, he will agree to have his story told in his own words. But he has not yet, because he believes that to do so would mean he was looking back at a career that has finished. Messier has played on and on and on, as a credible, vital presence in the game, in part because he tried never to speak about himself in the past tense, and he has taken offense at any attempt to press him on the subject of retirement. When he does retire, he will announce it on his own terms, keeping charge of the decision and of its dissemination as skillfully as he has kept charge of every other public aspect of his business and personal affairs.

In the meantime, his long and on the whole successful career has left in its wake a record of admiration that, if it were simply to be transcribed and printed up, would fill a book in its own right. All the quotes from so many of Messier's teammates and coaches praising him so fulsomely, so often, over so many years, begin to feel almost pornographic in their enthusiastic repetition;

if you were to search for a statement of sincere, positive appreciation for the various qualities of Mark Messier, you would have, I'd say, about 100,000 to choose from. I've tried to keep these to a minimum, but it remains true that at any point over the previous two decades, you'll find a lot of people expressing praise for him, for the same things and in the same terms. That fact is reflected in this book.

I've also tried to include as complete a record as possible of Messier's career, giving roughly equal weight to each portion of it. Past accounts of his life have tended to concentrate on one area at the expense of another—say, zeroing in on his first stint with the Rangers while glossing over his many accomplishments with Team Canada—but I felt that it was important to examine the whole thing. It has been at times a strange experience for me to be delving so deeply into Messier's life, almost as if he were a historical figure, then to be standing three feet away from him amid the general media scrum after a Ranger game, asking him how it felt to score a goal before the home crowd.

One time at the Rangers' training camp in Burlington, Vermont, I sat alongside Doug Messier, Mark's father, and we made small talk for a couple of minutes. Then I told him that I was the one he'd heard about who was writing a biography of his son, and he replied immediately, apologetically, but firmly that he never took part in such projects and proceeded to move to another seat several rows away. It may sound odd, and it certainly didn't make my job any easier, but I really do admire the way the Messiers value their own privacy and the consistency with which they guard it.

I'm also reminded of the portion of an afternoon I spent with Jim Matheson, who graciously agreed to meet with me while I was in Edmonton researching this book. Matheson has covered the Oilers for the *Edmonton Journal* since the team's inception in the World Hockey Association in 1972. He reported on Messier, on a daily basis, from Messier's teenage years all the way up through his fifth Stanley Cup and beyond. "He was so curious about the world," Matheson told me. "He shouldn't have been a hockey player. He should have been an explorer or a surfer or something."

Wow, I said, he sounds like an interesting guy—did you get to know him well?

"No, I never really did, not in all those years," Matheson answered. "He was very careful about who he let get close to him." In trying to tell Messier's story I have interviewed people who know or have known him; others I have spoken with in less formal, off-the-record conversations. I have also referred, as exhaustively as possible, to the published accounts of the events in which he has played a role. Sometimes it seems as though he has taken part in everything that has happened in the game over the last thirty years. His life, it seems to me, is very much a life of hockey, very much *the* life of hockey.

HALLSY

Mark Douglas Messier was born to the hockey life in Edmonton on January 18, 1961. He was the third child of Doug Messier and the former Mary Jean Dea. The oldest, Paul, was born in 1958 and was bound for a pro hockey career of his own. Mark arrived between his two sisters, Mary-Kay and Jennifer, the three of them separated by just one year apiece.

Doug Messier was twenty-five years old at Mark's birth and was attending the University of Alberta, where he played on the varsity team. Doug, craggy, flinty-eyed, and crowned with a regulation crewcut, was in many ways a typical hockey player, having come up through the youth ranks in Vermilion, Alberta, and on the south side of Edmonton. He was good enough as a teenager to make the grade as a defenseman with the Edmonton Oil Kings in the provincial junior league. Twice he made the league all-star team, and in his last season he led all defensemen in scoring with 20 goals and 20 assists. His NHL rights belonged to Detroit, but at twenty-one he went to England for a one-season stint with Nottingham, where Paul was born, then returned and played for the Lacombe Rockets of the provincial intermediate league for a couple of seasons. Around the time Mark was born, Doug made his North American pro debut, putting in five games as a defenseman with the Seattle Totems of the Western Hockey League.

Doug was on his way to becoming a minor-league lifer at a time when the minors meant a great deal more than they do today. Starting in the 1920s and continuing through the mid-'60s, the "bus leagues" comprised a world unto themselves, at varying times either strongly or loosely affiliated with the National Hockey League. Sometimes a career at this level was attractive and secure enough to make players pass up a job in the NHL: Jean Béliveau was content enough with the Quebec Aces, for instance, to force the Montreal Canadiens to buy out the entire Quebec Senior League to get him into the *bleu, blanc, et rouge*. Johnny Bower spent eight happy years with the Cleveland Barons of the American Hockey League, resisting offers from NHL sides, before the Maple Leafs finally landed him. Willie O'Ree, famous as the NHL's first black player for two brief stints with the Boston Bruins in 1957–58 and '60–61, ought to be better remembered for his twenty-one years of steady minor-league play, including fourteen with Los Angeles and San Diego of the Western league. Many other players of lesser renown also carved out long, respectable careers in the minors: Fred Glover was a Baron for sixteen seasons; Larry Wilson was a Buffalo Bison for thirteen; Guyle Fielder was a Seattle Totem, American, or Bomber for fifteen years, on top of which he logged seven seasons on various other Western league clubs.

But Doug Messier was not an entirely typical hockey player. He attended the University of North Dakota and then the University of Alberta en route to a degree in education. And the reason for his year in England with the Nottingham Panthers was not simply to try his hand at playing the pro game overseas; he also wanted to enroll at Nottingham University. According to a 1958 article in *Ice Hockey World*, a British weekly, he arrived in the fall of 1957 intending to pursue an engineering degree, only to find the courses full and the student list closed, so he concentrated on hockey and did some construction work. He played 53 games with the Panthers that season, recording 5 goals, 35 assists, and 107 penalty minutes. The article also says that Doug had been invited to the Detroit Red Wings' training camp in 1956, but he turned down the invitation; his own father was in the oil business, and at the time Doug was involved in a business inspecting shot holes for oil drillers. He would have to wait till the following autumn to continue his university studies, which, he figured, would take three to six years to complete.

In any case, Seattle was his first stop in the WHL, a loop whose cities were so far west of the westernmost NHL outpost, Chicago, that it was practically an alternative major league. Doug would play nine seasons in the WHL—a total of 487 games in which he scored 65 goals and 193 assists for a respectable 258 points, amassing a robust 790 penalty minutes. In the fall of 1961, when he was taking courses at the University of Alberta, Doug caught on with another WHL club, the Edmonton Flyers. In the first of his two years with the Flyers, the team won the Lester Patrick Trophy as league champions, and Doug contributed 12 points in 12 playoff games. He split '63–64 with four teams: the Pittsburgh Hornets of the American Hockey League, the Indianapolis Capitols and Cincinnati Wings of the Central Professional league (the Capitols' rink was destroyed in an explosion, so the team moved to Cincinnati), and finally, the Portland Buckaroos of the WHL, to whom he was sold as the second half of the season got under way. This last move would have a lasting effect on young Mark.

The Messier family lived well in Portland, a small, vibrant city set in a striking Pacific Northwest landscape. They resided on a small farm in nearby Beaverton, where they kept horses and the kids did farm chores, and they also had a log cabin on Mount Hood. They went to the cabin in the summer and, when Doug's schedule permitted, during hockey season as well. The Messiers were well known for doing things together. "They were a regular family," recalled Mike Donaldson, Doug Messier's defense partner for a few seasons in Portland, and one of perhaps a dozen Buckaroos who continue to live in the Portland area more than three decades after their playing careers ended. "They were very close, very nice. You'd always see them together, getting ready to drive off someplace. At the rink, Mark would come out and skate with Doug after practice. He was just seven years old."

Doug wore sweater number 11 for the Buckaroos, with whom he spent more consecutive years than at any other stop in his playing career. The stories that were later told, in the interests of spinning a good yarn, tended to exaggerate the toughness he displayed on the blue line, depicting him as a man possessed by a colorfully implacable rage. In fact, he was not exactly the one-dimensional, old-time blood-and-guts sort that some remember; he used his time with the Buckaroos to complete his master's degree in education at the University of Portland. On the ice, his penalty totals were fairly high for the era, but he was hardly in Dave Schultz territory; he usually was second on the team in penalty minutes, behind either Donaldson or Connie "Mad Dog" Madigan.

Part of the reason for the exaggeration may be put down to the nature of minor-league hockey in those days. Rinks had glass—or, more often, chicken wire—only atop the end boards. Along the sides of the rink, there was no barrier separating the fans from the ice, nor was there any behind the benches and penalty box; fans were, in effect, on their honor not to lean over and grab or punch players. Naturally, that arrangement proved impossible to abide by on those occasions when passions ran high. Donnybrooks involving fans and players were a fairly frequent occurrence from the nineteenth century all the way through to the 1960s, and there was little of the outrage and high dudgeon that commentators affect on those very rare occasions when a fan takes a swipe at a player at a North American sports event today. On the ice, there was no specific rule forbidding third men in or bench-clearing brawls, and although those types of shenanigans were fairly infrequent during the early and mid-'60s, they happened often enough to lend a hard-man sheen to an already rugged time.

That said, Doug Messier was unquestionably a hard-nosed player. And he was physically strong, spending some off-seasons loading cement trucks— "each bag weighed $87\frac{1}{2}$ pounds," he remembered, "and it was sort of a competition to load the truck three bags at a time." Donaldson said, "The way I would describe Doug is that he was authoritative, he had intensity, emotion, he was even crude at times. By crude I mean he would hit you so hard . . . You definitely got the impression that he was not to be fooled with." Donaldson could as easily have been talking about Mark as Doug.

Mark and the kids he ran with loved to play hockey, and they were at it all the time. "He and Paul both wanted to play so badly," Mary-Kay said. "They always wanted to go to practice. They played continuously for hours and hours. It didn't matter if they had skates on, or whether they had to play in the road, or whether they were shooting the ball against the wall and breaking neighbors' windows, or whatever." Mark started playing organized youth hockey in Portland at age five and was on what his boyhood friends recall as a "great team." His teammates included Patrick Schmautz, a boy whose family had a cabin on the other side of the Highway 26 footbridge, and Grant Sasser, a Portlander who would go on to a successful junior career and a brief stint in the NHL.

The members of the Messier family developed an unusual closeness early on, when the four children were still toddlers. It was a trait that would last through the decades to follow. "We traveled a lot, which was really fine because I think that contributed to us being a really close-knit group," Mary-Kay recalled in a video/DVD called *Mark Messier: Leader, Champion, Legend*, which is so far the only biography of Messier in any medium to receive the imprimatur of full cooperation from Mark and his family. "We had friends when we moved to cities and whatnot, but because we traveled so much together and moved a lot we became really close." There is a home movie of the four Messier kids, taken when Mark was two or three. They are sitting on the floor beneath a Christmas tree, arranged by age, with Paul getting into position at the end of the line. Mary-Kay is next, then Mark, holding one-year-old Jenny in his lap. When Paul takes his place, they all look up happily, but Mark's whole face lights up as he breaks into the thousand-watt, open-mouthed smile he would later become famous for. On his lap, Jenny's face lights up, too.

By the time they settled in Oregon, the Messiers were a model of togetherness, and when you talk to people who knew them in Portland, it is often the cabin on Mount Hood that they tell you about. "Their cabin was on the Salmon River, along one side of Highway 26," recalled Don Bucher, who played on the same team as Paul Messier when Paul was twelve and Mark was seven. "We'd play street hockey on the footbridge over the highway." Don's older brother, Sherm Bucher, remembered it, too: "They had a pond up there, and in the winter it would freeze over and the kids would come up and play. Doug never played—he was always afraid that he'd forget himself and act on impulse. He was so competitive, he was afraid he'd do something totally accidentally in the heat of the action and forget who he was playing with. So he never scrimmaged with the kids. He'd show them stuff and teach them some things, but as soon as they started playing, no matter what age they were, he made sure he was off the ice."

The cabin had a record player, but no telephone or television. According to an article by Tom Friend in *ESPN Magazine*: "The children complained of boredom, so Doug and his wife, Mary Jean (a former Miss Teen Edmonton), urged them to 'take a walk or pick flowers.' Mark began carving wood with his father, while others swam in a nearby creek, and at dusk, the family played its favorite card game, BS Poker. As a reward, Doug began playing the only music he'd brought along—two 45s: 'Raindrops Keep Fallin' on My Head' and 'Walk On By.' He'd play them over and over, and the Messier children soon realized they did not need to be entertained. They realized the power of conversation and listening."

Amid this idyllic family setting, Mark was something of a cut-up, doing impersonations of Miss Piggy and Tim Conway, fooling around with his friends and with his older brother's friends. "We always thought of Mark as 'the little Messier kid,'" Sherm Bucher said, and Don Bucher remembered him as "the little brother we always beat up on." Patrick Schmautz was the son of Doug's Buckaroos teammate Arnie Schmautz and played with Mark in the Portland Amateur Hockey Association, even though Mark was three years younger. "We played a lot of street hockey together because our fathers were together," Schmautz said. "Our dads would practice and we'd all get our skates after our practice, and we'd have time to go out on and play on the ice too. No one thought about guys like Mark very much, since we were ten-year-olds and he was just seven. We used to beat up on him."

Sherm Bucher said, "We used to think of Paul as the hockey player, as the future pro." But, Don Bucher remembered, "Doug always used to say that Mark would be the one who'd make it." One kid who used to pal around with the Messiers remembers something from when Mark was six or seven: "In Portland they used to live near the Portland Golf Club. One time Doug said, 'Let's go for a swim at the Golf Club pool.' Mark said, 'We can't.' Doug asked why not. Mark said we'd just had sandwiches, and we had to wait an hour before we could go swimming. Doug asked what would happen if we didn't. Mark said, 'We'd get craps.'"

Portland was an easy city to live in, and the Bucks were a winning team playing in Memorial Coliseum, a new rink built in the International style. In the six years of Doug's tenure with the club, they finished the regular season in first place five times in a row—an excellent record, even if the league had only five, six, or seven teams in those years. They got to the Patrick Trophy finals four times with Doug and won the title once, in 1965. Doug was also an early member of the first full-fledged hockey players union, the Professional Hockey Players Association. It was organized by Western leaguers, including some of his Portland teammates.

In the age before big media—Buckaroos games weren't even broadcast on local radio until 1970—to be a pro hockey player on a good club in the high minor leagues meant a comfortable middle-class existence accompanied by a modest amount of fame, the fun and camaraderie of being on a team, and fairly long-term job security without the cutthroat pressure of the NHL. Portland, like many minor-league clubs at the time, was run as an independent team rather than as the affiliate, or farm club, of a National league side. Today it's hard to conceive of a minor league team as a fully independent, self-sufficient, self-directed entity, but that's the way hockey worked then. Players were far less likely to get traded around by general managers based in distant cities, and players and their families had a chance to develop real roots in a community.

Just as important, if less tangible, under this arrangement was the sense of success and accomplishment it afforded everyone, even the young boys growing up together. "Our dads were doing something we thought was pretty cool," Patrick Schmautz said. "We all had it in our blood. One of my fond memories of that time is when our dads would be playing at Memorial Coliseum. We'd go up in the corner of the concourse, where the floor was almost perfectly smooth, and we'd play hockey with these little souvenir sticks or with our feet. We'd use a pair of shoes for the goal and a smashed paper cup as a puck. None of the ushers bothered us—they knew who we were." Mark's personality was shaped by the warmth and fun and high sense of self-esteem he experienced during the family's Portland years, and much of it had to do with hockey. He couldn't bear to be away from the game. "The family yarn," his future Oilers teammate Kevin Lowe wrote, "is that Mark would bawl his head off and run after his father's car down the street if Doug left for the rink without him." He wound up serving as the Bucks' stickboy.

Mark was seven when Doug retired from the Buckaroos, and his pro career, at the end of the 1968–69 season. The family moved back to

Edmonton, where Doug would serve as player-coach of the Edmonton Monarchs in the provincial senior league, and settled in St. Albert, a leafy town adjacent to Edmonton on the northwest, founded in 1861 as a Catholic enclave for French-Canadians and Métis. Doug soon hung up his skates for good to concentrate on coaching, and his two sons plunged eagerly into a more competitive minor hockey environment than they had experienced in Oregon.

At about the same time that Doug and his sons were making this transition, the World Hockey Association was emerging to challenge the NHL. The Alberta Oilers, one of the WHA's twelve original teams, debuted in the intimate Edmonton Gardens in 1972, part of an upstart league signing away NHL stars and causing a salary boom that briefly made hockey the highest-paying pro sport in the world. Just as importantly, the WHA was bringing big-league hockey to Canadian cities long shut out of the NHL's closed fraternity.

It was an exciting time in Edmonton, a dusty place dominated by train yards, refineries, and warehouses. The only city of any size located more than 100 miles above the 49th parallel, it lay so far to the north that the aurora borealis shimmered on midsummer nights and the winters were bone-crackingly cold, but it was also about to become flush with oil money and just a couple of years away from opening the Northlands Coliseum, which would be three times the size of the Edmonton Gardens.

Against this backdrop, Paul's youth career thrived. At the start of the 1973–74 season, at age fifteen and with two years of midget eligibility still remaining, he made the Edmonton Mets of the Alberta Junior league, the Tier II provincial junior circuit. For the 1974–75 season the team moved to the suburb of Spruce Grove, and there, with Doug as coach and Paul at center, working the point on the power play, and scoring at an MVP rate of nearly two points per game, the Mets won the 1975 Centennial Cup, the national championship of Tier II junior hockey. The following year father and son again reached the final with Spruce Grove, and though they lost, Paul was again a star of the team. Mark sometimes served as stickboy. Meanwhile, at home, Paul and Mark still shared a room, festooned with posters of Bobby Orr, Guy Lafleur, and Bobby Clarke.

As a player, Mark was coming up quickly, too. George Cassidy, the manager of Mark's peewee team, remembered the contrast between the ten-year-old's ease in social situations and his ferocity on the ice. "His dad would bring him to our house," Cassidy said, "and he would go in and play with my one-and-a-half-year-old daughter. It was hard to believe the difference when he was playing, because when he played, he forgot everything. He just would play with such intensity." Ray Lamer, his AA bantam coach, was impressed by that trademark focus as well. "I remember him as being the most intense player before a game I ever saw," he said. "Like all kids, he fooled around, but when it came time for games he'd get up for them. To be truthful, in those days I had no idea he'd end up being one of the best players in the world, but the thing I really remember that set him apart was that when he came into the dressing room, he sat down and got himself ready to play, and when it was game time, he had that look. He got quiet, didn't want to be bothered. He wanted to get going. Preparing himself like that—that probably came from Doug."

While Doug's influence was undeniable, at that point in Mark's development as a player, Mary Jean played at least as big a role. "My dad would be tied up with my brother playing junior hockey," Mark said in the family history, "and my mother would be the one who would be taking me to my games. And I could talk to her about the game just like I'd be talking to my dad." At this point in his hockey life, Mark's nickname was Hallsy, as in "Mess Hall."

At fourteen, when he was still eligible to play bantam, Mark was playing with Knights of Columbus Colts at the midget level. He says he scored "less than twenty goals" that year, which he found disappointing, and the team had a mediocre season. Still, he resolved to leap to the next level: the Spruce Grove Mets in Tier II junior, coached by his father. The next summer, with Paul on his way to study at Denver University and play for its NCAA hockey team, Mark tried out for the Mets. "We rode to and from training camp together in the same car for a month," Doug told Cam Cole of the *Edmonton Journal* in a 1977 article, "and I don't think he said two words to me. He never asked how he was doing or whether he was going to make it or not. Around the house he was grumpy as a bear, but to me, he never said a word. To tell the truth, I didn't think he could make the team. I had a few misgivings about whether to let him come up, just wondering if he was ready. But I knew he wanted to make it really badly because his brother came up as a fifteen-year-old." Doug really did have his doubts. One evening at home, Mark came across a copy of the Mets' roster in the dining room. Three question marks were written next to his name.

Mark did indeed make the team that fall, and after 41 games of the 1976–77 season he had tallied 48 points as a centerman, Cole wrote, of "startling poise." He stood five foot ten and weighed 165 pounds—fairly big for a fifteen-year-old—was a fixture on the power play, and had 23 goals, one short of the team lead. "I think it's the work on my skating that's helped me the most," he told Cole. "I couldn't skate when I got to camp and I thought I was finished." Mark said he was whipped into shape by the hard drills run by his father, who "doesn't treat me any better or any worse than any of the other guys." He added that he was inspired by his brother. "Yeah, I wanted to take after Paul," Mark said. "He's a heck of a hockey player. But I wanted it for myself, too. I wanted to prove—oh, I don't know." Mark, Cole wrote, didn't finish the sentence. He wound up that season with a 57-game total of 27 goals, 39 assists, and 91 penalty minutes. This early performance already bore the quintessential Messier trademarks that would define his professional career: excellent statistics, poise, the support and inspiration of family, a sense of enjoyment for the work of hockey, a mean streak, and a preternatural ability to fit into the social situation of the team.

The following year the Mets moved to St. Albert and became the Saints, and Doug and Mark came with them. Now Mark was the captain. His old bantam coach, Ray Lamer, came out to watch him play. "I hadn't seen him since he was about twelve, and he'd been really small then and not a good skater," he said. "The thing I couldn't believe when I watched that junior game was how he'd grown and how his skating style had changed. He used to have really choppy strides, but he'd become a really good skater." His teammates that season included future big-leaguers Mickey Volcan and Ken Solheim, and the team continued to be a powerhouse in the province. Mark, for his part now recognized locally as a phenom, played in 54 games and went 25–49–74 with 194 penalty minutes. Moreover, all his hanging around his father's teams over the years had made him intimately familiar with what to say and how to motivate. As captain, he took it on himself to take emotional charge of the players. When Doug would go into the dressing room to deliver one of his talks, he would arrive only to have the trainer tell him, "Don't worry, Doug, it's done. Number 11 already did it." As a coach, Doug believed in the motivational value of addressing his players. "I would have a lot of things to say verbally to a team about their commitment to the game, their commitment to each other," he said. "I always spent quite a bit of time trying to prepare teams for games." Before one particular game, he remembered: "I had a lot I wanted to talk to them about because it was a big game, and I walked in and I looked around the dressing room and everyone looked ready to go. And I realized then that Mark had already given the talk."

The Saints got to the league finals again but fell to the Calgary Canucks. Nevertheless, Mark had made an indelible impression. "He was big, strong, and very tough," Paul remembered. "Actually, he was a little bit mean. He always played with older kids, and he'd lose his temper. When he was seventeen, he already was 190 pounds. He was dominating the league, beating up everybody in Tier II." It was true enough, so it was not surprising when Mark moved up to major junior in what would be his only experience at the top rung of the junior hockey ladder. He joined the Portland Winter Hawks for the '78 Western league playoffs, and back in Memorial Coliseum, where he'd spent so much of his boyhood, he fit right in with a team full of incipient NHLers: Keith Brown, Larry Playfair, Wayne Babych, Brent Peterson, Paul Mulvey, Perry Turnbull, and Doug Lecuyer, among others. He was the youngest on the roster but still scored four goals and one assist in seven games. The Winter Hawks, though, crashed out of the playoffs.

Back in St. Albert, it seemed that more success lay ahead for 1978–79, with Mark returning and the Saints still a contender for the provincial title and the national title as well. But developments in the hockey world at large were changing the culture and economics of the game, in a way that would have an especially profound effect on Edmonton—and on Mark in particular. The WHA was starting its sixth season, and after some early rapid expansion some of its member clubs were now falling by the wayside. Originally, the league depended on Western and American league veterans to stock the bulk of its rosters and supply a fairly high level of play (Doug was approached about joining the original Oilers in 1972, when he was thirty-six, but he chose to stay in retirement), but after a couple of seasons the league, particularly Winnipeg, turned increasingly to Sweden and Finland for players—the first modest trickle of what would eventually become a flood of European talent onto North American rinks. Still, that wasn't enough to turn the ink in the teams' ledger books from red to black, so the WHA turned to another source of talent: underage Canadians. In the early '70s, NHL clubs would not sign anyone under twenty, leaving those players to their junior teams. But the WHA imposed no such restrictions, nor was it shy about paying teenagers well; in 1974, for example, the Vancouver Blazers signed Pat Price, a nineteen-year-old defenseman, to a six-year, $200,000-a-year contract.

Now the rebel league had its sights on even younger talent, namely Wayne Gretzky. The skinny kid out of Brantford had already been nationally famous, practically since he was a tot, for his enormous minor-hockey goal totals, and in 1977–78, at sixteen and in his only full season of major junior, he piled up 70 goals and 182 points for the Sault Ste. Marie Greyhounds. That June, Nelson Skalbania, who had made his fortune in real estate and was the owner of the WHA's Indianapolis Racers, entered into a brief negotiation with Gretzky's agent, Gus Badali, which was followed by a cross-country flight aboard Skalbania's private jet with Gretzky and his parents. During the flight, Gretzky signed a four-year contract for just under $1 million—a huge sum at the time, and that was that: Gretzky was going to be a seventeen-year-old pro in the World Hockey Association. The plane happened to land at Edmonton's Industrial Airport, and that's where the announcement of Gretzky's signing was made. "All my life, I've worked to become a professional hockey player," Gretzky said. "If I didn't take this opportunity and broke a leg or something back in the Soo, it could be all over."

The significance of this statement could not have been lost on Mark, nor could the rest of what Gretzky and his agent were talking about. "There's a war between two leagues, and I'm an agent with a client," Badali said. "How can I tell Wayne that he should not take nearly a million dollars from Indianapolis and go back to the Soo for $75 a week? What happens if he gets hurt? Better it should be $200,000 a year. Skalbania came to me. I did not go to him." As for Gretzky, he was happy that "the dream's come true," as he put it. "I never thought a player should be restricted from advancing because of his age. That's why I'm grateful to the WHA for giving me a chance to turn pro early." Signing Gretzky hardly seems like a gamble now, but nevertheless it did not work out for Skalbania. He had hired Gretzky (the contract was extended to seven years for a total of $1.75 million) to boost attendance in Indianapolis, where only 3,000 or 4,000 were showing up to games, and where the Racers reportedly needed to average 11,800 per game to break even. At first, Skalbania got a huge PR boost from the Gretzky signing, including a big feature in *Sports Illustrated*, perhaps the only place anyone in Indiana might stumble across any news about hockey. But Indianapolis is Indianapolis, and an average of fewer than 5,000 people turned out for Gretzky's four home games. Skalbania was running out of money fast, so he bailed. He told Gretzky that he was going to sell him to another team and offered a choice of Winnipeg or Edmonton. Badali told Gretzky to choose Edmonton, since the Oilers, he thought, had a better chance of making it to the NHL should the two leagues agree to a merger. Gretzky agreed, and he, forward Peter Driscoll, and goalie Eddie Mio were sold to the Oilers for $825,000.

In the November 3, 1978, edition of the *Edmonton Journal*, under the headline "Gretzky Is Now an Oiler!", Jim Matheson wrote about Gretzky's arrival in the city the day before. But the ninth and tenth paragraphs of the story stand out:

> In a strange twist, Skalbania also tried to sell centre Richie Leduc and defenceman John Hughes to Quebec Nordiques Thursday, but Nordiques couldn't come up with the necessary dough to complete the transaction.
>
> But that's a mild turn of events compared to this one. In the wake of the sale of the Boy Wonder, [the] Racers extended a five-game trial Thursday to St. Albert Saints forward Mark Messier. You guessed it. Messier is seventeen, and he plays centre like Gretzky.

Mark had started the season with St. Albert in October, but, as Doug later recounted, "He was in his third year and he'd gone from five-eleven and 155 to six-one and 195, and he looked like he was ready for more. But he didn't have a desire to play Tier I." His sister Mary-Kay remembered Mark itching for a higher level of play. "My dad could sense the fact that he was becoming stagnant," she said. "He was becoming frustrated with his own players, which wasn't like him, at practice. So I think they just decided that they had to let him go." Mark wanted to try the pros, and the WHA was clearly the place to do it. The whole league was keen on finding teenage diamonds in the rough; in the aftermath of Gretzky's initial signing with Skalbania, Birmingham Bulls owner John Bassett noted that he had six underage juniors he wanted to sign.

During the summer, Doug negotiated with the Colorado Rockies of the NHL on behalf of Paul, who wanted to turn pro after two years at Denver University. At the same time, Doug had started talking with his old Buckaroos teammate Pat Stapleton, who happened to be coaching the Racers, about Mark. Also during that summer, Mark tried out at the Edmonton selection camp for the Canadian Olympic Team that would play at the 1980 Games, still two years off, and is said to have done fairly well.

Paul wound up signing with Colorado, and Mark, soon afterward, signed for a five-game amateur trial with Indianapolis. The Racers thought that young Messier could be their replacement for the departed Gretzky, and they actually wanted to sign him outright to a pro contract. But Doug and Mark decided it would be better to go with the tryout instead; in case it didn't work out, Mark could return to junior with his amateur status intact. As it turned out, this was the beginning of both brothers' professional careers, and of Doug's career as his sons' agent, though he would not officially take that role for several years. In the same November 3 edition of the *Edmonton Journal* that recorded Gretzky's arrival, Cam Cole wrote an article headlined "St. Albert Junior Tries WHA":

> While the city is still buzzing about Edmonton Oilers'
> acquisition of a seventeen-year-old millionaire, here's an
> even stranger tale.
>   Mark Messier is a seventeen-year-old Tier II junior
> with St. Albert Saints who's going to Winnipeg Sunday
> to suit up with the Indianapolis Racers. That is, after he

plays today (vs. Taber Golden Suns) and Saturday (vs. Calgary Canucks) in St. Albert.

Nothing like this has ever happened in hockey before.

In the article, Doug sounded ambivalent about Mark's tryout with Indianapolis. "It's quite a decision," he said. "Whether he should play out his junior years or, if he can make a good buck right now, whether he should try to play pro hockey. I don't have the answer. Where would he develop better?" Doug added that if Mark did lose his amateur status by staying more than five games, and then the Racers folded, Mark would return to Edmonton to attend school, then go to the Portland Winter Hawks in major junior for the following season. But, he said of his son, "I think he can play pro, given the right circumstances." Mark's mother, Mary Jean, remembers the difficulty of the decision. "We had controversy over that," she said years later. "He was so young—he was only seventeen. I didn't want him to leave."

Mark departed to join the Racers after playing 13 games for St. Albert. His WHA debut came in Winnipeg on November 5, just two nights after Gretzky debuted as an Oiler, and he did nothing to appear in the summary of the game, a 6–2 Indianapolis loss. He didn't score in his next two games for the Racers, defeats at Cincinnati (4–0) and Quebec (8–2), but wearing sweater number 18, he did somehow register a plus-3 mark. The fourth game was a 6–1 loss to Edmonton in his hometown, and although he didn't score and went minus-2, he played aggressively and, according to Stapleton, "well enough to play pro hockey." Glen "Slats" Sather was the new coach of the Oilers, and he liked the way Messier played, too. "He made some mistakes defensively," Sather said, "but he wasn't afraid to bump people and go into the corners."

Mark returned to St. Albert for a couple more games, scored eight points, then played the fifth and final game of his tryout with Indianapolis on November 28, another outing at Northlands against the Oilers in which he went scoreless and his Racers lost yet again, by an 8–2 margin. The tryout was complete, but the Messiers held off on signing with Indianapolis—sensibly, as it turned out, and not only because the Racers lost all five games by a combined score of 32–7 while Mark was in the lineup. The club folded on December 15. Mark received one paycheck from the Racers. It bounced.

Nevertheless, Mark liked what he saw of the WHA; it was a challenge that suited him. He played another couple of games with St. Albert, then finished up with his father's team for good, compiling final totals for the season of 17 games played, 15 goals and 18 assists for 33 points, and 64 penalty minutes. Shortly before Christmas, he and Doug signed a full contract with the Cincinnati Stingers. Mark was a professional hockey player at last, if the phrase "at last" can be applied to a seventeen-year-old.

NOT EXACTLY
WAYNE GRETZKY

"**B**ig. Strong. Fast. Great shot. Physical. Mean. Durable. Great leader. What else could you possibly ask for in any individual?" That's what Ric Nattress said when asked to sum up Mark Messier's career. This assessment was made in December 2002, just before what may well have been Messier's final visit to the Calgary Saddledome, and Nattress, a Flames defenseman in the 1980s, was simply naming the qualities that most everyone cites when they talk about Messier. It's all true enough: Messier possesses all these traits. But there is one that Nattress left out, indeed which most analyses of the quintessential captain overlook: his intelligence. Messier is smart, and not just in a street-smart way, but in a way that is curious about the world, that can process information, analyze it, weigh its value. In later years, to listen to Messier talk to reporters game in and game out was to listen to someone with an expert facility with words and ideas. He never misspoke and rarely made a gaffe—instead displaying night after night the kind of sustained ease with words, the knowledge of how much to reveal and how much to gracefully obfuscate, that most politicians must strive to attain.

It is impossible to say, as it is for anyone, where Messier's intelligence came from. But while most people have looked to his father's influence to find precedent for his usual roster of attributes—Mark is tough like Doug, mean like Doug, strong like Doug, learned how to lead by watching Doug— their tendency to overlook Messier's intelligence may be a function of their equally glaring tendency to overlook his father's. As much as anything, Doug was a bright guy, the kind of guy who pursued an education overseas and then, while raising a family, a master's degree, in a time and environ- ment in which such a pursuit was highly unusual. And to do so while living the life of a professional hockey player, in an era when only about 17 per- cent of hockey pros completed their *high school* education, made it more remarkable still.

Doug and Mary Jean were raising their sons as hockey players, but they were also raising them with an eye toward a university education. That was why Doug kept both Paul and Mark at the Tier II level, with Spruce Grove and St. Albert, rather than let them play major junior. At Tier II, they retained their eligibility for collegiate play. "I was always a strong advocate of junior teams and against the major junior system, because education is not a big factor at major," Doug told Roy MacGregor in MacGregor's 1995 book *The Home Team: Fathers, Sons, and Hockey.* "I tried to stress the positive side of going to college on a scholarship." Paul did indeed go to college, if only for two years. For Mark, though, the attraction to professional hockey out- shone everything else, and his brief playoff stint with the Winter Hawks had complicated his chances of playing NCAA hockey anyway. Doug's plans for Mark's education were not working out quite the way he had envisioned, but to his credit he gave his son his full support.

"School just wasn't for me," Mark told MacGregor many years later. "I knew it, and he knew it, too. We're pretty liberal. He basically just let us do what we wanted to do."

But letting Mark quit Grade 12 to do what he wanted did not entail Doug taking a completely hands-off approach. An article in *The Cincinnati Enquirer* on December 30, 1978, the first feature the paper did about the newest Stinger, tells of Doug's presence in town to visit his son while on hol- iday break from teaching ninth-grade special education classes. "We wanted him to finish school," Doug said, "but this was a great opportunity for him.

I'm going to send him course material during the season." For his part, Mark wasn't talking about finishing high school but rather about his new job. "I always thought I'd play pro hockey," he told the *Enquirer*. "But I never thought it would happen this soon. I'll just have to keep trying, keep working, and see how it goes." He is reported to have said this with a grin. He also sounded understandably starry-eyed about the prospect of playing that night's game, against the New England Whalers and Gordie Howe. "Wouldn't it be great if I could get a picture of myself skating on the same ice with him?" he asked, a quarter-century before challenging Howe's standards for scoring and longevity.

There is practically no published record of what Messier did with Cincinnati. Perhaps Floyd Smith had an inkling of some sort when he told the *Enquirer*, "Mark is the kind of player who will be the future of the Stingers." Given what the future of the Stingers would turn out to be, it is apt that Messier had little impact in the scoring summaries. It took him three games to log his first points, a pair of assists on goals by another teenager, the highly touted bonus baby Mike Gartner, during a 6–5 loss to Birmingham at Riverfront Coliseum in Cincinnati on December 28. He also went to the penalty box for the first time as a pro, picking up a coincidental double minor in a shoving match with Bulls defenseman Serge Beaudoin. He assisted on a goal by the lightning-fast Gartner again a couple of nights later, the game-winner in the third period of a 2–1 victory over Howe's Whalers, the one Mark was so eager to play—although Doug looked back on that game many years later and remembers feeling something other than eagerness when he saw his son on the ice for the opening face-off. "What the hell did I get this kid into?" he thought. "There was Mark, and he was playing center with Mike Gartner and Dave Forbes. And across from them were standing Dave Keon, Gordie Howe, and Mark Howe. I turned to Mary Jean and said, 'I'm not sure we did the right thing.'"

That burst of three assists in two games was about as productive as Messier got during his maiden season in the pros, yet he was very much in his element. Shaggy-haired and wearing a perpetual squinty-eyed grin, he was earning at age seventeen a salary of $35,000—quite good in 1978 for a half-season's work—had rented his own apartment, and owned two cars. In an interview one year later he would look back on his Cincinnati experience and call it one of his happiest, acknowledging that most teenagers don't get the chance to "do what they like best and get well paid for having fun." Smith remembered Messier twenty-five years later: "We knew him from his tryout with Indianapolis, and we knew he could play. So when we were on a trip to Edmonton, he came to a practice, maybe it was two. I talked to Mark's dad, and we set it up. We really talked about whether the club could afford to take on another young player. We already had Mike Gartner, who was nineteen, and a young goalie in Mike Liut and a few other young players, but Mark was too good to pass up. So he lived with some of the other young guys. He was never alone, and his family came out and visited him. You could tell he had a real passion for the game. He just packed his bags and came."

Messier wore number 27, and sometimes he centered Gartner, who was a year older, and Peter Marsh, who was four years his senior. On other occasions, he played left wing, and while Gartner stayed on the right side, Robbie Ftorek, the WHA's most valuable player the season before, took over in the middle. "When Mark and Garts first came in there, I played center for them a bit," Ftorek said. "I remember calling my dad and I said, 'Dad, I've got Gordie Howe on one side and I've got Steve Shutt on the other side.' Mess just had that body type, the shoulders and the neck, the size and the speed and the shot, while Garts was just speed personified. You knew that both of them were going to make big splashes in whatever league they were going to be playing in. They were naturals." Gartner himself was impressed with Messier. "We were roommates together," he said, "and you could see that Mark was going to be a player. He had all the tools and all the attributes, even at a very young age." But while Gartner was already showing some stuff—he would wind up with 27 goals, 52 points, and a surprisingly scrappy 123 penalty minutes in his 78 games as a Stinger—Messier's abilities lay entirely in the realm of potential. He would finish the season with just one goal and 11 points in 47 games, along with 58 penalty minutes.

Unlike Ftorek and Gartner, most people who encountered Messier in Cincinnati did not see him as a surefire future star. "I coached against Mark Messier in the World Hockey Association," said Jacques Demers, who ran the Quebec Nordiques that season, "and he was a tough, skilled teenager, but he wasn't the Messier we would know a couple of years later." One of Messier's teammates was Barry Melrose, then a defenseman for the Stingers, now a commentator for ESPN. "I'd be lying to you if I told you I thought he was going to be a great player," Melrose said. "He was big, he was strong, but he was seventeen years old and he didn't have that work ethic he has now. He was a kid, just out of Tier II hockey. He had a lot of physical skills, but he was very young and childish at that time. I don't think anyone would have told you he was going to be a Hall of Famer and win six Stanley Cups and be considered one of the great leaders in hockey."

Predictably, given his age, Messier seems at times to have enjoyed his independence to an excessive degree. "He was a kid who suddenly had all that money, and he didn't handle himself very well," someone described only as "a source from the St. Albert Saints organization" told *The Edmonton Sun*. "He's a good lad, too, but he likes to party. He didn't go for a big, expensive sports car like Pat Price did, but he wasn't handling his big money and freedom at Cincinnati all that well. He's much better than his points total with the Stingers shows."

Whatever Messier may have done off the ice to provoke such tut-tutting, his issues on the ice stemmed from his inability to put the puck on net. He had managed seven shots on goal during his five games with Indianapolis, and he was getting his chances with Cincinnati. But he couldn't control his shot. "He was raw," said Don Helbig, who attended many Stingers games as a teenager and is now a vice president with the Cincinnati Mighty Ducks of the American Hockey League. "He was very good on face-offs, and they used him to kill penalties, because he was responsible and intelligent and he was faster than everyone else. But he didn't have control yet—everything he did was at about 100 miles an hour. I remember him missing a lot of breakaways. It seemed like every game he had a breakaway, and the puck always sounded good going off the glass." It got so bad that Floyd Smith wondered about the effect of all those missed breakaways. "He was physically developed beyond his years, and he skated really well and was fast," Smith said, "The only thing he couldn't do was score. He had numerous breakaways, and I mean numerous, but he couldn't score. That was the one thing I was a little worried about. He missed so many breakaways, I was afraid he'd get into a state of mind that he couldn't score."

One thing upon which everyone looking back through the mists of time can agree is that young Messier did not lack for spine. "Did he get into some scraps?" Smith asked rhetorically. "More than most young guys? Well—yes, he did. Let's put it this way: he was always standing at the end. That's what matters most. That was the one area we weren't worried about with him." Helbig remembers Messier mixing it up against the Birmingham Bulls, who were known as the "Baby Bulls" because they carried several underage players, including Rick Vaive, Rob Ramage, and Craig Hartsburg. With Young Turks drunk on testosterone peopling the rosters of both teams, Bulls–Stingers games often devolved into donnybrooks. "Messier would steamroll 'em into the boards," Helbig says. Terry Flynn, who covered the Stingers for the *Enquirer*, recalls Messier as "a pretty tough kid. He wasn't big, but he obviously had muscle. I don't recall that he was picked on, and that tells you something."

However tough he was, Messier got into only two fights in the WHA, both while wearing the black and yellow of the Stingers. His first was in Edmonton on March 2 against Dennis Sobchuk, a wiry and pacific junior star who enjoyed a modest amount of success in the World association but never made it as an NHLer. It was the final dustup in a game that had several and which Cincinnati lost by a score of 5–2. Doug claimed that Sobchuk started the scrap, and he was quoted as saying, "Dennis thought Mark was one guy he could get some points with." But that seems hard to believe, given that Sobchuk totaled only 31 penalty minutes all season and was in no way the fighting type. Mark remembered it more plausibly than his father. "Sobchuk was a very talented player," he said, "but he wasn't very tough." In any case, Messier is said to have thrashed Sobchuk so soundly as to convince Glen Sather, the Oilers coach, to grab Messier when he became available after the season. "The fight made a hell of an impression on Slats and everyone, and I could see why," said Bryan "Bugsy" Watson, an Oilers coach who witnessed the punch-up as a Stingers defenseman finishing a nineteen-year big-league career as a specialist in fistic mayhem. Messier's other set-to came on March 31 in Birmingham, where, with the Stingers up 2–0 in the first period, he threw down with another third-line forward, Tony Cassolato. Cincinnati went on to lose, 6–3.

The famed meanness that Messier exhibited in subsequent years never really surfaced in his season in the WHA. All he was trying to do was to prove to himself and everyone else that he belonged. His highlights were subtle and few, but they were there all the same. On January 26, nine days after Messier turned eighteen, he and the Stingers were in Edmonton to play the Oilers. It was Wayne Gretzky's eighteenth birthday, and at center ice the club staged a pregame ceremony at which their Boy Wonder signed a twenty-one-year contract, making him an Oiler through 1999, and was presented with various gifts. But Cincinnati won the game handily, 5–2, and Messier earned an assist on a Rick Dudley insurance goal in the third period. The lone goal Messier scored in the WHA was less than glamorous. It came on March 20, in Messier's forty-second game as a pro, at 11:53 of the second period at Riverfront Coliseum and with the Stingers already ahead of the Bulls, 3–1. "It was a bit of a fluke," he told Jim Matheson in a 1979 article for *The Hockey News*. "I let a shot go from just inside the blue line against Birmingham's Pat Riggin. It took a crazy bounce over his stick." Messier was on his way to the bench when the puck went in.

He also had his moments as a two-way player. Against Quebec, he was given the difficult if prestigious assignment of shadowing 75-goal man Real Cloutier. ("That," quipped Messier, "was a real treat.") Overall, Messier's plus/minus stats were respectably fair to middling. In those years a complicated formula was used to figure plus/minus: the statistic was expressed as a percentage, which supposedly yielded a truer picture of a player's two-way abilities. In the first 45 games he played for Cincinnati (the latest total that can be located), he had a mark of minus-3 percent. That put him at about the middle of the Stingers' lineup in the plus/minus department, not bad at all for a kid.

After Indianapolis folded, the WHA was down to just six teams, and by the latter stages of the season, it was all but certain that four of the teams—Edmonton, Quebec, Winnipeg, and New England—would be absorbed into the NHL for 1979–80. Cincinnati and Birmingham would be paid off, to the tune of $3.5 million each, to drop any claim on a place in the NHL and go to the Central Hockey League instead. General managers started to ogle various players they coveted for their own teams once the Stingers and Bulls bit the dust, and the Oilers' coach, Sather, wanted Messier. In March, he told Matheson: "If he's available in the draft of kids this summer, I'll take him in a minute. He's good in the corners and big and strong. Surprisingly so. I remember him knocking 215-pound Dave Langevin over once."

Of those six teams playing out the last days of the WHA, five of them, it was decided, would make the playoffs, with the fifth- and fourth-place sides meeting in a best-of-three miniseries, ostensibly for the right to play in the semifinals but actually to provide a couple more home dates for the cash-strapped clubs before time ran out. As it turned out, Cincinnati took the last berth from Birmingham. They faced New England in the miniseries and lost, two games to one. Messier did not dress for any of the three playoff games. His WHA adventure was over, and he had passed the test. He had shown poise on the ice and independence off it, but he was still a teenager, and he also probably sensed the appropriateness of keeping more or less to himself in certain situations. "At that point he was a kid," Flynn said. "You almost had to draw him out to get him to talk to you. To me he was kind of quiet at first, but once he got to know you he opened up a bit. But I was always with the team. When it came to the rest of the media he was kind of reserved." As Melrose aptly put it, "It's very hard for a seventeen-year-old to be a leader when he's with guys like Robbie Ftorek and Rick Dudley, veteran players."

The WHA playoffs ended on May 20, with Winnipeg beating Edmonton in six games; the NHL playoffs ended on May 21, as Montreal dispatched the Rangers in five. Mark returned to St. Albert and helped pay for a two-month family vacation in Malibu Beach, starting a tradition of sea-side retreats for the Messier clan. Meanwhile, the four surviving WHA teams were making the first payments on the onerous price of admission to the NHL. In addition to the $6 million entry fee, each team was allowed to protect only two skaters and two goalies from its WHA days; the rights to the rest of the players either reverted to the clubs that had held their NHL rights, or went up for grabs altogether. Edmonton, for example, protected Gretzky (who had wound up third in the WHA with 110 points in 60 games), Bengt-Ake Gustafsson, Dave Dryden and Eddie Mio. On June 9, an expansion draft restocked the four denuded teams. Winnipeg, an innovative and powerful side throughout the WHA years, was decimated in the process and never recovered, but other teams were able to make some back-door agreements that ensured they would get some key players back. The Oilers' general manager, Larry Gordon, was able to hang on to 11 players from their last WHA season: Gretzky, Dryden, Mio, Brett Callighen, B.J. MacDonald,

Garnet "Ace" Bailey, Stan Weir, Peter Driscoll, Ron Chipperfield, Dave Hunter, and Al Hamilton. The next step was the entry draft, for which all junior-age players not already protected by the four ex-WHA teams were eligible. Here too the Whalers, Jets, Nordiques, and Oilers were put at a disadvantage; they were placed at the end of the draft order, in places eighteen through twenty-one.

Messier was in this pool, and although he was admired for successfully making the jump from Tier II to the big leagues, he was not considered a blue-chipper. There was so much young talent available, from prominent junior prospects to a number of successful World association players only slightly older than Messier, that Messier was more or less lost in the shuffle. The draft took place on August 19 and was conducted, quaintly, by telephone. A listing of the first-round choices illustrates the high quality of the 1979 draft: Rob Ramage from the Birmingham Bulls went first, chosen by Colorado. Next came Messier's brief Winter Hawks teammate Perry Turnbull, Mike Foligno, Messier's Stingers linemate Gartner (chosen by Washington), ex-Bulls Rick Vaive and Craig Hartsburg, ex–Winter Hawk Keith Brown, Ray Bourque, Laurie Boschman, Tom McCarthy, Mike Ramsey, Paul Reinhart, Doug Sulliman, Brian Propp, Brad McCrimmon, Jay Wells, Duane Sutter, Ray Allison, Jimmy Mann, ex-Bull Michel Goulet, and Kevin Lowe, chosen twenty-first by Edmonton.

Gordon did some wheeling and dealing in the second round. In order to retain Dave Semenko from the Oilers' WHA roster, he swapped draft choices with Minnesota, who held Semenko's NHL rights. The upshot was that the North Stars took Neal Broten with Edmonton's second-round pick, and the Oilers took Messier with Minnesota's third-round pick, the forty-eighth over all. Edmonton now had the two youngest professionals in the NHL in Gretzky and Messier. No one knew it yet, but those two players would provide the foundation for one of the greatest teams ever to play the game.

Nevertheless, Sather had a feeling that the Oilers had made a steal in getting the big youngster. "He has unlimited potential," Sather said of Messier, who seemed happy to be playing with his hometown side. "I really didn't know what to expect, where I'd go or how high," Mark said. "It's just a good break to be coming here." He sold the two cars he had in Cincinnati and moved back into his parents' house. Now he was driving one of the family cars, a '69 Ford, and for fun, he told the *Edmonton Journal* just before the 1979–80 season started, "I hang around with the St. Albert friends I've always known."

Messier exhibited a precocious sense of perspective, or at least the words he chose did. "I guess I've done more than the average eighteen-year-old and seen a lot more," he reflected. "Maybe I do feel older than I am at times." He seems to already have been forming the ethos that would define his long professional career as well, the complete comfort with discipline, a breakneck enjoyment of life, and an understanding of how the two can coexist: "When you go to school, a teacher makes sure you attend. When you work in an office, the boss is always watching. There's always somebody—in my case it's a coach. I've never felt that the pressure is too great. The minute I stop enjoying the game, I'd leave the ice. I just can't see that happening." Asked what he would say to other teenagers who experience early success, he replied: "They've got to keep living in the same way. A totally different act is impossible to keep up. They've got to be ninety-nine percent the same person as before." The other one percent, he said, should be reserved for living the good life. As he would soon demonstrate, however, he'd be expending a lot more than just one percent of his effort on having fun—and it came close to costing him his life.

Messier kicked off his Oilers career with another trait that would sometimes mark his later years: the avoidance of training camp. Messier held out before Edmonton's rookie camp, seeking a four-year contract at $50,000 a year with a bonus. The Oilers were offering a four-year deal with a two-way clause that would pay him considerably less if he were sent down to Houston of the Central league; the alternative was a one-year deal for about $20,000 with an option on a second season. Messier was forthright in explaining his objection: "I won't come to camp without a signed contract. Last season I went to two teams and had to try out. I just decided I'd like a contract here." Messier's agent, Gus Badali, whose services he shared with Gretzky, said that if Edmonton didn't come around, Messier would try for reinstatement as an amateur and return to Portland, or simply sit out the year and sign with another NHL club later on. Sather's reply to this shot across his bow was to fire a salvo of his own. "The kid can be a hell of a pro one day," he said. "He's big and strong and he might just be the tough center I'm looking for. But he only scored one goal last season. He's not exactly Wayne Gretzky."

Messier missed rookie camp but signed in time for the exhibition season, and now Sather felt free to praise his young charge. "His puck handling has improved from last season," he said. "But then, here was a seventeen-year-old boy jumping from Tier II to pros without even the benefit of a training camp. The game was a little too fast for him to make good plays right away. But he'll get better. He's much more mature now. He can skate, shoot, and he's rambunctious, with a little bit of a belligerent streak to him. I don't think I'd mind having a tough center like him on the Oilers. I'm not going to put him in the minors just because people seem to think that's where he should go." Messier himself seemed already to have advanced light years from his WHA days. "I feel more confident," he said. "Last year I wasn't sharp enough with the puck. The coach was right to put me there, but on left wing sometimes I stood around. I didn't get the puck as much."

The Oilers' PR director at the time, John Short, remembers the specific incidents that gave Messier that confidence. "In Mark's first NHL experience, in preseason games," said Short, "we came up against a couple of tough guys—John Paddock in Philly, and a guy named Al MacAdam in Minnesota. Mark was eighteen years old and got into scuffles with both of them, and he did very well. In the room after those games, he'd say, 'I'm stronger than them,' and he was so surprised by that. That was the first time he realized that he could go into another arena and do that."

Kevin Lowe was a twenty-year-old rookie defenseman at the Oilers' first NHL camp. Two decades later he looked back on his first encounters with Messier: "He showed up with a bang. He held out at camp, and he'd scored one goal the year before—I don't know too many guys that would do that. But being a local boy, there was a lot written in the papers about him. So when he showed up at training camp, all eyes were on him. It was clear that he was something special, even at that time."

Like Gretzky, who since boyhood had lived in and coped with the glare of intense national media attention, and like Messier, Lowe had begun to acquire poise and leadership skills at an early age. In Lowe's case, it came from growing up in one of the few families in Lachute, Quebec, for whom English was the household language. That alone would not have been any special reason to develop a sense of responsibility. But his father owned a dairy, and the dairy sponsored Lowe's peewee hockey team; in part for that reason, Kevin was made captain. He spoke little French at the time, but almost all his teammates were francophones, so at his father's insistence he learned to communicate with all his teammates and their families in their own language. It served Lowe well; he became fluently bilingual and, after he reached juniors, the first-ever anglophone captain of the Quebec Remparts. He, Messier, and Gretzky, all of them remarkably poised, intelligent, and verbally adroit, would within a short time become a kind of leadership triumvirate at the head of the Oilers.

Sather immediately decided that Lowe and Gretzky should room together. It was a pretty bold move on Sather's part; after all, Gretzky had always boarded with families, and Lowe had never lived outside Québec. But at their coach's urging they moved together to an apartment on the south side of Edmonton. Their neighbours were teammates Doug Hicks and Dave Lumley, and Messier would often drive down from his family's house in St. Albert to hang out and sometimes stay over. Lowe wrote about the sense of togetherness this fostered in a 1988 book, *Champions: The Making of the Edmonton Oilers*, which he coauthored with Stan and Shirley Fischler: "Doug was a seasoned pro—Minnesota, Chicago—by the time he reached Edmonton and knew the meaning of teamsmanship. One of the first bits of business he initiated was 'The Original Team Beer.' Dougie decided that every couple of weeks it was mandatory for *everyone* to go to a certain place, have a steak sandwich and a couple of beers. It was like a fraternity bash where we could unwind, hash out any problems and, most of all, cultivate the team spirit that would very soon be evident on the Edmonton Oilers." The Oilers were certainly not the first team to exist in an atmosphere of strong camaraderie, nor could they have been the only team in the league at that time to do so. Nor, it might be added, is it even necessary for a team to have a special sense of togetherness to become a champion—witness the Montreal Canadiens of the 1960s and '70s, whose dressing room was often torn by factions, blow-ups, and various other forms of strife. But the Oilers were distinguished by their all-conquering sense of fellowship, and Messier came of age in the midst of it, helped foster it and bring it to new heights, and carried it with him when he left Edmonton.

The Oilers opened their NHL existence on October 10, 1979, at Chicago Stadium before a meagre 9,000 fans. All the Oilers were nervous, even the eight who had prior NHL experience. Messier said: "It really hit me in the afternoon. Until I sat there at about 3 p.m., I hadn't really let it get to me. But I sat in my hotel room and all I could think was, 'Hey, we're in the NHL.'" Gretzky remembered sitting with Messier in that room, "just sort of staring at each other."

The eighteen-year-old Gretzky took the team's first-ever face-off, lining up against Stan Mikita, who was in the last of his twenty seasons in the NHL. Mikita seemed old and slow in that final campaign, and indeed he would retire after playing just sixteen more games. He was thirty-nine, an age that would seem increasingly ancient as the '80s proceeded and the youthful Oilers established their hegemony of speed over North American hockey. In the club's first NHL season there still were some ageless wonders plying the rinks, most notably Gordie Howe at fifty-two, Bobby Hull at forty-one, and Dave Keon at forty, all with the Whalers—by then known as Hartford rather than New England. A handful of other players from the pre-1967 Original Six days were still in the league, but by the end of the '82–83 season, when Serge Savard, Wayne Cashman, and Carol Vadnais retired, they were all gone, victims of the Oiler-sparked youth movement that took over the game. By the mid-'80s, any player over the age of thirty-three was considered old and on his last legs, almost as impossibly ancient as Mikita seemed on opening night in 1979. How ironic that Messier was one of the players in that opening-night game—the second-youngest, in fact—and that he would still be going strong at age forty-two. In the NHL world of the new millennium, he would be the second-oldest player, and there would be many players in their late thirties. Unlike the old guys still barely hanging on in the '70s and early '80s, thanks to expansion the old guys of the 2000s—Steve Yzerman, Brett Hull, Chris Chelios, Al MacInnis, Ron Francis, Adam Oates, Scott Stevens—weren't merely hanging on, they were the best players in hockey. Messier, then, was a catalyst in the greening of the NHL, and he would still be around for the league's greying.

The Oilers lost that first game in Chicago, 4–2. The club's second game, three nights later, was their home debut. It came against Detroit, and it featured a fight between Lee Fogolin and Mike Foligno, perhaps the only time in big-league history that anagrams traded blows. Also in that game, Messier scored his first NHL goal. It came against another Original Six veteran, Rogatien Vachon, at the 17:36 mark of the third period, unassisted, and it forged a 3–3 tie. In the Oilers' fourth game six nights later at home against Quebec, Messier earned his first NHL assist, helping set up a Doug Hicks goal that tied the score at 1–1 en route to Edmonton's first NHL victory, by 6–3.

The schedule was under way, and Messier was getting a regular shift on the third line. He was much more in the thick of things than he had been the season before in Cincinnati, but he still had some trouble hitting the net. Part of the problem was his penchant for taking slap shots; the sound of the puck clanking heavily off the glass, the same sound the fans heard so often at Riverfront Coliseum, was now echoing through Northlands Coliseum. "A lot of work went into shaping Mark up as a big leaguer," said Barry Fraser, the Oilers scout who had been a strong advocate of drafting Messier, of the young player's '79–80 season. "After he joined the Oilers, Slats got him to cut down on the slap shot, and that alone took a year."

Off the ice and in the company of his friends on the already close-knit Oilers, Messier was having a good time, with a vengeance. A couple of years later he would admit that he went out when the lights went on and came home when they went off. And Sather would look back at Messier from that same vantage point and say: "Hell, name me one kid who's seventeen or eighteen who gets a fistful of money, a new car, new clothes, and tell me he doesn't get into a little trouble. You can't expect a kid to handle drinking and girls and things like income tax when he's that young."

Sather tolerated the antics of the young Oilers and even participated in them himself. He and Larry Gordon consciously cultivated a young team, figuring that they would grow together into a contender within a few years. That was hardly an innovation; the history of pro sports is littered with the corpses of teams that invested in the future with young rosters, endured losing seasons, and then when those young rosters matured, proceeded to lose some more.

But there was method to the Oilers' madness for youth. For one thing, it's easy to see a bright future when you have Wayne Gretzky in your lineup. But early on Sather also recognized the value of Lowe and Messier, beyond their nascent stardom on the ice. While he paired Lowe with Gretzky, he made Messier room on the road with Lee Fogolin, a young veteran defenseman who within a year would become the Oilers' third NHL captain. Lowe remembers that Sather "pushed" him and Messier into leadership roles, "straight out" telling them: "Hey, you guys take charge. You tell 'em when they're screwing up." But they sometimes screwed up themselves.

Lowe described the early Messier, the party animal, in terms that deftly tiptoe around specifics. "We had some great times, to say the least," he wrote in a long tribute to Messier in *The Hockey News* in 1990. "Mark loves to have a good time. He and I probably went out on the town a little more than Wayne. Wayne did his share of it, but right from day one he had that great sense of responsibility. He knew from the time he was ten years old that all eyes were on him. He was very diplomatic about his public life and not ever stepping out of line. On occasion he did, like any other eighteen-year-old, but Mark and I were out more often because we weren't Wayne Gretzky." Messier stepped out of line more than once at the start of the Oilers' season. He missed a team bus at one point and showed up late for a few practices, behavior that was difficult for Sather to countenance with any player, much less one he'd tabbed as a future leader of the team. Sather chewed him out, but soon there came the proverbial straw that broke the camel's back, as the Oilers made ready for a trip from Edmonton to St. Louis at the end of October.

According to Lowe, who recounted the tale in *Champions*, the team flight was to depart from Edmonton's international airport, but Messier thought it was taking off from the municipal airport. To make matters worse, Messier and his mother got a late start from the family house. They drove downtown, to the wrong airport, where Messier found that no planes were flying to St. Louis. "As quickly as possible," Lowe wrote, "he turned his car in the direction of the international airport—as he tells it, driving on the wrong side of the road because there had been an accident, facing traffic for about two or three miles—almost killing himself and his mom.

"They arrived at the international airport just in time to watch the TWA flight climbing into the sun.

"Mark headed for the nearest phone and called Bruce MacGregor, who by now was assisting Slats in the front office. 'I missed the flight to St. Louis,' Mark announced.

"'That's all right,' MacGregor replied. 'I have one for you.'

"'Good,' said Mark with the utmost naïveté. 'Can I catch the team?'

"MacGregor paused momentarily. 'Yeah, you can catch the team. But the team you're catching is the Houston Apollos.'"

Messier was indeed sent down to Houston in the CHL. Wearing number 10, he tallied three assists but no goals during his four-game exile with the Oilers' farm club, and picked up a couple of minor penalties as well. There were a number of other Oiler prospects on the team, plus a few others sent down for a short period, but most of them would never make an impact in the NHL. Among the Apollo regulars that year, only Charlie Huddy and, to a lesser extent, Tom Roulston, would later play significant roles in Edmonton's Stanley Cup conquests.

Messier was recalled from his demotion after a week and a half, and although he wasn't exactly scared straight, he did claim to have learned something from it. "It was my own fault," he later said. "I was hurt, but I thought if I busted my butt I'd never have to go back." According to Lowe, the rest of the team "learned a lesson" from the incident. Sather had sent a "chill" through everyone, and they bucked up. But Sather and Gordon were also to be credited for returning Messier to the big club after only four games rather than leaving him to languish in the CHL, as some coaches would have done. It is also true, however, that the Oilers were 1–5–0 in Messier's absence and 2–9–4 overall, so the team also could not afford to exclude anyone who might help out. At the end of the season, Sather looked back and claimed to have found further motivation for recalling Messier in the fact that he had been "far and away the best player in the Central league" during his short stint, although that seems a little hard to believe.

Even though Messier was very much the club-hopping hellion in need of discipline that first season, he remained as firmly grounded in his family as ever. Lowe recalled that for Christmas Eve 1979, the Messiers invited some of the single Oilers to the house in St. Albert, where a friend who was a priest was going to say a family Mass. Lowe and the backup goaler Jim Corsi got lost on the way and arrived very late, at 1 a.m. "We land in," Lowe remembered, "and they're all still up, in their pajamas and opening up their Christmas presents. It was like, 'Come on in, what took you guys so long, we've been waiting for you.'" On the other hand, he took part in such high jinks as driving Dave Semenko's Trans Am with Semenko, Lowe, Dave Lumley, and Dave Hunter packed in, then rolling right into Northlands and up to the dressing room door—just as team owner Peter Pocklington and a livid Sather walked through it.

Despite Edmonton's awful start, they still had every reason to believe they had a shot at the playoffs. The schedule was perfectly balanced that season, with each team playing the other twenty clubs four times apiece. Although the standings were printed as if divisions and conferences meant something, they in fact meant nothing at all. For playoff purposes, the clubs would be ranked first through sixteenth, solely according to their final point and victory totals. When the regular season ended, the sixteenth-place team would play the first-place side, number fifteen would play number two, the fourteenth would play the third, and so on. It was the least complicated, fairest set-up the NHL has ever employed, the only fault being the ridiculously high ratio of teams (76 percent) allowed into the postseason. That last aspect was manna for the Oilers. They sputtered through the regular season and endured into the stretch run with a shot at a playoff spot. Then, Gretzky and Lowe leading the way, the Oilers finished the year on a 7–0–1 roll, and that, coupled with a Washington swoon, put Edmonton into the sixteenth and final berth by a single victory. Nevertheless, the fact remained that Edmonton finished eleven games below .500, and were in the postseason only courtesy of the NHL's generous playoff system.

To a certain extent, Messier was still something of a bit player at this point, having scored just 12 goals and 33 points in 75 games, as well as registering a pretty poor minus-10 mark. Like everyone else on the team, he was overshadowed by the Great Gretzky, who'd had an unbelievable NHL debut, with 51 goals and 137 points. But Messier had definitely made an impact. Wearing the flimsy Jofa helmet that everyone on the Oilers favored, he played a banging, crashing style, always skating at full throttle and looking to stir things up. Matheson noted in an article for *The Hockey News* near the end of the regular season that Messier had been in ten fights (he finished the season with eleven fights and 120 penalty minutes) and had won, by Matheson's own reckoning, seven of them, with two draws at the hands of Dennis Ververgaert of Philadelphia and Al MacAdam of Minnesota; the only loss, Matheson wrote, came against Bert "Long Arms" Wilson of Los

Angeles. As had happened the season before, a run-in with the big defenseman Dave Langevin, now with the Islanders, was cited as stark testimony to Messier's brute strength. The two squared off in a game on Long Island, Matheson wrote, and "the 195-pound Messier hit the 215-pound Langevin so hard with a left hook, Langevin's helmet exploded in the air. 'I wasn't really ready for a southpaw,' said Langevin, sheepishly.'" Messier was so intimidatingly ferocious that his teammates called him Mad Dog, which became the nickname he carried through that first season in the NHL.

But Messier did more than just charge around trying to keep his opponents off-balance with his unpredictability on the ice. In February, he was moved off left wing and put at center, giving him a significant increase in ice time. By the stretch run, he was taking most of the key face-offs and shouldering a lot of the penalty-killing chores. "Name me one other team," Sather said, "that's got a third-rounder playing regularly. He's better than some number one picks." Sather pointed to Messier's skating ability in particular. "I don't think there's a faster guy on the team. When he's in full flight he just pulls away from guys. He catches defensemen a little flat-footed by his speed. The only thing he really has to do is slow down a little inside the other team's blue line. He tends to go full out all the time. Inside the other team's end he could slow down a little and use his strength." For the first time, Messier was being touted as a future star. All in all, it was a big improvement on his WHA season.

Edmonton's opponent in the best-of-three preliminary series was Philadelphia, who had finished first overall with 116 points, 47 more than Edmonton had. The Flyers swept the Oilers, but twice Edmonton held third-period leads that Philadelphia had to overcome, and twice they made it to overtime before finally falling. Messier scored a goal and two assists, meaning he was in on half the goals Edmonton scored in the series, the same as Gretzky. The Oilers had acquitted themselves well, and the Flyers' captain, Bobby Clarke, singled out two Oilers, Gretzky and Messier, as the reason Edmonton would soon be a team to be reckoned with.

The Edmonton players were in a buoyant mood. The day after the season ended, Doug Hicks suggested an "instant vacation" to Hawaii, and he recruited Lowe, Gretzky, Lumley, and Messier to come along. Lowe had never been on a vacation in his life and packed four suitcases for the trip to the far-off islands. Messier, however, was already a veteran of oceanside holidays; according to Lowe, he showed up at the airport wearing shorts, running shoes, and a denim shirt, his only luggage a little tote bag, and carrying "about $4,000 stuffed into the top of his pocket." They had a great time.

Meanwhile, Philadelphia got all the way to the Stanley Cup final, but there they fell to the New York Islanders. The Isles had risen quickly from a terrible expansion team in the early 1970s to one with huge expectations sparked by a core of young phenoms in mid-decade, to one with a reputation for devastating underachievement in the playoffs in the late '70s. But in 1979–80 they put it all together and embarked on an astonishing reign atop the hockey world. The Oilers would run into them soon enough.

Edmonton got ready for 1980–81 by adding a trio of future stars in the draft: defenseman Paul Coffey in the first round, right winger Jari Kurri in the fourth, and goalie Andy Moog in the seventh. All would join the team in the coming season. Also coming on board was a fourth-rounder from the previous draft, right winger Glenn Anderson, who had spent '79–80 as the best player on the Canadian Olympic Team, the sixth-place finishers at Lake Placid.

The rest of the Oiler roster was ready to come back, including winger Don Murdoch, whom Edmonton had picked up at the 1980 trade deadline as the stretch run got under way. Murdoch had enjoyed a spectacular NHL debut with New York Rangers in 1976, scoring 12 goals in his first month with the club, cooling off a bit, but still winding up with an impressive 32 goals his rookie season. Two years later, however, he was arrested for cocaine and marijuana possession and was suspended for half a season by the NHL. His play never returned to the level of his first two years, and Sather dealt for him, making him one of the first of many "reclamation projects" Sather would undertake over the years.

Murdoch was Messier's cousin. In terms of population, Canada is not a large country; maybe that's why it can sometimes seem as if practically every Canadian NHLer is related in some way to another Canadian NHLer. In Messier's case, however, the extent of the family ties is remarkable. There was, of course, his brother, Paul, whose tenure with the Colorado Rockies was brief, lasting only nine games in '79–80, and who was by this time playing in the CHL. His younger cousins Mitch and Joby Messier would eventually appear in the NHL—Mitch for some brief stops with Minnesota in the late '80s and early '90s, Joby for cups of coffee with the Rangers alongside Mark in the mid-'90s. An uncle on Mark's mother's side, Billy Dea, had had a long and prosperous minor-league career in the '50s and '60s, like Doug, and he also made it up to the NHL for all or parts of eight seasons. There was Don Murdoch, also related through Mark's mother's side of the family, and a great uncle, Murray Murdoch, who just happened to be the first man ever signed by the New York Rangers all the way back in 1926. Murray Murdoch set a record for consecutive games played by appearing in every one of the club's 508 regular-season contests over its first eleven years of existence (and all 55 playoff games as well), then went on to serve as longtime head coach at Yale University. Messier was even for a time the brother-in-law of John Blum, a journeyman defenseman who began his NHL career in Edmonton, where he met Jennifer. Mark could also have wound up with a family tie to Ken Danyeko, the longtime hard-rock New Jersey defenseman who knew the Messiers as a teenager and went out briefly with Mary-Kay. There was even a family connection to hockey's sister sport, boxing: Mark had an uncle, Larry Messier, who was once a member of Muhammad Ali's entourage.

The Oilers' 1980–81 season was the one forever preserved in Peter Gzowski's classic *The Game of Our Lives.* At the time, the book seemed afflicted with a mild case of the elegaic; nevertheless, it already read like a great work. Revisiting it now, more than twenty years later, it is even better, a remarkable whiparound of the world of North American hockey at a very special moment in its history, when memories of the game's golden age were still fresh, when the debate over goonery versus firewagon élan still raged, when the attitude towards Europeans was just starting to tip from suspicion to appreciation, when the business equilibrium between Canadian and American was just about perfect, when the phenomenon of female reporters in the dressing room was still new and strange, and most of all, when the Edmonton Oilers were young and famous and only beginning to come into their own.

Gzowski began his book with a passage introducing Messier, the only player on those Oilers who actually came from Edmonton. "Messier was still a teenager that fall, although he had a body sculptors would kill for," he wrote. "On the ice, he played with what he liked to call 'reckless abandon,' probably unaware that the phrase echoed back to players as ancient as Sprague Cleghorn, a face-breaking defenceman of the 1920s. Messier sometimes played with reckless abandon off the ice, too. He had a wide-eyed look when he was excited, and his nostrils seemed to flare. In the dressing room he would occasionally break into song. With his head thrown back, his eyes closed, his Praxitelean body naked, one hand cupped over his genitals, he would bellow, 'Been down so long it looks like up to me.'"

As the Oilers pick up steam through the season, Messier appears in Gzowski's account as a kind of trickster figure always ready to play some kind of Zen joke. In Buffalo, his victim is Oilers play-by-play announcer Rod Phillips: "This morning, Mark Messier, the irrepressible teenager, emptied the scotch from the mickey Roddy sometimes packs to relieve the tension of his broadcasts and filled it with water." Arriving in New York, Messier solicits quarters from his teammates for, as Gzowki puts it, "the flesh machines of 42nd Street," and at practice, he strides out onto the ice and shouts, "And now, live, from Madison Square Garden, it's the pesky Edmonton Oilers!" Leaving New York, Messier wears newly bought "stereophonic headphones" and has them on from the Garden all the way to the plane and on board it as well. "'Pretty good sound, eh, Mark?' another passenger [presumably Gzowski] said. Messier smiled in silent reply, pointing to his covered ears and snapping his fingers in rhythm. . . . Messier took off his earphones and offered them to the passenger, who placed them carefully over his ears. There was no sound in them." In sum, Gzowski sees Messier as "so young in many ways" and "so old in others. He can be the best player on the ice, or the worst, and sometimes he is both on the same shift. In conversation he can be solemn, reflective, articulate, or as surly as a punk rocker."

Kurri, Coffey, and Anderson were regulars practically from the start, and soon the Oilers gained renown around the league for their youth. They became famous for playing road hockey with wadded-up tape in the corridors of rinks around the league in the hours before their real game began. At one point in his account, Gzowski echoes a point a lot of other commentators were making at the time: that the Oilers "were almost certainly (there

were no statistics from the early days) the youngest team in NHL history."
This was in fact not entirely true. The 1980–81 Oilers averaged 24.3 years
of age, while that season's Colorado Rockies averaged 23.6—proving that to
be a young team was not necessarily to be a good team or even a promising
one. Nevertheless, the '80–81 Oilers were very much a team of the young
and the restless, and they were on the move.

No one, of course, was moving faster than Gretzky. He wound up breaking Bobby Orr's single-season assist record (102) and Phil Esposito's point
record (152). Messier, playing as a left winger, also improved, getting better
as the season proceeded. He scored 28 points over his first 48 games, which
already put him within five points of his entire total of the previous season.
Then he caught fire, counting 35 points over the final 24 games—as hot a
pace as he would ever maintain, even in his best years. On March 3, he
notched the first four-point game of his pro career, getting two goals and two
assists against the Islanders. Two weeks later, he scored his first pro hat trick,
against Pittsburgh. He burned brightest when he played on a line with the
taciturn Finn Matti Hagman at center and the mustachioed free spirit
Glenn Anderson on the right wing.

Messier, like the team as a whole, did not move in a straight line from
promising to accomplished. He played inconsistently over the first half of
the season. At one point he suffered a groin pull that kept him out of a few
games, the first of an almost countless series of small injuries that would sideline him briefly, but never for too extended a period, over the next two
decades—but the injury wasn't the cause of his sometimes spotty play.
Rather, there seemed to be a lack of focus. "One night you'd be looking and
you'd say, 'Jeez, this kid dominates,'" Ron Low remembered many years later.
"And then the next night he wouldn't play as well." Messier often seemed
to be drifting aimlessly on the ice, stretches of lassitude that stood out all the
more in contrast to the high-speed crashing game he played the other half
of the time. In early February, Sather, now both coach and general manager,
sent Murdoch, Messier's cousin, to the Central league, and threatened to
send Messier himself down again, too. Things very nearly came to a head, as
Gzowski reported: "If he wanted to stay with the Oilers, Sather told him, he
would have to get his head back into the game and cool down his social life.
He was to be home at night, subject to bed checks."

Messier has a stubborn streak that goes hand in hand with his independent spirit, and Sather's ultimatum, apparently, was almost too much for him to take. "Messier, newly turned twenty," Gzowski wrote, "did not react as quickly to this lecture as Sather might have hoped. In fact, as he was to say later, he gave very serious thought to shoving the whole business and devoting his youth to enjoying himself." But he enjoyed being a pro hockey player too much to give it up, and he bore down, resolving to mend his ways. It was at this point that he began his late-season tear. When it ended in early April, he had 23 goals and 63 points in 72 games, twice the output of his previous season.

Edmonton finished fourteenth and drew as their first-round opponents the storied Montreal Canadiens. It would become the most famous best-of-five series in league history. The Habs were only two seasons removed from their four-year reign as Cup champions, and they still had Guy Lafleur, Steve Shutt, Bob Gainey, Larry Robinson, Serge Savard, Guy Lapointe, and a number of other immortals on the team. They were so confident of victory that one of their goalies, Richard Sevigny, committed the cardinal sin of predicting a romp, telling the papers that Lafleur would have Gretzky "in his back pocket." Sather's response was to agree that the series would probably be lopsided—"the biggest mismatch in hockey history," he called it—and then made two key strategic moves: he assigned Dave Hunter to shadow Lafleur, and he put rookie Andy Moog in the nets. The excited Oilers basked in the atmosphere of the Montreal Forum before game one. "I can still remember siting in the visitors' locker room before the first game in the Montreal Forum, the cathedral of hockey," Gretzky recalled in his 1990 autobiography. "I remember it had old blue carpeting and ancient wooden benches. There was an old training table in the middle of the room, and I thought of how many great players had lain there in pain and defeat after games here."

The game under way, Hunter covered Lafleur like a blanket, leaving him no room to maneuver and frustrating the Canadiens. Lapointe and Hunter got into a fight, and Lapointe took off Hunter's helmet and started whacking him over the head with it. The Forum fans booed Lapointe. At another point, Messier squared off with the towering Robinson, though no blows were exchanged. After two periods, Edmonton was ahead, 3–1. In the dressing room during the second intermission, Gzowski reports, Oilers assistant coach Billy Harris told Messier he thought he would fight Robinson. "Not out in the open," Messier replied. "I'm going to wait until I get him against the boards, and then I'll beat the crap out of him." The Oilers pulled away in the third to win, 6–3, with Gretzky earning a record-tying five assists and making sure to pat the back pocket of his pants as he skated past the Montreal bench after the final Edmonton empty-netter. Now they were the cocky young Oilers. They took game two, 3–1, with Moog brilliant for a second straight night and the Forum fans applauding the Oilers. The series returned to Edmonton, where to further inspire his players Sather put together a videotape of all the Oiler goals set to the strains of Tom Jones singing "The Impossible Dream"—a ploy that seems irredeemably hokey today but which in 1981, with videotape still a new product and music video in its infancy, was bold, innovative, and inspiring. Pumped up in front of an ecstatic crowd at Northlands, the Oilers finished off the Canadiens, 6–2, marking the first time since 1952 that *Les Glorieux* had been swept from the playoffs.

Next up were the Cup-holding Islanders. The Oilers fell behind two games to none (in one of those games the Isles' great but violently berserk goalie Billy Smith laid a two-handed slash on Gretzky's ankle, foreshadowing more notorious antics in the years to come), won one, then fell further behind, three games to one. Game five was played at Nassau Coliseum, and most figured the Isles would close out the series. They were young, efficient, tough, and practically flawless. They were also businesslike—in sharp contrast to the boyish Oilers, who still played ball hockey in the pregame corridors and blasted rock music in their dressing room, another innovation that has since become commonplace but was then brand new. With Edmonton clinging to a 3–2 lead late in the fifth game a scene unfolded that would forever define the young Oilers. Gzowski describes it thus:

"Then, in the third period, a stirring thing happened: the Oilers began to sing. Mark Messier started it. Sitting on the bench, his stick clutched like a spear in his gloved hand, he began to chant, 'Here we go, Oilers, here we go.' Down the line, Kevin Lowe picked it up, then [Curt] Brackenbury, then everyone else, and all through the arena, amid the din of the suburban Long Island crowd, you could hear them singing.

"'Here we go, Oilers, here we go.'"

The Oilers hung on to win, and if they weren't already the darlings of Canada, they were now. The series returned to Edmonton, but the Isles had too much talent and experience to fold. The Oilers got as close as 3–2 after Messier scored in the third, but Duane Sutter and Mike McEwen put the game and the series away for the Long Islanders.

Still, the Oilers won the hearts of a lot of fans and the respect of everyone with their exuberance and their scrappiness. However, they did not necessarily endear themselves to the Islander players. There was the slashing contretemps between Smith and Gretzky, and according to Mike Bossy's autobiography, Bob Bourne was angered by the Oilers' "Here we go" chant on the bench. Bossy also remembered that "Anderson and Messier were skilled players, but they showed no respect for me whatsoever in that series. If those guys could have injured me on a particular play, without a doubt they would have." The Isles' great defenseman and captain Denis Potvin distilled the contrast between the two teams before the series, when he was asked about the Oilers and said: "You're not supposed to enjoy the playoffs. It's supposed to be work."

It was not work for the Oilers or for Messier, which is why everyone liked them so much. They would have to learn what Potvin already knew before they could taste victory themselves, but in the meantime, for better or for worse, they were having too much fun.

A LONG ROAD TO CLIMB IF YOU WANT TO ROCK AND ROLL

There is a phenomenon in hockey that might be called the Mandatory Suffering Rule. It's not a formal rule; it's more a law of nature. It states that, before any team can experience the fulfillment, joy, and acclaim of winning the Stanley Cup, it must first undergo at least two stunning reverses, disappointing to the point of devastation, in the years immediately prior to their victory. If you think of all the teams that have won the Stanley Cup over the last thirty seasons, with the exception of the Montreal Canadiens, who are an exception to everything, you will find that there is not one that has escaped the iron dictate of the Mandatory Suffering Rule.

The joy of the Oilers' summer was broken only by the unpleasantness of the 1981 Canada Cup tournament, in which Gretzky was the club's only Team Canada representative. That tournament, like most North American defeats in major international play, is glossed over in most histories, but certainly the 8–1 thrashing the Soviet Union dealt Canada in the final match—in Montreal, yet—has to rank as one of the greatest victories in the history of hockey, although Canadians cannot be blamed for thinking of it in less glowing terms. Gretzky was the top scorer in the tournament, but the Soviets blanked him in the decisive game. (Igor Larionov tallied two of the USSR's goals in the finale; twenty years later, he would be the only NHL player older than Mark Messier.) It was the second time in a row that the Soviets had completely embarrassed a North American select team in a tournament final in North America, the previous occasion coming in 1979 at Madison Square Garden, where they slaughtered the NHL All-Star Team, 6–0. The NHL and Team Canada would have to await the arrival of Messier before they could finally tangle with the Soviets as equals.

Edmonton started the 1981–82 season in white-hot form and never let up. All the players on the team were scoring like mad, the first sparks of an offensive explosion that would transform the game in the 1980s. Gretzky, true to form, rocketed to what would become the biggest goal-scoring season any big-league player has ever had, but Messier, now known by teammates as "Moose" and still playing on a line with Glenn Anderson and Matti Hagman, was on fire too. So were Jari Kurri and Paul Coffey.

Just seven games into the season, Gretzky confidently told reporters that the Oilers would finish first in their division, which now comprised Edmonton, Los Angeles, Vancouver, Colorado, and the Oilers' new archrivals, the Calgary Flames, who had moved from Atlanta in 1980. In the thirty-ninth game of the regular season, against Philadelphia at Northlands, Gretzky scored four times. The last of these, into an empty net with three seconds left, was his 50th goal, shattering the previous standard of 50 goals in 50 games set by Rocket Richard in 1944 and tied in '81 by Mike Bossy. The first Oiler to reach Gretzky in the joyous rush to gang-tackle him was Messier.

By now, everything was coming together for him—the wild insouciance with which he lived his life was meshing perfectly with his play on the rink. Gone were the lapses of inconsistency; everything flowed together seamlessly in a rocking slipstream of good times on the ice and off. "His motto," Kevin Lowe wrote of the Messier of '81–82, "is to live every day as if it's his last, and he plays that way as well. If I were to choose one word to describe Mark it would be 'fierce.'" There was no need for discipline, because he did everything he did at 100 miles per hour, and it worked. "Mark runs over life like it was an enemy defenceman," Lowe wrote, "and in no time at all he became the soul of our team. 'Fellas,' he would say, 'there's nothing left to save it for. There's nowhere for us to hide out there, so let's play with reckless abandon.'"

Cured of his addiction to the slap shot, Messier developed a new offensive weapon that proved remarkably effective and that he would use for the rest of his career. Probably the best description of it was given by Rick Carpiniello in his biography of Messier: "Messier, a left-handed shooter, developed a snap shot off the wrong foot, the back foot, a dangerous shot he'd often fire while skating down the right wing. Goalies, who are used to players shooting off the front foot, were fooled even when they knew it was coming. . . . His right leg would kick straight out toward the right-wing boards as he unleashed the shot, which often sliced. Often, the shot wasn't terribly hard, but it was always difficult to handle. Because Messier lifted his leg, goalies could not detect the moment of release by watching his skates."

During the second month of the season, Messier revealed publicly for the first time his admiration for someone who could serve as Messier's role model, doppelgänger, and professional ideal. "I'd love to be Mick Jagger," he told Jim Matheson of the *Edmonton Journal*. "To be a rock 'n' roll star and have the fans going crazy. Would that be a rush or what?" Messier also professed to have fantasies about being a pro water-skier—he was already an excellent wakeboarder and water-skier—and a race-car driver, and he also talked about what it might be like to earn the kind of money Gretzky, who was pulling down almost a million dollars a year, was making: "I guess someday I'd like to make $1 million a year, too, but that might take forever. I might be 1,000 years old." About the amount he actually was making, he said: "I almost feel guilty making the money I do. My father worked his butt off when he was younger. He had three jobs and played hockey, and he still passed with honors in school. He sweated for everything he got. I'm going to get a house pretty quick, but I don't think I'll ever get one that costs more than my dad's. His is unbelievable . . . but on top of that I don't know if it would feel right."

Although he still resided in the family house, Messier lived quite independently, and he loved his fast cars. At this point he owned a black Corvette, having recently given up a motorcycle and a Jeep because of the

Oilers' concerns for his safety. Those concerns were well founded: in December he was stopped by police and failed a Breathalyzer test, just one in a number of dangerous driving incidents involving NHL players that give the story of his driving from airport to airport against traffic to catch the plane to St. Louis a somewhat less humorous tint than it might otherwise have.

But on the ice, there was no possible basis for concern; everything was going perfectly, and Messier was continuing to score and run people over, despite an ankle injury suffered in early November that would nag him all year. At the halfway point of the season, the Oilers had 56 points from 40 games, a .700 winning percentage, tops in the entire NHL. With Gretzky pulverizing every conceivable scoring record and opponents concentrating vainly on stopping him, the rest of the Oilers were free to gambol un-impeded. And, with the Great One now besieged by the media on both sides of the border, that applied to off-ice activities as well. "It doesn't bother me at all," said Messier when asked whether he minded playing in Gretzky's shadow. "In fact, I don't want the responsibilities Wayne has. He doesn't have his summers to himself like I do where I can water-ski, something I've been doing since Grade 3. He has got all his endorsements and he's travel-ing so much. Everybody on this team is going to get their day; it's only a mat-ter of time. Wayne has just matured faster than us." The preference he expressed here for his privacy, even at the expense of making money through endorsements, is something Messier would exhibit throughout his career.

Messier was chosen to play in the 1982 NHL All-Star Game, his first such honor. When he got word of his selection, he told Doug he wanted to fly the entire family to Washington for the All-Star Weekend. Doug told him it was too expensive, but Mark's response, as Doug remembered it, was "What's the use of making the team if I can't share it?" The entire family went to Washington.

Messier was one of the core of young Oilers who were scoring at better than a point-a-game pace; besides Gretzky and Messier, there were Glenn Anderson, Paul Coffey, Jari Kurri, and even Dave Lumley, who was installed for a while as Gretzky's right-winger. Edmonton wound up with 417 goals, more than any NHL team had ever potted before. And if the Oilers were a traveling carnival, Gretzky's quest to break Phil Esposito's record for most goals scored in a season, 76, was the feature attraction. Esposito followed the

Oilers from city to city, ready to appear at a rinkside ceremony the moment The Kid scored number 77, until he wound up at Memorial Auditorium in Buffalo on the night of February 24. Goldie Hawn and Burt Reynolds were in town filming a movie, and they provided an appropriate Hollywood sheen to the proceedings in the event that Gretzky, who had 76 goals, finally got the magic 77th. Gil Perreault, an idol of Gretzky's when he was a little boy growing up in nearby Brantford, Ontario, was showing some of his old Gallic flair for the Sabres. He scored a hat trick, and Reynolds, a Floridian who played college football and for whom hockey was a mystery, could be seen leaping to his feet rooting for Buffalo, the flamboyant, aging former box-office draw cheering on the flamboyant, aging former scoring sensation. But with the count tied at three and just six and a half minutes left, Steve Patrick—the player many Sabres fans will still tell you was the worst ever to wear the blue and gold—fumbled away the puck at his own blue line to Gretzky, who swooped in to score the record-setting goal, break the tie, and bring Espo onto the ice for hugs and handshakes. Gretzky went on to score two more before time ran out.

After the game, the scene moved to the Aud's wood-paneled interview area, which looked more like an exceptionally nice basement rec room than a pro sports facility. There, flashbulbs popped as pictures were taken of luminaries in street clothes, celebrating Gretzky's achievement. One of the photos features prominently a homemade tapestry of a Sabres crest, made of plush carpeting and hanging on a wall. Before it, a line of smiling celebrants stand with their arms draped over one another's shoulders. At the left is Oilers owner Peter Pocklington, followed by Sabres owner Seymour Knox III, then Goldie Hawn, and on the right is Burt Reynolds. Between Reynolds and Hawn, his arms stretched widest, his mouth spread in the broadest grin, his body torqued in the most suggestive Jagger-like stance, his jacket opened the widest, and his straight shag haircut the most moplike of all, stands Messier. Hawn is looking up at him, amused, while Reynolds seems to be doing one of his signature Johnny Carson double-takes at the young hockey player whom he had probably never heard of. Messier squints blissfully at the camera as if he just doesn't care.

The season rolled on like a dream, and the charismatic Oilers drew sellout crowds to each of their final sixteen road games. The seventy-ninth and penultimate match of the year was against Los Angeles at Northlands, and there was talk that Gretzky, who came in with 92 goals, actually had a shot at 100. As it happened, he would score no more that season, but in this game he did set up Messier for two goals, including his 50th, which came with 23 seconds left in a 7–3 victory. Messier broke into a jubilant dance when he saw the puck go in. "Helping Mark get to 50," Gretzky said after the game, "was as important as anything I could do for myself." Perry Berezan, who went on to play for the Calgary Flames, was playing for Doug Messier's St. Albert Saints at the time. He was on the Saints' team bus as it drove up Highway 1 from Calgary at around 1 a.m. that night and was overtaken and cut off by a sleek black Porsche. "And there," Berezan told the *Calgary Herald*'s George Johnson in an interview twenty years later, "was Messier, face against the windshield of the bus, literally hanging onto the wipers, yelling, 'Where's my dad? Where's my dad?' He had just scored his 50th goal and wanted to celebrate with Doug."

Messier finished the campaign with 50 goals, making him one of ten players from among the league's twenty-one teams to reach the plateau. He would never again score as many goals in a single season. He also rolled up 38 assists for 88 points, 119 penalty minutes that were far more intimidating than that total indicates, and for the first time finished with a respectable plus/minus mark, plus-21, which put him in the middle of the pack on the Edmonton roster. An impressive showing, if understandably overshadowed by Gretzky's 92 goals, 212 points, and plus-81 mark.

Big things were expected in the playoffs from Edmonton, who had finished second overall in the league standings, trailing only the Islanders. Their opponents in the best-of-five opening round were the L.A. Kings, which was probably to the Oilers' liking not only because they had finished 48 points ahead of the Kings and had gone 5–1–2 against them in the regular season, but also because they loved L.A. Now that the Oilers were a phenomenon, they were treated like celebrities in a way that no hockey players ever had before. In Hollywood, there were parties, dinners, photo opportunities, tours, and so on, resulting in pictures of *Penthouse* Pets batting their eyelashes at the clearly delighted twenty-year-old Canadian boys; or in tales of visits to the Playboy Mansion, at which Messier marveled at Hugh Hefner's appearance amid the revels in his signature pajamas and pipe; or to the set of M*A*S*H, the most popular television show of the time, at which Messier stood wide-eyed and delighted, taking it all in; or to the homes of Muhammad Ali—an invitation they wangled through the connection to Mark's Uncle Larry—Michael J. Fox, and Gretzky's pal Alan Thicke, where they met some of the big TV and movie stars of the day.

But the distracting glamour of L.A. could not be blamed for what happened in game one at Northlands, where the Kings rallied from a 4–1 deficit to take an 8–6 lead. The Oilers managed to tie the score, but L.A. got the final two goals for a ridiculous 10–8 result that exposed the weakness of Edmonton's defense-be-damned style. In game two, Messier gave the puck away behind the net, leading to an easy goal that gave the Kings a 2–1 lead, but Gretzky eventually scored the 3–2 overtime winner to tie the series.

Things got worse for Edmonton in game three, played at the Forum on Manchester Boulevard in Inglewood, California. The Kings drew only their third sellout crowd of the season. The Oilers raced to a 5–0 lead through two periods and were on their way to a laugher. The Forum crowd was booing another futile Kings power play, and the Oilers on the bench joined in, booing, laughing, singing songs and squirting water bottles at one another. "Hey, the fans were booing, so we did too," Gretzky said. "We did that a lot that year. We had a lot of fun. We thought we were God's gift to hockey." But then came what many still consider the greatest episode in Los Angeles Kings history: the Miracle on Manchester. With eighteen minutes to go, Jay Wells scored for L.A., then Doug Smith, then Charlie Simmer bounced it past Grant Fuhr off Randy Gregg's skate. With four minutes left, Mark Hardy skated around the defense and Fuhr to make it 5–4, and with only five seconds left on the clock, Steve Bozek found the net through a crowd to send the game into overtime. If the Kings scored next, it would cap the greatest comeback in NHL playoff history. Messier had a breakaway in the second minute of the extra session, but shot over the crossbar. Soon thereafter there was a draw in the Oilers' zone. Messier took it, but was beaten by Smith, who sent the puck to Daryl Evans, who fired a twenty-five-foot slapper that beat Fuhr and sent the crowd, and the entire hockey world, into a frenzy. The cocky Oilers, who had jeered the Kings from the bench during the game and were generally "young and obnoxious," as Gretzky put it several years later, had been taken down a humbling notch.

The next day, as the depressed Oilers sat in their team bus on the way to practice, Dave Semenko broke the silence by piping up, "Can you believe what we did last night?", which cracked everyone up. They hung on to beat the Kings 3–2 the next night, but lost the fifth and deciding game in the return to Northlands, 7–4. It was a catastrophe, the first abject failure the NHL Oilers had ever experienced. Terry Jones of the *Edmonton Sun*, a columnist whose relationship with the Oilers was always somewhat adversarial, wrote, "From today until they win a playoff series again, they are weak-kneed wimps who thought they were God's gift to the NHL but found out they were nothing but adolescent, front-running, good-time Charlies." The assessment would stick in every player's craw. When assistant coach Billy Harris insulted Sather by calling the team "antagonistic toward opponents, officials, and referees" and "a reflection of Glen Sather's personality," he was immediately fired, to be replaced eventually by John Muckler.

For his part, Messier had not played very well in the Kings series; after the playoffs, he revealed that he was unable to turn his injured ankle and that his arm was numb from deep bruises, where calcium deposits had formed. Nevertheless, the notion of Messier being beaten on a key face-off in a big playoff game is a difficult one to grasp. It must have left a bitter taste, because from that point forward his competitiveness on face-offs, to the point of viciousness, would become a personal trademark. Still, he had had a fantastic season, and in June he was voted to the NHL's First All-Star Team at left wing, joining Gretzky and Bossy on the front line.

The Oilers approached the '82–83 season with a sense of purpose. Gretzky looked back on the Kings debacle as something his team needed, a "cream pie in the face" that taught them "we didn't need to be rubbing people's noses in it when we beat them." Meanwhile, Sather, a scrappy journeyman spear-carrier as a player in the '60s and '70s but by now an excellent teacher as coach and manager, stepped up the pace to take his team to the next level. As Harris had pointed out, the Oilers were indeed a reflection of their coach's personality, and Sather schooled his young players in matters like handling the press and the importance of cultivating outside interests, as well as in matters of hockey. He had also taken psychology courses at Memphis State and Oklahoma State, like Doug Messier pursuing a degree

while playing minor-league hockey, and he applied that knowledge by sub-
jecting the young Oilers to endless seminars and focus sessions they usually
found baffling, something he had done right from the start. "We were
eighteen, sitting in a seminar all day, shooting spitballs at each other and
playing hangman," Messier remembered. "It must have sunk in." Sather was
smartening them up for the mental and emotional rigors of a run at the
Stanley Cup.

From a more tactical standpoint, Sather told Gretzky that his ice time
would be cut from 26 minutes to 22, to preserve him for the springtime playoff grind. Hagman was not re-signed, and Sather also told Gretzky that he
would move Messier from left wing to center to take Hagman's place. But
when Sather dealt away defenseman Risto Siltanen and acquired Ken "Rat"
Linseman in a three-way deal that involved Hartford and Philadelphia, he
chose to keep Messier at left wing on the second line, with Linseman at center. The Swede Willy Lindstrom would be their right winger.

Before the season started, Kevin Lowe decided that he wanted to live
in a house, so he moved out of the apartment he shared with Gretzky, who
stayed in penthouse digs near the university. The oil boom was on in the
north of Alberta, and real estate was hard to find, but one day Messier called
Lowe and told him that his father had found a house. "It's unfinished," Lowe
reports that Messier told him, "but we can take it over and finish it ourselves. This way we won't have to pay rent anymore, and you and I can own
our own place." Thus did Messier move out of the family home in St. Albert,
the second time he set up housekeeping more or less on his own.

Mark's move from the family home coincided with Doug's as well—the
Oilers started an AHL franchise in Moncton, New Brunswick, and chose
Doug as coach. He spent the season 3,000 miles to the east. Mark's new
house, in the upscale west end of Edmonton, was a beautiful structure built
into the side of a hill. Within a fairly short amount of time Messier and Lowe
filled it with features, gadgets, and amenities. Lowe described the contrast
between living with Gretzky and with Messier as being crystallized by the
sports they watched on television. Gretzky loved to watch baseball and
sports reports, knew all the players' stats, and kept tabs on the times and
channels the various highlight packages aired in whatever city they were in.
While Gretzky was "so relaxed," Messier was "fiery." "Mess loved to watch

boxing on the tube and became passionate over the fights," Lowe remembered. "I've never seen a person more excited about a boxing match than Mark." Beyond that, though, he didn't spend a whole lot of time in front of the tube; perhaps those summers in the cabin near Mount Hood had had a lasting effect. "Mark wasn't interested in television. If a boxing match or stock car race came on, Mess would get involved, but otherwise he couldn't care less."

The Oilers got off to another fast start and once again plowed through the league. Gretzky set a record by scoring in each of the first thirty games. In a 5–2 victory over Montreal at Northlands on December 19, Messier, now wearing the Robocop-like WinnWell helmet he would use the rest of his career, scored four goals for the first time as a pro. He was still playing with the reckless abandon of his first seasons, still running opponents, using his stick maliciously, and generally scaring the hell out of people on the ice. "You look at his eyes, you think there's a screw loose," was how the hockey commentator Don Cherry admiringly put it. But now he tried a more measured approach, cutting down on the penalties so that he could increase the amount of time he was on the ice. He still tended to give the puck away on overly hopeful cross-ice passes, a problem he would have throughout his career. But that never stopped Messier; he always tried to make the risky play if the potential payoff was great.

"He was never afraid to try anything," Semenko wrote in his autobiography, *Looking Out for Number One.* "He wasn't afraid of screwing up. He knew he was good, but every now and again he would try to do too much and it would cost us. But where a lot of guys might try something, fail, and never try to do it again, Mark always went back for more. If he insisted on doing something one way, then he was going to do it that way, period. His attitude was, 'Hey, if it causes a goal against us, tough luck, I'll get two back.' Mark had confidence. He knew that even if he did make a mistake, Slats was going to put him back out there on the ice. It wasn't just that he was talented. You simply couldn't keep a person with his competitive drive on the bench unless you had a chain. A thick chain."

The Oilers romped through the Smythe Division once again and took third place overall, just four points behind the league-leading Boston Bruins. Their 106-point total was five off their performance of the previous year, but they topped their own scoring record by notching 424 total goals. Gretzky led the NHL in scoring again, this time with 71 goals and 196 points. Messier finished second on the team, piercing the 100-point barrier and cracking the league's top ten scorers, both for the first time—his 48–58–106 total was seventh best in the NHL. He took only 75 penalty minutes, but his two-way play suffered a bit, as he registered a plus-19 mark, three below the team average. Nevertheless, his performance was so impressive that he earned a second straight First Team All-Star berth at left wing.

In the playoffs, the Oilers did not trip up as they had the year before. They started by sweeping Winnipeg, then knocked off Calgary, four games to one, with Messier contributing a four-goal outburst in game two, one of a record three hat tricks he would get that postseason. He credited his four-goal effort to the presence of Doug, who'd been away in Moncton. It was the first time that both he and Mary Jean were in their usual spot in Section V, Row 17, Seats 11 and 12. "Mom and Dad were my inspiration tonight," Messier said. "It was weird all year with my dad in Moncton, to look up at those seats and not see them watching me. I wanted to win this for Dad. He's the one who got me here. And Mom always sits in Seat 11 because that's my uniform number. A gorilla couldn't take that ticket out of her hands. That's her lucky seat." Doug's response, as recorded by Terry Jones in the *Edmonton Sun*, was, "I'm pretty proud of him, but mostly I'm just happy for him that he's healthy this year and that he's been able to do what he's doing. Last year he was one hurt buckaroo. He was hurt a lot worse than anybody knew." Doug continued with an oblique observation: "I've seen it so many times as a coach and way back when I was a player. But it's pretty pleasing watching as a parent when you see the maturing. It's always difficult for a young player like that when they discover the glamour and the bright lights. Like a lot of them, he stumbled. Now he's succeeding."

Doug's statement was remarkable for what remained unspoken—the suggestion, so widely understood that a mere allusion was the only thing needed, that Mark's wildness was a thing that had to be gotten under control. But further concerns over that would have to wait. Next up, the Oilers swept past Chicago, bringing them to the Stanley Cup final with a playoff record of eleven wins and one loss. Lying in wait were the three-time defending Cup champions, the Islanders. The Isles, experienced and confident, had beaten the young and cocky Oilers in all three of their regular-season meetings, but had still finished with ten fewer points in the standings.

The sniping came early and often, as though the ill will from their 1980 series was still simmering. "We want to beat them more than anything," Clark Gillies said before the series. "You know why? Because they think they're the greatest thing since sliced bread." Bob Bourne said: "The Oilers are so damned cocky. The thing that really bugs me is that they don't give us any respect. The Flyers respect us. So do the Rangers and Bruins. Edmonton doesn't respect anyone. There isn't any team we want to beat more. If we win, it will be the sweetest victory we've ever had." Enough resentment was flowing out of the Islanders camp that a little damage control was in order, and the team's fine Swedish defenseman Stefan Persson tried to provide it. "They're a cocky bunch, pretty confident, which is probably deserved," he said. "They're riding high. We have no dislike for them. How can anyone work up a hate for Gretzky? He's so good."

But no matter how much some of the Isles tried to damp down the ill feelings, someone would come along to reignite them. A reporter from a Canadian TV station interviewed Bourne, who was especially touchy about the attention being given the Oilers, and the reporter never once mentioned the Islanders, even going so far as to say that many believed no team in the world could beat Edmonton. "It amazes me," Bourne replied, inwardly fuming, "that our team doesn't even get any credit for being there." Sather tried to spark some kind of David-versus-Goliath sentiment by talking about how his country boys were vast underdogs to the team from the Big Apple, who "have got the most fans" and "come from the richest area in North America." However well this may have played at home, Sather's spin-doctoring was comical to fans in the American northeast, who knew that the Isles were a team from the suburbs that, despite their incredible achievements, played fifth or sixth fiddle in the New York metropolitan area behind the baseball and football teams, and even the Rangers. A replica of a Bryan Trottier sweater was more likely to be seen on the street in Toronto than in New York's tri-state area.

The final opened at Northlands, with the Isles missing Bossy, who had been sidelined by an attack of tonsilitis. Still, they got an early goal from Duane Sutter, after which the two teams settled in for one of the most intense displays of action seen in any series. Billy Smith was incredible in the Islander nets, stopping all 35 shots he faced, while Andy Moog stopped 22 of 23. An empty-netter near the end made it 2–0 for the Isles. It marked the first time in 198 games that the Oilers had been shut out. "I didn't think anybody could do that to us," an uncomprehending Messier said. "We kept coming and coming and they kept turning us back, especially Smith."

Predictably, game one provided plently of melodrama, given the high stakes, the pre-series rancor, and the presence of Billy Smith—almost certainly the dirtiest goalie ever to play in the NHL. In the third period, Anderson skated around the net and was slashed in the knee by Smith. Smith received a two-minute minor for his work. The next day the knee swelled up and Anderson was unable to practice, and Sather blasted the Islander goalie, saying he was playing "like a maniac" and engaging in "a degrading form of hockey." The Edmonton papers plastered Smith's face on their front pages and labeled him "slasher," "creep," and "Public Enemy No. 1"—all of which only stoked Smith's contrarian fires. "That's the first time I ever hit someone in the arm and he got hurt in the knee," Smith said, before calling Edmonton fans "a bunch of sheep" and "fools." Things were getting entirely out of hand, and what should have been worrisome for the Oilers was that Gretzky was totally on the periphery, practically irrelevant. The same was true for Linseman, who was rendered invisible throughout the series, and his wingman Messier, whose wrist and shoulder were hurting, though no doubt several players on both sides were nursing similar injuries.

In game two the Oilers finally beat Smith, but it was Semenko who did it. The Isles replied with three straight goals and outdistanced the Oilers the rest of the way, 6–3. Gretzky finally did get involved, but in another stick-wielding incident involving Smith, and again in the third period. This time Smith unnecessarily but lightly tapped Gretzky on the thigh with his goal stick as Gretzky circled the Isles' net, and Gretzky fell ostentatiously to the ice. Gretzky claimed he was actually hurt; others, including Bossy, believed that he had taken a soccer-style dive, trying to get Smith called for a penalty. Either way, within a few moments Gretzky was on his feet, screaming at Smith and pointing his stick at the goalie's head. Smith stood in his crease and pointed his own stick at Gretzky's head, and the confrontation went no further. Smith was issued a five-minute slashing major. A minute and a half later, Dave Lumley stabbed his stick into Smith's upper chest, and now *Smith* went down. Lumley was given a major for spearing and the booing in Northlands was deafening. After the game, Smith spoke with typical bombast: "If you ask Gretzky and he is the man I think he is, if he can say what I did was intentional, it would totally blow my mind. I was just swinging for the puck. But Lumley was trying to take my head off."

The series moved to Long Island, and the Oilers already sounded as if the whole experience was a learning exercise, which in fact it was. "Sure, we're down," Paul Coffey said, "but you don't realize how much you learn: patience, experience, execution, how to deal with pressure situations. The Islanders have mastered all of that. We need to learn that." Assistant coach Ted Green pointed out helpfully that "they have eleven regulars between the ages of twenty-eight and thirty-two. Of the guys we have in the final, three are twenty-eight and one is thirty-two. That makes a difference." It was probably the last time for a decade and a half that an NHL coach would tout the value of age over youth.

At Nassau Coliseum, where the faithful had become quite used to winning Stanley Cups, no one was worried when the score in game three was tied 1–1 after two periods. Sure enough, the Isles scored four unanswered goals in the third to put a stranglehold on the series. In game four, New York took a 3–0 lead into the first intermission, and as the Oilers trudged into their dressing room Messier quipped, "All right, we got 'em right where we want 'em!" Edmonton staged a brief comeback in the second period, and Messier scored his first goal and point of the series to make it 3–2, but Smith shut the door the rest of the way. In the third period, Glenn Anderson lifted his stick in Smith's general direction, and the goalie dropped as though felled by a bullet, an utterly feigned dive that he saw as payback for the Oilers' theatrics. Still, it was convincing enough to get Anderson a five-minute major. When Ken Morrow closed things out by scoring into an empty net, the third goal of the series for the unprolific defenseman, the Islanders had won again—an incredible fourth straight Stanley Cup championship.

Smith was awarded the Conn Smythe Trophy as MVP of the playoffs and he used the presentation by NHL President John Ziegler as a bully pulpit for his petulance. "I'll remember the bitterness more than anything," he said as Ziegler stood by uncomfortably, eyeing possible exits. "I've never been so hurt, for all the abuse I took, all the crap I took emotionally that I didn't deserve. It put fuel in my body, made me do things I didn't know if I could do." Asked about the third-period incident with Anderson, Smith said: "When I hit Gretzky he rolled around and cried like he was dying. So that's what I did. I threw myself and I squirmed. I want to tell people in Canada and all over the world that two could play that game." Ziegler looked on, barely masking a desire that the interview end in mid-sentence. Needless to say, Smith had not taken part in the traditional handshake line at game's end.

The series was over. The Oilers had reached the final in only the fourth season of their NHL existence, the fastest for any team since the 1920s. But the Islanders had just won their sixteenth consecutive playoff series, an unprecedented total, and their fourth straight Cup title in only their eleventh year. Sather had already professed his open admiration for the Islanders after game three, and his words provide a good deal of insight into what he did to make the Oilers a dynasty in their own right. "We took our approach to building this team from the Islanders," Sather said. "They have good scouts, a great organization, and a strong front office. They go out and get draft picks and let them play. They give the players the feeling they have confidence in them. When you are drafting kids, as they did and we have done, you have to have room to play them. You let them grow up in your system and they become accustomed to it."

Messier led the Oilers with 15 goals in 15 playoff games, and in the Cup final he had creamed Tomas Jonsson and Anders Kallur with hits that bordered on the illegal. But his offensive contribution in the finals consisted of a single measly goal. The whole team had managed only six goals the entire series—three of them by Kurri, none by Gretzky. Messier had seen the Islanders pick up the Stanley Cup and seem as jubilant as if they had won it for the first time. No player seemed as ecstatic as Bryan Trottier, the center-man who played the same kind of high-scoring, highly physical, sometimes dirty, and, most of all, inspirational role as Messier. Trottier's personality was as reserved as Messier's was outgoing, but his jubilation was completely unbridled as he paraded the Cup around the Coliseum ice.

The Oilers learned still more lessons that night. Long after everyone had dressed and all the interviews had been given, the Oilers got ready to leave the Coliseum. "Kevin and I loaded up our troubles and our junk and made our way to the bus," Gretzky remembered in his autobiography. "We both knew we were going to have to walk by the Islander locker room, and we were dreading it: having to see all the happy faces, the champagne shampoos, the girlfriends' kisses, the whole scene we wanted so much. But as we walked by, we didn't see any of that. The girlfriends and the coaches and the staff people were living it up, but the players weren't. Trottier was icing what looked like a painful knee. Potvin was getting stuff rubbed on his shoulder. Guys were limping around with black eyes and bloody mouths. It looked more like a morgue in there than a champion's locker room. And here we were perfectly fine and healthy. That's why they won and we lost. They took more punishment than we did. They dove into more boards, stuck their faces in front of more pucks, threw their bodies into more pileups. They sacrificed everything they had. And that's when Kevin said something I'll never forget. He said, 'That's how you win championships.'"

Now the Oilers turned serious. Having gotten close and seeing exactly what it took to win it all, they grew up. They gained focus, learned the need for preparation, and finally understood that their raw talent and frat-house enthusiasm weren't by themselves enough. Just before the season started, Lee Fogolin, twenty-eight years old and by Oilers standards a member of the old guard, voluntarily handed over the captaincy to Gretzky, a move that Gretzky said made him "feel like a leader." Messier and Lowe asserted themselves, too; both of them talked a lot in the dressing room, Messier appealing through emotion, Lowe expressing more rational concerns such as who had to check whom. They weathered the criticism that already labeled the Oilers, despite their youth and the track record of other teams for whom mandatory suffering preceded ultimate glory, as perennial bridesmaids. "From the baby Oilers," Messier recalled, "it didn't take long till we were having all kinds of things written about us: we didn't have enough character, didn't have the determination, didn't have the guts, didn't have what it took to be winners."

As a sign of their new sense of seriousness, the Oilers could have concentrated more on defense, but they did not. "We were different than any other team in the league at that time," Messier remembered years later. "We were new. We played the game differently. It was a break from traditional hockey teams and the way hockey was played back then." But the Oilers weren't different for very long. Inspired by Gretzky's enormous scoring totals, Coffey's Orr-like numbers from the blue line, and the point-a-game rates of so many other Oilers, the entire NHL forgot about defense in the early '80s, choosing to focus on goals, goals, goals. It became a sort of mania: from the late '60s through the end of the '70s the average game featured about 6.5 goals; in 1980–81 the average shot up to 7.7, and in '81–82, it reached a hyperinflated 8.0. Goals were like Deutschmarks in the Weimar Republic, devalued to the point where you had to cart them around in wheelbarrows just to get the same value you used to get with only a couple. Everywhere, team scoring records fell; a 50-goal season, once the hallmark of a titan, became the sign of merely a pretty good player, and scores of 10–7 became the overactive norm in a game desperately in need of Ritalin. From the '81–82 high-water mark of 8.0 goals a game—the highest figure in the NHL since 1943–44, when World War II left NHL teams to fill rosters with minor-leaguers and teenagers—the average receded a bit to 7.7 in 1982–83. But if Edmonton's wide-open style of play was no longer exactly new, they still were the best at it by far, and they stuck with it in their quest to hunt down the Islanders and the Cup. Instead of changing their style, they vowed simply to get better.

The dawn of the 1983–84 schedule saw the Oilers charge out of the gate even faster than before, and Gretzky started a new point-scoring streak that broke the one he had set the year before. Once he got well past the thirty-game mark, he later said, he should have rested for a few games; he'd hurt his shoulder and it was killing him, but he felt compelled to continue the streak. Messier got off to a slow start, with only one goal in the first eleven games, but he picked up steam. In December, he tallied a career-high six assists in a 12–8 travesty against Minnesota. Finally, Gretzky's streak was snapped by the unlikely specter of Kings goalie Markus Mattson, but only after he had scored in each of the team's first 51 games, in which he notched 61 goals and 92 assists for 153 points. He then sat out the next six games, the last five of which were on the road. His linemate Jari Kurri missed them, too, and the Oilers lost those five road games, the last of them in Hartford by the incomprehensible score of 11–0.

That schneid finally persuaded Sather to make the move he had long considered. When the team returned to Edmonton, he moved Messier off left wing for good and put him at center. Now he was the number two pivot, second only to the greatest player in the world. "That turned around our team," Gretzky remembered, "because that's when it became evident we had a one-two punch that other teams didn't have. We had two guys who could score; we had one guy who could score a lot and one guy who could play really physical and score. It worked out well because neither of us had any selfishness toward the other. He would come off, and he would push for me to go, and when I would come off, I would push for him to go."

The first game Messier played at centre was at home against Winnipeg on February 15, and the Oilers won, 7–4, starting an eight-game winning streak. In fact, once Messier had moved to center, they went 18–4–0 through the end of the season. It pushed their record to 57–18–5 for 119 points, by far the best in the league, and their best ever as well. They set yet another record for goals scored, with 446, and Gretzky's 87 goals and 205 points, while just shy of his '81–82 totals, were actually a bit more impressive because he had amassed them in only 74 games rather than the full 80. Coffey scored 126 points, Kurri 113 in only 64 games, and Messier 101 in 73 games. It was Messier's second straight 100-point season. Moreover, his two-way play improved vastly; he registered a plus-40 mark, 15 points better than the team average, and was voted to the NHL Second All-Star Team at left wing. Messier, said Sather, was "like a young racehorse."

But the most noteworthy feature of the way Messier played in 1983–84 was his abandonment of the more measured approach he had taken the season before. Everyone called him Moose, but this season the mad dog was back: he racked up 165 penalty minutes, the most on the team, and was using his stick to punish and intimidate more than ever before. As Semenko put it, "You don't really see what Mark does to a lot of other players. The last thing you want to do is beat him clean on the draw. I've talked to centermen on other teams, and they've told me how they never wanted to embarrass Mark, because if they beat him, he was going to leave a mark on them with his stick or his elbow. Mark has such a competitive fire in him and gets so caught up in things that I've often wondered if he realizes what he does sometimes."

In October against the Toronto Maple Leafs, Messier was given a match penalty for high-sticking Greg Terrion, and he would eventually have to sit out a one-game suspension for having accumulated three game misconducts. All that was mild compared to the way Messier celebrated his twenty-third birthday in January against Vancouver, when he clubbed the Canucks' peaceable Swedish center Thomas Gradin over the head and gave him a mild concussion. There was some dispute over exactly what happened, but Gradin said, "I was blocking him out after winning a face-off and he just hit me after I turned around. I didn't see it coming. I wasn't knocked out, but I was seeing some stars." Messier said: "I didn't feel I hit him that hard—I've been hit harder at practice. It was a good play on Gradin's part, interfering with me as I tried to get to their point man. As I swung around to free myself, my stick hit him." Sather's version of this *Rashomon* tale was simply, "Aw, it was only a one-hander." Dutch van Deelan, a supervisor of officials who saw the play later on a videotape supplied to the league, described it as "an overhanded, one-handed swing of the stick on top of the head." That was the explanation the NHL went with. A few days later, Messier was given a six-game suspension, yet he was still unrepentant. "The film didn't do anything in my favor," he said, probably because it revealed what had actually taken place. "I know what happened, and I didn't think there was much severity to the blow at all. It was a glancing blow. I administered it, and I know how hard I hit him." In subsequent years it seemed Messier continued with some regularity to go after players who happened to be European.

But whatever the moral implications of his renewed maliciousness—as Semenko put it, Messier "has a mean streak that's unequaled"—there could be no arguing with its effectiveness. He inspired his teammates. "You could see it in his eyes; he was pushing guys a little bit more the next year," Sather said of the season that followed the loss to the Isles. "All of them pushed, but Mark was the guy who stood up and said it when it had to be said in the dressing room." Lowe remembered that "Mark did whatever it took. If it happened to be a game where Wayne was being checked, he went out and took charge offensively. If Wayne was doing his thing like he did normally, Mark would be a physical force. The point I'm trying to make is that he made a commitment to just wanting to win."

The Oilers rolled into the playoffs armed and ready. They knocked off Winnipeg again in three straight, but against Calgary they struggled, needing a seventh game to win a hard-fought series that was the first real expression of an increasingly bitter provincial rivalry. In the deciding game, Messier put two Flames in the hospital. First he ran Mike Eaves into the boards with a huge, unpenalized hit from behind that gave Eaves a concussion and a broken wrist. He also hit Al MacInnis and left him with damaged ligaments in his left knee. "He ran over a few people, nothing major," Fuhr said. "That's part of the game. Mess runs over people. Sometimes, people don't get up. That's life. That's what happens when you stand on the train tracks." The semifinals, against Minnesota, passed easily, a four-game sweep. That put the Oilers through to the final, against the inevitable Islanders.

Twenty years have passed since the end of the Islanders dynasty, and it is saddening to see how that team has been treated by history. They are regarded primarily as a precursor to the Oilers dynasty, the obstacle that hockey's darlings had to confront and finally overcome before they themselves could ascend the plinth of greatness. Generally, when the roll call of the best teams in history is sounded, the names you always hear first are those of the Oilers, or of the Canadiens of 1956–60, or the later Habs juggernaut of '76–79. Only then are the Isles of 1980–83 considered. Too often they are used as a literary device, their own story valuable only as a preface to that of the Oilers. There are a number of reasons for this. The players who were central figures in the Islanders dynasty either retired as Isles (Denis Potvin, Mike Bossy, Bill Smith, Bob Nystrom, Ken Morrow, and Stefan Persson, as well as the coach, Al Arbour) or played important but less than central roles elsewhere for a couple of seasons at the end of their careers (Bryan Trottier, John Tonelli, Clark Gillies, Butch Goring, and Bob Bourne), while practically all the Oilers' central figures went on to play starring roles with later teams. The result was that the Isles' saga concluded with the end of their dynasty, while the Oilers' story acquired a second act that plays on to this day.

More to the point, the legends of hockey are recorded and recited in Canada, where the Oilers played. Not only did the Islanders flourish in America, but in a part of the U.S. where hockey is usually an afterthought— far from the myth-making machinery where the game's stories are told, repeated, and become part of the collective imagination. There was no muse for the Islanders, no Peter Gzowski to record their ascent in finely turned phrases or Roch Carrier to capture their essence in a work of children's fiction, nor were there cereal boxes, television commercials, SCTV skits, twice-weekly appearances on *la Soirée du Hockey*, or crowds of wide-eyed passersby who would recognize and stare google-eyed at them on the street. The Islanders did not play in utter anonymity—that experience would be reserved for the New Jersey Devils in a later era—but compared with the fame that attended and still follows the Oilers, their achievements are sorely underappreciated.

Indeed, the Islanders may have been the very best of all the dynasties, Edmonton included. When their regal procession reached the 1984 Cup finals against the Oilers, the Isles had just won their nineteenth consecutive playoff series—an astonishing run that no team has come close to equaling before or since. The Canadiens of 1956–60, winners of five straight Stanley Cups (but in an era in which there were only five other teams to beat, not twenty), won ten straight series during their reign; the Canadiens of '76–79 won twelve in a row; the Oilers of Gretzky, who hoisted four Cups in five years in the '80s, won sixteen of seventeen, but never more than eight in a row. Moreover, the Islanders trod a much more difficult path in winning the Cup each year than the Oilers did, because throughout the '80s the Prince of Wales Conference (made up of the eastern teams) was much better than the Campbell Conference (the west). Within their own Patrick Division, the Isles faced stiff competition from Philadelphia and the Rangers and, over in the Adams, tangled with strong foes from Montreal, Boston, and Buffalo. Those tight-checking eastern clubs provided a nightly gauntlet of strong goalkeeping, small rinks, and rugged play that grew only more punishing in the spring. In contrast, the Oilers had little to challenge them in the wide-open west, where only Calgary provided consistently tough opposition. The case for the Islanders' overarching greatness is a persuasive one, and while there will never be a way to say for sure which team was the greatest of all, it is a gross injustice that so many speak up for Montreal and Edmonton, while so few speak up for the Isles.

In fairness to the Islanders' legacy, their four playoff series with the Rangers between 1975 and 1984 electrified the metropolitan area like nothing in hockey had ever done before. The atmosphere at any given Islanders-Rangers game bordered on the maniacal and sometimes veered well over the line into madness. The rivalries between Edmonton and Calgary in Alberta and between the Canadiens and Nordiques in Quebec were fierce and feverish and even held important political and cultural overtones. But the sense of menace in the stands at Nassau Coliseum or Madison Square Garden when the Isles and Rangers hooked up was pervasive and inescapable. It was often literally dangerous to go to a game, just about the only instance in North American pro sport where the roiling hatred in the stands approached that of the terrace culture in soccer overseas. The only other places and times on this continent where that also occasionally held true were when baseball's New York Yankees hosted the Boston Red Sox in the 1980s, and when the fans of the Vancouver Whitecaps and Seattle Sounders of the old North American Soccer League actively emulated English football hooligans and traveled back and forth across the border to bust up each other's city centers in the 1970s.

The pressurized atmosphere surrounding the Islanders' dynasty made them stronger, but unlike the Oilers they were not a charismatic bunch, and this, too, contributes to history's unfair consignment of the Isles to second-tier status. Where Gretzky was preternaturally charming and unfailingly good-natured and Messier a Jumpin' Jack Flash *méchant*, the Isles' stars were much less flashy, much less ready for prime time. Bossy and Trottier were such close friends that they didn't mix much, even with their teammates; Bossy was seen as irascible and even egotistical in his push for scoring records and in his outspoken stance against fighting, while Trottier patrolled the ice stone-faced and fuming, allowing an outward show of emotion only when he hoisted the Stanley Cup. Billy Smith's personality was completely unsalvageable, and Potvin came off like a hail-fellow-well-met Rotarian. When the Isles won their fourth Cup title in 1983, Potvin brought it with him to an appearance on the NBC-TV show *Late Night with David Letterman*. He was interviewed briefly, but when he went offstage, the Cup was kept behind and propped in a chair for the rest of the show. Paul Shaffer, Letterman's bandleader, who hails from Thunder Bay, Ontario, was genuinely flabbergasted, in awe over actually being able to touch the sacred mug, but also seemingly a bit ashamed that it was being used as a comedy prop for an entire hour, the same way an American might feel if the original draft of the Constitution were Scotch-taped to Canadian talk-show host Mike Bullard's desk. Presumably, Potvin hung around to pick up the Cup after the show was over, but certainly Gretzky and Messier would not be treated quite as cavalierly when they appeared with Letterman in later years. Today you can buy videotapes of their appearances, but you can't buy a copy of Potvin's guest shot, nor does there seem to be any demand. If the Islanders had played in Ontario or on the Prairies instead of on Long Island, they would surely be a more storied team today, their amazing run of excellence remembered with all the respect and detail it deserves.

When they reached the final in 1984, the Islanders hoped to complete their "Drive for Five." Entering the series, they had beaten the Oilers in ten straight meetings, but they had also experienced two uncharacteristic hiccups in the playoffs, needing overtime to beat the Rangers in the deciding game of the opening round, then having to rally from a two-games-to-none deficit against Montreal in the semifinals. Moreover, they had finished second overall to Edmonton in the NHL during the regular season, a full 15 points behind the Oilers. Worst of all, they were banged up, physically and emotionally. Bob Bourne was out with an injured knee, Stefan Persson was playing with a shoulder separation, Bob Nystrom and the rookie wunderkind Pat LaFontaine had bad knees, and Potvin and Dave Langevin were mourning their fathers, who had passed away during earlier rounds. Finally, the NHL had chosen this year to experiment with a travel- and money-saving 2–3–2 final-round format borrowed from baseball, a sport where home-field advantage doesn't count for much, which meant that the Isles would be in real trouble if they split the first two games at Nassau Coliseum. All in all, the odds were stacked nicely in the Oilers' favor.

But nothing was a foregone conclusion, and the two teams still had it in for each other. "I can't begin to tell you how much aggression had built up in us concerning the Islanders," Lowe recalled. "The bottom line was that by this time we really hated the Islanders. We hated them because they got so much publicity and they were 'The Almighty Islanders.'" In fact, the opposite was true, but athletes often need to feel slighted for extra motivation. The Oilers used other forms of motivation as well. They toted around a big poster, a collage of photographs clipped from magazines of players from other teams celebrating with the Cup. Sather gave the players inspirational, power-of-positive-thinking speeches: "You're going to win, and you're going to win easy," he told them. The Oilers also came into the series more prepared than they had ever been before. The video guru Roger Neilson was on the coaching staff, and he prepared elaborate video breakdowns of the Islanders, one of which exposed previously unseen weaknesses in Smith (he had trouble with the puck when it went behind the net) and Ken Morrow (he sometimes stumbled when he turned quickly). John Muckler, Ace Bailey, Ted Green, and the rest of the coaching staff all pitched in to further prepare the Oilers. By the time the series started, they were ready, but there was still that nagging shadow of a doubt.

"We were expected to win, and we knew we could win," Messier later said. "But when a team has won four straight Cups, well, they just knew how to win. We weren't quite sure that we knew how to win."

Gretzky had been labeled a playoff choke artist by many in the press—hard as it is to believe that anyone could hold that opinion of a twenty-three-year-old—and he was out to prove differently. The year before, he hadn't played badly; he led the Oilers with four points, all on assists, but of course so much more had been expected of him. Messier had contributed far less the year before, and he had not stepped up when Gretzky was shut down. He had things to prove, too, even if there was relatively little pressure on him to do so from the press and public.

Game one was a goalie's duel, just as the first game at Northlands had been the year before, only this time it was between Smith and Grant Fuhr. Finally, in the third period, Kevin McClelland scored for Edmonton, and the goal held up for a 1–0 win. The Isles bounced back to win game two, 6–1, in a contest that featured no fewer than four fistfights, including a scrap between Messier and Gord Dineen. But the Oilers had what they wanted: a split on Long Island and the next three games at home. And they were further buoyed by the sight of Messier leveling the normally unmoveable Islander captain. "Mark hit Denis Potvin on the goal line just to the right of their net," Coffey remembered. "And at that time when you hit Denis Potvin you just went down. We were all, 'Wow, yeah, yeah.' It really brought our emotion up. We said, 'Hey, we can play with these guys.' Because up to that point the Islanders were so superior to our hockey club."

Nevertheless, the first half of game three at Northlands belonged to the Islanders, and when Clark Gillies put them up, 2–1, early in the second period, it looked as if they might assert their supremacy yet again, especially with Gretzky still being silenced. Then, in the game's twenty-ninth minute, came the pivotal moment of the series—and, one could easily argue, of the next decade, for it was the tipping point, the moment when the Oilers took it away from the Islanders and claimed everything for themselves.

The Islanders were moving into the Oilers' zone on a fairly routine play when Pat Flatley overled Brent Sutter with a pass. Lee Fogolin tipped the puck back into the neutral zone, where Messier swooped onto it and turned. The space between the Isles forwards and defensemen was empty, and Messier was able to pick up speed as he cut diagonally across the Islanders' line, alone against Potvin on the right and Gord Dineen on the left. He skated directly at Dineen, as if he were going to round him on the outside, and when the defenseman fell for the deke, Messier shifted his weight to the inside. He was in the clear for a moment, twenty-five feet from the net, and he snapped off a wrist shot, his stick bending and recoiling like a fishing rod. The puck lasered past Smith and into the net off the inside of the goalpost to Smith's right, finding a gap just a couple of inches wider than the puck itself. The score was tied, 2–2. "That," Lowe remembered, "was the goal."

Messier remembered it as "a real typical Oiler goal. Down through the middle, through the defensemen and a goal. And it gave the rest of the guys on the team the confidence to say, 'Hey, we can do this against this team, too.'" Grant Fuhr remembered it as pure inspiration. "We could only count on Gretz for so much," he said. "We needed somebody else because they were checking Gretz very well. And that's something that we were all looking for, looking for someone to follow." Lee Fogolin remembered it as a devastating blow to the Islanders. "It really took the wind out of their sails," he said. "You could tell. They were just deflated. They sagged." And Gretzky remembered it as the key epochal moment it turned out to be. "From that point on," he said, "Oiler hockey was there to stay. It really took our team to a level of confidence where we never looked back." With two minutes left in the second period, Pat Hughes pushed Pat LaFontaine into Fuhr, and the teams started scuffling. That set up four minutes of four-on-four play, the Oilers' bread and butter. Within a minute and a half, the

Oilers had go-ahead goals from Glenn Anderson and Paul Coffey. The floodgates stayed open in the third, with Messier contributing one of a trio of unanswered goals.

In the dressing room after the 7–2 rout was over, Messier struck a balance between caution and exuberance. "It's only two wins," he said. "As the saying goes, 'It's a long road to climb if you want to rock and roll.'" Game four started with Gretzky finally breaking through for a goal in the second minute, but it was only 2–1 for Edmonton late in the first period— until Messier scored unassisted on a dash from the red line while both teams had just three skaters on the ice. That broke the game open, and it ended in another 7–2 rout with Messier adding an assist on a Willy Lindstrom goal, his last point of the postseason (Messier wound up 8–18–26 in 19 playoff games). The Isles hung on bravely in game five, but when Dave Lumley scored into an empty net with thirteen seconds to go, the celebration was on.

Red and blue balloons poured down from the rafters as Messier shot the puck off the final draw into the Long Island end. He skated down to the right-wing corner in that end, where his family sat, and as time expired and the other Oilers poured over the boards for a massive dogpile atop Andy Moog in the Edmonton zone, Messier faced his family all by himself, whipped his stick around in the air and flung it away, and in the same motion, leapt in the air and threw both gloves to the ice. Cameramen and fans ran out onto the ice as the players embraced amid the pandemonium. The Islanders lined up to shake hands, and now all the mutual hatred was gone, replaced by true mutual respect. Duane Sutter wept as he congratulated the Oilers. Bossy, who had been shut down in the final series as Gretzky had been shut down the year before, wrote about that handshake line in his autobiography: "When I lined up for the ceremonial post-series handshakes, I looked into the eyes of every Oiler and recognized the joy. I've never forgotten what it was like to win for the first time. They looked like we did in 1980."

The Isles skated off the ice and left it to the Oilers. Messier flashed his huge grin as he went from player to player. NHL President John Ziegler handed the Stanley Cup to Gretzky, and eventually it was given to Messier, who held it aloft triumphantly in the corner to show his family. "I've been rehearsing this moment for years," he said. "Every night when I went to bed I went over what I'd do, how it would feel with the Cup in my hands. I've been dreaming about skating around with it since I was six years old." A couple of minutes later it was announced that Messier had won the Conn Smythe Trophy as playoff MVP, and he skated through the tumult at center ice in tears. Dick Irvin, the longtime *Hockey Night in Canada* commentator who was on the ice at the time, vividly remembered "Messier leaning over the boards, bawling his eyes out in the midst of bedlam." Accepting the trophy in the dressing room, Messier provided the strongest imaginable contrast to last year's winner, Smith. Beaming, he told the television audiences, "God, I went to my mother's place before we went to Long Island and I asked her about what she thought about this series. Usually she doesn't say too much, but she said, 'I can feel it in my blood,' and that was all I needed to hear." Mark, Doug, and Paul huddled around the Smythe trophy's big gilded maple leaf for photos with Mark, and the celebration went on and on in the dressing room as the stereo blasted some of the players' pregame favorites by the Thompson Twins and Aretha Franklin.

The celebration continued for three days straight, through the taking of the team picture the next day, to a public ceremony at City Hall, and, of course, the victory parade, for which as many as 100,000 cheering Edmontonians stood along the sidewalks as Messier passed, drinking beer and shaking hands with fans. There were visits to bars and restaurants all over town—where, according to Semenko, "we were going to give anybody in Edmonton who was thirsty a sip out of that Cup." He, Messier, and Lowe drove to St. Albert and took the Cup with them. "We had the sunroof open," he remembered, "and every once in a while we'd pop the Cup up through the hole in the roof and watch the reaction of the people in the cars around us. It was unbelievable. We'd have the horns honking and people in other cars smiling at us, clenching their fists, yelling, screaming, and applauding in midafternoon as they drove down the road."

One of the Cup's stops in St. Albert was the Bruin Inn, a small, white stucco building that has since been demolished. From the 1920s through the 1950s it was quite popular because it was one of the only places in the Edmonton area where men and women could drink together. In the 1980s it was a funky relic from another era. "We went to the Bruin Inn in St. Albert,"

Semenko said, "and there weren't many people in there at all. It was Mark Messier's neighborhood pub. So we put the Stanley Cup on one of the tables and played a little pool. Next thing you knew, the few people who'd been in the place when we got there were all lined up behind one another at the pay phone, waiting to call their friends and tell them what was happening so they could come down and see for themselves. We kept filling the Cup with beer and made sure everybody got a chance to have a drink from it." It must have been a marvelous, unforgettable night. Messier would orchestrate many more like it.

A week after the Stanley Cup was paraded around the Northlands ice, Jack Falla wrote an article for *Sports Illustrated* in which he heralded the coming of age of the cocky young Oilers. Falla enthused that "The Oilers may well have launched a new era in the pro game," adding that "the sleek may yet inherit the ice."

Perhaps so, but by voting to award Mark Messier the Conn Smythe Trophy, the hockey reporters seem to have concluded that, if the sleek were truly to inherit the ice, they would still need a big, combative hustler to lead the way.

FAST, HARD, AND
OUT OF CONTROL

All of Edmonton had watched its hometown boy grow up, and now in 1984, it celebrated with him. All along, Edmontonians had looked at Messier in that characteristically Canadian way, combining admiration for the local kid who made good with a dose of who-does-he-think-he-is. Edmonton is not a large city, and when Messier did things like hold out for a bigger contract, party hard and often, or drive his European sports cars recklessly, word got around town fast, and some people disapproved. But by 1984 he had also helped forge a Stanley Cup–winning team, and that made up for everything.

John Short was the Oilers' public relations director for the first two years of their NHL existence. Before, during, and after he held that post, he was able to watch Messier's maturation at close range. "I watched Mark play in the Alberta Junior league," Short says, "and I remember Doug [Messier] telling me, when Mark was fifteen, 'He's big and strong and he'll be a big star.' I said, 'Maybe he'll play in the NHL.' Doug said, 'No, he'll be a star, end of story.' Doug was a teacher, and a good one, and he was a good minor pro player who could've played in the old WHA and who would've been a star in a thirty-team NHL. He was tough and competitive, and obviously that's where genetics came in. Mark's dad was a driven man, and Mark was a driven man. And environment [played a role] too, because Mark was just immersed in the game—he had to be, he was so close to his dad when his dad was coaching. Then you get the obvious physical advantages that Mark had: he could skate, he was big and strong, and again, he was driven.

"The first thing about Mark was that he had this intensity, and this incredible strength. But he was a kid. He missed planes, he got disciplined, and Slats had to kick him in the rear, but he grew up. Mark always had the intensity, early. If there was a prank to be played, Mark was in the middle of it. In his first year in the league they were all so young, they had no sophistication. What they learned at that level was from Slats. He taught those kids every trick there was. He lined them up to be interviewed by radio, TV, and print people, and he taught them when they were nineteen years old how to carry themselves, that being interviewed on radio was different than being interviewed by TV and print guys. After a while, they understood that not every reporter was a good guy, and they learned to manage the media as well as Slats manages the media. That was only part of the education he gave them. The beginning of Mark's understanding of himself came from Slats force-feeding [the young Oilers] an appreciation of their own talent, because Slats himself didn't have any as a player—he was a guy that hung on and got a living from the NHL, but he taught these guys to appreciate their talent and put them in a position where they could benefit from it.

"Eventually, Mark got to a point where he was the guy who'd speak up. In the early years, if something needed to be said, Gretzky wasn't a talker; Gretzky wanted to get along with everyone. Lowe had the same leadership [ability] Mess had, but wasn't the demonstrative leader Mark became. Lowe would do whatever he had to in the room to get the guys going, but Mark took it to another level. The better a player he became, the better a leader he became. I see it as an evolution—starting with the first fights he had in his first NHL exhibition season, when he took on John Paddock and Al MacAdam and started picking up confidence from there—and I see him also as being incredibly fortunate to fall into that group of young men. Gretzky, by his talent, made so much room for everybody else. There was no pressure on Mess or on anyone else, because the pressure was on Gretzky. They repaid it quickly by taking the pressure off Gretzky, and he didn't always have to go out and score 212 points.

"Gretzky was the brigadier boy, but he had a bunch of generals and colonels. He realized he was the emotional leader of the Oilers, of all of the gifted Oilers—Gretzky, Lowe, Anderson, Kurri—but Mark was the only physical one. Mark was the big, strong, tough guy. They had Semenko to be a policeman, but Mess didn't ever do that kind of job. Mess did it emotionally. If he got fired up, he knew he could go do anything he needed to do. Lee Fogolin said that in motion, when skating, the strongest man in the world is Mark Messier. That kind of persona, with the confidence that comes from knowing you can go into the toughest rink in North America and come out the other side, that's what Mark had.

"When he was given latitude here, he got that latitude from his teammates. It wasn't imposed, it wasn't imported, it was developed from within. They were babies together, and they evolved into roles that fit them. The melding that these kids did was as much through instinct as anything else. Lowe and Mess lived together, and Gretzky was over there all the time. If they had a team party, they had a *team* party, even the jerks. It evolved with Mark in the middle of it, and because it worked and worked so early they just kept doing it. The sheer intelligence of that group can't be underrated, either. It's dangerous to fail to realize how brilliant they were off the ice. Mess was one very alert piece of work, always was."

The author Douglas Hunter touched less on the emotional development of Messier and more on his tactical, on-ice maturation when he wrote about the Oilers' first Cup in his book *The Glory Barons*: "It was Mark Messier, not Gretzky, who was awarded the Conn Smythe Trophy as playoff MVP. Gretzky produced the most assists (22) and points (35) of the playoffs, but in the trench warfare of the series against Calgary and especially the Islanders, it was Messier's physical play that carried the Oilers forward. . . . The weakness of Gretzky's style was revealed in the heavy traffic of an aggressive physical game. Unlike Messier, he could not fight his way through and still contribute to scoring. Gretzky needed a linemate who could ride shotgun for him . . . and when abused, rather than retaliating the way Messier could, he had to turn to his on-ice bodyguard or take dives to draw the referee's attention to the abuse he was taking. . . . Messier's Conn Smythe win was not a repudiation of Gretzky's skills, but an indication that a championship team needed more than playmaking finesse. It was the first indication that the Oilers might be able to win without Gretzky, and that they could lose if Messier was not completely effective."

Hunter may overstate somewhat the notion of Gretzky's "weakness" in physical situations, but he does aptly summarize the cruciality of Messier's presence to the Oilers' Cup dreams, as well as the emerging awareness of the fact among everyone who followed the game. It's kind of strange that over the next decade and a half, Gretzky would serve as the prime example of a nonviolent ideal for those who wanted to see hockey become a game based more on speed and creativity, and less on size, brawn, and pugnacity. At the same time, Messier would serve as the ideal for the opposing faction, who prized toughness and hard hitting over what they saw as a trend toward softness and effete European pussyfooting. No two players could better exemplify opposite extremes of excellence, yet they meshed together perfectly in every way.

It was a short holiday for Messier and seven of the other Oilers. Just a couple of months after they squired the Stanley Cup all over town, they convened in Montreal for Team Canada's 1984 training camp. The national professional team was to have a new look, to make a break with the disasters of the recent past. Since the razor-thin victory in the Summit Series of 1972, when the Canadians established that they had enormous heart and would stop at nothing, including appalling viciousness, to win, but when the Soviets established that they were just as good, Canada's NHLers had been embarrassed repeatedly. Soviet club teams toured North America in 1975–76, and NHL clubs won only two of the games, in one of which the Philadelphia Flyers hacked, speared, and slashed Central Red Army players while the NHL referee and linesmen looked the other way. Canada won the inaugural Canada Cup tournament in 1976, but in '79 came the NHL All-Star debacle at Madison Square Garden and in the 1981 Canada Cup, the home side was again demolished by a vastly superior USSR team.

The Canadians refused to play the Soviets unless they were first granted every conceivable concession. Big Olympic-size rinks? Out. Smaller NHL rinks would have to suffice. Games both at home and abroad? Nix: Team Canada's policy of never again playing on Soviet ice, or on any ice outside North America, ossified into a hard and fast rule that would not be superseded until 1998. One-game championship matches? Nope. When the Soviets creamed the Canadians in the 1981 tournament's one-game final, it was decided that all future finals would be best-of-three affairs, to give Canada a chance to recover in case of future setbacks. Possession of the Canada Cup itself? Not if the Soviets won it; tournament organizer Alan Eagleson gracelessly refused to let the Soviets take it to Moscow after they won it in '81. But for all the shenanigans intended to give Canada an extra edge, none had worked so far. In the end it was clear that the best way to win back prestige for Canada was to actually become a better team on the ice.

To that end, the selectors of Team Canada chose Glen Sather, the architect and builder of the new Oilers juggernaut, as head coach. He brought with him Messier, Gretzky, Glenn Anderson, Kevin Lowe, Paul Coffey, Randy Gregg, Charlie Huddy, and Grant Fuhr. But an Islanders contingent was recruited as well: Mike Bossy, John Tonelli, Bob Bourne, and Brent Sutter. Denis Potvin was invited but didn't come because he was being treated for high blood pressure, the cause of the leg cramps that had sharply limited his effectiveness in the previous spring's Cup finals. Bryan Trottier didn't play, either. He was part Chippewa, Cree, and Métis and thus eligible to play either for Canada, which he had represented at previous tournaments, or the U.S., and because he lived and worked in the States and had married an American, he opted for the latter. Trottier's decision caused some controversy in Canada, but it was in keeping with the deeply individualistic, sometimes idiosyncratic personality that marked the Islanders, which stood in contrast with the Oilers' atmosphere of close-knit tomfoolery. Those two factions within Team Canada would clash as the tournament got under way.

It was Bossy who touched off the rift. As deft as Gretzky was with word and gesture, Bossy was clumsy, and his own account of the miserable time he had at the 1984 Canada Cup tournament is unintentionally hilarious. First, he blurted out criticism of Trottier, his close friend, when he learned that Trottier would be playing for the U.S.. They ironed out their differences in a subsequent discussion (as always, Bossy claimed that "I answered difficult questions frankly, but only the negative half of my answers were written"), but Bossy admits to sticking his knee out and tripping Trottier when they played opposite each other in the tournament, prompting the fallen Trottier to mutter, "You lazy bastard, you little rat." Bossy also stayed at home in Laval while everyone else on the roster stayed at a Montreal hotel, and later he asked to be given his own room when the team moved to Banff. At one point Sather tried to lure Bossy into a greater sense of involvement by offering him the co-captaincy, getting a response of "Sure, fine" from the star winger. In the end Gretzky and Larry Robinson were chosen instead. Through each of these episodes—all as recounted by Bossy in his own autobiography—he can't seem to understand why his simple statements and requests keep getting misunderstood.

Later in the tournament, Bossy would ignite the Islanders–Oilers powderkeg. Team Canada started the tournament well enough, crushing West Germany in Montreal, 7–2, in the first real game Messier ever played for his country. (He wore the number 12 sweater; Mike Gartner wore number 11.) But then they stumbled to a 4–4 tie with the U.S., and the third match, in Vancouver, wound up a shocking 4–2 loss to Sweden. Afterward, Bossy was asked whether things would be different if Al Arbour were coaching instead of Sather, and Bossy was honest, impolitic, and naïve enough to answer yes. His remark was taken the wrong way by the Oilers in the dressing room, and now the Oilers and Isles, who had seemingly patched things up after the previous spring, were at loggerheads again. It was, Gretzky remembered, a far more difficult problem for Team Canada to overcome than any presented by the Soviets, Swedes, or Americans. Getting the two factions on the team to work together, he said, was "like getting rival street gangs together for a prom." Finally Sather directed the co-captains, Gretzky and Robinson, to gather everyone into a hotel room and clear the air. There, over beers, Bob Bourne told the Oilers, "Let's face it. We just don't like you guys." It took a while, but finally everything got talked out. The two factions were at peace and united in common cause. The necessity and effectiveness of what Gretzky and Robinson had just done was not lost on Messier.

Canada bounced back to dominate an especially wan Czechoslovakian side, 7–2, in Calgary, thus clinching one of the four semifinal berths. Their fifth and final round-robin game was against the USSR in Edmonton. A

Canadian win or draw would give them second place, and even a loss would likely leave them in third; either way their semifinal would be against the USA or Sweden. The setting was perfect for Messier to act: in his hometown, in an important game against the feared and hated Soviets.

He acted right away. Halfway through a scoreless first period, Messier crashed into Vladimir Kovin with his hands high and his stick on both of them. Kovin went down, and the ice turned red with his blood where he lay. Messier was given a mild two-minute elbowing penalty by the Swedish referee, although many maintain it wasn't Messier's elbow that opened up Kovin's face, but rather the butt end of his stick. In their book *The World Cup of Hockey*, Joseph Pelletier and Patrick Houda called it "one of the more infamous moments in Canada Cup history." Messier's stick, they wrote, "viciously carved into Kovin's face, sending him to the dressing room for over twenty stitches. . . . Kovin was perhaps the toughest man in all of Soviet hockey, at least the toughest since Boris Mikhailov. Despite being the all-time leader in penalty minutes in Russia, Kovin was no match for a moose named Messier."

The Soviets punished Messier and Canada by scoring on the ensuing power play to take a 1–0 lead. The Canadians struck back to go up 2–1, but the Soviets were too good, and they won by a convincing 6–3 margin. From Team Canada's standpoint, the whole scenario backfired from the start. Messier's rearrangement of Kovin's face should have intimidated the Soviets, but never in its history was the Soviet team put off by intimidation, and would not be in this game, either. Even the atmosphere at Northlands was off: only 12,400 were in the stands. And because of the combination of results elsewhere that night, Canada finished a humbling fourth. They were a 2–2–1 team headed for an immediate rematch in the semifinal with the unbeaten, untied Soviets.

This would be the famous game in Calgary that Canada won on Paul Coffey's heroics. Doug Wilson's goal with six minutes left in regulation tied it at 2–2, and Messier had two point-blank chances robbed by Soviet goaler Vladimir Myshkin, including one with 90 seconds left. In the thirteenth minute of overtime, Coffey stopped a two-on-one rush by Kovin and Varnakov with a brilliant diving lunge. He then got to his feet, lugged the puck up ice into the Soviet end, dished it off and, when he got it back a moment later, fired it on net. Bossy was there, having just knocked the goal stick out of Myshkin's hands, and he tipped the puck in for the winner. The fractious Canadians had finally come together as a team to beat their *bête rouge*.

Now only the anticlimactic formality of playing the Swedes in a best-of-three final lay ahead. But Sweden's coach, Leif Boork, restored a sense of drama. He said the Soviets would have been a tougher opponent than Canada, because Sweden had lost forty-one straight times to the USSR but had beaten Canada the previous week. Then he accused Messier and Glenn Anderson of throwing cheap shots. "They play like children," Boork said. "My team is not intimidated by Messier and Anderson. They do such stupid things on the ice. I do not understand why the coaches allow them to play that way. It's difficult to understand why they do this, because they should be outstanding players. They have not been outstanding in the Canada Cup." Told of Boork's remarks, Messier said, "Some unknown from Sweden makes some statement about me and I'm going to change my style? Are you crazy?" When asked about what he'd done to Kovin, Messier replied, "I don't regret that one bit."

Game one in Calgary went smoothly for Canada, a 5–2 victory that included a Mike Gartner goal assisted by his old Stingers linemate Messier, even if Messier did appear to be offside on the play. Game two in Edmonton went less smoothly. After Messier scored to help the Canadians to a four-goal lead, they allowed the Swedes to mount a stirring comeback. But it fell just short, and Team Canada won, 6–5. Now Messier and his fellow Oilers had another trophy to carry around the Northlands ice, the Canada Cup. The nation's wounded pride was restored; for the first time in five years, Canadians could legitimately say they were the best in the world. After the game, Messier gave the Swedes their props for playing with heart and pride, but he couldn't resist one last veiled shot at Boork, saying that the real tournament final had actually been the USSR–Canada game.

The Canada Cup was a valuable, if mixed, experience for Messier. He learned about leadership from seeing firsthand what had to be done to change the dynamic that divided Team Canada. But he had not asserted himself as the statesman or the nuanced speaker he would later prove to be. As far as his play on the ice was concerned, Boork was right: Messier's series had not been outstanding; in fact, the Islanders' John Tonelli was named tournament MVP for doing the kind of things Messier had done in the Stanley Cup playoffs. And his one fearsome hit, the one that cut open Kovin's face, probably did nothing to intimidate or slow up the Soviets, either.

But that hit, and all the cocky, tough-guy quotes he gave in defense of it, helped forge the legend of the indomitable Messier, the player who was a law unto himself and for whom conventional rules simply didn't apply. All of Canada saw that what he had done for the Oilers, he was just as willing to do for his country.

Messier signed a contract extension with Edmonton during the summer, passing up a chance at the limited free agency that would have been available at the time. He chose to stay with the Oilers, and when the NHL schedule started soon after the Canada Cup, they were not merely cocky; they were now justifiably confident. They continued to rely on offense, and Gretzky continued to mow down scoring landmarks, becoming the fastest to amass 1,000 career points and 500 career goals. Messier strained ligaments in his left knee in Winnipeg on November 4, and he sat out fifteen games. But he was now seen as the toughest, meanest son of a bitch in hockey, and as soon as he returned he proved it. Early in the second period of his seventh game back, what would be a 6–5 win on December 26 in Calgary, Messier attacked Jamie Macoun, a big, talented defensive defenseman who was developing his own reputation for the occasional cheap shot. In the first period, Macoun had rammed Messier into the boards, more or less from behind, and was given a boarding minor. "I guess he didn't like it," Macoun deadpanned many years later. "He jumped me and punched me from behind. Cracked my jaw." More specifically, Messier's sucker punch cracked Macoun's cheekbone in two places and bruised a nerve in his face that left Macoun's top teeth numb for about a month, injuries that would sideline him for five matches.

After the game, while Macoun lay in hospital, Messier explained what happened. "I snapped," he said. "But if I don't get even for a thing like that I have a short career. Macoun's hit was a deliberate attempt to injure. I don't regret anything at all." It was actions like those he took against Macoun and

Kovin, and his cavalier responses about them afterward, that cemented Messier's reputation as a player who was as volatile, unpredictable, and destructive as a vial of nitroglycerine. "Messier doesn't play the game square," as Don Cherry said. "He's like Gordie Howe. You bother him, and there's nothing he won't do to you. He could end your career."

The NHL took an inexplicable nineteen days to review the Macoun incident before handing down its decision. Messier was suspended for ten games. "The act by Messier was premeditated and unprovoked, since there were approximately thirty minutes between the time Macoun received a minor penalty for boarding Messier and the retaliation by the Edmonton player," league vice president Brian O'Neill said in announcing the suspension. "In addition, the Calgary player was attacked from the rear and was unable to defend or protect himself."

Messier returned from the suspension for the second half of the season and didn't play quite up to his standard. Nor did the Oilers. They still dominated, Gretzky set another record by scoring 135 assists to go along with 73 goals, Kurri and Coffey put up huge numbers, and both Andy Moog and Grant Fuhr were excellent in the nets. But Edmonton finished the 1984–85 regular season with 109 points, 10 off the previous year's total, and second in the league behind Philadelphia. Messier finished with an unremarkable 23–31–54 in 55 games and was a subpar plus-8.

Still, the Oilers never lost their signature looseness. Music still blared from their dressing room only minutes before game time. A Ping Pong table stood in the middle of the floor, and carrots dangled on strings from the ceiling, an embodiment of the incentives Sather and Pocklington used, like paid trips abroad, to motivate and positively reinforce. The Oilers' 1984 Stanley Cup rings bore an engraving of a carrot, as they would each subsequent year. The atmosphere was so loose, in fact, that Sather took a week's vacation in Hawaii at the beginning of March and left the club in the hands of his assistant, John Muckler.

Messier stayed loose, too, while keeping his eyes on the prize. "I was in the home that Mark had, after Kevin moved out," Short said. "It was almost submerged. It was really quite a lavish place buried in the hillside with every possible amenity. He was twenty-three. There were team parties at his place, though they didn't party there all the time. They were a bunch of guys, all young, all aggressive, all by contemporary standards attractive to the oppo-site sex. There were women around. They liked girls and they spent a lot of time with girls, and they also learned quite early that that was less important than winning games—because by winning, they got enhanced opportunity for financial gain or for whatever. The realization that they couldn't piddle it all away was at least started by Sather."

Still, some of the Oilers were getting into trouble, and people around town noticed. "They eventually learned to be quiet about the way they behaved," Short said. "A number of stories in the early days had policemen saying one of the Oilers was not in very good shape, but the policeman got him home."

If the Oilers were not overwhelming in the regular season, they were in the playoffs. They swept past Los Angeles in three close games, making up in part for the embarrassment of 1982, and swept past Winnipeg in four. Chicago gave them a tough time, but the Oilers prevailed in six and reached the final round for the third year running. Messier was back in form, having contributed 19 points in 13 postseason games. Their opponents in the Cup finals were the only team that had outdone them in the regular season, the Philadelphia Flyers.

Edmonton had some cause for concern: their record against the Flyers since November 1982 was 0–7–1, and sure enough, they lost the opener at the Spectrum, 4–1. For game two, Sather imported Esa Tikkanen, a Finn who spoke no English, and put him on Gretzky and Kurri's left wing. He didn't get a single point in the game or in the series, but he looked good, and the move was so bold it seemed to energize the Oilers. They won game two 3–1, buoyed by Tikkanen's presence—and by Messier's faceoff record, an impressive 36–14 in the series so far. Back at Northlands for the next three games, Philadelphia's big 54-goal man Tim Kerr went down for the series, and with one of the club's two best defensemen, Brad McCrimmon, already out, the Flyers slowly wore down. Their overworked goalie, Pelle Lindbergh, became dehydrated and therefore pioneered the practice of leaving a water bottle atop his net. In game four, a 5–3 Edmonton win, Ron Sutter was pulled down in the open by Messier and was awarded a penalty shot, but Fuhr stopped it. In the clincher, an 8–3 walkover in game five, Messier scored his first two goals of the final, both on unassisted breakaways.

Yet again, the Oilers paraded their championship silverware around the Northlands ice. Gretzky was awarded the Conn Smythe Trophy, but Coffey and Fuhr were also strong candidates, and as Sather said, "I would have split that trophy and given it to all three guys, then hand a chunk to Mark Messier." Most of the players said that winning this second Stanley Cup title wasn't as exciting as it was the first time around, but that it gave them a deeper sense of satisfaction.

That summer, the Messier family visited Mark's brother Paul in West Germany, initiating a new household tradition. Paul's career in North America had been bumpy. After leaving Denver University and signing with Colorado, he stayed up with the Rockies for only nine games, then kicked around with four Central league and two American league teams before landing with the Oilers' farm team, the Moncton Alpines, for the 1982–83 season. There he was reunited with Doug, who had also had an eventful few years. At the end of the 1979–80 season, the Alberta Junior Hockey League suspended him for the remainder of the campaign after a huge brawl between the Saints and Red Deer Rustlers. He coached St. Albert to a couple more provincial championships, and for '82–83 the Oilers hired him to make the jump to the pros, at the helm of the Alpines. There, Paul, under his father's direction again, recorded his best scoring totals as a North American pro: 77 points in 77 games.

But they were together only one season before Paul went over to Germany. In '84–85 he played for Iserlohn, then moved on to a long stint as first-line center with Mannheim. Some have written that Paul Messier did not have a successful hockey career, but that is an unfair and incorrect assessment. His career, in fact, resembled his father's, even to the extent that he used it to go overseas. There he stayed for several years and enjoyed something that many people would be glad to have: a well-paying job that allowed him to live abroad, doing what he loved to do. Doug, meanwhile, coached Moncton for two years, finishing five and eight games below .500, respectively, and missing the playoffs both seasons. He was fired after '83–84 and sold the St. Albert Saints before the next season started, soon to give himself over entirely to representing Mark, whose agent, Norman Caplan, died in October 1984.

Mark was still living life hard and fast, but soon before the 1985–86 season started, he pushed *too* hard, and it nearly killed him. At about 1 a.m. on Friday, September 6, he was driving his black Porsche down a city street when it swerved over the center line and crashed into three parked cars. He then left the scene of the accident. Three hours later he called the police and reported the collision. Messier was charged with hit and run and careless driving, and eventually paid a fine. This incident came on the heels of Dave Hunter's repeated instances of being stopped for impaired driving, an offense for which he had been convicted in June. Dave Semenko had had his license revoked for six months in 1982 after a drunk driving conviction. And the Oilers had a new centerman that season, Craig MacTavish, who had just finished serving a one-year sentence in a Massachusetts prison after being convicted of vehicular homicide.

Where Messier's behavior had only been rumored to be out of control, it was now demonstrably so. Some believe that his close scrape with death and the embarrassment of his three-hour disappearance awoke Messier to the need to rein in the worst excesses of his lifestyle. He never said whether that was the case, but just one month into the season, on November 10, Pelle Lindbergh, the Flyers goalie whom Edmonton had just faced in the Cup finals, smashed his Porsche into a concrete wall at 80 miles per hour. He was brain dead, and his two passengers were seriously injured. Lindbergh, it was soon revealed, had been out late and was drunk when he crashed. He was taken off life support and died four days later.

The Flyers' first game after Lindbergh's death happened to be at the Spectrum against the Oilers. It was an extremely emotional night that began with both teams lining up at their respective blue lines for a memorial service. The most difficult part came when Bernie Parent, whom Lindbergh had idolized, stood in a spotlight at center ice in the darkened arena and spoke of his grief. As Parent eulogized Lindbergh, Lowe remembered, "a lot of our guys looked down the blue line at all the faces and thought about the good times" and of how quickly it could all disappear. The teams retired to their dressing rooms, then returned for the game, which the Flyers won, 5–3.

In the weeks following Lindbergh's accident, there was a lot of discussion about NHL players' penchant for mixing drink and fast cars, a surprising number of which were Porsches. (Owner Peter Pocklington even gave his Oilers players Porsches as a playoff bonus.) That discussion coincided with increasing general awareness of the high prevelance and dangers of drunk driving and an accompanying tightening of laws and penalties across the continent. As it happened, it was at this time that Dave Hunter had several hearings over his impaired driving conviction and was sentenced to jail. He was released in February after serving one week. As a result of the Oilers' driving mishaps and the perception that their partying had now crossed the line to reckless disregard for others, the team's image suffered. Newspapers noted that, instead of the large crowds that had gathered in previous years, waiting for autographs in the corridor outside the team's Northlands dressing room after games, now only about a dozen adults and children were hanging around after games.

On the ice, the Oilers rolled on unabated. They finished with 119 points, matching their 1983–84 figure, and took first place in the league, nine points ahead of Philly. They led the league in every conceivable offensive category again, paced by Gretzky's record 163 assists and 215 points, marks that still stand today. Coffey set scoring records for a defenseman that still stand, too, with 48 goals and 138 points. Fuhr and Moog were excellent in goal again, with Fuhr facing a league-high 35.6 shots per game while his teammates cavorted in the other end, heedless of defense because they didn't really need any. Messier's performance improved over the previous season's, as he went 35–49–84 in 63 games, which, prorated to the full 80 games, would have meant 107 points and a ninth-place finish in the scoring race. His problem was that he suffered a left foot injury on December 3 during an 8–4 shellacking of Minnesota, and missed the next 17 games. He also clocked in with a strong plus-36 and a hearty but sane 68 penalty minutes.

Despite the clouds gathered over the Oilers, they looked unstoppable in their quest for a third straight Cup win. In the first round they met Vancouver, a team that finished the season with a 23–44–13 record (yet were still not the worst team to make the playoffs!) and wiped them out in three straight. Next up were Calgary, who wound up 30 points behind the Oilers in the standings. Another Battle of Alberta loomed.

Calgary had made a couple of important additions before the trading deadline, getting the Islander and Canada workhorse John Tonelli and the nifty American Joe Mullen. They already had Joel Otto and Jim Peplinski among the forwards, two huge bruisers meant to counteract Messier with their size. The Oilers had gone 6–0–1 against Calgary until their final regular-season meeting, when, with Tonelli and Mullen in the lineup, the Flames won, 9–3. That was a sign that the bulked-up Flames would not be physically dominated by the Oilers anymore. Calgary won game one at Edmonton in stunningly easy fashion, 4–1. Messier started game two by ramming Paul Reinhart into the end boards with a clattering body check just 15 seconds in, but the Oilers needed Anderson's overtime goal to win it. The series see-sawed back and forth until the Flames went up 3 games to 2 with a chance to clinch on home ice at the Saddledome. Sather took the extraordinary measure of putting Messier in Gretzky's place between Kurri and Tikkanen, and it worked. Down 2–0, Edmonton rallied, tying the game on Messier's shorthander, and went on to win, 5–3.

The seventh game would provide one of the most famous moments in hockey history. With everything on the line, Messier went all out, at one point smashing into Calgary's Calder Trophy–winning defenseman, Gary Suter, whose left knee ligaments were torn to shreds on the play. Still, the Flames were up 2–0 again—but Edmonton came back, with Messier tying the score on a shorthanded breakaway near the end of the second period. The Oilers seemed to have the momentum in the third period, but with 15 minutes to go, defenseman Steve Smith stood behind his net with the puck, ready to start a routine fast breakout play. Calgary's Lanny McDonald moved in to chase him from behind the net, and Smith passed dangerously across his crease. The puck hit the back of Fuhr's leg, rebounded—and dribbled across the goal line. It was a horrible miscue, which happened to come on Smith's twenty-third birthday. He broke down in tears on the bench, but his teammates were confident. During a stoppage, Lowe and Messier skated around the ice, Lowe telling Messier, "I think you'll probably get the winner in OT. You or Gretz." Messier laughed and said, "Yeah, this is great, isn't it?" But it never happened. Though they had several chances against Flames goalie Mike Vernon, they never got the equalizer. Calgary won, 3–2, and afterward Sather made sure to spread the blame among everyone, not just the disconsolate Smith. Sather didn't name names (although Gretzky was miffed that the coach blamed the players without accepting any himself), but Messier, for example, had contributed just two goals in the series and was neutralized by Otto. Edmonton's Stanley Cup reign was over.

It was a shocking result, but another shock just as big awaited. As the Flames moved through a memorable and hard-fought seven-game semifinal with St. Louis en route to the Cup final against Montreal, *Sports Illustrated* hit the newsstands with a big story on the Oilers' hard-partying ways, including allegations that at least five Oilers had "substantial" cocaine problems, that at least three people had seen Oilers at parties using marijuana or cocaine, and that a player on another NHL team told of having used coke with three Oilers during the 1985–86 season. The players and sources went unnamed (the article, written by Donald Ramsay and Armen Keteyian, was heavily vetted by *SI* lawyers, and large portions were deleted from the final version because of legal concerns). One agent quoted a player he represented as saying, "Every time we go into New York City, it's a real blizzard, and I'm not talking about the weather." Neither the agent nor the player were named. One of the few named sources in the piece, Staff Sergeant Hal Johnson, head of the RCMP's Edmonton drug squad, said, "We do not have evidence to lay charges, but we have information that there are users on the club." (Johnson later said that he had been misquoted, and that his department was aware of "the same rumors that have been floating around for two years," which were "not worth investigating.")

The article also cited various pay garnishments and lawsuits involving Oiler players, including a 1985 out-of-court settlement Messier had reached with Gus Badali—the agent he had retained before Caplan—after Badali sued him over unpaid fees, and referenced Messier, Hunter, and Semenko's driving incidents. One relative of an Oiler told *SI* that before Christmas in 1984, a list of drunk-driving checkpoints had somehow been leaked from the Edmonton police department and circulated among the Oiler players. The magazine also took a critical view of Sather's remarks regarding the alleged drug use. "Any kind of drugs you want to find I'm sure has been exposed to this team at one point or another. If a guy goes to a party, gets drunk, or sniffs a line of cocaine or smokes a joint, that doesn't make him a compulsive user or dealer or anything. That makes him a guy who went to a party and had a good time. If it becomes a habit, if he gets caught, then you've got a problem. But until it's a problem I can't do anything about it."

The financial problems of Grant Fuhr, whose cocaine addiction would become public in later years, were also brought up. The goalie was constantly neglecting his bills and seemed to have no sense whatever for managing his money. The Oilers handled all his financial affairs, which included paying him a salary of only $70,000 a year; the team even held a lien on his house, and Sather charged a monthly fee of $100 to handle his bills.

The article caused a sensation; for the first time, widespread drug use was being attributed to hockey players, the only major sport that had so far escaped such allegations during the drug-drenched '70s and '80s. *The Hockey News* ran a follow-up article and ran a cover picture of an Oilers crest reflected in a mirror, upon which rested a vial of white powder, a razor, a straw, and a couple of coke spoons. In the *Hockey News* article, the Oilers denied the allegations, and Sather called the *SI* piece "absolute innuendo." (Ramsay, one of the authors of the *Sports Illustrated* story, had been fired five years earlier by *The Toronto Sun* for writing an article that was found to have falsely alleged a cabinet minister's involvement in stock fraud, and this was cited by some as evidence that the *SI* article was faulty.) The *THN* story, by Stan Fischler, also mentioned an *Edmonton Journal* article in which Cathy Dea, described as Messier's girlfriend, was quoted. "When Mark is high on life and hockey," Dea told the *Journal* in the article, which ran before *SI*'s drug story came out, "he's high on it to the max. After a game he comes out of the dressing room, and he's still shaking a bit." The *THN* article noted the quote as "curiously ironic."

The fallout from the story carried over into the summer, with league president John Ziegler and NHL Players' Association head Alan Eagleson labeling the *SI* and *THN* articles "McCarthyism" and a "smear" while at the same time promising stiff antidrug policies. One absurdly distorted result of Ziegler's new get-tough policy was to suspend the great Maple Leafs defenseman Borje Salming for half a season merely for telling a Toronto newspaper that he had tried cocaine on one occasion five years earlier.

Lowe distilled the Oilers' feelings about the twin shocks of the Calgary upset and the *SI* story: "It was an education in what it's like being at the top, plain and simple. We were a high-profile hockey team. We had a great deal of success over the years. For the first few years, everybody loved the Edmonton Oilers. They were Canada's team; they loved to see Gretzky and the Oilers, they loved to see us win. But that only goes so far. Eventually people get tired of the success story, and they like to see a loser. And it was that much better this time. They loved to say, 'Aha, you see, those Oilers couldn't handle the success. Aha, the Oilers had problems, they weren't so glamorous. They weren't the boys next door.'"

The only way to deal with the taint of the drug story, the Oilers correctly believed, was to go back and recapture the Cup again. The club tightened up on defense, and that signaled the beginning of the end of the age of air hockey. League-wide, scoring would drop by more than half a goal per game from the 1985–86 average, to 7.25, and the Oilers were among the leaders in the sudden new trend toward responsible play. They still led in every offensive category yet again, but because of the lower scoring, games were closer, and commentators had the impression that the Oilers were struggling. That was true, however, only *vis à vis* the Flames, who beat the Oilers the first four times they played and wound up taking the season series, 6–1–1. Even so, Edmonton was the best team in the league. The Oilers would finish first overall in the newly straitened NHL with 106 points, six ahead of Philadelphia.

A new side of Sather took over in 1986–87, and the Oilers' paradise was shaken up. Before, the players looked upon him as their mentor, someone who took part in their dressing-room badinage and still enjoyed the camaraderie of team life, while at the same time helping turn them into more sophisticated people. "There's no doubt in my mind that he sort of cultured us along the way," Lowe said in 1987. "Ask the guys now, they might say, 'Oh, we did it all on our own. We learned about the theater in New York on our own and we learned about restaurants' . . . Glen encouraged that stuff. He just allowed us to grow. He's almost like a good parent." More than ten years later, MacTavish looked back on the coach the same way. Sather, he said, "really brought those qualities to the locker room, where everybody became not only a much better hockey player, but a more well-rounded person and had other interests and enjoyed doing a lot of different things."

But in '86–87, that side of Sather that needled and prodded and sometimes insulted his players became more pronounced. He still blamed them for the loss to Calgary, which irked Gretzky, and he started publicly questioning Coffey's effort. In the first month of the season, he traded Semenko, one of the most popular players on the team, to Hartford, which broke Semenko's heart. During one team meeting, Sather even went after Messier, who shouted back. Later, Messier was visibly upset, with tears in his eyes. Sather apologized to Messier and then to the entire team for what he had said. He had already dressed down some big stars and eventually would even single out Gretzky, but he would never again choose to confront Messier in the same way. "It was so strong," Jeff Beukeboom, then a rookie defenseman, told Rick Carpiniello. "Everything that happened at that instance affected the team tenfold. Slats is always proud and confident, and it's the only time I've ever seen him back down a little bit from anyone."

The fun was over. Winning had become a serious business—still immensely enjoyable, but the associated emotions were now more complex, more ambiguous, and varied enough to include bitter tears.

In February, instead of the usual pointless ritual of the NHL All-Star Game, the Quebec Nordiques staged Rendez-Vous '87, a two-game set that pitted the NHL All-Stars against the Soviet National Team. It was a brilliantly staged event, run as a joint sport/cultural festival in conjunction with the *Carnaval de Québec*. It was remarkable in many ways; for one, it was the first time the NHLers and Soviets met without the ugly Cold War rancor that had marked, and in some ways marred, previous meetings. This was partly attributable to the era of *glasnost* already in full swing under Soviet Leader Mikhail Gorbachev, but probably more so to the fact that it was staged in the province of Quebec, where there had always been much less of the knee-jerk hostility that greeted Soviet teams in the rest of Canada and the United States. Several top Canadian hockey figures—antediluvian Maple Leafs owner Harold Ballard, NHL Players Association and Canada Cup supremo Alan Eagleson, even Bobby Orr, to name a few—still looked askance at the games with the Soviets, but Rendez-Vous turned out to be an enormous success, largely because the hockey itself was so fantastic.

The first game was so fast-paced that there were no offside calls for the first two periods, and the five Oilers skaters in the lineup were flying, while Fuhr was strong in the nets. Messier played on a line with Glenn Anderson and with the young New Jersey Devil Kirk Muller. The Flyers' Dave Poulin won it for the NHL, 4–3, when he tipped in Mario Lemieux's shot with 1:15 left. Even though Messier did not get a point in the game, he was named the first star. In the second game, NHL ref Dave Newell called a blatantly pro–NHL game. He whistled down Sergei Nemchinov for tripping when everyone saw that Lemieux had stumbled on his own, and did nothing on the ensuing power play when Jari Kurri tripped Vyacheslav Fetisov in front of the net, took the puck, and passed to Messier, who scored. But the Soviets won, 5–3, on two spectacular goals by Valeri Kamensky.

It was a thrilling experience all around, and it also displayed a new quality in Messier, whose resemblance to Mick Jagger was receding along with his hairline into more of a Schwarzenneger-as-Terminator look—the assured leadership that would be his hallmark from then on. "I remember at the '87 Rendez-Vous tournament," Poulin said four years later, "Mark took over the dressing room. I don't think there was any question of that. Of course, Gretzky's presence is always a factor, but Messier just stood up and took it over. He said, 'This is the way we're going to do this, and this is how we'll warm up,' and then he said, 'Okay?' He scared the hell out of me. You played your best because you were afraid of answering to Mark."

Back in the storm of the NHL stretch run, the seriousness of the Oilers' intent was further demonstrated at the trade deadline, when the former captain Lee Fogolin was dealt away to Buffalo. One of the players Edmonton picked up at the deadline was Kent Nilsson, a high-scoring Swedish forward for Calgary and Minnesota, nicknamed the Magic Man both for his wondrous now-you-see-it-now-you-don't stickhandling skills and for his alleged penchant for disappearing when the going started to get rough at playoff time. That deal provided the basis for one of the Messier legends, when he supposedly pinned Nilsson to the wall of an Edmonton bar during the 1987 playoffs and threatened to send him "back to Sweden in a box" if he didn't straighten up. No one has ever been able to confirm the story, which Lowe, on several occasions, has said never took place, but other Oilers of the era have not denied that it happened. Either way, Nilsson's addition to the Messier–Anderson combination made for an especially potent line. Until Nilsson arrived, Kevin McClelland or Mark Napier was their wingman. "Before Kent got here," John Muckler said, "Mess and Andy had a tendency to play with each other and ignore the third guy."

Messier finished the season third on the Oilers in scoring at 37–70–107 in 77 games, one point behind Kurri and 76 behind Gretzky, although it is important to remember that unlike Kurri, Messier was not on the ice with Number 99 very much. Moreover, he finished fourth in scoring in the entire NHL. His plus-21 mark was a little better than average on the Oilers, and his relatively restrained 73 penalty minutes showed a level of discipline that clearly did not compromise his effectiveness.

That year, according to Gretzky, "we took every single shift in those playoffs dead seriously." The team's usual dressing-room boisterousness was tempered, the tone businesslike. After losing the first game to Los Angeles, they rebounded with a 13–3 win, a record for most goals scored in an NHL playoff game. Gretzky passed Jean Béliveau to become the all-time leading postseason scorer, and Messier scored the eighth shorthanded playoff goal of his career, another record. The Oilers went on to take the series, four games to one, then swept Winnipeg and got past Detroit in five, with Messier scoring two goals in the come-from-behind clincher. After that last game, Sather said, "Messier sums it up. He's got that unbeatable spirit. When he gets that look in his eyes, it spills over to everyone else. I played against Rocket [Richard], and he had that look. Messier decided that was enough, and away he went." Jacques Demers, the Red Wings coach, said, "There's just too much Mark Messier as far as I'm concerned. Mark Messier is phenomenal. We shut down Gretzky as much as we could, but Messier was there."

After a one-year hiatus, the Oilers were back in the Stanley Cup final, and they would face the Flyers once again. In game one at Northlands, Messier gave the puck away in the first period, which led to a Brian Propp goal. But he atoned in the first minute of the third period by bamboozling the Flyers' best defense pair, skating around Mark Howe and faking Brad McCrimmon to the ice, then setting up Glenn Anderson for the go-ahead goal in a 4–2 victory. The Oilers were behind, 2–1, after two periods of game two, and were being outshot as well, 27–16. They came back to win in overtime, but afterward Sather credited what happened during that second intermission. "I just wish you guys could have been in the dressing room between the second and third periods to hear Mark Messier talk," Sather said. If Nilsson felt any possible resentment toward Messier for what Messier had supposedly done, it didn't show. "Mark is the best all-around player in the world," Nilsson said. "He gets everyone going."

Messier opened game three at the Spectrum with a breakaway goal as the Oilers jumped to a 3–0 lead, but Philly roared back for a stirring 5–3 victory. Tensions ran hot carrying over into game four. Messier broke up a potential brawl between Flyers and Oilers during warmups when he ordered the glaring participants to knock it off. Philadelphia goalie Ron Hextall pulled a Billy Smith and slashed Nilsson in the legs. But the Oilers recovered to win, 4–1, behind Gretzky's three assists.

With Edmonton just one win away from the Cup title, the teams reconvened at Northlands. Messier talked about the previous year's upset by Calgary. "It's very tough to win once, let alone twice. No matter how mad we get, we're never going to get it back." About the way the drug abuse reports affected the team, Messier said, "I don't think it pulled anybody closer. For the most part, it kind of left unanswered questions. The big thing is we were all very disappointed after last year. Everyone was anxious to prove a lot." But Philadelphia wasn't ready to roll over quite yet. Mike Keenan pulled a motivational stunt that worked, getting the Stanley Cup wheeled into the Flyer dressing room before the game. Charged by its mystical energy, they came from a 3–1 deficit to silence the Edmonton crowd with a 4–3 win that sent the series back to Philly for game six. There, Keenan got hold of the Cup once more, and once again they rallied from a big deficit. Down 2–0, the Flyers rose up again for a 3–2 victory.

For the first time since 1971, the Stanley Cup final was going to a seventh game. And now fingers were being pointed at Messier, because although he was the leading contender for the Conn Smythe Trophy after the first three rounds and had played well in the final, he had only one goal and three assists in the series so far. And he was getting testy. When asked about Keenan's ploy of putting the Cup before his players, Messier shot back, "I hope they took enough time to read all our names on it." Before game seven, Keenan tried to get the Cup to show his players once again, but this time the Oilers' trainer, Sparky Kulchisky, foiled him by locking it away in a secret location; three minutes before the opening face-off, it mysteriously reappeared. In the Oilers' dressing room, the players were bouncing off the walls. "'This is the game you dream about playing *your whole life!*'" people were shouting, according to Gretzky. "Guys had eyes as big as dinner plates."

Just 34 seconds into the game, Messier was sent off for cross-checking, and at 1:13, Coffey was whistled down for holding, setting up a rare two-man advantage in a Cup final game. Murray Craven struck at 1:41, and the Flyers were ahead. But midway through the period, Anderson, Nilsson, and Messier worked a perfect tic-tac-toe passing play that ended with Messier directing it past Hextall for his 12th goal of the playoffs. With five minutes to go in the second, Kurri put the Oilers ahead with a shot from the left face-off circle. And then the Oilers did something they had never done before: they clamped down on defense. The Flyers tried to engineer a fourth come-back victory, but they were absolutely smothered, getting off only two shots in the final period. Edmonton got a 57th-minute goal from Anderson, and that was that. The Oilers had won again, but this time they won with defense. They had learned their final lesson and won the best Cup final series in a decade and a half. They were champions again.

In the joyous scrum at center ice, Messier and Nilsson embraced, Messier fighting back tears even as he laughed that open-mouthed laugh of his. He took Gretzky's head in his hands as if he would plant a wet one on him, but instead buried his own head in Gretzky's neck and shoulder. Then Messier looked up, and the two of them screamed in each other's faces with joy. John Ziegler materialized with the Stanley Cup and presented it to Gretzky, who, in a gesture prearranged with Messier and Lowe, turned and gave it to Steve Smith. Hockey fans around the world recognized the import of Gretzky's gesture: Smith was redeemed. In the victorious dressing room afterward, Smith held the Cup over his head. "This is not coming down," he said, beaming. "It's going to stay up there forever."

All in all, the Oilers' third Cup celebration was relatively subdued. There was a feeling of satisfaction, not only at having won, but at being able to put to rest any possible lingering questions about drugs, about having experienced too much success too young, about choking, about somehow squandering their enormous talent. All those questions were irrelevant now, and the Edmonton Oilers took their place as one of history's greatest teams.

Downtown after the game, a crowd of 30,000 assembled to celebrate and, in a phenomenon that became commonplace in championship-winning cities across North America in the late 1980s and into the '90s, violence broke out, causing some property damage and injuries to a few police officers and civilians, and resulting in some arrests. While the situation developed downtown, at Northlands the celebration was still peaceful. Messier took the Cup from the rink to the bar across the street, called the Forum Motor Inn, where strippers used it for a prop. "The boys called it the ballet," Oilers PR director Bill Tuele told Kevin Allen for a book about Cup celebrations. "But some have suggested that players were egging on the dancers to get involved in the Cup. That's not true. Players were mindful of the history. When a girl jumped on the table and tried to get in the Cup, she was quickly moved away." A couple of days later there was a parade, attended by only about 5,000 people—a far cry from the 100,000 who lined the ten-block route in 1984. It was inevitable that Edmontonians would become blasé about winning Stanley Cups.

In the off-season, a ninety-minute TV documentary about the Oilers was broadcast. *The Boys on the Bus*, narrated by Lowe and directed by Bob McKeown, followed the team through the tumultuous and disappointing 1985–86 season and on through the Cup victory in 1987. "Boys" shows the Oilers at work and at play, with plenty of fly-on-the-wall peeks at the goings-on in the dressing room. The players come off as fun-loving, charismatic, and above all, close-knit. The film offers an intriguing look at the Oilers as they mature, and it is a process you can literally see in Messier in particular.

The film opens with him as a twenty-five-year-old, eighth-year pro, his hairline already receding, but playing with a wild, uncontrolled force. We see Messier very dangerously cross-checking the Rangers' John Ogrodnick from behind along the boards—not once, but *twice*, actually breaking his stick in the process, then complaining to referee Bill McCreary when he gets called for it ("That's a fuckin' joke!"). We also see him trading bombs with, and pummeling, the Flames' Jim Peplinski in a rollicking fight. He skates and shoots beautifully, sits in the very rearmost seat at the back of the bus as it rolls into Manhattan, and cuts up at a team photo shoot, donning a pantomime bishop's mitre and mugging broadly. In the dressing room, he shows off Craig MacTavish's stitched-up brow and declaims for the camera, with a bright smile, "This is what it takes to win the Stanley Cup!"

In his narration, Lowe says that Messier is "certainly the soul of the team," someone "very capable of showing his emotions and letting people know where he is. A lot of times people question those emotions and whether or not they want to get too close to a guy who appears to be as ferocious as he is." In sum, Lowe says, "That's how most players in the National Hockey League perceive Mark Messier, like, 'This guy is way out of control.' And they stay out of his way."

But the most telling Messier moment comes during a team dinner before the cameras, with Messier questioning Gretzky about what inspires him to play his best, and each player distilling what they get from being great at what they do. Certainly "distilling" feels like the appropriate word for Messier here:

> MESSIER: Okay, then maybe it's not such a challenge that you've got to go out and match this or match that, but you can't tell me that you don't have a challenge in your own mind, that when you step on that ice, that you have enough pride and challenge to go out there and to challenge even yourself, if it's a challenge.

> GRETZKY: Well, as far as going on the ice and having fun, I do. That's the only way I can sum it up. All I'm trying to say to you is I can have fun playing with you and him and him and him because I'm playing with the best players in the world. But I can go out on the ice and play with Joe and Ed and have just as much fun.

> MESSIER: But even though you're having fun, you're still challenging it. You're challenging yourself, or you're challenging something.

It is unfair to draw too many conclusions from a filmed snippet of a dinner-party conversation, especially one in which Messier seems to have had perhaps half a glass of wine too many and uses a form of the word "challenge" a remarkable eight times out of seventy-nine total words. Nevertheless, the

Messier we see yukking it up in the photo shoot and engaging in what sounds like a dorm-room dialectic with Gretzky comes off as a bit of a rube—hardly lacking intelligence, but a bit raw and unpolished, too.

The Messier we see at the start of the 1986–87 season seems more focused. He sits in the Forum dressing room before Montreal's home opener, reeling off the names of his teammates, accompanying each with a staccato exhortation. It's a glimpse of the Messier who will take charge in the Rendez-Vous dressing room and who will help lead the Oilers back to the top, the Messier no longer just fierce or fearsome or intent on victory, but one who is now keen on leading others to victory with him.

APOTHEOSIS OF THE MOOSE

The National Hockey League had never been in better shape than it was in the summer of 1987. There were twenty-one teams in the league—a number large enough to yield a wide scope of competition and variety of styles, but still small enough that fans could keep track of who was on each roster and what was going on in every city. Moreover, none of the twenty-one were in dire economic straits; after more than a decade of instability, things had settled down into a secure calm. Clubs were distributed nicely on both sides of the border, fourteen in the United States, seven in Canada, and there were no complaints about under- or overrepresentation from fans in either country. Most of the game's best players were in their twenties. The champions were young and charismatic, and they played an entertaining, creative, high-scoring brand of hockey; yet defense, which had been abandoned for a few years in the aftermath of the WHA merger, was making a comeback. Tickets were affordable, rinks were full, and salaries—though high enough to propel players into the uppermost reaches of the middle class and beyond—were not seen as skyrocketing out of control. The boards and ice surface were still pristine white, unsullied by advertising, and no one had yet uttered the terms "revenue stream" or "retail point." Any team had a reasonable shot at the Stanley Cup, whether it hailed from a big city like Montreal or New York or from a small market—another as-yet-uncoined term—like Edmonton or Buffalo. There was balance on the ice and off, and the only worries people had about the NHL concerned matters of tactics or refereeing, not the cultural or economic survival of the game itself.

This was the hockey world that Messier stood atop at this particular moment in history. It was very different from the one he grew up in—his father's world of independent minor leagues and provincial senior leagues and a staid, six-team NHL—and it was different, too, from the wild and woolly days of the WHA that had enabled him to get such an early and lucrative start as a pro. Messier's NHL was one that looked to the wider world: managers, coaches, and players were losing their suspicion of foreigners—Europeans and Americans alike—and the Canadians who still comprised the vast majority of players were themselves becoming more worldly. No one epitomized this new breed of player better than Messier, with his overseas holidays and hunger for new experiences. But at the same time, he played as traditionally Canadian a game as anyone ever had. Commentators were just beginning to compare him to Gordie Howe, the most quintessentially Canadian player there ever was, as someone who combined great scoring ability with fearsome physicality and a mile-wide mean streak.

The Rendez-Vous games had done much to bring the NHL and European strands of hockey into some kind of harmony. But that was an exhibition series, something Europeans would call a "friendly." Another Canada Cup tournament was set for the summer of 1987; these games would be played in earnest, and there was pressure on Team Canada to prove that their 1984 victory was no fluke. With hostilities subsiding between Canadian hockey and its Soviet counterparts, the Canadian side seemed headed for a more European approach, one more in tune with the skills of their best players, Gretzky and Mario Lemieux, who would emerge as the tourney's biggest stars. But the 1987 Canada Cup would also mark the real emergence of the Messier we know today.

Glen Sather was no longer the coach of Team Canada. He was now one of the managers (Serge Savard, Bobby Clarke, and Phil Esposito were the others), and he demonstrated a willingness to put aside whatever rancor he might have felt after the finals with Philadelphia in agreeing to choose Mike Keenan as coach. Edmonton's John Muckler was named one of Keenan's three assistants. In August, thirty-five players convened in Montreal to try out for the twenty-three places on the team, but coming as it did after the longest NHL season in history, some players balked at attending training camp. Gretzky was one of them; he did not decide to take part until just a couple of weeks before camp began. Larry Robinson decided to sit out the tournament, while Kevin Lowe and a couple of other defense candidates were injured. Flyers goalie Ron Hextall did not help matters once camp started when he swung his stick and broke the arm of the high-scoring Hartford forward Sylvain Turgeon; some considered it a healthy sign of Team Canada's passion and commitment, but it was in fact a boneheaded move that should have cost Hextall his place on the team. In the end, five Oilers made the roster: Grant Fuhr, Paul Coffey, Gretzky, Glenn Anderson, and Messier.

Gretzky was made captain again, and he led through peerless example and unfailing nice-guy exhortation. Messier was another story. Washington defenseman Larry Murphy remembered entering the Team Canada dressing room for the first time. "Gretzky, who was the captain, came over to greet me," he said. "I glanced across the room and caught Mess's eye. I looked away right away but looked back a few minutes later. He was glaring at me, straight through to the bone, real mean-like. I knew the party was over. Wayne may have been captain, but Messier was the boss, no question."

Before and immediately after the first game of the tourney, several players were upset about how little time Keenan had given them to spend with their wives and families while the team was in Banff. Messier, Gretzky, and Ray Bourque of Boston had already gone to Keenan with players' complaints about the difficulty of training camp, and now, it was Messier and Gretzky who spoke up about the Banff issue. They led a small delegation who went to Keenan to clear things up, and the team came together as a result.

The Canadians struggled to tie Czechoslovakia 4–4 in Calgary in their first game, played before the heart-to-heart with Keenan, then moved on to Hamilton, where they had little trouble with Jari Kurri and Finland, winning 4–1. Messier chimed in with a goal. Keenan had been juggling countless different line combinations, but against the United States in Hamilton, the Canadians were given six power plays over the course of the chippy evening, and Keenan stuck with a power-play unit that featured Messier, Gretzky, and Lemieux up front, the three top centers in the sport, with Coffey and Ray Bourque on the points. They were sent out for a face-off in the American end with the score tied 1–1 and seven seconds left in the middle period. Lemieux won the draw, got the puck back to Coffey, who relayed to Messier, who passed to Gretzky, who shot wide. Lemieux retrieved the puck and, while Messier went to the front of the net to tie up U.S. defenseman Kevin Hatcher, slipped it past goalie John Vanbiesbrouck for the score. That took four seconds. In the third period the trio combined again on a power play, and the Canadians held on to win, 3–2. Keenan decided to keep the threesome together as a line at even strength, too.

Next up for Canada, at the Forum in Montreal, were the Swedes, a strong side that had just beaten the USSR for the first time in tournament play since 1977. It was 3–3 going into the forty-sixth minute of play, but Gretzky made a brilliant move, faking Swedish defenseman Tommy Albelin to the ice to set up Lemieux for the go-ahead goal en route to a 5–3 victory. The Gretzky–Lemieux–Messier combo was Canada's best line, with Gretzky notching a goal and three assists and Lemieux scoring two goals. Messier had registered no points at all in the game, yet afterward it was he whom everyone praised. "The guy who created the openings and took the punishment in front of the net was Messier," Gretzky said. Sweden coach Tommy Sandlin said, "Gretzky and Lemieux could be regarded as the best scorers in North America, but I like Messier. He is a complete hockey player." There were no complaints this year about Messier's dirty play; more mature than he was in '84, Messier had yet to take a single penalty in the tournament. And his ability to motivate was publicly endorsed by the highest authority, Gretzky himself, who told reporters that he and Messier had met privately for twenty minutes before the game to talk about what they had to do. "I wanted to play my best tonight," Gretzky said. "Talking to Mark helped. He wants to win every shift of every game."

The Canadians returned to Hamilton for the last round-robin game, a 3–3 tie with the Soviets. Canada scored the last two goals—including one by Gretzky with less than three minutes left—and Messier assisted on both of them. In the semifinal in Montreal, Czechoslovakia took a 2–0 lead in the first period, even though Messier delivered his first thunderous bodycheck of the tournament, drilling defenseman Miroslav Horava so hard during a penalty kill that Horava went pinballing into the end boards and landed in a heap. He made it to the bench but was unable to return to the game. Canada awoke for three quick goals in the second period en route to a 5–3 win and a best-of-three showdown with the Soviets in the final.

In game one at the Forum, the Soviets led by 4–1 late in the second, but Canada roared back. Halfway through the third, Messier appeared to tie it when Gretzky's shot went in off his skate, but referee Don Koharski ruled, despite Canadian protests, that Messier had kicked it in. Canada tied it nonetheless with 5:21 left on an Anderson goal set up by Messier, then pulled ahead when Gretzky scored with just three minutes to go. But the Soviets tied it only thirty-two seconds later, and won the game, 6–5, on Alexander Semak's goal in the sixth minute of overtime.

Back at Hamilton's Copps Coliseum for the second game—which many still consider the greatest hockey game ever played—Messier set up the opening score with a nifty pass to Normand Rochefort just forty-three seconds in. Messier started the game not with Gretzky and Lemieux, but at center on a line with Anderson and the smallish, high-scoring Winnipeg star Dale Hawerchuk, a unit meant to check and contain the Soviets' stellar KLM Line of Vladimir Krutov, Igor Larionov, and Sergei Makarov. They did indeed shut the élite line down, but the Soviets got scoring elsewhere, fighting back from deficits of 3–1, 4–3, and 5–4 to tie the game with just 1:04 left on an incredible solo effort by Valery Kamensky, who split between Rochefort and Doug Crossman and, falling, flipped the puck over Grant Fuhr's shoulder. More than thirty minutes of heart-stopping overtime ensued, and the game finally ended well past midnight when Lemieux, standing at the side of the crease, stuffed in a misdirected Gretzky shot. The crowd went insane.

The apocalyptic finale at Copps is also on the short list of the greatest games ever played. Messier's checking line stayed intact but couldn't shut down the KLM unit completely; they struck for two of the Soviets' three early goals as the USSR jumped to first-period leads of 3–0 and 4–2. But this time it was Canada who battled back, taking the lead with three unanswered goals in the second period. At the same time, Koharski swallowed his whistle while Soviet players were victims of a Messier elbow, a Craig Hartsburg punch in the face, a Brian Propp slash after a goal, and a Rochefort high stick that the Soviet linesman had to finally step in and call. But as always, the Soviets failed to be intimidated by such tactics; they tied the score at 5–5 on Semak's goal with 7:39 left in regulation time.

The stage was set for one of the most famous goals in hockey history. With less than two minutes to play and a face-off in the Canadian zone, Keenan sent out his number one unit. Gretzky, Lemieux, Coffey, and the fine rushing defenseman Larry Murphy went over the boards, but Messier did not. Keenan sent Hawerchuk out in his place—a risky move, given that Messier was Canada's best face-off man. Hawerchuk, though, won the draw and tied up Vyacheslav Bykov. Lemieux swooped in for the puck, and Kamensky collided with Bykov and fell down. Suddenly the Canadians were breaking out on a three-on-two rush. As it happened, coach Viktor Tikhonov did not have his best defense pairing, Vyacheslav Fetisov and Alexei Kasatonov, on the ice, a huge and bewildering tactical gaffe. Young defenseman Igor Kravchuk was out instead, and he tried to stop Lemieux along the boards—only to fall down as well, while Lemieux pirouetted deftly past and sent the puck ahead to Gretzky. Keenan's move had trumped Tikhonov's, and now it was a three-on-one, Gretzky and Murphy, with Lemieux trailing, on Igor Stelnov, who was all by his lonesome. Stelnov finally went down and took away the pass to Murphy, so Gretzky dropped a backhand pass to Lemieux, who shot past the goaler Mylnikov for his eleventh tally of the tournament. The final few seconds counted down with the Copps crowd in a deafening, flag-waving delirium while Tikhonov bawled out the downcast Kravchuk on the bench in full view of everyone.

Messier scored a goal and six assists in the tournament's nine games—a decent output—and his plus-2 mark was okay, if nothing to write home about. Yet the 1987 Canada Cup truly marked Messier's apotheosis as a leader. "The thing that was most striking about Mark was his ability to mix with the group without taking away from anybody, and his relationship with Wayne," Keenan remembered. "Wayne was an artist and an exceptional player. Mark was the passionate leader. The mix was fantastic." Keenan recalled for Rick Carpiniello the effect Messier had at a crucial juncture during the final series with the Soviets. "In game two in 1987, we were tied after regulation. He came in and just jacked the room right up. It was really an incredible experience. And the team stayed jacked up, even more so for game three. Honest to God, you could feel the energy in the room, like I've never experienced in any situation before or after. The energy was so high, it was like they were walking on air after he spoke."

NHL training camps were about to get under way, but the Canada Cup players were given a few days' leave. Messier, Coffey, and Anderson took more than a few days: they held out for bigger contracts. During the 1986–87 season, the Oilers had for the first time discussed with one another how much money each was making, and had discovered wide discrepancies within the context of the team and of the NHL as a whole. The Oilers were no longer docile kids, happy just to be playing on a great team and having a great time. Naturally, Messier's holdout reflected his cosmopolitan flair: he took off for West Germany. "I felt like dancing," Mark said later. "So it was off to Mannheim to visit Paul and do some club-hopping." Paul Messier remembered Sather's efforts to get in touch with his holdout centerman. "The phone would ring and it would be Slats, and I'd say, 'Mark isn't in right now, Glen. I'm not sure where he is.'"

Messier had other financial concerns, and characteristically, they involved his family. He now lived near Gretzky in an eleventh-floor condo near the University of Alberta in a leafy riverside neighborhood. Mary-Kay lived there too, and Paul was often there when he was in town, as were Jennifer and her husband at the time, Bruins defenseman John Blum. Messier also owned a small clothing company called Number Eleven Manufacturing. Operating out of a small factory on Jasper Avenue in Edmonton and with a store in the sprawling West Edmonton Mall, Number Eleven used old denim as material for new vests, skirts, and jackets (an idea that would become popular about fifteen years later); some pieces included a trim made of "carp-skin leather," derived from the fish. It also sold a line of resort wear.

Messier explained to *The Toronto Star*'s Frank Orr how it worked: "In 1985, my dad and mom went to West Germany, where Paul was playing, on a holiday and spent some time in Europe. When they were in Paris, they went to a fashion show, and my mother, who has always been interested in fashion, got the idea of importing some European sportswear. Well, that was the start of it. My mother had plenty of ideas, my sister Mary-Kay had studied marketing in New York, and my dad could handle the business side of it. So we put our resources together along with Paul, and what started as one sewing machine in my folks' garage now is a big, complex business." Doug was the company's general manager, Mary Jean the design and production supervisor, Mary-Kay the marketing director, and Paul was a kind of scout, sending trendy items from Europe. At one point in the mid-'80s the company had a store in Vancouver and was present at ready-to-wear shows in New York. Mark even appeared in print ads for some of the jean jackets, which sold for a hefty $270 to $345, in all his rolled-up-sleeve, 1980s-fashion glory. The Messiers had high hopes for the company, but whether because the clothes were too expensive, the style was not attuned to customers' tastes, or some other vagaries of small business intervened, Number Eleven went into receivership in January 1988.

Still, the main branch of the Messier family business was Mark's hockey career, and while he held out in West Germany, Doug represented him in negotiations with Sather. As Sather quipped later, "How would you like to spend three weeks staring across a table at Doug Messier?" Anderson ended his holdout in late September, but Coffey stayed out. He had been stung by Sather and Pocklington's shabby treatment of him in 1986–87, when Pocklington had publicly questioned his courage and Sather had sharply reduced his ice time while throwing in a few choice quotes of his own for public consumption. The idyllic mood in the Oiler dressing room had been broken, and the coming season would be one of adversity.

There was discontent elsewhere on the team as well. Mike Krushelnyski was unhappy with his ice time and skipped training camp. Kent Nilsson and Reijo Ruotsalainen, both of whom had made important contributions in the Oilers' Cup run the previous spring, went back to Europe to play. Andy Moog had finally had enough of playing second fiddle to Grant Fuhr at playoff time and joined the Canadian Olympic Team.

Most significantly of all, Gretzky was unhappy as an Oiler for the first time. He played the whole '86–87 season under the cloud of contract problems, as Gretzky wrote in his autobiography and as Douglas Hunter detailed in *Glory Barons*, which delves into the Oilers and Pocklington's financial and political dealings. Sather, meanwhile, started to publicly criticize his superstar, even though Gretzky's performance continued to be of Hart Trophy caliber. Gretzky and his agent Mike Barnett were renegotiating the contract Gretzky had signed in 1978, the one that tied him to Pocklington through 1999. A contract that allowed for free agency at some future point was not an option—the players had pretty much given that away in the collective bargaining agreement signed the year before, in exchange for enhanced pension benefits. Nor were Gretzky and Barnett able to obtain a no-trade clause. But what they did get, when a four-to-five-year contract was finally signed, was a retirement clause. That would mean that any team that acquired Gretzky before the contract was up would have to sweeten the deal to keep him playing. It was, in effect, a very cleverly crafted form of free agency.

Gretzky sought the deal because of the turmoil that had arisen in Pocklington's financial empire. Pocklington was a Mulroney/Reagan-era Tory with provincial and national political ambitions (in 1981, he made an unsuccessful bid to lead the federal Conservative Party). One of his holdings was a meat packing company called Gainers, and when contract talks between labor and management broke down and the workers went out on strike in 1986, Pocklington acted in a fashion typical of businessmen of the era: he tried to bring in "replacement workers," the go-go '80s euphemism for "scabs." He also tried other tactics to win the strike, among them cutting off workers' pension payments and hiring strikebreakers, along with drivers to take them through picket lines in buses. It was an ugly, protracted affair, and money hemorrhaged from Pocklington's holdings. Suddenly, the foundation for the Oilers' financial stability was beginning to look shaky. Players Sather had once declared "untouchable" Oilers-for-life—Gretzky, Messier, Lowe, Coffey, Fuhr, Anderson, and Kurri—no longer seemed quite so entrenched.

Messier missed the entire preseason, but just before the regular-season opener, Sather and Doug Messier struck a deal for a contract that made Mark, who had been earning an estimated $320,000 a year, one of the five or six top-earning players in the game and putting within his reach the million-dollar-a-year salary he'd joked about a few years earlier. He was in uniform when the Stanley Cup was dramatically lowered from the Northlands rafters on opening night, and he scored a goal, the only one for Edmonton, in a 4–1 loss to Detroit. "Mess suddenly showed up out of the blue, playing the first game cold!" as Lowe put it.

Three weeks into the season, Messier was forced to confront a personal issue he had not had to deal with while playing in the Canada Cup or holding out in Europe. On October 31, he was served with papers in a paternity suit by Leslie Young, a twenty-three-year-old woman who worked as a model and whom Messier had met in New York. She gave birth to a boy on August 16 near her parents' home in Virginia and was seeking child support from Messier. The suit became public on November 7 in an article in *The Edmonton Sun*. In the end, Messier acknowledged the child, named Lyon, as his own, and developed an affectionate relationship with him. Over the years Messier has said little about Lyon, just as he has remained tight-lipped about his private life in general. But he did seem to mature during his later years in Edmonton, and he has never commented on whether or not his becoming a father had anything to do with that. In the event, his fatherhood would be raised as an issue again later in his career.

Six weeks into the 1987–88 season, Sather dealt away the first of his untouchables. Coffey, Dave Hunter, and Wayne Van Dorp were sent to Pittsburgh for Craig Simpson, Dave Hannan, Moe Mantha, and Chris Joseph. Simpson, a handsome young goal-scoring prospect, would be the key addition to the Oilers. And Messier found himself in a slightly different role within the team dynamic: he was now a kind of elder statesman, someone who ushered new players into the fold and inculcated them with the Oilers ethos.

Simpson remembered what it was like to go from the last-place Penguins to the Stanley Cup champions and meet Messier, his new linemate: "Slats said, 'I brought you here to play a big role. I'm going to play you with Glenn Anderson and Mark Messier.' That first day, at the morning skate for a game against New Jersey, I went to Mark and asked nervously, 'How do you want me to play?' He said, 'In our own end take care of our end, make sure the puck doesn't get in, and hey, let's have some fun.' I learned the balance of being committed and being as good as you can be, but not so that you can't have fun. He was one of the superstars of the team, I was twenty, it was my third year in the NHL. What I instantly liked about being around him and playing with him was his energy and intensity. He had a balance, that intense look and attitude, yet he was carefree and enjoyed every minute and remembered why he was playing the game—to be great, and to have some fun. He was great at combining all of those things and not losing the focus you need to be successful."

As Simpson's first season with the Oilers unfolded, he took note of the chemistry that percolated between Messier and Gretzky. "Mark knew and understood his importance and had an understanding with Wayne," Simpson recalled. "There was no animosity, but a good competition between them. They pushed each other, but they also knew where the other one stood. It was important for me, coming from Pittsburgh, a team with superstars—you've got to have ego and cockiness, but the bottom line is everyone working toward the same goal and working together.

"There was an interesting dynamic within the team. It was Wayne's team, but everyone in the room knew we were different people with the same goal. Mark was more a stand-up-and-yell type, or he'd challenge guys. He was known to stand up and talk from the heart, sometimes with a quivering voice, almost in tears, and you never knew which one was going to be there. Wayne talked, but the thing with him was that he was unbelievably prepared for every game. And then there was Slats, who put pressure on different guys. As a twenty-year-old, if I had a bad game, I thought I'd be ripped apart by Slats. But the guy he picked on was Mess. It wouldn't do anything for the team to rip me apart, but to do it to Mess sends a message. And it sends a message to me, Mark getting ripped over something I did.

"Give and take, little ingredients of everything—the combination of all that was what made that team. Mark's laugh is infectious. He brought out a little fun and the commitment that comes of saying, 'Let's play hard on the ice, then go out and enjoy the fun.' We'd eat together, four or five people before every game. We'd all talk about what challenges us. In a big game you'd look down the bench at people you had gotten to know and trust. You didn't have to stand up and yell, 'Hey, we need a big shift.'

"There aren't that many teams in the NHL that start the season with the notion that they're going to be champions. That team had that mindset, and part of the burden that comes with that is to push yourself. One thing that was great about having Wayne Gretzky is that he drove that ship pretty hard. I don't think you've seen a guy that driven to be the best. It was pretty infectious, and I think that when Mark was young, he looked at Gretzky and realized, 'Hey, I can be that, too.'"

With Simpson on his left wing and Anderson on his right, Messier thrived as a playmaker as never before. By the time the season ended, he'd poured in 37 goals and 74 assists, totals that included 33 multiple-point games. He had five four-point games, and once, a five-pointer. Simpson wound up with a career-high 56 goals, and Anderson notched 38. At one point late in the season, Messier even centered a line with Kurri on his right and Gretzky on his left. One night, in a 7–6 victory over Vancouver, Messier totaled three goals and an assist, Kurri two assists, and Gretzky just one assist. Messier finished fifth in the league in scoring, and his plus-21 figure was a little above average on the team. Overall, his 111 points in 77 games was second on the Oilers only to Gretzky, and he also weighed in with a rambunctious 103 penalty minutes. On the night Gretzky tied Gordie Howe's all-time assist record, a 7–4 victory on March 5 over Philadelphia and their stick-swinging goalie Hextall, Messier was thrown out for being the third man involved in a fight. The festivities had broken out after Messier scored while Hextall was tangled up with Simpson in the crease, and Hextall cross-checked Simpson after first jawing at referee Bob Myers.

Despite Messier's fine play, however, Edmonton did not do quite as well as in years past. Their 99 points represented only the third-best mark in the NHL, and the Oilers finished second in the Smythe Division behind hated Calgary, whose 105 points topped the NHL. The Flames also scored more goals than Oilers did, the first time since '81–82 that Edmonton did not pace the league in scoring. The team missed the firepower of Coffey—and of Gretzky, who lost sixteen games to an eye injury and won neither the Ross nor the Hart Trophy for the first time in eight years. Both those honors went to Lemieux, who had clearly learned his Canada Cup lessons well.

Sather saw that his team needed a boost, and at the trading deadline he acquired swift, clever wingman Geoff Courtnall and backup goaler Bill Ranford from Boston in exchange for the rights to the disgruntled Moog. Fuhr would play in 75 regular-season games—an NHL record—and all 19 playoff games, but Ranford was still an important member of the club, and Messier made sure he was in tune with everyone. "When Ranford started to play he was a talented young goaltender but an absolute hot dog," one Oilers insider remembered. "One time he got run over in the crease and was laying there, getting all the attention in the world, but the players knew he wasn't hurt. Mark skated over, looked down, and said, 'Don't pull this shit. Get up and play.' That was a major step in the evolution of Bill Ranford as a player."

Edmonton's Cup defense opened against Winnipeg, and the Oilers disposed of their traditional whipping boys in a quick five games. At one point in the series when the Jets had a two-man advantage, Messier stole the puck, swooped down the ice on a breakaway, and scored. Next up were the Calgary Flames, with their new coach Terry Crisp, the league's two top-scoring defensemen in Al MacInnis and Gary Suter, and memories of their seven-game upset of cocky Edmonton in 1986. But these Oilers were cool and efficient, and they calmly jumped to a two-games-to-none lead with narrow wins in Calgary. For this series, Sather moved Messier to another line, between Courtnall and the bulky youngster Normand Lacombe, and their swirling forechecking shut down the Calgary attack. In game three in Edmonton, Messier leveled forward Perry Berezan, who as a St. Albert Saint had seen Messier's Porsche buzzing the team bus the night Messier scored his fiftieth goal in 1982. Berezan was taken to hospital with a concussion. Messier had three assists in a 4–2 victory. In game four, Messier added his third goal of the series as Edmonton won, 6–4, and completed an emphatic sweep in the fourth edition of the Battle of Alberta. "We certainly jelled together for this series better than I can remember," Messier understated in the victors' dressing room. Calgary withdrew to lick their wounds and learn the lessons of the Mandatory Suffering Rule.

Next, for the second straight year, the Oilers disposed of Detroit in the semifinals. During the series, a profile of Messier appeared in *Sports Illustrated,* one of the very few times he has ever met separately with a reporter for an article. In it, the writer, Austin Murphy, finds himself with Messier "as he red-lines his Porsche down Edmonton's 104th Avenue on his way home from practice. Messier knows where Edmonton's finest have set up speed traps." That detail is glossed over without comment.

The finals pitted Edmonton against Boston, who now had Andy Moog in their nets. It was practically no contest. The only game that was close was the opener at Northlands, a 2–1 Edmonton win in which Messier was held

without a point for the first time in fifteen playoff games. The Bruins managed only 14 shots on Grant Fuhr, a testament to the more well-rounded
team the Oilers had become since their victory over Philadelphia in game
seven of the '87 finals. In game two, a 4–2 victory, Edmonton outshot
Boston by 32–12. Acting on the advice of the Oilers' Boston-based scout
Ace Bailey, Sather had his forwards obstruct the Bruins' forecheckers to give
the defense time to move the puck. When the Bruins had the puck, the
Oiler forwards hit Ray Bourque every chance they got, and he tired in a
hurry. Game three at Boston Garden was another easy win, 6–3.

Game four was tied at 3–3 in the late stages of the second period. The
spring weather was very warm, and inside the decrepit old Garden, which
lacked air conditioning, a fog continually rose up off the ice. Play had to be
stopped periodically to literally clear the air. With 3:23 left in the period, an
overloaded transformer across the street blew up, cutting off the power to
the lovable old dump. The teams retreated to their dressing rooms in dark-
ness, the crowd was sent home out of concerns for their safety, and after an
hour's delay the game was abandoned. "We were 23 minutes from the
Stanley Cup," Messier lamented.

The abandonment of the game meant that the series would return to
Edmonton, where the Oilers could raise the Cup yet again before their home
fans. The game, designated "game 4A," was close until the end of the second period. The Oilers were ahead, 3–2, when Gretzky crossed into the
Boston zone with a few seconds remaining. He held the puck until a single
second remained, then passed to Simpson, who fired it home. There was a
tenth of a second left in the period, so the goal counted. Edmonton breezed
to a 6–3 victory.

The time had come again for Gretzky to pick up the Cup. It passed from
him to Lowe, to Messier, and then all around the team. Nine of the Oilers
were celebrating for an incredible fourth time in five seasons, and they were
still so young: Grant Fuhr and Kevin McClelland were 25; Messier, Gretzky,
and Anderson were 27; Kurri and Huddy, 28; Lowe, 29; and Randy Gregg, 32.
Gretzky was also given the Conn Smythe trophy, having gone 12–31–43 in
just 19 playoff games (Messier was second at 11–23–34). Then Gretzky, sporting a buzz cut that sounded the death knell for the mullet as the hockey hairdo
of choice, convened all the Oilers to take a team picture with the Stanley

Cup, right there on the ice. It was another beautiful moment among so many orchestrated by Gretzky, who had an unerring instinct for *la geste juste*. The laughing players, coaches, trainers, and office personnel crowded around the old goblet while the fans continued to cheer in the Northlands stands. It was, in effect, the last thing Gretzky would ever do in an Edmonton uniform.

In the dressing room, Messier poured a steady stream of Dom Perignon into the bowl of the Cup so that everyone could drink from it. Later, the players went to a local bar called Barry T's, where, as was their tradition, they invited anyone present to see, feel, touch, and of course, sip from it. Today the Cup is accompanied everywhere by a minder from the Hockey Hall of Fame; while the public still has full access to it, in Edmonton the arrangement was less formal. "What I liked about the Oilers' relationship with the Cup," the team's longtime PR director, Bill Tuele, told Kevin Allen, "was that we had unbelievable access and we made it unbelievably accessible to Edmontonians. It went everywhere without security, without any concern that we needed to be careful or it might disappear. Mark was the most social with the Cup, along with Glenn Anderson. They would go from bar to bar to bar. They would go on three-day howls with the Cup."

Simpson recalled sharing the Cup not just with late-night revelers, but with others as well. "Everyone felt a responsibility to have the Cup make a difference in someone's life; everyone took it to a school or to a hospital," he told Allen. "The healing power of the Cup is special. Everyone on that team knew that the Cup had to be shared with fans. And there was nothing quite like walking into a children's ward in a hospital with the Stanley Cup."

The big event of the off-season was to be the Gretzky-Jones nuptials— "Canada's royal wedding," as it was widely known. But there was another wedding at least as important for Messier to attend: that of his sister Mary-Kay on July 7 to Darrell Morrow, an Edmonton businessman. The ceremony took place on Kauai, considered by many the most beautiful of the Hawaiian islands. Mark was the best man, and he spent two weeks on Kauai helping with arrangements for the wedding, which was also attended by Gretzky and Jones.

The Gretzky-Jones wedding was held on July 16 at St. Joseph's Basilica in Edmonton, the biggest church in the city. Neither bride nor groom was Catholic, but it was chosen because it was the only house of worship large enough to accommodate the 700 guests for the ceremony and all the pomp and glitter that went with it. Gretzky's best man was Eddie Mio, who had come from Indianapolis to Edmonton with him in Nelson Skalbania's fire sale back in '78, and Messier, Lowe, Coffey, and Gretzky's three brothers were the groomsmen. Among the guests were Gretzky's friends from the hockey world, including all the Oilers, as well as his idol and spiritual mentor, Gordie Howe; the premier of Alberta and a few scattered showbiz types, such as the television actor and emcee Alan Thicke, were also on hand. Three thousand people waited outside to catch a glimpse of the newlyweds when they emerged. At the reception at the Westin Hotel and a later party at the private Centre Club, Messier took the mike and belted out his impression of Elvis Presley singing "Spanish Eyes."

Immediately after the wedding, Gretzky learned that Peter Pocklington had been sending out feelers to other clubs for more than a year about trading him. Gretzky would say that he had wanted to end his career in Edmonton and that he and Jones had been looking for a house in the city. But according to Gretzky, while he was on his honeymoon in Los Angeles he received a call from Bruce McNall, the new owner of the Kings: Pocklington had given him permission to contact Gretzky. Over the course of the next few days, Gretzky decided to okay a trade to L.A., a choice fueled by a combination of his resentment over Pocklington's trade feelers and a growing rapport with McNall. Now the trick was to keep the deal a secret from everyone until it was done, even the other players who were to be involved. (Marty McSorley and Mike Krushelnyski were to accompany Gretzky to the Kings in exchange for Jimmy Carson, Martin Gelinas, three first-round draft picks, and $15 million U.S.) One particular concern for Gretzky was to keep Messier, who had heard rumors of a trade, out of the loop. "Mess must have called me eight or nine times during the negotiations, but I knew I couldn't call him back," Gretzky wrote in his autobiography. "I knew if I called him, he'd go crazy and maybe talk Peter out of the deal. Mess is just that persuasive."

On August 8 in Los Angeles, McNall told Gretzky that the trade would be announced the next day in Edmonton. The morning of August 9, Messier was golfing at the Edmonton Country Club when he heard that a press conference would take place later in the day. He and Gretzky spoke by phone before Gretzky took the dais, and a little later Sather met with Gretzky for almost an hour to try to dissuade him, but Gretzky had made up his mind, and there was no turning back.

Canadians, and hockey fans the world over, retain vivid memories of the press conference. Gretzky, with Pocklington at his side and McNall standing behind him, announced that, by mutual consent of all parties, he was being traded to Los Angeles, but the moment that remains the most vivid, the most telling, comes when Gretzky suddenly stops in midsentence, daubs at his eyes as they well with tears, and says, "I promised Mess I wouldn't do this." Pocklington later suggested that those were crocodile tears, but they were genuine. "I started thinking about my friendship with Mark Messier," Gretzky explained a few weeks later. "The friendship has really been important to me. Mark used to say, 'Gretz, learn to enjoy life; don't be so serious.' We were together all the time. Boy, I don't know whether I was crying because I was losing him as a teammate or because I'll have to play against him now."

The next day an article by Jim Matheson in the *Edmonton Journal* quoted Pocklington as saying that Gretzky had "an ego the size of Manhattan" and that he was "a great actor" for making a show of his sadness at the press conference. It was true that, however reluctant Gretzky may initially have been about the trade, he soon embraced it and was instrumental in managing the backroom dealings that made it happen.

The immediate instinct among Canadians was to blame Jones—known as Janet Jones Gretzky during the twenty-five days since the wedding—who was pregnant, as Gretzky told reporters at the press conference. Starting their family in L.A., he said, would be a side benefit of the trade.

Rancor and a sense of betrayal surrounded the announcement of the Gretzky trade, and even today many look at it as the single event that changed nothing less than the course of hockey itself. The official National Hockey League line is that in moving to California, Gretzky, like a sporting version of Johnny Appleseed, sowed a Sun Belt revolution, popularizing the game in parts of the United States that had never seen ice. The game grew, according to this view, and so did its wealth. Many Canadians and hockey traditionalists, however, see the trade as the start of the hijacking of the game from its northern roots, to be transplanted into arid, cultureless soil.

The modest means of the places where hockey was inextricably woven into the cultural fabric were simply no match for the rich, taxpayer-backed regional economies that now all clamored for hockey teams as a requisite step toward "major-league" status. The result, according to this view, is the presence of NHL teams in Carolina, Phoenix, and Tampa Bay and their absence in Quebec, Winnipeg, and Hartford. General managers, who work in the game at its bottom-line level, see the trade as the start of the in-flationary spiral of player salaries, spurred on by profligate owners. Gretzky's base salary of $1.4 million a season, atop a $5 million signing bonus, set new benchmarks and raised expectations among players and agents.

There is truth in all of these views. It is an interesting exercise to spec-ulate on what might have happened if Messier had been able to persuade Gretzky and Pocklington to call off the deal, beyond preventing the sudden appearance of bands of kids playing roller hockey under the shade of palm trees or the rollout of the latest "Mighty Ducks" movie. Had Messier been able to talk Gretzky and Pocklington out of a deal with the Kings, McNall may well not have emerged as the key figure in the National Hockey League at that critical moment. McNall was just thirty-nine at the time of the Gretzky trade, a young, appealing, self-made millionaire who had made his fortune dealing in antiquities and valuable coins. He was a wheeler-dealer with regular-guy charm, and Gretzky fell for him in a big way. Moreover, he had gained enormous stature among his fellow owners for pulling off the Gretzky deal and for seeming to have money to throw around boldly. McNall was a far cry from the pinched, inward-looking cabal of owners who had dominated the NHL for so long, a type embodied by Bill Wirtz, the elderly, miserly yachtsman who owned the Blackhawks and chaired the NHL Board of Governors. Very soon, the other owners would decide that Wirtz and the league's president, John Ziegler, were holding the NHL back in its pursuit of that elusive, money-spinning payday: a U.S. TV network contract and the nationwide exposure that was expected to come with it. Ziegler's tenure had been conservative and pokey, in the mold of the previous seventy years of league leadership, but it was also marked by occasional public gaffes, as when he was literally unreachable for a couple of days when referees called a wildcat strike during the 1988 playoffs, and in the perceived con-fusion that followed the power failure at Boston Garden during the '88 final.

Soon enough, the owners would want him out (even though it was they who had approved the ruinous cable TV deal that left the NHL all but invisible through much of the '80s), and they would look to McNall to lead them out of the wilderness.

Buoyed by the enhanced status the Gretzky trade afforded him, within three years McNall would sponsor the successful candidacy of Gary Bettman as head of the NHL. Bettman was a lawyer from New York who had been among those running the NBA when that league took off in the mid- to late 1980s; he knew little about hockey, and he would wind up importing a number of deputies who shared his cluelessness. The idea was that the NHL was such a mess and in such need of fresh blood that only a whole new administrative team would do. Under Bettman, and with McNall serving as chairman of the board of governors, a policy of aggressive southward expansion and franchise shifts was pursued, as were a slew of rule changes and a general desire to do away with anything seen as hidebound tradition in favor of innovation. Over the course of the '90s and into the twenty-first century, this attitude on the part of the league would alienate countless fans in hockey's heartland across Canada and in the northern United States.

In the early '90s, McNall ushered the rich, prestigious presence of the Walt Disney Company into the league through its ownership of the Mighty Ducks of Anaheim, and pocketed $20 million of the expansion fee as his commission. He arranged for a series of nonsensical "neutral-site" games that inflated the regular-season schedule from 80 games to 84. Clubs played in such non-NHL markets as Sacramento, Cleveland, Orlando, Halifax, Phoenix, Hamilton, Dallas, Saskatoon, Cincinnati, Milwaukee, Atlanta, Providence, and Oklahoma City (and, later, Minneapolis, whose North Stars had been the first to move south, hijacked in 1993 to Dallas), and McNall accepted a fee for his efforts. No one minded that he was raking in a little extra on the side, because he had taken the lead in the NHL's American campaign, and Gretzky was his—and the league's—glittering sign of legitimacy. Gretzky was the proud cheerleader for hockey's expansion, and he made the Kings a hot ticket and a celebrity magnet. Within five years of his arrival, they were playing for the Stanley Cup itself, and Southern California was definitely along for the ride.

But disturbing questions were beginning to surface around McNall. In a profile in GQ magazine, he openly boasted of smuggling antiquities out of Turkey, a form of theft even more reprehensible than simple larceny because he was bragging about stealing a nation's patrimony. Not long afterward, he was indicted on fraud charges wholly unrelated to smuggling; he was keeping a false set of books that inflated his wealth, which turned out to be more or less nonexistent. In 1994, he pleaded guilty to defrauding banks of $234 million. The man in whom both Gretzky and the National Hockey League had invested so much trust, the man who had decided on and directed the course that hockey would take in the 1990s and beyond, went to jail.

If Messier, the one man whose intercession Gretzky feared the most, had succeeded in talking any one of the principals out of the trade, would McNall *not* have risen to the chairmanship of the board of governors? And would the NHL therefore not have undertaken a headlong rush into the Sun Belt, nor its massive, talent- and interest-diluting expansion? Would it have avoided alienating so many of its fans and an economically precarious spiral of inflation that threatened so many clubs' survival? One can only speculate. But the fact remains: the Gretzky trade set in motion a series of events that lie at the heart of everything, good and bad, that hockey is experiencing today. And Messier could have changed it all with a single phone call. As Gretzky said, he was just that persuasive.

Messier's reaction in the immediate aftermath of the trade was one of shock and an impulse to take action. Three days after the press conference, Messier called one of his own, then canceled it. He and some of the other Oilers were considering a teamwide strike or demanding that Pocklington sell the team. "I thought Gretz would always be an Oiler," Messier told the *Edmonton Journal.* "I'm analyzing the events of the last few days." In the end, however, the players took no public action against Pocklington.

The Oilers would wander through the 1988–89 season as if they were orphans. Glenn Anderson said that playing without Gretzky was like mourning the death of a brother; meanwhile, in L.A., Gretzky was missing the friends with whom he had came of age. (He would later say that throughout his first two or three years there he often found himself thinking about what was going on in Edmonton.) Messier was now the Oilers' captain, and he made a brave show of rallying his teammates to move on, but his heart wasn't entirely in it. The trade, Lowe wrote a couple of years after, "was devastating to Mark, perhaps more than to anyone else because he is so sensitive, caring, and emotional."

What Lowe observed in Messier was something very much like mourning: "His emotional side was just uncontrollable when it came to Wayne. He just didn't understand it. He couldn't believe it. He really thought it was all a joke at first. He went through stages. At first, it was disbelief. Then the leader in him showed through. He said, 'What are we going to do, sit around and piss and moan about it, or are we going to get our asses going?' But mostly through that first season without Wayne, it was a feeling of disbelief.

"To Mark's credit, he never showed any bitterness around the team. But it was tough on him because he was playing a mental tug of war with himself. We spent countless hours talking about the trade We were trying to figure out the reasons for the deal. How much of a part did Wayne play in it? How much of it was Peter Pocklington and Glen Sather? Was it purely a business decision? Were they really thinking about the future of the team?"

The Oilers started strong, thrashing Long Island in the season opener and rallying to beat Winnipeg behind Messier's four assists in the next game, including Lowe's winner with 55 seconds left, but all thoughts still centered on their departed superstar. "We really had a difficult time forgetting how important Wayne was," Messier said after the Jets game. "We watched him playing for the Kings on television in their opener. Watching him brought back so many memories, some as recent as last spring. Of course, we were all hurt by the trade."

The schedule threw the Oilers and Kings together right away. The first post-trade meeting of the two teams took place in Edmonton on October 19, the seventh match of the season. Before the game, Gretzky said he wouldn't know how to react when he saw his friends on the other side of the ice. Messier said he was at a loss, too. "It's something I've never had to deal with before," he said. When the Kings came out for the pregame skate, the Northlands crowd gave Gretzky a four-minute standing ovation and chanted his name, stopping only when the public-address announcer persisted in introducing the national anthems. Anderson scored early, Messier took a penalty, which was killed off, for holding Gretzky in the seventh minute, and Gretzky wasn't too much of a factor, generating a relatively modest two assists in an 8–6 defeat for the Kings. At one point, Messier drew boos for knocking his former teammate down. (Messier left him with "a pretty good bruise" after "steamrolling" him, as Gretzky later put it. "Now I know why people cringe at the sight of him.") Messier scored two goals, including one off an errant Gretzky pass that started a three-on-one break the other way. "Messier's a great player," Gretzky said. "I wish he was for sale."

In the other dressing room, Messier told reporters what he was thinking of when Gretzky stepped onto the ice before the anthems. "To be honest," Messier said, "twenty thousand thoughts and memories of all the fun we had and how we won four Stanley Cups together went through my mind. The fans were cheering, and I thought, 'He used to be on our side.'"

If there was still any question whether Messier would change his style without Gretzky around, those doubts were dispelled just four days later, with the Vancouver Canucks in town. Rich Sutter was cutting across the ice as he entered the Oilers' zone. Messier, going the other way, skated past him with his stick up at head level. Sutter crumpled, his mouth a bloody mess, yet no penalty was called; neither referee Rob Shick nor his linesmen had seen it. In the Canucks' dressing room, the doctors found four of Sutter's teeth broken and, according to Canucks' coach Bob McCammon, hockey tape "embedded in the roof of Sutter's mouth and between his teeth." Canucks general manager Pat Quinn chewed out Schick and the other officials in their changing room after the game, and the team sent an official complaint, a videotape, and Sutter's dental records to the league office. A week later, the NHL suspended Messier for six games, ruling that although the incident was inadvertent, Messier had not kept control of his stick; in light of the general high-sticking crackdown then in force, a suspension was warranted. It was the third such punishment of Messier's career and entirely in character for the fearsome Moose.

"He didn't have to fight," John Short said. "He could hit with an elbow or stick or absolutely lose it. He left guys almost comatose on the ice. That was the game for him; he was by today's standard a dirty player, because he did whatever he had to. You were allowed to do that to him, too, if you were tough enough, but few were. Opposing players always knew where Messier was on the ice during any given shift. You were quite at liberty to hit Mark Messier with a butt end—if you wanted take your life in your hands." Two players who were willing to risk it were Calgary's hulking pair, Joel Otto and

Tim Hunter. In the second period of a game in early December, Otto split Messier's lip in a fight. A few minutes later, Hunter high-sticked him in the mouth, chipping two teeth. "He stuck me," Messier said. "The referee didn't see it because I was already bleeding."

The Oilers limped through the first half of the season, while Gretzky's Kings surged. After the October 19 game in Edmonton, Sather told reporters that as matters currently stood, L.A. had got the better of the deal, and the Oilers were on "the down side." As it happened, the 1989 NHL All-Star Game was to be held in Edmonton, and what had in the past been a fairly meaningless occasion in which Gretzky would score a bunch of points and win yet another car as MVP of the game now took on undertones flavored with bittersweet nostalgia. Before the game, the Edmonton papers ran a formal portrait-style photo of Gretzky with his wife and six-week-old daughter—of whom Messier was the godfather—heightening the general civic sense of a family reunion. For Gretzky, any homecoming to Northlands was still emotionally charged, but this one also carried the knowledge that he would sit on the home team's bench for the last time.

Symbolic of the changing balance of power in the Smythe Division was the fact that five Oilers were in the lineup for the game—but so were five Kings. Gretzky centered a line with Kurri of the Oilers on his right and Luc Robitaille of the Kings on his left, while Messier was flanked by two of his Calgary archrivals, Joe Nieuwendyk and Joe Mullen. "It was like old times on the bench—Slats, Mess, Kevin, and Grant," Gretzky said. "I realized it was the last time I'd be sitting here again." The Campbell Conference team triumphed, 9–5, and Gretzky, selected the MVP, won the fourteenth car of his career. He closed out the love-in by turning the keys over to his old Oiler teammate and bodyguard, the now-retired Dave Semenko.

Messier was put out of action a week later, courtesy of a bodycheck by Rangers defenseman Michel Petit—a rare instance of someone doing to Messier what he usually did to others. He missed a couple of games, but it didn't matter much. Edmonton finished the regular season with a record of 38–34–8, their worst in nine years, as was their third-place finish in the Smythe. Messier was the third-leading scorer on the team, his 33–61–94 in 72 games putting him just behind Kurri and Carson. He rolled up a hefty 130 penalty minutes, and his minus-5 was below average on the team. It wasn't a bad individual year, but it wasn't particularly great, either. He stickhandled and passed more than he had in the past, as if to compensate for the departure of those traits with Gretzky, and he didn't drive to the net as often as he had before. He was bothered by a series of minor injuries to both knees, which began with Petit's check. And teams felt free to concentrate a little more on stopping him now that they didn't have to worry about Number 99. Meanwhile, the Kings, who had finished 12 games below .500 without Gretzky the season before, now finished 11 games above with him, good for second place. The Calgary Flames dealt an even more punishing blow to Edmonton's morale by finishing first in the entire league.

As if the season hadn't already been fraught with enough irony, the Kings and Oilers met in the first round of the playoffs. Messier scored a goal and two assists in the opener, a 4–3 win for Edmonton at the Fabulous Forum. The Kings got back on track the next night, a 5–2 victory in which Gretzky scored only his second goal in ten games against the Oilers. Halfway through the game, he was run over at center ice by Messier and left in a heap. "Obviously, we're going to have to put friendships aside," Messier said, "but when the smoke's cleared, I'm sure we'll still be friends."

Back in Edmonton, the love affair with Gretzky went cold as the fans booed him roundly; they were reacting to TV and newspaper interviews in which he had made public his complaints about Sather over the previous two seasons. During the game, which the Oilers won, Messier crunched Gretzky again, this time with a shoulder along the boards. "The first thing that went through my mind? That Janet wouldn't like it," Messier laughed after the Oilers won, 4–0. Edmonton won game four, too, when Lowe swatted in Messier's rebound with just 25 seconds left for a 4–3 verdict and a three-games-to-one series lead.

Messier was the star of the series so far, but Gretzky was not done. He notched three points in a 4–2 victory in L.A. to keep the Kings alive, and after the game, adding to the air of surreality that had started to envelop the series, he learned that former President Ronald Reagan had sent the team a telegram urging them to "win one for the Gipper." Back in Edmonton, L.A. snapped the Oilers' 14-game playoff home winning streak with a 4–1 victory. Afterward, Messier was among the first Oilers to sprint from the dressing room rather than face reporters' questions.

Now it was down to game seven back at the Forum. The game started tense and tight and stayed that way, tied 3–3 halfway through. But Gretzky set up Bernie Nicholls for a goal during a two-man advantage, and goalie Kelly Hrudey held the Oilers at bay in the third. Two late goals made the final score 6–3 for L.A. Gretzky and Messier had each finished with 12 points, most in the series—but it had ended in a stunning comeback triumph for Gretzky and the Kings, and a devastating foldup and defeat for Messier and the Oilers. Gretzky took his place at the end of the handshake line, embracing each Oiler in turn. Yet when he got to Lowe, Messier, and Sather, their exchange was brief and pro forma; the circumstances were too painful to do more. "I know that no one takes losing harder than Messier and Lowe," Gretzky said afterward. "Those guys are champions. I enjoyed playing with them, and I feel deeply sorry for what they're feeling now. Going through the line was difficult. I wanted to talk with them, but I also wanted to let them alone."

Messier was so devastated he barely said anything to reporters, and when asked about Gretzky could only summon the words to say, "He's a pretty good player." Messier's disappointment was to be expected, but over in the Kings' dressing room, rarely has a pro athlete expressed such ambivalence in victory. "Personally, I didn't enjoy the series at all," Gretzky said. "It wasn't fun for me. For fifteen days or whatever, I saw those guys every day, and no words were spoken. That's not what life should be about. You're supposed to be able to talk to your best friends."

The Kings were swept out of the next round by Calgary, who went on to win the Stanley Cup, doubly embittering the cup of gall that Oilers fans were forced to drink that postseason. Messier could have taken the whole off-season to fume about how awful it felt, but instead he joined the Canadian team playing in the annual World Championships being held that May in Sweden. As if he hadn't had enough hockey over the previous decade, he played in six games and scored three goals and three assists in helping Canada to a silver medal. They fell only to the Soviets.

The tournament helped Messier get over the trauma of the Gretzky trade. When summer arrived, "Mark finally got it all out of his system," according to Lowe. "He finally faced up to the whole situation. He truly put the past in the past and focused on the present." He vowed to take charge and forge a different outcome for the season ahead. "His motives became more team-oriented," Lowe said. "Mark is smart enough to realize he's getting older. He's curtailed his off-ice activities because he knows there's a necessity there; that if he's going to have a Mark Messier-type of year, he has to perform every night, and at his age he can't afford to be out all the time." He was maintaining, Lowe said, "the right balance now."

It was a good thing for the Oilers that Messier had found the right balance, because the summer of 1989 in Edmonton was still all about Gretzky. In late August, the city of Edmonton paid tribute to Gretzky's ten years in town by unveiling a statue of him holding the Stanley Cup over his head. It was installed outside Northlands Coliseum, and inside the arena 13,000 fans paid to attend a two-hour benefit in his honor. The Oilers sent no official representative—neither Pocklington nor Sather, who had given up the coaching reins to John Muckler—but several players came on their own, including Messier. At one point Gretzky was presented with a painting of three boys playing hockey on a pond in front of the Edmonton skyline; two of the boys are waving goodbye to the third. Gretzky said, "Then I realized it was me leaving and Kevin and Mess waving goodbye."

The '89–90 season was only four games old when the focus was again on Gretzky, who came into Northlands needing just two points to pass Gordie Howe as the NHL's all-time leading scorer. He set up a goal early to tie Howe, then had his bell rung on a clean check by defenseman Jeff Beukeboom. In typical storybook fashion, he returned to the ice in the last couple of minutes, with the Kings trailing by 4–3, and scored the historic goal with 53 seconds left. Messier was on the ice for the play. The game was stopped, and Gretzky was joined on the rink by his wife and family, by NHL President John Ziegler, and by Howe, and presented with various gifts and tributes. On behalf of the Oilers, Messier gave him a gold bracelet studded with diamonds that spelled out "1,851," for the number of points he had now scored, and said a few unmemorable words to the crowd. Then he and Gretzky embraced for a long time and whispered to each other. "We didn't need any words," Messier said later. "It's obvious how Wayne and I feel about each other." After the ceremonies ended, the game went into overtime. And, of course, Gretzky scored the winner.

But unlike the previous season, Messier was not flustered. He soldiered on, embracing and mastering his role as captain. Just before the Gretzky game, Jimmy Carson quit the Oilers; the twenty-one-year-old had felt as strongly about staying with the Kings as Gretzky had about the Oilers, but unlike Gretzky he never adjusted to his new team and decided to force a trade by walking out. His departure left the Oilers with a new, devastatingly effective line: Messier–Kurri–Tikkanen, and Messier pretty much blew Carson off. While Muckler said, "It's difficult on everybody, missing a 100-goal scorer," Messier disagreed openly: "It's not going to hurt us, not having a guy who doesn't want to play for us. I'm confident Slats will make the right move."

Sather was with Messier on that one, and fanned the flames still further. "Jimmy Carson is no longer with us because he couldn't stand the heat from Kevin and Mark," he said. "He didn't like Messier always saying he'd beat the shit out of him if he didn't produce." That quote, when it appeared in the *Hockey News*, is probably what gave everyone the persistent impression that Messier ruled by intimidating some of his teammates. Whether Messier actually made the threat or whether Sather was just embellishing for the sake of sticking it to Carson is unclear. Neither Messier nor Carson has commented on it specifically.

Sather traded Carson to Detroit for Petr Klima, a Czechoslovak who had deft hands but who had been considered a lazy underachiever during his four and a half seasons with the Red Wings. Klima made some comments about playing the next season in West Germany, hinting that he wasn't keen on coming to Edmonton. But the day he arrived, Messier picked him up at the hotel, took him to practice, and told him, "This is the way we do things around here—we're teammates, all on the same page." Klima later said that, more than anything else, that first day made him feel welcome, which in turn made him more willing to contribute. It may have even saved Klima's NHL career. He was given the stall next to Messier's, and he was put on a line with Messier and Anderson. This would be one of Messier's roles for the next decade and a half: to mentor a revolving door of linemates assigned him by coaches who believed his influence could put magic in the stick or steel in the spine of any player.

The first half of the season was up and down for the Oilers, but Messier's leadership was stalwart. All his energy was focused on forging ahead toward another championship. "We've still got a lot of Stanley Cup rings in the dressing room," he said, now an elder statesman at twenty-eight, "so when the young guys come in, we try to give them a sense of what was going on in the past so we can continue the tradition." There were a number of young bucks to be schooled, including a second-year Messier wannabe named Kelly Buchberger, who was a littler taller and leaner than his idol but, if anything, even more in love with the idea of intimidation. He rolled up 493 penalty minutes in his first 140 games as an Oiler, and emulated Messier's look by wearing the same discontinued WinnWell helmet. He would eventually become the Oilers' captain. Another young charge was Adam Graves, who had come over from Detroit in the Carson–Klima trade. In Edmonton and in New York, he would become Messier's most fervid acolyte and, after Anderson, his most frequent and productive linemate. Bill Ranford, whom Messier had broken in the year before, would take over the number one job in goal when Fuhr got hurt later in the season. Thanks to the captain's influence, he was now a stolid, focused netminder.

Messier handled his duties with unerring poise. He stayed around to answer reporters' questions after every game, no matter how difficult or tedious the task was. It was a job he had seen Gretzky do night after night for years, and now, after a tentative start in '88–89, he mastered it. He became good at slipping encouraging comments about players into his postgame spiel, as well as coded messages designed to prod underperforming players to improve. Lowe said that Messier did not grab lagging teammates by the throat and threaten to kill them, as the rumors had it, but he did imply that a certain amount of pressure was sometimes applied: "He has enough respect for an individual that he might take a guy aside and say, 'If you don't start playing, I'm going to do this or that to you.'" As Messier put it, "sometimes you have to give them a little positive reinforcement, or a kick in the ass."

Glenn Anderson was amazed by Messier's transformation. "He's shown all sorts of character, on and off the ice," he said. "He's the dressing-room leader day in and day out, and he constantly carries his attitude onto the ice with performances of 110 percent. But now he's also taking care of new guys on our team. He's always having team functions, taking guys out for a couple of beers or dinners. He's doing everything to help guys feel more comfortable with the idea of making the team a winner."

Muckler saw the transformation too. "Now Mark has learned how to handle the pressure better, to become a better leader" he said. "With Gretzky gone, this is Mess's team now. All the responsibility was dumped in his lap when Wayne left. He had to grow with the responsibility. It's not an easy thing to do."

But all Messier's leadership counted for only so much. His real value was in his play, which in '89–90 was better than it ever had been before, or has been since. Of the 79 regular-season games he played, he scored multiple points in 41. At Northlands in January against—who else?—the L.A. Kings, Messier scored a goal and four assists in a 7–6 victory, a performance that completely overshadowed that of Gretzky. He scored hat tricks three different times, the last of which was a four-goal game. He was unstoppable. Gretzky finished the season as the scoring leader for the first time in three years (Mario Lemieux missed a third of the schedule with injuries), but the number two man in the entire NHL was Messier. He wound up with 45–84–129, his best performance ever and just 13 points off Gretzky's pace. He kept the penalties down, just 79 minutes' worth, and played hockey, intimidating through the scoreboard more than with his elbows, shoulders, and stick. His plus-19 mark was third-best on the Oilers, signifying a new conscientiousness in his own end of the rink. His dominance of the Oilers' statistical summaries that season (Kurri finished second on the team in scoring, 36 points behind) was positively Gretzky-like.

The Oilers finished second in the Smythe, nine points behind Calgary, and fifth overall in the league, a small but significant improvement over the season before. But everyone knew they had a real chance at the Cup. In the first round they faced the hapless Winnipeg Jets, yet fell behind, three games to one. But they rallied to take the next three games, then swept Gretzky and the Kings in the next round, exacting sweet revenge for the year before. Then they met Chicago and fell behind, two games to one. Game four at Chicago Stadium has gone down in legend as one of the most terrifying one-man-wrecking-crew performances in hockey history.

In a move that was completely out of character, Messier arrived at the Stadium early, long before everyone else. He sat at his stall, dressed for the game, and rocked silently back and forth. "You should have seen his eyes," Graves remembered. The game started and, according to Mike Keenan—at this point the coach of the Blackhawks—"Mark came out, and I knew after the first shift the game was over. The series was over. The first two shifts he broke two sticks, one over Denis Savard, another over Doug Wilson, and he didn't get a penalty. That was the end of us." Messier ran roughshod all over the ice, slashing and elbowing. At one point he was sent to the box for elbowing Hawks captain Dirk Graham, and as Messier sat there he looked at Graham and motioned with his finger on his chin, as if to say, "Keep your head up." He set up the first goal and scored the next two, then ran over Steve Larmer and Jeremy Roenick, the latter yelling "Fuck off!" as Messier skated away. With the score 4–2, he took off on a breakaway, and Chicago defenseman Doug Wilson tried to hook him but stabbed him in the neck instead. Messier scored, then went over to the bench and told the trainer, "He got me in the fuckin' throat." Messier warred with the Blackhawks throughout the third period as he had all game long, but there was no further scoring. Messier had won the game singlehanded. The only thing he was reported to have said to his teammates all night was, "Don't take any stupid penalties."

The Oilers never looked back after that performance. They won the next two games to eliminate Chicago, then took four out of five from Boston to win the Stanley Cup—for the fifth time in seven years, and for the first time without Gretzky. The Cup was handed first to Captain Messier, and he took it, held it aloft, and skated over to his family's corner of the rink. He stood there, his huge mouth open all the way in joy, and shared the triumph with his mother and father and the people of Edmonton one last time. It was a famous picture, and it ran on the cover of *The Hockey News* with a one-word headline: "Redemption." In the corridor on the way to the dressing room, a happy Muckler was being interviewed by *Hockey Night in Canada*. Messier clomped right up to him and gave him a big kiss on the cheek. "Greatest coach in the world, right here," he beamed. In the dressing room afterward, he clutched the Cup and said, "This one's for you, Gretz."

Messier reaped a bounty of postseason honors: he was named to the First All-Star Team at center, won the Lester B. Pearson Award as the players' choice as MVP, and finally won the Hart Trophy itself. Usually he was off vacationing by the time of the annual NHL awards show, but this year he attended for the first time. When he took the podium at the Metropolitan Toronto Convention Centre before a national TV audience, he started to give a speech, then choked up and said, "Oh, this is wild." It took several moments for him to compose himself. He looked back on his eleven years with the Oilers and thanked Muckler, Ted Green, and Sather. "To Wayne Gretzky," he finished, "who's been such a big part of my life. And my family."

Then, in his tuxedo, he posed with the Hart Trophy and Stanley Cup. There with him, all smiling the same broad Messier smile, were his sisters, his brother and sister-in-law, and his mother, father, and grandmother. They looked a bit like that Christmastime home movie in Portland, when the kids were toddlers.

GOODBYE TO ALL THAT

After the Oilers' Stanley Cup victory of 1990, Mark Messier stood atop the hockey world. He was no longer simply a crasher and banger who could score a lot and injure a lot and scare the hell out of opponents. He was still all those things, of course, but he was now also an inspirational leader who could will his team to victory through force of character as well as through indomitable personal example. He had earned the recognition he deserved, and craved, as the third-best player in all of hockey, behind only Gretzky and Lemieux. And he sought to convert that status into the third-highest salary in the NHL. He was entering the fourth year of a six-year deal, making about $1.1 million annually—not bad, but he wanted $2 million per season, more than anyone except Numbers 99 and 66.

Messier was one of several Oilers who, in the wake of the Gretzky trade and the greater awareness of money matters it touched off among players, took a harder line in salary negotiations with Sather and Pocklington. Jari Kurri held out, and wound up missing the season altogether, playing in the Italian league with AC Milan, an organization better known as a soccer superpower. Glenn Anderson held out as well, although he returned once the season got under way. Messier and his father, who represented him in talks with Sather, did not issue any ultimatums, but with Pocklington's finances in an increasingly precarious state, it was understood by everyone involved that the time might come to sell off the valuable but expensive Messier just as Wayne Gretzky had been dealt away.

The Cup champions reconvened for training camp and played part of their exhibition schedule in Germany, where they edged the German league champions, Düsseldorfer EG, by 2–0, but also lost to the touring St. Louis Blues, 10–1. The Oilers were already feeling the repercussions from an *Edmonton Journal* article that appeared on August 31, in which Grant Fuhr admitted to a long involvement with drugs and to having spent two weeks at a Florida clinic in August 1989 to try to kick the habit. Fuhr told the paper he had stayed off drugs since that visit. By the time the team returned from Europe, the whole affair had boiled over. Fuhr had a hearing with NHL President John Ziegler on September 26, and the next day Ziegler issued his verdict: Fuhr was suspended for one year without pay for having abused cocaine for seven years, between 1983 and 1989. It was a draconian deci-sion, stoked by the "Just Say No" rhetoric of the Reagan years, but it was in keeping with NHL policy. Fuhr was the fifth player suspended under the league's antidrug rules. If nothing else, the affair exposed the fallacy under-lying Sather's contention, oft-repeated in the aftermath of the 1986 *Sports Illustrated* drug article, that no NHL player could possibly stay in fit enough shape to compete while doing drugs.

When Fuhr's suspension was announced, Messier became among the most vocal critics of the league's regulations. "We definitely have to come out of the ice ages and come up with some sort of drug policy," he said, "because obviously what we have right now suppresses people from coming forward and trying to get help." Messier saw as objectionable the idea that admitting to past drug abuse and having obtained help in overcoming it could still result in suspension and the possible loss of a player's livelihood, threats that he felt would dampen players' willingness to seek help in the first place. "This might end his career," Messier said of the league's actions toward Fuhr. "If our poli-cies had been different perhaps ten years ago, this might not have happened." Messier added that the next collective bargaining agreement between the players and owners, due to be negotiated in a year's time, ought to contain more progressive provisions for drug treatment. It was the first public evidence of his taking a leadership role in union matters.

The Oilers would begin the 1990–91 season without yet another of their mainstays: Randy Gregg was waived just before the season began, and he chose to retire rather than to report to Vancouver, the team that claimed him. And on October 16, they lost perhaps their most irreplaceable component: Messier himself. He got tangled up in a scrum along the boards at Northlands, fell over St. Louis's Dave Lowry, and badly sprained his left knee. Edmonton dropped that game, 5–2, won the next one, then lost the next nine in a row. Two of the losses were consecutive 1–0 results, marking the first time ever that the Oilers had been shut out twice in a row. By mid-November, Edmonton was in last place—ignominy enough, but further compounded by *The Calgary Sun*'s decision to run Terry Jones's columns on the team under the rubric "A View From the Cellar." Muckler resorted to a time-honored "oh yeah?" retort: "Let them have their fun. We may be in the cellar, but tell Calgary we can still see sunlight, because it's bouncing off our five Stanley Cup rings."

Given the dire circumstances, Messier returned to service in mid-November—a full month sooner than expected. He wore a knee brace that he would have to wear the rest of the year, but sure enough, playing 20 minutes between Anderson and Esa Tikkanen, he contributed two assists and an empty-net goal in a 5–3 win over Vancouver. His performance only underscored how critical he had become to the Oilers' fortunes. "They aren't a one-man team," Chicago defenseman Chris Chelios said. "But they don't go without Messier. He pulls other players together." Blackhawks' center Troy Murray added, "Most NHL players agree Mark Messier is the best all-around player in the world. There aren't many players who can change the outcome of a game, or know how to win it all. Gretzky and Messier are probably the only two."

With Messier out of the lineup, the Oilers scored just 14 goals in 10 games. In the first three games after his return, they scored 12. In the '80s, a lot of people had thought that Gretzky was the whole Edmonton team and that most of the other players were essentially superfluous. The events of 1989–90 proved that theory wrong, and now the evidence seemed to support a new, unexpected conclusion: that *Messier* was the Oilers. Maybe they were a one-man team, after all, except it was a different man than everyone originally thought. His teammates started to speak of him in downright mystical terms. "You look at Mark and there's almost an aura about him," Adam Graves said. "I don't know how to explain it, but he knows how to win, and he's able to transmit that to the rest of the players."

The Oilers rolled on, going 4–2 on an eastern road trip, with Messier setting up four goals in a 7–3 rout in Pittsburgh. Things were going well even though Messier admitted to playing at three-quarters speed because of his injury. "I'm trying to stay out of traffic, stay out of the way as much as I can," he said. "The ligaments and the joint are still weak. The only alternative I had was sit out another month and let them heal, but I didn't want to do that." But after leading the Oilers on a 10–4 tear that took them out of the wilderness of last place, he was forced to sit out a few games on either side of New Year's Day. In the second game after his latest return, he scored his 1,000th point. It came in a 5–3 win over Philadelphia, an assist on a shot that Anderson tipped in for a milestone of his own: his 400th goal. Afterward, Messier confessed uncharacteristically to taking pride in his statistical achievement. "I've never been much for goals, assists, and personal accomplishments," he said, "but it's kind of exciting. I've joined a pretty elite group of hockey players." Messier was again playing like a force of nature, and only his shaky knee could stop him. His value was undeniable, which made for a sticky situation for Pocklington and Sather, who were offering him an upgraded contract of $1.6 million—an amount representing only half the raise Messier wanted.

"The offer we made proves he's one of the great players," Sather told Jim Matheson. "But as far as money goes, let's get serious. He's not Wayne Gretzky or Mario Lemieux. They're ahead of everybody else." Messier told Matheson that he wanted to stay in Edmonton and finish his career there; but, he figured, if no agreement was reached, the Oilers would do with him as they had done with Gretzky and deal him away before he could become a free agent. "After this season, I have two years left on my contract, then I'll be a free agent without compensation," Messier said. "There's two things that will happen. I'll get a new contract for five or six or seven years or I'll be traded. History says they won't let me play out my option." Messier, who had just turned thirty in an era when thirty-five was a ripe old age, aspired to a quality that no one at the time could have thought would mark his career: longevity. "I'd like to play until I'm forty, until the year 2000," he said. "I'd like to play in four decades."

Less sentimental was Doug Messier, who accused the Oilers of rushing his son back into uniform too soon. "Mark feels there has been a concerted effort to suggest to the public that his knee injury was not as severe as it was," he told Matheson. "We don't want to be in this position again. Obviously, there would have to be clauses in there to protect the Oilers, if he couldn't play after a few years. But Mark would like the Oilers to make him a contract offer that would take him through the end of his career, like Wayne's in Los Angeles. Mark is asking that he be fairly paid through the remainder of his career.

"Generally," he continued, "if you go over the Oilers' contracts over the years, players have been trying to catch up. Paul Coffey left because of money. Wayne left because of the clause in his contract, which Peter felt made him a diminishing asset. . . . Look at Jari Kurri. Players have had to battle and hassle for money all their careers here, and it wears on the tremendous job Glen has done establishing loyalty and unity."

Sather's response: "I'm prepared to keep talking all season. I'm used to it. He can play until he's thirty-five years old, but it depends on the terms. It's give and take. I don't want to trade him. He's Mark Messier."

Messier was taking advantage of, and in turn fueling, the new policy of *glasnost* about salaries, encouraged by the NHLPA on the correct assumption that shared knowledge would drive salaries up. As Messier made his demands, for example, it was known that his salary was lower than those of Gretzky, Lemieux, Brett Hull, Steve Yzerman, Denis Savard, Patrick Roy, Ray Bourque, and Scott Stevens. He also told reporters that the $7 million in expansion fees the Oilers were about to receive proved the team could afford his desired pay raise. It was indeed true that the owners had decided to expand, a move that would yield short-term injections of millions of dollars, diluting the talent pool but providing money in the absence of a fat U.S. television contract. The unforeseen fallout from that policy was already apparent in Messier's salary demand. Thus began the inflationary spiral that would drive costs sky-high over the next decade, triggering franchise relocations, bankruptcies, and near ruin for several clubs over the coming decade.

But all of that was still in the future. For the moment, Messier was reviving the Oilers. In histories of the team, the 1990–91 season is usually glossed over as a postscript, a year in which the club's flame of dynasty was finally extinguished. But in fact there was the very real and widespread belief that the Oilers could repeat as Cup winners yet again. In '89–90 they had started slowly, finished the regular season with a modest record, then surged to the Stanley Cup. This season was on track to follow the same pattern.

It was, that is, until the February 11 game in Pittsburgh, when Pens goalie Tom Barrasso tripped Messier and sent him crashing into the boards, breaking his thumb. Messier played the next three games, and endured some unwarranted criticism in the press about his lack of physical play. Even Muckler joined in, saying, "Messier is most effective when he's aggressive. Everybody knows that. In that aspect of his game, he hasn't been the old Messier. It's pretty obvious that's been hurting us." But the pain and swelling would not go away, and doctors finally decided that he would have to sit out indefinitely, though no surgery would be necessary. The Oilers went 6–14 in their captain's absence. So much for his supposedly counterproductive pacifism.

They closed out the season at .500 (37–37–6), a dim achievement brightened a bit by Fuhr's early return from his drug suspension. Their record was good only for third place in the Smythe Division, behind vastly improved Los Angeles and still-powerful Calgary, and eleventh place overall. Messier wound up playing only 53 games and went 12–52–64, just five points off the team scoring lead, but well off his pace of the previous season, as were his 34 penalty minutes. But he registered a plus-15 mark, third-best on the team and unusually good for Messier, who usually hovered at or below the halfway point on the Oilers' plus/minus lists. All in all, it was a mixed individual season for the injury-racked Messier.

In the first round, Edmonton met Calgary for the fifth time. They split the first two games at the Saddledome. In the second, Messier elbowed Ric Nattress viciously in open ice. The Calgary defender crumpled, struggled to his feet, and stumbled to the Flames' bench like a punch-drunk prize fighter. "It was a standing eight count," Muckler chortled afterward. "He was standing. I give him credit." Nattress fumed darkly: "What goes around, comes around. We'll see what happens." The series was shaping up as a typical Oilers–Flames stretcher-fest, and for the occasion Messier had left behind the gingerly play that marked his regular season. But in overtime of game six, Messier threw a poor pass into center ice, where it was picked off by Calgary's Theo Fleury. Fleury broke in alone on Grant Fuhr and scored, sparking the famous celebration wherein Fleury slid half the length of the rink on his pads, back, and belly, waving his arms in a prostrate, spastic dance of joy. Messier thought it prudent to blot the error from his memory. "It will be a good idea for me not to dwell on that one because we have to think postive," he said afterward. "What can I say? Everybody saw it."

Ultimately, the Oilers prevailed in a classic game seven, overcoming a 3–0 deficit to win, 5–4, on Esa Tikkanen's goal in the seventh minute of overtime. Messier, hobbled by his various injuries and a couple of new ones, finished the series with a strong two goals and six assists, giving him a career total of 39 points in 30 games in the Oilers' five playoff wars with the Flames.

Against Gretzky and the Kings, Messier and the Oilers had a much easier time of it, perhaps because, as L.A.'s Larry Robinson said of Messier, "Even skating on one leg he's as good as most hockey players—any Mess is better than no Mess at all." Certainly Messier's sense of pragmatism was intact: in game one he two-handed Kings defenseman Steve Duchesne with a slash in the legs while Duchesne was looking the other way. Playing between Craig Simpson and Anatoli Semenov, he contributed little offensively (one goal and one assist) to what became an Edmonton sweep, but he did level big, dangerous defenseman Rob Blake in game four. Tikkanen, meanwhile, limited Gretzky to just five points, all assists. The 80-point Oilers moved on to the semifinals, having dismissed teams with 100 and 102 points. Their record in playoff series since 1984 now stood at an amazing 23–2.

All that blocked their path to a seventh Cup final in nine years were the Minnesota North Stars, whose regular-season record was a paltry 27–39–14 for 68 points. But after the North Stars took game one, 3–1, and Messier was silenced in the scoring column again, questions about his fitness arose. "All I'm going to tell you is that I feel as good now as I've felt all year," he said, deftly making it clear that he was injured without actually complaining about it. "I can also tell you that it's frustrating playing hurt, but if you play in this league long enough you're going to reach a point where you're going to have to get used to playing hurt. All I know is that we've won five Stanley Cups in the last seven years, won another Smythe Division championship this year, and now are in the semifinals again. Seems all we do is keep winning while people keep wondering what's wrong with me."

The Oilers won game two, 7–2, but that was where it ended. The North Stars knew Messier was hurt and went after him in game three in Bloomington, slashing him on his bad hand, forcing him to go to the bench doubled over in pain. He bravely set up two Simpson goals in a 7–3 defeat, but the season was as good as over for him and for the Oilers. Edmonton gooned it up in a 5–1 loss in game four, then the series returned to Northlands. Messier scored to tie the fifth game 2–2 early in the third period, but just 41 seconds later Bobby Smith restored Minnesota's lead and the North Stars held on the rest of the way. The Oilers were finally done. Messier, who in this series had surpassed Kurri to become the number two playoff scorer of all time, contributed a goal and four assists to the Edmonton effort against Minnesota. But somehow it was seen as insufficient; everyone had grown used to him being transcendent, something he had not managed this time.

Battered, Messier retreated to Hilton Head to recuperate. Hockey had become an unending challenge for its best players in the 1980s, and it continued to be so in the '90s. The season now extended until the end of May, and the new year began as early as August whenever an international tourney was to be played. A player like Messier would have little time to recover from his wounds before the 1991 Canada Cup, in which Team Canada was expected to defend the championship it had won so spectacularly in '87. Messier was counted on to be a big part of Canada's title defense, but exhausted and jealously guarding the downtime he so cherished, he turned down the invitation. He did tell Team Canada coach Mike Keenan that he might reconsider, however, and Keenan agreed to leave the door open for him.

While the players at the Team Canada training camp in Toronto were vying for jobs, Messier went inline skating on Hilton Head—ten miles a day—and relaxed by golfing, deep-sea fishing, and wakeboarding. After a while he started getting calls from Wayne Gretzky, asking him to change his mind about joining the national team. Finally, three weeks into training camp, Messier's old friend persuaded him to join the cause. "Gretzky has called me three days in a row," Messier said from Hilton Head when reporters heard the news. "I'd really like to go. I'm feeling pretty good right now. I think I can do it now." He was concerned that the Team Canada players might resent his showing up on the last day of the twenty-five-day camp, and indeed, Keenan made Calgary's strapping winger Gary Roberts the odd man out to make room for him. "A lot of guys put a lot of time in there," Messier said, rather lamely. "Although I wasn't putting in time, I was there in thought and mind." When he showed up at Maple Leaf Gardens looking tan, fit, and nothing like the bedraggled man he was at the end of the playoffs, he pronounced, "I'm here to help Canada keep the title," and, after making obligatory statements about not wanting to ruffle anyone's feathers by showing up late, he said: "If Gretz hadn't called, I don't think I'd be here. When I first left for Hilton Head, which was around the time that camp opened, I never planned on being here. I knew the invitation was there and always knew that there might be a chance I'd play, but until I got the call and started to think about it, I hadn't given it much thought. I feel great, the best I've been in a long time. Besides, I'd reached the point where I'd had enough of golf."

Messier said he thought he might miss the first two matches while he got into game shape, but in fact he was in the lineup right from the start. Whereas previous editions of Team Canada were built for speed and scoring, this one was built to grind and check. Just as the governing ethos of the NHL was changing from the wide-open air hockey of the mid-'80s to the tight constriction of the mid-'90s neutral-zone trap, so too was Team Canada undergoing a similar transformation. But it didn't matter—Messier could play it either way. Something had changed since '84 and '87: Messier now played second banana to no one. Everyone, Keenan included, saw him as every bit as critical a component of the national team as Gretzky or Lemieux—more so, in fact, because Lemieux's rapidly deteriorating back forced him to miss the tournament. Team Canada '91 retained the flash of Gretzky, Messier, Coffey, and Luc Robitaille, but the core of the team was made up of such two-way players as Steve Larmer, Dale Hawerchuk, Theo Fleury, Rick Tocchet, and Brendan Shanahan, and outright grinders like

Dirk Graham, Shayne Corson, and Brent Sutter. Surprisingly, it would turn out to be the most successful team that Canada ever assembled.

No one said anything bad for attribution about Messier joining the team at the last minute, although one unnamed player who was cut was quoted as calling Messier's late arrival "brutal" and added "there's just so much politics involved." But the general feeling was summed up by Michael Farber of the Montreal *Gazette*: "This isn't just anyone Team Canada imported but a real ringer, Death-Stare Mark, a clenched fist of a forward who is even more fierce than he is skilled. Messier has played on five Stanley Cup winners and two Canada Cup champions. He has earned a lot of accolades, a lot of money. Mostly, Messier has earned some slack."

Once on board, Messier made his usual emphatic first impression. Eric Lindros, 18 and the only member of Team Canada not to have appeared in the NHL, was an admirer right from the start. He had grown up with an autographed poster of Messier in his bedroom, and in his autobiography (written when he was all of 19) Lindros described the scene when his idol sauntered into the Canada dressing room after agreeing at the last minute to play in the tournament. "How ya doin', kid?" Messier said when he saw him. "Good to meet ya. Let's get busy." Bill Ranford, whom Messier had set straight when the goalie first joined the Oilers, looked at Lindros and said, "Well, there he is. There's our fearless leader." The starstruck teen described Messier as "downright scary" and tried to emulate everything he did. "I'd watch the way he skated around in the warmup," he enthused. "He'd get that intense stare going, and I'd try to get a stare going too." Lindros even got to room with Messier near the end of the tournament. "He was a riot!" Lindros reported, and many years later they would room together again, under very different circumstances.

Messier assisted on the tournament's first goal in a 2–2 tie with Finland, and he was in midseason form as he exchanged elbows with his erstwhile linemate Tikkanen. Against the USA he was outplayed by his Calgary nemesis Joel Otto in what was still an easy 6–3 win; in a way, the role of Messier was played in this game by Lindros, who tangled with Otto all night long. Canada followed with a 4–1 defeat of Sweden and a 6–2 trouncing of Czechoslovakia, then closed out the round-robin phase with a 3–3 tie against the USSR. This would prove to be the last-ever tournament for the

Soviet team; shortly afterward, as the Soviet Union melted away, it competed briefly under the banner of the CIS (Commonwealth of Independent States), before the individual republics (Russia, Ukraine, Kazakhstan, and so on) formed their own national teams.

The Canadians finished the first stage at 3–0–2, second to the Americans' 4–1–0. But their performance was somewhat overshadowed by news reports that the Oilers were not going to re-sign their big stars. Messier was rumored to be headed to one of three or four deep-pocketed clubs. Anderson also seemed to be at an impasse with management over his re-negotiated contract. Adam Graves' contract expired, and when negotiations went nowhere, he signed with the New York Rangers. Tikkanen's contract was also up, and on the day after Graves signed with Rangers, Tikkanen called the Oilers "cheap, cheap, cheap." A couple of days later, on September 4, Messier decided that he'd had enough of the Oilers. "I don't think you'll see me in that uniform again," he told *The Edmonton Sun*. "I'd say I've probably played my last game as an Oiler." Messier's mood was not lightened, either, by how difficult the collective bargaining agreement made it for free agents to move from team to team. Draft choices had to be given up, and sometimes arbitrators were called in to rule on disputes. When the New Jersey Devils signed defenseman Scott Stevens, formerly of the St. Louis Blues, during the tournament and were forced to give up Brendan Shanahan as compensation, Messier's terse opinion on the matter was, "It's fuckin' bullshit."

Like Tikkanen, Messier was frustrated over the Oilers' tightness with a dollar, although he expressed it in more statesmanlike terms. "It's about winning," he said. "I thought we could win again this year with a couple of moves before the deadline. And we came close. But I see it starting to fall apart now. And at this stage of my career, the only thing that matters is winning." About Graves' departure, and the way the club had let other players depart, he said: "We still respect the organization and we still respect ourselves and the fans of Edmonton. But there was no reward given back to those players. I wouldn't say those players kept the franchise alive. Edmonton is a great hockey city. The franchise will survive. But those are the players who kept the dynasty alive. If that's the way it's going to be in Edmonton, I don't want to be there."

Typically, Sather got in a zinger when asked to respond. "Mark is a good guy," he said. "Mark is a good player. When he didn't get the big paycheck, I think he made up his mind he wanted to get more money wherever he could." It was an uncomfortable situation, because so many of the principals were at the Canada Cup—Messier, Sather, Stevens, Shanahan, Tikkanen, and of course, Gretzky, who said of his old friend: "This guy wore his [Oilers] crest on his heart. I remember when I went through it, how tough it was for me. I'm sure all of this is really weighing on Mark's mind. His family lives in the town. He's from there. He grew up there." Reporters descended on Messier and asked whether he now expected Sather to trade him. "I think he will," Messier said. "I hope he will."

The other Oilers seemed sad and resigned to the situation. "It eats me up inside to see the likes of Mark Messier and Grant Fuhr discontented," said Steve Smith, who was also playing for Team Canada. Bill Ranford added: "Are we going to see the Edmonton Oilers next year, or another team? A lot younger team, basically the Cape Breton Oilers [Edmonton's farm team]. I'd hate to see that happen. It's a situation where all last year they were trying to get the contract taken care of. They had a year to do it. And I'm sure now it's to the point where Mark's just fed up." Kevin Lowe, who sat out the tournament, said: "It's extremely frustrating. I know the organization is having a tough time, but so are we. We're seeing guys we've gone to war with leaving. You're looking at the exact same situation as Gretzky. Mess has meant so much to the organization, the city, his teammates. Don't even think how are you going to replace that." Tikkanen plaintively asked, "What's happened to my team?"

Now that the cat was out of the bag, Messier spoke freely about what had gone wrong and where he figured he'd wind up. "I haven't talked to Glen hardly since the middle of the playoffs last season, for whatever reason," he said. "Renegotiating the contract came to a complete halt somewhere around January and I never talked to him about it after that. They've been trying to deal me for the last year. Glen's been made aware that I wanted to be traded at the draft this summer. I don't expect to hear from him until something happens. I'm not trying to concern myself with that right now. I'm going to concentrate the next couple weeks on this tournament. Hopefully, things will get settled. It was a great twelve years. I see friends of mine on the team having trouble, and it's just gone too far. I just think it's best for me at this time to go somewhere else. Toronto certainly has to be considered. I'd have to say New York and Philadelphia are probably the two teams in the running. Also L.A. or Detroit."

The Canada Cup had been upstaged by the Oiler upheaval and leaguewide labor-management strife, and was nudged further out of the spotlight after the Soviets failed to qualify for the semifinals while Team Canada coasted uneventfully past Sweden, 4–0, to get to the final. Keenan's team found itself defending its title in a best-of-three series against what, for Canadians, was the only other country besides the USSR that could be cast as a natural villain: the United States. That matchup boosted Canadians' interest, while everyone was taken aback by news of the illness that had stricken U.S. coach Bob Johnson, the former Calgary Flames bench boss who had taken over in Pittsburgh and led the Penguins to the Stanley Cup in May. Johnson was in a Pittsburgh hospital undergoing surgery and radiation treatment for brain tumors, and the end was near for the widely beloved coach.

In game one in Montreal, Canada led by 2–0 halfway through the contest when U.S. defenseman Gary Suter blindsided Wayne Gretzky from behind. Gretzky fell headfirst into the boards four feet away and got up slowly, his back clearly hurt. No penalty was called. (Gretzky, who missed the rest of the game, did not blame Suter for the hit.) Less than two minutes later, Suter scored, making Canadian fans and players even more livid. Team Canada had lost its focus by the the second intermission, and Messier stepped forward to win it back. In the dressing room he addressed his teammates, an experience that the young Lindros described as "amazing." "He just got that look," Lindros remembered. "With Messier, it's in the eyes. They're like lasers. Man, do they ever get you going. I was sitting on the other side of the room to the right when Messier stood up to make a speech and said what had to be said."

Messier backed up his words with action when he took the ice for the third period. At 11:42 he beat Mike Richter on a shot that made it 3–1 and for all intents and purposes ended the Americans' chances. "Mark Messier took charge," Gretzky said after the 4–1 victory was sealed. "When Wayne went down, there was Number 11, playing great," Theoren Fleury added. After a decent but more or less unremarkable tournament, Messier had come alive.

With Gretzky sitting out game two, Messier lit up the early minutes of that contest as well. He opened the scoring, beating Richter on the stick side at 13:39. Twenty seconds later, Steve Larmer made it 2–0. But the Amerks fought back and tied the game after two periods, 2–2. Now it was Dirk Graham's turn to step up in the dressing room, delivering an inspirational speech that was worthy of Messier himself, and which everyone later said was the catalyst to victory. In the third period, poetic justice was served when Larmer stole the puck from the vilified Suter and scored the go-ahead goal on a shorthanded breakaway. Messier set up Graham for the clinching empty-netter, and the Canadians were tournament champions for the third straight time, their patrimony fully restored after the crushing setback against the Soviets ten years before. Messier was there for each triumph, in 1984, '87, and now '91, playing a greater role each time. In the 1991 tournament he finished third on the team in scoring, with two goals and six assists in eight games, and with a high plus-7 rating to boot. The seeds of leadership planted within him as he watched Gretzky and Robinson in '84 now bloomed as he took charge of the team after Gretzky's injury. Despite the public acrimony between Messier and the Oilers that hung over the 1991 Canada Cup, the tournament only added to his legend.

With the tournament over, Moose hunting season began. Speculation ran rampant as to where Messier would wind up. He did not attend Oilers training camp, simply sitting tight as the field of suitors narrowed to the Rangers, Islanders, and Keenan's Chicago Blackhawks. Detroit dropped out of the running, presumably because they didn't want to part with Steve Yzerman, and so did Philadelphia, reluctant to give up first-round draft choice Mike Ricci. The players reportedly being offered for Messier included Pat LaFontaine, Jeremy Roenick, and Bernie Nicholls. Meanwhile, Sather dealt Steve Smith to Chicago and Ken Linseman to Toronto, and juggled holdouts by Craig Simpson and Grant Fuhr. The whole Edmonton house of cards was coming down.

The Oilers went to Calgary to open their season, but Messier did not make the trip. He was in Hilton Head, playing golf with Doug. By now the drama had been sucked out of Messier's departure; everyone just wanted it over with. That day, the months of impasse and acrimony finally ended: Sather announced that Messier had been traded to the New York Rangers. Messier got the news by cellphone while he was on the fifteenth tee, and he got ready to head to New York.

Messier flew to New York on October 3, but he wasn't yet a Ranger. He would have to pass a physical first. Given the damage to Messier's left knee during his previous, injury-filled season, the fact that he had played so many high-intensity playoff and international games over the previous ten campaigns, and the prevailing belief in hockey in 1991 that a thirty-year-old player was entering the twilight of his career, there was no guarantee he would pass. But when Rangers team doctor Bart Nisonson phoned Neil Smith in Boston, while New York was in the process of losing its season opener to the Bruins, he reported that Messier was a "specimen," and the deal was on. Smith would make the announcement in a Boston hotel the next morning: the Rangers were sending to Edmonton Bernie Nicholls, a flashy second-line centerman miscast as a first-liner in New York; tough guys Louie DeBrusk and Steven Rice; and cash, an amount later reported as at least $1.5 million. In exchange, they were getting Mark Messier. Smith called it "the biggest day in the sixty-six-year history of the New York Rangers."

In Calgary, while the Rangers were losing to the Bruins half a continent away, the Edmonton Oilers played an NHL game for the first time ever without Mark Messier as part of the team. They lost, 9–2.

THE COACH KILLER

The first time Mark Messier played in New York back when he was an eighteen-year-old hellraiser, so the story goes, he drank so much after the game that his Oilers teammates had to prop him up and sneak him past the customs officers at the airport. That may or may not actually be true, but Paul Coffey does remember the Oilers arriving in Manhattan for a game and the young Messier taking it all in and announcing, "Another beautiful day in the Big Apple, and I want to take a big bite out of it!"

There was no question that Messier was going to enjoy being a New York Ranger, and there was also no question that Messier was being brought to the Rangers to be more than simply a superstar player; he was to be their new captain. The club had allowed its previous leader, Kelly Kisio, to be claimed by the new San Jose Sharks in the expansion draft of 1991. Kisio was a small, earnest centerman and the living embodiment of the hard-working plugger who has made the most possible out of his limited talents, but he was neither the fire-eating type, nor a statesman, nor someone who led through superlative performance. That he wound up wearing the

Rangers' C was illustrative of just how rudderless the club had become as it cast about futilely for its first Stanley Cup in half a century.

Neil Smith realized this and when he exposed Kisio, who like Messier wore number 11, he already had Messier in his sights. Smith was trying to add leadership, character, and winning experience to New York, a process he had already set in motion when he signed the free agent Adam Graves. (When Graves reported to the Rangers camp he took Kisio's number 11 sweater in tribute to Messier. As soon as word was out that his hero was coming to Manhattan, Graves gladly surrendered it.)

The Rangers arrived in Montreal on Friday for a Saturday-night game against the Canadiens. That morning, Messier hooked up with his new team, but the news was already out. Papers all over North America had the story, quoting coaches, general managers, and players who had played with and against Messier. All paid tribute to his ability and predicted big things for the Rangers. Back in Edmonton, Ted Green, who was now coaching the Oilers, said he was "a little saddened" that Messier was gone. Glen Sather said, "We had a great relationship over the years. It's too bad these things happen, but that's business." Joel Otto, Messier's main Calgary tormentor in the Battles of Alberta, was less valedictory. He said he was glad his rival was gone. "We never spoke," Otto said. "No, that's not totally right. Once in the playoffs, they were beating us and near the end of the game he said something. What did he say? They weren't friendly words."

Meanwhile, the Rangers had suddenly become a serious contender, not so much because of the tangible benefits Messier added to their lineup, but because of the intangible qualities he brought. Smith later relayed a conversation he had with Sather after the trade was completed: "Slats told me, 'He will solve every problem you have, every time something comes up,' meaning in the locker room. That's what everybody says: 'Messier will always find a way to lead the team.'"

Smith called a news conference at the Montreal Forum and presented the club's twenty-second captain, who pulled the blue number 11 sweater over his head. "Whenever he leaves here," Smith told the assembled media in the world capital of hockey, "if it's seven months or seven years from now, he'll leave us with something we didn't have before he arrived. We'll be a better organization for having had him. He will put something into the

Rangers logo that you won't be able to see. He will make the Rangers believe they can win, and I'm not sure anybody has ever made the Rangers believe they can win. You will sit there and say there is something dramatically different about this team."

Then it was Messier's turn to speak. He stepped up to the mike, his laser-intense gaze amplified by the TV lights and flashbulbs. "I accept the challenge, and everything that goes with New York," he said. "Everybody seems to want to tiptoe around the issue that the Rangers haven't won a Stanley Cup in fifty-one years or whatever it is. Well, in Edmonton I always felt pressure was good for us. I've met every challenge I've ever faced head-on. I never want to duck any issue or challenge that comes my way. I welcome this one."

It would not have been unexpected for Messier to comment on his acrimonious departure from Edmonton, but for the moment any ill feelings seemed to have been swept under the rug. "I lived in Edmonton for thirty years, and this was one of the biggest decisions of my life," he said. "It was a fantastic twelve years, but I'm looking more than forward to the new challenge in front of me. I'm starting a so-called second career, and I'm every bit as confident that my second career will be as good as my first."

From that point on, whenever Messier commented on the end of his Oiler days, he always said that it had simply been time to move on, that he had done all he could do there and it was time to find new challenges. This has become the *leitmotif* of everything written about Messier's rupture with the Oilers—not the disappointment and bitter sense of betrayal over the Gretzky trade, the lowballing in salary negotiations that took advantage of the youth and naïveté of the players, or the accusations that Messier was dogging it in his final year. All of those factors have more or less disappeared down the memory hole, mostly because Messier himself refused to dwell on any of it. "One thing I can say for Sather is that he's a winner," Messier said on the day the trade was announced. "I don't think anybody in hockey has been as good a coach or general manager." And he graciously characterized his desire to leave Edmonton as a mutual decision between team and player that it was "time to move on." Messier remained close to Sather, Muckler, and his Oiler teammates, and they would return to play key roles during the many years left in his playing career.

Doug Messier, Mark's father, mentor, coach, and later his agent, spent the 1957–58 season with England's Nottingham Panthers. © *Hulton-Deutsch Collection/CORBIS/MAGMA*

Eighteen-year-old Mark Messier stick-handles his way past Stefan Persson of the New York Islanders early in his rookie season, 1979–80. © *Brian Winkler/BBS*

At the July 13, 2000 news conference to announce Messier's Broadway return, he and Dave Checketts, CEO of Madison Square Garden, bury the hatchet—literally. © *Bruce Bennett/BBS*

Messier takes charge of the festivities, filling the Cup with champagne after Edmonton's first championship in 1984. © *Bruce Bennett/BBS*

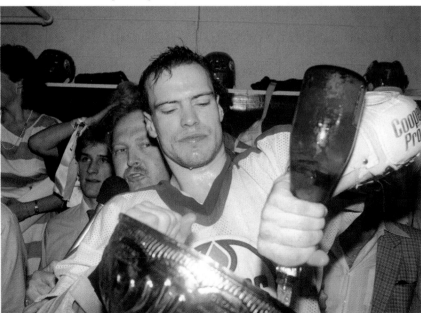

Messier shares a laugh with Phil Esposito (left) and teammate Wayne Gretzky (right) after Gretzky scored his 77th regular-season goal, breaking Espo's 11-year-old record. © *Bruce Bennett/BBS*

The same night, February 24, 1982, Messier hobnobs with actors Goldie Hawn and Burt Reynolds at Buffalo's Memorial Auditorium. © *Bruce Bennett/BBS*

Messier flashes the Hawaiian "hang loose" signal and shows off the Conn Smythe Trophy after being named MVP of the 1984 playoffs. © *Bruce Bennett/BBS*

(top) Captain Mark sprints down the ice at Boston Garden with the Cup after the Oilers defeated the Bruins in the 1990 finals—their first and only win without Wayne Gretzky. © *Bruce Bennett/BBS*

(above) Messier winds up for a slap shot on the Rockefeller Center rink to promote the 1994 All-Star Game in New York. Ranger legend Rod Gilbert is at right, in the white jersey. © *Scott Levy/BBS*

(opposite) Messier hoists the Cup before the hometown faithful after the Oilers' 3–1 win in game seven of the 1987 finals. © *Bruce Bennett/BBS*

Messier raises his stick after scoring what would prove to be the Cup-winning goal against Vancouver during the 1994 finals. © *Bruce Bennett/BBS*

The conquering heroes flaunt the Cup during a ticker-tape parade through Manhattan's "Canyon of Heroes" on June 17, 1994. Messier is flanked by Brian Leetch (left) and Adam Graves (right). © *Bruce Bennett/BBS*

On November 12, 1995, Messier scored a hat trick to become the 21st NHL player to reach the 500-goal plateau. He is seen here with Kevin Lowe.
© *Bruce Bennett/BBS*

Ranger fans welcome their former captain with open arms on November 25, 1997, as Messier plays his first game at the Garden since signing with the Canucks.
© *Scott Levy/BBS*

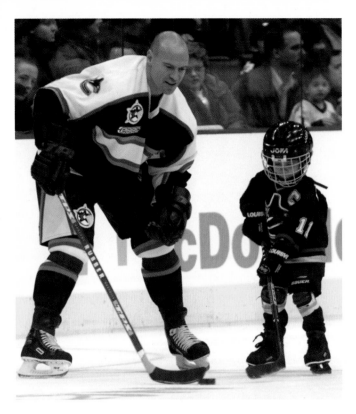

During the 2000 All-Star weekend in Toronto, Messier spends some time on the ice with his four-year-old nephew—also named Mark Messier. *CP (Ryan Remiorz)*

At the Rangers' home opener on October 7, 2001, firefighter Larry McGee presented Messier with his helmet; attached to it is a photo of Deputy Fire Chief Ray Downey, who was killed when the World Trade Center towers collapsed. Eric Lindros is at left. *© Bruce Bennett/BBS*

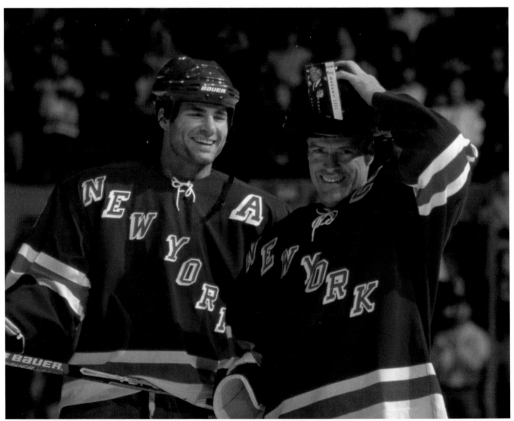

After the news conference, Messier went to the visitors dressing room, where he suited up and introduced himself to his new teammates—literally approaching each one, shaking his hand, and saying, "Hi, I'm Mark Messier." As Rick Carpiniello wrote in his Messier biography, Messier then stepped onto the Forum ice and started taking businesslike turns around the rink. A few Rangers came up to him for some quick words, but many preferred to look on from a safe distance. Several seemed in awe, from former 50-goal men John Ogrodnick, Tim Kerr, and Messier's former Cincinnati linemate Mike Gartner, to the promising young defenseman Brian Leetch, who turned to his fellow blueliner James Patrick and said, "Do you believe Mark Messier is on our team?" Another up-and-coming youngster, Tony Amonte, was told he would play on Messier's line. "I don't know," the rookie winger replied nervously. "I don't think I'm going to be able to do it." Graves, the son of a Toronto policeman who raised several foster children, said, "Aside from my father, there is nobody I respect more than Mark Messier." It was as if a warrior saint had suddenly materialized in the Rangers' midst.

The Rangers played the Canadiens the next night. Sitting in the visitors' dressing room before the game, Messier said nothing. Later, he admitted that he was thinking about his first NHL game, in 1979, when the baby Oilers sat expectantly in Chicago Stadium. "I actually thought about that first game before this game. That's bizarre. I don't know if that happens to other guys after they've been traded. It was a little bit of the same feeling tonight as it was back then." Out on the Forum ice, where the Rangers had not beaten in Montreal in twelve games over the course of six years, the Habs went up 1–0 before Messier, just out of the penalty box, set up Doug Weight to tie the score. Then, in overtime, Sergei Nemchinov, recently a star for *Krylia Sovetor* (Soviet Wings of Moscow) of the Russian Elite League and a stalwart on the Soviet national team, now playing his first season in North America, scored his first NHL goal to give the Rangers the victory. Messier wore number 11, but his sweater did not have a C sewn onto it.

The home opener lay two nights ahead. Smith, who at thirty-eight was one of the youngest executives in the league, nevertheless had a very strong sense of hockey tradition, having grown up in Toronto with a mother who, highly *un*traditionally, had actually played the game. He planned a spectacle that would transform the notion of Ranger history—which, when it was acknowledged at all, was viewed as a source of shame—into a basis for pride and celebration. Messier, Smith had already noted, had five Stanley Cups to his credit in his twelve-year career while in sixty-six years the Rangers franchise had but three. The new captain, therefore, was to be the centerpiece, or perhaps more accurately, the altarpiece, of the opening-night ceremony.

That evening, the crowd at Madison Square Garden was more excited than for any opener since the brief heyday of the Ooh-La-La Rangers of the late 1970s, the last time the club had gained any kind of hold on the city's imagination, when Ron Duguay was the cover boy of Andy Warhol's *Interview* magazine, Phil Esposito and John Davidson danced clumsily in television commercials for designer jeans, and the Rangers met the Canadiens in the '79 Stanley Cup finals. In the intervening dozen years, there had been nothing to get excited about, except perhaps coach Ted Sator's Smurfs, who won a couple of playoff rounds one year before fading back into the team's usual murk of obscurity. But on this night, fans genuinely believed that with the arrival of Messier, something different and new was beginning.

The house lights were brought down, and nine Ranger captains of the past were introduced to stride or totter out on a carpet to center ice. There were such recent alumni as Ron Greschner, Barry Beck, and Dave Maloney; older legends Rod Gilbert, Harry Howell, Andy Bathgate, and Camille Henry; and then, going really way back, Don "Bones" Raleigh. Finally, there was Messier's distant relative, the man who was literally the original Ranger: eighty-seven-year-old Murray Murdoch, the first man signed when the team got started in 1926 and a player in each and every one of the team's first 563 regular-season and playoff games.

Next, as the public address announcer intoned, "And the newest Ranger captain . . .", Messier stepped into the spotlight, the C now proudly affixed to his sweater. Grinning broadly, he skated out to center ice and shook hands with all the old captains, one after the other, ending with Murdoch. "It's kind of eerie, isn't it?" Mary-Kay said later. "Murray is a man we have known all of our lives. Uncle Murray. There always have been family stories about him playing with the Rangers. Now, to have Mark here . . . it's like it was meant to be." After embracing Murdoch quickly, Messier turned and thrust his arms in the air, proud to be a Ranger. From the stands, the cheers rained down like thunder.

The game itself, against Boston, finally began. Once more the Rangers played to a 1–1 tie in the regulation sixty minutes, and once again they won in overtime, Ogrodnick netting the winner. Messier assisted on both New York goals and sported an attractive gash above his lip, courtesy of Ray Bourque's stick. It made for the perfect image of the knight victorious that Ranger fans craved. The next game was at home against the Islanders, the renewal of a rivalry almost as bitter as the Oilers–Flames antipathy. Messier scored his first two Ranger goals in a come-from-behind victory, while Kris King netted the winner with just fifteen seconds left. So it went that first month with Messier on board: everything worked out as if in a storybook. The Rangers went 9–4–0 in October, the new captain leading the way and the whole motley roster fired up and producing in response. In New York, Messier was no longer the Moose; he was the Messiah.

The honeymoon would last the entire regular season, and just as effusive as anyone in his praise for Messier was Roger Neilson, the Rangers' coach. The fifty-seven-year-old was a lifelong hockey coach who had made his name during a decade-long tenure at the helm of the storied Peterborough Petes of the Ontario Hockey Association (now the Ontario Hockey League) in the '60s and '70s. He moved up to become the bench boss of the Toronto Maple Leafs and soon gained renown as the first coach to analyze videotape and use it as an instructional aid. Neilson was successful everywhere he went—including that brief stop in Edmonton in 1984, when Sather brought him in to contribute his video breakdowns to the Oilers' effort to unseat the Islanders—but he never lasted more than a couple of seasons in any NHL job, gaining a reputation as someone who could make a bad team good but never good enough to win it all. Although he was himself soft-spoken, he favored teams that clutched, grabbed, and, especially, fought. Despite his innovative use of videotape, he was in fact an exemplar of old-time Canadian hockey, the hard-nosed kind that worked in the Ontario junior ranks.

After head coaching stints in Toronto, Buffalo, Vancouver (where he led the Canucks to the 1982 Stanley Cup finals), Los Angeles, and Chicago (as something called a "co-coach"), Neilson was hired by the Rangers' new GM, Smith, for the '89–90 campaign. He guided the team to a 36–31–13 record, good enough to top the Patrick Division—the first time the Blueshirts had finished first since 1942, such was the depth and breadth of their chronic mediocrity. The next season the Rangers compiled the same record, but exited the playoffs after one round instead of after two, prompting Smith to bring in Messier so that the Rangers could make the leap to true contention. Neilson was delighted. "When a player of his stature stands up," he said of Messier's inspirational qualities in the dressing room, "players listen. Not all captains do that."

For now, at least, Messier and Neilson were in accord. But behind the scenes, there was a secret rift: very soon after his arrival in New York, Messier began to have doubts about Neilson's tactics. He later revealed that in only his second month after joining the Rangers, he told Smith of his misgivings. He believed that Neilson's dump-and-chase system might work in the regular season, particularly with the two fine young goalers Mike Richter and John Vanbiesbrouck covering the team's defensive mistakes, but he also believed that it could easily fail in the playoffs.

There were no outward signs of the divide between Neilson and Messier, although D'Arcy Jenish, writing a profile of Messier for *Maclean's*, may have unknowingly stumbled across one. He described a scene at the end of a 90-minute workout following a third straight loss: "Nielson summoned his players to one side of the rink for a brief lecture on puck pursuit in the opposition's end. He then headed for the locker room—and Messier took over. With his teammates gathered around him, the captain spoke quietly for 10 minutes. Neither he nor the other players would reveal what he said." The next night the Rangers won.

Any doubts about Neilson's tactics remained in the background as long as everything else was going so well. Messier, his father, and the Rangers front office were certainly on the same page when it came to Messier's contract. The newly militant NHL Players' Association, seeking leverage in a simmering dispute with the owners, conducted a salary survey. It revealed that Messier's $1.1 million stipend was only the fourteenth highest in the league; Smith and his Garden bosses quickly worked out a new deal with Doug: Mark would become the third-highest paid, after Gretzky and

Lemieux, making $1.75 million for 1991–92, with incremental increases leading to $2.75 million in '95–96. The deal also included a signing bonus and incentive clauses covering playoff series wins, championships, and various individual honors. Messier even had the right to renegotiate if New York won the Cup.

Life in New York City was also agreeing with Messier. He first lived in the Westbury Hotel on East 69th Street, a tony address, and ate at the hotel's Polo Restaurant, where the maitre'd assigned him an exclusive table and introduced him to celebrities like Howard Cosell and Cyndi Lauper. Then he found an apartment that was almost egregious in its glamor—a huge place on the seventy-third floor of one of the tallest residential buildings in the world, a huge black monolith on West 57th Street next to Carnegie Hall. "A number of times before I ever came here, I envisioned what it would like playing in New York," he said. "I wanted to live downtown. I wanted to experience the whole thing—playing in a major media market and feeling the pulse of the city. I wanted the whole adrenaline rush of doing it all, and now I've got it. When I'm in my apartment, looking out the window, I sometimes feel like I'm in a movie."

He shared his place with Mary-Kay, Paul—who had just retired from his playing career in Germany—and his housekeeper from Edmonton, Maria. Other aspects of his former life he left behind. "When he moved, he left all his trophies, all his awards, back in Edmonton," Mary-Kay told *Sports Illustrated* writer Leigh Montville. "I kept asking him when he wanted me to ship them. He kept cutting me off. I couldn't figure it out. Why wouldn't he want this stuff? It's all in the basement of the house in Edmonton. Then it hit me. He was making a break. Nothing else counted. He wanted to concentrate on being a Ranger."

Messier drove an '89 Bentley, which he'd bought from Gretzky, to practices in the suburbs. He appeared in skits on David Letterman's late-night talk show on NBC. He dated a Swedish model, Carrie Nygren, who a couple of years earlier had appeared in a movie called *King of New York*. He met Madonna on the set of *A League of Their Own* over the summer, got her phone number from Janet Jones, and spoke with the Material Girl a few times during the Canada Cup tournament. They don't seem to have ever actually gone out more than once, but Ranger fans were ecstatic at the notion that their new hero might be sleeping with the biggest pop star of the era, a rumour fueled by *The New York Post.* Under the headline "N.Y. Hockey Hunk Putting the Move on Madonna," the tabloid's dependably cheesy Page Six gossip column reported phone conversations between the two "may soon lead to pillow talk," even though Messier demurred: "Madonna and I talked on the phone, and we plan on meeting when she gets to New York. But I haven't had a lot of time to think about her right now." A couple of weeks later he again played it coy, saying, "With her schedule—she's working on her next album right now—and our schedule, there hasn't been much time to get together." Later, he said they had canceled three times, once because of a team function for a child-abuse prevention program, and "It darn near killed me." No action on the Madonna front having transpired, he stopped talking about it altogether, though the belief persists to this day among many Ranger fans that they were once an item.

On the ice, all was still good. The night before Messier's homecoming to Edmonton on January 23, he stayed at the family house in St. Albert with Mary-Kay and their mother, who now lived in Hilton Head with Doug. The next evening, he arrived at Northlands Coliseum more than four hours before game time. During the pregame introductions, the crowd gave him a ninety-second standing ovation (impressive, but about three minutes shorter than the one Gretzky received in his return). Then in the 900th game of his NHL career, he scored his 1,100th career point on a fifteen-foot slap shot—which the crowd booed—and set up Amonte for the game-winner in a 3–1 triumph. "I wasn't too uptight about coming back here," said Messier. "It was a chance to see some friends and some family, and my mom and my sister are here, so I'm glad the game's over with and I'm glad I don't have to do this four times a year."

Clearly, Edmonton was in Messier's past. It was midseason, and Messier stood fourth in the league in scoring, the Rangers were battling the Washington Capitals for the Patrick Division lead, and New York was genuinely excited about the team. "We're in the news," Messier said. "It's fun. That's what it's all about. It's show business, and it's entertainment, and you try to put on a good show."

In the dressing room, things were even better. With literally a lifetime of experience in winning rooms, Messier understood, both innately and intellectually, how to create an atmosphere of camaraderie. One of the first things he did was ask for the removal of a large table that stood in the middle of the Rangers' dressing room at the Garden; it was usually stacked with coolers, cups, and rolls of tape, which often blocked the view of players sitting across the way. Messier said he wanted to be able to look anyone in the room in the eye. The table was promptly removed. He also noted the bareness of the walls, the absence of anything that would instill pride in the players. In response, old team photos and plaques were quickly put up, and where once the gaze of Rangers players and staff fell only on bare cinderblock, it now met the eyes of Lester Patrick, Frank Boucher, Bill Cook, Ching Johnson, Bryan Hextall, Davey Kerr, Phil Watson, Emile Francis, Jean Ratelle, Eddie Giacomin, and two-thirds of a century's worth of history. For the first time in many years, being a Ranger was starting to carry the same kind of institutional pride that seemed to come naturally for the other so-called Original Six clubs.

All season long, every player and member of the coaching staff marveled at the change in atmosphere wrought by their captain. He held players-only meetings in which he argued passionately for a commitment to excellence; some players were surprised by the utter lack of physical threat from Messier, a threat they had heard about from his rumored run-ins with slackers in his Edmonton days. "We lost a game in Los Angeles," Richter told Leigh Montville. "Mess called a meeting. It wasn't a real bad game—we outshot them, their goalie made the saves—but still we weren't as good as we should be. Mess was very emotional. I don't want to say things I shouldn't be saying, but there were tears in his eyes. He was saying, 'I will not take losing as a habit. I will not stand for it.' He wasn't blaming anyone else. He said none of us should blame anyone else, that you never have to look further than yourself when you lose." In St. Louis, Messier ordered the bus driver to pull over to a bar so everyone could celebrate that night's victory. In Los Angeles, he took the team golfing at a country club in Thousand Oaks and set up a tour of the Paramount studios. He arranged for the players to give each coach a set of expensive luggage for Christmas. On New Year's Eve in Chicago, he arranged a team party. Impromptu get-togethers, team dinners, new suits for hayseed rookies—everything Messier did fostered and strengthened bonds within the team.

Graves was his left winger (Amonte played on the right side) and was more extravagant in his praise than any other Ranger. "He's more valuable to this team than he ever was to Edmonton, and in 1990 he won the Hart Trophy," Graves told *Sports Illustrated*. "I'd say he has to be the premier leader in professional sports right now. Any team. Any game. Who'd be better?" And indeed, Messier was having a Hart-quality year. When the regular season ended, he would rack up 35 goals and 72 assists for 107 points, sixth best in the league. His plus-31 figure was great, the second best on the team and perhaps the best showing of his career in that department. Tony Amonte led all NHL rookies in scoring with 35 goals and 69 points—for which he credited the constant stream of encouragement and advice from Messier on the ice—and finished a close second in the Calder Trophy voting behind Pavel Bure. Brian Leetch, Messier's road roommate, fellow passenger on limo trips to practice, and perhaps closest friend on the team, amassed 102 points to become only the fourth defenseman in NHL history to break the century mark. Messier was whistled down for 76 minutes in penalties; he left the fighting to several others on the roster, namely Graves, Kris King, Joey Kocur, Jeff Beukeboom (who came over from Edmonton a month into the season as a future consideration in the Messier deal), and especially the inimitably crazed Tie Domi.

Other players' perception of Messier changed. He had long been respected for what he'd done in Edmonton and with Team Canada in '84 and '87. But with another Canada Cup victory under his belt the previous summer and now as the skyscraper-dwelling leader of the Rangers, equal measures of statesmanship and glitz seemed to accrue to him; he was looked upon almost as if he were royalty. The Penguins' Jaromir Jagr, the second-year Czech sensation whose English was still somewhat rudimentary when he was chosen to play in the NHL All-Star Game in 1992, observed the scene from a certain remove when the Ranger captain arrived in the Prince of Wales dressing room. "In comes Mark Messier," he wrote in his memoir *Jagr: An Autobiography*, "wearing a long black coat and looking like some kind of mysterious big shot. He spots Coff, and the two of them sit down together and talk about the old days in Edmonton, obviously enjoying their reunion. Then Mario walks by, and even though he and Messier barely know each other, having played together only briefly on the Canadian national team, they shake hands like old friends too—just a couple of all-time hockey greats glad to have the chance to say hello."

The season was almost going *too* well for anyone who had been involved with the Rangers for any amount of time. Isolated from the hockey mainstream for decades, Ranger fans lived in a hermetic world bounded by Long Island to the east, Philadelphia to the south, New Jersey to the west, and nothing, really, to the north, except perhaps Boston. Ranger fans truly believed their team was the only one that suffered injuries at key moments, the only one to get jobbed by referees, the only one to hit goalposts when the game was on the line. As blinkered as this view was, it was also borne out by fifty-one years of bitter experience. In 1979, for instance, the Rangers made the Stanley Cup finals, but lost their star winger Ulf Nilsson en route when he collided with the Islanders' Denis Potvin and broke his ankle. It was an accident, acknowledged by Nilsson and by everyone else on the ice, but Ranger fans were certain that the loss of Nilsson cost them the Cup, and they blamed Potvin for it. Twelve years later, in Messier's first season, they still chanted "Potvin sucks" at every game, no matter whom the Rangers were playing and despite the fact that Potvin was long retired. They continue to do so to this day.

This notion of a Ranger jinx seeped down to the players, and Richter was concerned enough about it to approach Messier. "I was talking with him the other day about the problems we've had in the past," Richter said. "We always seem to do well during the season, then fall flat when the biggest moment comes during the playoffs. Two straight years we've done that. It seemed we were spent at the end. I told him that we seemed burned out. You know what he said? I think now I probably never should have asked the question. He said he doesn't believe in burnout. Of course."

And there would be no burnout this season. On March 22, Messier scored four times in a 6–3 win over New Jersey and cracked the 100-point barrier. On March 26, the Rangers clinched first place overall in the NHL, the first time they had done so since 1941–42.

But on April 1, the NHL Players' Association, newly empowered by the disclosure of player salaries and newly assertive under the leadership of Harvard-hockey-player-turned-lawyer Bob Goodenow, voted 560–4 in favor of a work stoppage over the long-expired collective bargaining agreement.

The players wanted free agency restrictions lifted, as well as a greater share of pension benefits and hockey card revenue, but they were at least as interested in signaling an end to the supine position they had taken in labor-management relations for so many years under the corrupt leadership of Alan Eagleson. "We have to make a stand," Messier said. "I don't think they're going to give us anything without taking us seriously. It seems it has to come down to the last minute to make them feel we're serious."

The players walked out, and the last few games of the regular season were postponed. Of course Ranger fans saw it as being all about their club. "This might be the best team I've seen," one longtime fan was quoted as saying. "But like everything with the Rangers, the strike was meant to be." The Ranger players were disappointed, too. They pooled money to rent their practice rink at Rye in suburban Westchester County and held informal skates to keep fit. Rick Carpiniello was there on the second day, when Messier's black stretch limo pulled up outside. Messier walked up to the rink-side boards, and when his teammates skated over and gathered round, he told them that by staying fit they were sending a message to the owners that they were less than serious about the strike, that they expected it to end shortly, and that their main intent was to be ready to play—all of which was what the owners wanted. This admonition was enough for them: they stopped skating and did not return for the duration of the strike. Within a couple of days, all the other teams that had been working out informally also stopped. Messier, whose father had been solidly behind the first hockey players' union when it was organized by his Portland Buckaroo teammates, was taking a hard-line, pro-union stance three decades later.

Negotiations stalled, and Messier took Graves, Richter, and rookie Doug Weight with him to Hilton Head for a few days of golf and inline skating. He returned to New York, where league president John Ziegler and the owners were still at loggerheads with Goodenow. The playoffs were supposed to begin on April 7, but that date came and went and still no settlement was at hand. Messier talked tough, at one point saying that he was considering becoming involved in a players' league that would be completely independent of the NHL. After all, said Messier, the players were the reason that people paid to watch hockey, so why shouldn't the players employ themselves? The suggestion angered Stanley Jaffe, the CEO of Paramount

Communications, which owned Madison Square Garden and had recently agreed to pay Messier at least $13 million over the next five years.

That ploy might have opened the door, however inadvertently, to a settlement. A few days later, Messier said that in the aftermath of his players' league statement, he spoke with Jaffe. "I explained to him that it was said more out of frustration," Messier said. The two spoke on three or four more occasions, part of a channel that opened between key players—such as Wayne Gretzky, Kevin Lowe, and Steve Yzerman—and the owners. "We just wanted to let them know we were serious about what we were doing," Messier said of the players' contact with the owners, "but we all wanted to do what was best for the game." That contact seemed to play a role in lessening tensions between the two sides; a tentative settlement was proposed on the eighth day of the work stoppage, Messier, Gretzky, and Yzerman addressed Goodenow, NHLPA President Bryan Trottier, and the player representatives via conference call and urged them to adopt the proposal, so that the regular season and playoffs would not be canceled, while the association continued to seek a permanent solution. "We wanted to know that if we had a long strike," Messier said, "we could look at ourselves and at each other over the summer and know that we had done everything possible to get a settlement."

The solution came in the form of a one-year agreement, approved by a vote of 409–61, that yielded modest gains for the players but essentially tabled most big issues until 1993. Nevertheless, the message had been sent: the players had struck on a leaguewide basis for the first time in NHL history. Messier had played a key role in making the strike vote stick among the players and showing a militant face to the public; then, he was central in reopening channels of communication to help facilitate a settlement and in persuading the players to accept a settlement.

The stoppage lasted ten days, and when the schedule resumed, the Rangers split their final two regular-season games, finishing at 50–25–5 for 105 points, seven better than anyone else. Ziegler presented Messier with the Presidents' Trophy, the first honor of its kind that the team had earned in half a century. Messier politely took it, then placed it aside. Only the Stanley Cup counted, and now the time had come to find out whether Messier's unspoken doubts about Neilson's coaching were justified.

The Rangers' first-round opponents were the New Jersey Devils, who were laying the foundations for the championship-caliber team they would become within a couple of years—and would still be a decade later. They finished only seven games over .500, but they had Scott Stevens, Ken Daneyko, Scott Niedermayer, and a rookie goalie named Martin Brodeur, all of whom would form the team's bedrock defense for years to come. They also had one of the best postseason irritants ever in Claude Lemieux, whose job it was to shadow Messier. Although Messier scored a pair of shorthanded goals in game two, he also took three penalties and finally broke his stick across Lemieux's in frustration in a 7–3 loss. The teams battled back and forth, the heavily favored Rangers bearing the yoke of perennial postseason disappointment as well as a surprisingly tough and up-and-coming Devils side. After the Devils won game six at the Meadowlands—amid the New Jersey fans' chants of "1940!"—a ten-minute-long all-hands brawl broke out, one that resulted in $25,000 in fines against each team. Laurie Boschman and Messier squared off during the donnybrook, prompting Domi to jump in in defense of his captain. Game seven was played at the Garden; it was only the fifth such encounter in Rangers history, and they had lost the previous four. Neilson was able to get the Messier–Amonte–Graves combination away from Lemieux, and the Rangers opened up, Messier contributing two goals and two assists in an 8–4 romp.

Pittsburgh came next, and now Messier was hurting. A muscle in his back was torn—injured, apparently, during the Devils series in a collision with Claude Lemieux. The club trainers wanted him to sit out two weeks to recover, but he wound up missing only two games. Game two, which the Rangers won without Messier, became famous for the slash on the hand Graves gave Mario Lemieux. The Penguins superstar crumpled to the ice, prompting the Garden fans to yell that he was faking an injury, but it was revealed after the game that his hand was broken. It had not been a deliberate attempt to injure, but rather a half-slash on the gloves that referees had been allowing for at least a decade (part of a general deterioration in the enforcement of rules that had been ongoing since the 1970s). Graves, though apologetic, was suspended.

The Rangers took a two-games-to-one lead, but Messier's misgivings about Neilson were surfacing. He seemed sullen whenever the coach addressed the team. He didn't like the way Neilson wanted the Rangers to lie in wait in the neutral zone for Lemieux, Jaromir Jagr, Ron Francis, and the rest of the offensively powerful Penguins; he wanted the team to go full-tilt, Oilers style, in every zone, with or without the puck. He didn't like the way Neilson was matching lines with the Penguins' coach—the master of the art, Scotty Bowman. Neilson often sent out a checking line against the Pens' big guns. Every shift for the checking line meant one less shift for Messier's line. Messier found fault with the dump-and-chase style Neilson called for; he thought the Rangers, armed with five forwards who had scored 30 or more goals during the regular season, were talented enough to carry the puck in. Nor did he care much for what he thought was an overemphasis on hitting, which he felt was wearing down the team; he felt that the mere act of hitting does nothing to win hockey games if other tactics aren't working.

In game four, the Pens were on the ropes, trailing by two goals, but a routine shot by Francis from the neutral zone beat Richter, and the tide turned. Messier himself would play the goat. While killing a penalty, he skated in front of his own net with the puck and gave it away to Francis, who scored again for the game-winner. The Pens went on to win the next two games, winning the series. Ranger fans seemed to expect the collapse; they pointed to the strike as a momentum-killer, as if theirs were the only team affected by the stoppage, and to the fluke goal allowed by Richter as yet another entry in a long litany of fatal gaffes.

"This team is going to win a Stanley Cup, no question about it," Messier said in the immediate aftermath of elimination. "It definitely has the desire, it definitely has the talent, and it definitely has the dedication. It's just a matter of when. I'm willing to shoulder the blame for the loss. Every time I lose I feel responsible. Sometimes to taste the sweetness of victory you have to taste the bitterness of defeat. I've tasted the bitterness before and bounced back. I think this team can do it, too." He also blamed the strike for the Rangers' defeat, saying the team never recovered the "tempo of play" it had maintained before the stoppage. But the one thing he did not say was what he believed most: that Neilson's tactics doomed the team to defeat. New York reporters noted that, while Messier had praised all the players and management of the Rangers, and even Pat Riley, the coach of New York Knicks basketball team, he had said nothing about Neilson. The blowup was coming.

The Penguins, led by league scoring champion Mario Lemieux, managed not to lose another game en route to winning their second Stanley Cup championship in a row. Yet when it came time to tally the ballots for the Hart Trophy, Lemieux wasn't even among the three finalists. Messier's resuscitation of the dormant Ranger franchise so impressed the members of the Professional Hockey Writers' Association that he won in a landslide, earning 67 of a possible 69 first-place votes. Leetch enjoyed a similar runaway victory in the Norris Trophy race.

Messier attended the 1992 NHL awards ceremonies in Toronto with his family, just as he had done two years earlier, when he won his first Hart Trophy. He told reporters that playing in a city the magnitude of New York had helped him "grow as a person." Onstage, he thanked his family, got a little *verklempt*, congratulated Lemieux and the Penguins, and paid tribute to his teammates. He said that "the goal is the Stanley Cup, and I want to tell the Ranger fans to be patient." All that, and he never once mentioned Neilson, who was in the audience as a finalist for the Jack Adams Award as coach of the year. Indeed, some wags quipped that Messier was disappointed that he—Messier—didn't win the Adams.

Neil Smith, who was also in the audience and who was loyal to Neilson, was angered by the snub. Later, in Hilton Head, Messier continued his deafening silence on the subject of his coach. "I haven't said anything one way or the other about Roger," he said. "When you don't win the Cup and you have as good a team as we do, everybody has to be evaluated. We have a young, talented, creative group of people. We have to evaluate everybody in the organization to make sure we have gotten the most out of them." Newspaper stories bore headlines about Messier's problems with Neilson—namely, what he saw as Neilson's passive tactics, and the coach's contention that the Rangers lost to the Penguins because they weren't sufficiently committed to defense. "When you've got a team that can skate like ours, you want to apply pressure all over the ice," Messier told *The New York Times*. "It wasn't our defensive problems. If we have the puck 75 percent of the time, we're going to win. Defense doesn't mean waiting for the other team to bring the puck up."

That August, Stan Fischler met Messier at an outdoor café near the player's apartment to interview him. At first, Messier told Fischler nothing remarkable. But, as Fischler later wrote, when the talk turned to Roger Neilson, Messier "almost furtively leaned over the table and whispered, 'Turn off the recorder.'" At that point, Messier went into a long explanation of, in Fischler's words, "why Neilson was unfit to be a Ranger coach."

Neil Smith spent much of the off-season trying to patch up the relationship between Neilson and Messier, but to no avail. Smith re-signed Neilson anyway, to a three-year deal worth about $1 million, though of course any coaching contract can be as ephemeral as gossamer. Meanwhile, the atmosphere around the Garden was changed by the rift between coach and captain. "I was hoping to have a great summer after the year we had," assistant coach Colin Campbell said in Frank Brown's book *Broadway Blues*. "But obviously, from the awards on, with Mess not acknowledging Roger, there seemed to be tension. And probably, other people focused on it more than Mess or Roger. They had their opinions, and they're very strongly opinionated people about their hockey thoughts. It seemed like when you were a kid; you're riding in the car and your parents had had a fight. There was that tension between them, and it made you feel uneasy. They wouldn't say anything, but you knew there was something wrong; you just wished they'd be back together again."

On the eve of training camp in Rye, Neilson and Messier finally met, and they emerged from the summit to tell the press that any misunderstandings were now resolved. Messier spoke of the "mutual respect" between him and Neilson, of how the "differences in philosophy" were "not a problem," and of how there could be no doubt that Neilson, as coach, had the final say. "I think we can work with each other and help each other out," Messier said. "I certainly respect my coach, as I've been taught my whole career, and I told Roger, 'I've come to play my butt off, as I did last year.' . . . The one thing that got lost over the summer was that I really enjoyed last year and I really enjoyed Roger. I never blamed any of the coaches for us losing last spring." For his part, Neilson said: "There is no issue. Things get blown up. All's well. He said there is no problem whatsoever."

The Rangers started the 1992–93 season by picking up 15 of a possible 20 points in their first 10 matches—but in many of those games they were outshot and needed to be rescued by their goalies, Richter and Vanbiesbrouck. Messier called a team meeting, and according to Leetch, he said, "We're 7–2–1, guys, but we've got to change some things. We've got to take pride in what we do." The discussion covered the poor team defense that was exposing the goalies to a nightly barrage of rubber. The next game was a 6–3 loss to Quebec in which Richter was bombarded with 43 shots. It got no better over the next several games, reaching a new low with a 5–1 loss at home to the nondescript Tampa Bay Lightning.

That night happened to coincide with the announcement of Neilson's contract extension—and, after the game, with a long address to the media in which Messier criticized the club, "right from the top of the organization to the bottom of the organization," for shuffling people in and out of the lineup and creating uncertainty among the players. He charged that the result was that "you don't have good feelings chemistry-wise, feelings-wise, in the dressing room." It was the first overtly negative public statement Messier had made since joining the Rangers, and although he said no one in particular was to blame, it was an unmistakable shot at Neilson—and even Smith. The truce that had held since training camp was over.

The Rangers continued to slump. Messier was playing poorly, bothered by the lingering effects of the muscle tear in his back that he had suffered in the Devils series the previous April. Adam Graves, protecting his hobbled hero, dropped the gloves with anyone who so much as glanced at Messier the wrong way. In mid-December, Messier was buoyed by the arrival of Kevin Lowe, one of the last remaining members of the Oilers' Stanley Cup core group, in a trade with Edmonton for the promising but ultimately undistinguished Roman Oksiuta and a draft choice. But a few days later, Leetch injured his shoulder trying uncharacteristically to cream Philippe Bozon along the boards in St. Louis, and the Rangers' tailspin continued. Messier kept giving quotes that questioned Neilson's approach. "To change the lineup for no rhyme or reason doesn't work for the competitiveness," he told Brown, who covered the Rangers for the New York *Daily News*. Neilson offered no rebuttal to Messier's criticism, except to say that he did not think he was making an undue number of lineup changes. In Washington on December 29, the Rangers tried to baby a one-goal lead in the third period and wound up getting outshot, 21–6. The Capitals tied the score late in the period and won in overtime. Messier went minus-2. On New Year's Eve in Buffalo, New York was blown out by the inconceivable score of 11–6, and Messier went minus-5.

That was the last straw for Neilson. To him, it seemed that a disgruntled Messier had simply quit playing. The team flew to Pittsburgh the next day, and there Neilson summoned three veterans into his office. "We called a meeting with Mike Gartner, Kevin Lowe, and Adam Graves," Neilson later said. "I told them, 'Mess just isn't leading us, and you guys are going to have to do that job. And once we get the team going, I think Mark's competitive spirit will bring him back to take charge again.'" It was incredibly bold of Neilson to ask Messier's teammates to replace a man who was regarded as the most respected leader in hockey. It was even more so to ask this of Graves, who clearly idolized Messier, and of Lowe, who had been with the club only three weeks and who was widely seen as the Boswell to Messier's Samuel Johnson. Even Gartner, an avid union man, had a long association with Messier dating back through the Canada Cups to the WHA days. "I knew about the meeting," Messier said a few days later. "Obviously, that was one of the problems Roger and I had. Our relationship deteriorated. Having a meeting like that behind my back didn't help. I'm captain of the team until someone takes it away from me."

The night of the meeting, the Rangers were again terrible in a 5–2 loss to the Penguins that included a Messier giveaway that resulted in a short-handed goal by Mario Lemieux. New York's record was 19–17–4 and fading fast. Neil Smith felt he had to act.

On the morning of January 4, Smith came to Rye and fired Neilson, whom he liked and respected, and who was twenty years his senior, and replaced him with Ron Smith, the coach of the Rangers' farm team in Birmingham, New York. "I was completely devastated, just devastatingly sad," Smith told Frank Brown about breaking the news to Neilson. "I could hardly pick my head up to tell him. I hated myself for it." Smith then went to talk to the players, and, he told Brown, "I said, 'Now you've made me go and do this. I want to be paid back.' I was really angry. 'Fuck' was probably used 30 times in a minute. I stared at all of them. A lot of them put their heads down." Smith's public statement contained an unmistakable warning to Messier. "The players know they're the next ones to go," he said. "That's the next step. To make the big trades. Their jobs are on the line now, not Ron's."

It had become a very public dispute, and now that it was over, both sides defended themselves in the newspapers. Neilson—who, it could be argued, had erred in not standing up to Messier and engaging him in a battle of wills—no longer needed to hold his tongue. "Last year," he said, "Mark came in and gave us all hope for a Stanley Cup. He was as good a leader as you can get on a hockey team. This year, he just didn't lead us. Last year, he was leading by example, calling regular meetings, picking guys up, noticing things. He was excellent. This year, those things just didn't seem to be getting done." Messier replied that he had no desire to coach the team, but that the Rangers had been "bullheaded" and had failed to "adapt," and were getting beaten as a result. Colin Campbell, the assistant coach who took Ron Smith's place in Binghamton, told the papers that it was a dispute that "to be blunt, Mess won."

Before the Rangers' first game under Ron Smith, the new coach called a private meeting with the team leaders: Gartner, Lowe, Graves, and—pointedly—Messier.

Mess had indeed won, but at what cost? Rick Carpiniello saw Messier away from reporters in the players' lounge after the first game under Ron Smith. "I don't feel so good right now," Messier said, his eyes downcast. "What the fuck was I supposed to do?"

Messier struggled through the rest of the season. At home against Ottawa in the first game after the firing, a 5–1 victory over the lowly Senators, Messier was killing a penalty when he ragged the puck in his own zone. During his protracted skate with the puck, the Garden fans started to boo him. A couple of days later, the Devils' defenseman Alexei Kasatonov saw reporters heading to the Rangers' room to interview the captain and quipped, "Who's the new coach? Messier?" Soon thereafter Messier sprained ligaments in his wrist against Detroit and had to miss six games.

In late January, Messier, now being called a "coach killer," sat down with *Newsday*'s Greg Logan and offered a defense of his actions in the Neilson affair. "I have to admit it's been tough," Messier said. "As right as I know I am, it's always tough. But as a leader of the team, it's so important to hide those feelings and seem unaffected by it. You're living a double life.

At home, you're climbing the walls, but when you come to the rink, you have to hold it together so people around you feel positive and secure that things are going the right way. I didn't try to purposely hurt anybody. The easy thing would have been to sit here and shut my mouth. But I've felt the responsibility has been on my shoulders to bring a Stanley Cup here. If we win, I'll get praise, and if I lose, I'll get criticism. If that's the way it is, I might as well do the things I feel are right, having been successful five times before."

Lowe spoke out in defense of his friend. "The part that needs clarification is it's not like he was coming into the dressing room and criticizing Roger," Lowe said. "This is one of the tougher challenges of his career." Tie Domi, who had been Messier's inseparable sidekick ("he was like a big brother to me") until he was traded just before the New Year's Day blowup, called the notion that Neilson was fired because of Messier "a crock of shit" and said that Neil Smith "should have put his foot down and said, 'Mark Messier didn't get Roger Neilson fired. I fired him. It's my job.'" Most Rangers who were not such strong Messier loyalists simply voiced regret that things had deteriorated so badly between two respected and strong-willed men that one of them, Neilson, had to go.

The Rangers returned to Edmonton late in February. Messier set up the only goal of the game. But ten seconds from the end, Oilers defenseman Igor Kravchuk threw an open-ice body check that Messier never saw. The ribs on his right side tore painfully away from the cartilage. Now both his ribs and his back were damaged. By March, he would have to take a regular regimen of painkillers and anti-inflammatory drugs under the supervision of the training staff. On March 5, Penguins defenseman Ulf Samuelsson—whom NHLers would later vote the dirtiest player in the league in a *Sports Illustrated* poll—ran Messier into the boards of Madison Square Garden, and like a wounded beast Messier responded by dropping Samuelsson with either a punch or a butt end, depending on which account you accept. Either way, Samuelsson lost three teeth, and a stick fight between the two very nearly ensued. Both players were given short suspensions.

Things got even worse in the early-morning hours of March 20, 1993, after an encouraging 8–1 victory at home over San Jose. Leetch, back in the lineup for five games after recovering from his shoulder injury, reportedly stepped out of a cab near his apartment on West End Avenue, stumbled on a ridge of snow, and hurt his ankle. He showed up for practice the next day, but his ankle was so swollen that he was taken for X-rays, which revealed that it was broken. He was through for the season. New Yorkers started calling the city's all-sports radio station to say they'd seen Leetch on the fateful night, out with Messier at a bar. Some said it was a place called Avalon, others said it was the Tavern. Some claimed the two of them had been play-fighting when Leetch got hurt, while others testified that Leetch was being chased down some stairs and tripped. Leetch acknowledged that he'd been out for a couple of beers with Messier and Amonte, but said that there had been no horseplay, that he had not been drunk, and he had simply turned his ankle awkwardly when he got out of the cab.

For all Leetch's protestations, the story took on the irrefutable air of urban legend for Ranger fans, who believed the episode was yet another in a long line of disasters for their jinxed club. Later, Messier would be asked to name his greatest regret of the year. He paused for a moment, then dead-panned, "Probably beating the shit out of Brian and breaking his ankle."

The season deteriorated inexorably, and the Rangers plummeted in the standings. Messier played his 1000th regular-season game, but there was no ceremony to mark the occasion; he didn't want one. In the last game of the season, a 2–0 loss to Washington, the Garden fans summoned up decades of bile and frustration and expressed it with their characteristic sarcasm, chanting "Same old shit," and mockingly, "1940," as if they were rooting against the Rangers. They booed Messier continually. The team that had finished first overall with a 50–25–5 record in 1991–92 wound up last in the Patrick Division with a 34–39–11 mark—and out of the playoffs altogether. In 75 games Messier, the previous year's Hart Trophy winner, topped the Rangers with a respectable 25 goals and 66 assists for 91 points, but he didn't even come close to cracking the NHL's top 25 scorers. His minus-6 rating was one of the worst plus/minus numbers on the team. On clear-out day in Rye, Messier stood by his locker and said, "Right now, I don't feel like ever playing another game in my entire life. My mind's about ready to explode." He talked about how the past season, of all the years he had played to date, had been "the least amount of fun ever."

"I don't want to end my career in New York on this note," he said. "It's easy to be a great team guy, a great leader, and a great player when you're 50–25–5. This is the other side of the coin. So what do you do next, when you are under a little adversity? Do you fold your tent and say, 'I want to leave?' Or stick to your guns, fight back, and try to make it better? That's what I intend to do."

Messier was justifying what he had done to Neilson, both to the press and to himself, one more time, and then he looked ahead to the Rangers team in 1993–94.

"It may sound crazy," he said, "but I don't think there's a lot wrong."

THE MESSIAH

There was little chance that Ron Smith, who had been hired with the title of interim coach, would be retained for the 1993–94 season. He had come up through the coaching ranks with Roger Neilson and shared the latter's belief in a conservative approach to the game. The feeling within the Garden front office was that it was time to bring in a different kind of coach altogether. That coach turned out to be Mike Keenan, who had been behind the opposite bench when the Oilers beat the Flyers in seven games in the 1987 final and the Blackhawks in six in the '90 semifinals and who, as coach of Team Canada in the '87 and '91 Canada Cup tournaments, had been so impressed by Messier's leadership. He had seen Messier from every angle, and there was nothing about him he didn't like.

Keenan was a martinet whose incessant mind games had yielded remarkable results in the first couple of years of each of his tenures at Philadelphia and Chicago—two Presidents' Trophies and two trips to the Cup finals—but ultimately alienated vast swaths of those teams' dressing rooms. With his RAF mustache, slicked-back hair, and black, beady-eyed glare that suggested imminent volcanic irrationality, Keenan ruled by challenge, insult, and mockery, but many players regarded him as a sort of drill sergeant who weeded out those unwilling to pay the high price for victory, pushed those who remained to new extremes of endurance, and gave the team a real chance at victory, which would be worth all the physical and spiritual pain needed to attain it. As Blackhawks defenseman Doug Wilson described life under Keenan, "No team won so often and had less fun doing it."

Tactically, Keenan wasn't markedly different from Neilson, who was actually ahead of his time in his advocacy of the neutral-zone trap and of a defense-first philosophy. Like Neilson, Keenan's favored strategy on the attack was to dump and chase, followed by endless mucking about in the corners and cycling the puck along the endboards. These were to become the unimaginative staples of North American offense that would eventually allow Europe to eclipse Canada and the United States on the world hockey scene. These methods had worked for Keenan at the Canada Cup, in part because he could also call upon the unearthly talents of Gretzky and Lemieux to transcend the Canadian style and score goals, beautiful goals, that papered over the style's shortcomings. In the second half of the 1990s, the tactics of Neilson and Keenan would quickly proliferate and predominate: goal scoring would plummet, and deeply mediocre teams such as the Florida Panthers and Washington Capitals would reach the Stanley Cup finals by playing a kind of anti-hockey that strove for a 1–0 result.

But really, for Keenan, commitment, will, sacrifice, toughness, leadership, and other impalpable qualities were what he prized, far more than Xs and Os. His ideal player was Messier: someone who had all the intangibles, yet was good enough on the ice to create speedy attacks that complemented the grinding trench warfare in which the other forwards would engage.

Thus Messier arrived at the season that would crown his career, the perfect juncture in history where the offensive philosophy of the Oilers of the '80s coexisted in harmony with the defense that would dominate the later '90s. The sport would change after the 1993–94 season, in ways that Messier would no longer be able to master. But in the season about to take place, on the ice, on the bench, and behind the scenes, he would draw on every attribute he could summon to realize the dream of bringing the Stanley Cup to the Rangers.

Neil Smith hired Keenan on April 17, 1993, the last day of the disastrous '92–93 season when, with Ron Smith behind the bench, Messier and the Rangers were jeered relentlessly by the Garden crowd. In making the hire, Smith understood that Keenan would scorch the earth and upset everyone at one point or another, but for the moment Keenan was given carte blanche to implement whatever tactics he deemed necessary, and Smith vowed to make any personnel moves Keenan wanted. Smith knew Keenan and Messier were mutual admirers from their Canada Cup experiences, and he knew that Keenan's stubbornness would be a match for Messier's should the two square off over any issue. As Smith succinctly put it a few months later, "The team needed a coach who would come in and kick its butt."

Messier decided to intensify his own level of commitment. He knew Keenan would be testing everyone's fitness from day one of training camp, so he installed a gym at his house in Hilton Head. "I decided to follow the team's regimen," he told *Sports Illustrated*, with "about twenty machines, some Cybex, some other stuff." Messier arrived at camp in even better shape than usual, and with a shaved head that gave his skull the taut, hard look of a bullet.

Early in Keenan's tenure, he borrowed an old trick from Glen Sather's bag and had an inspirational video prepared. Scenes from various ticker-tape parades up lower Broadway were edited together—celebrations held for the Yankees and Mets after World Series wins, as well as those staged for astronauts and various other heroes. He hired a team psychologist, Dr. Cal Botterill, who had worked with him at his previous stops in the NHL. At Rye, Keenan placed motivational signs above the urinals that read, "Attitude—a little thing that goes a long way." He also terrorized the staff with his mercurial mood swings, irrational and trivial demands, and raging tantrums, all of which he justified as ways to keep everyone around him on their toes. He told Smith that the team was too weak to contend for the Cup and listed the players he thought had to be replaced. It was going to be a wild ride, but Mark Messier was definitely on board.

The Rangers opened their exhibition season overseas, in London, where they won a two-game "tournament" at the Wembley Empire Pool. But after a loss later in the preseason, Keenan publicly blamed Smith for the Rangers' supposed softness. He insulted his players in front of the others. To Leetch, he screamed, "You're no fucking Chelios!", referring to the rugged Norris Trophy winner he'd coached in Chicago. To the three Russian Rangers, he yelled, "That's why we always wanted to play you guys in the Canada Cup!" He told reporters that one of them, the gifted blueline prospect Sergei Zubov, was the team's "least fit athlete." He yelled at practically every player, though not at Messier.

Meanwhile, he laid down a rugged regimen: practices were run full tilt, at game speed, and focused solely on the fundamentals—skating, stickhandling, passing, and shooting. Weight training was a constant; players rode stationary bikes immediately after every game to cut down on the buildup of lactic acid in their legs; and they were expected to exceed certain fitness thresholds or else face Keenan's wrath. If a practice didn't go the way the coach thought it should, he made everyone skate until they were sick to their stomachs. All of this was meant to build the players' strength and stamina for the long fight for the Cup. It was the same level of physical dedication and willpower to which Messier had been pushing himself since his later years in Edmonton, and he thrived under Keenan's regimen.

The Rangers stumbled to a 4–5–0 start, and Keenan raged. He benched regulars James Patrick and Tony Amonte, belittled them in public statements and in private meetings, and marked them for trade. There immediately followed a fourteen-game unbeaten streak that made it clear the team was a contender again. During the streak, Smith went along with Keenan's demands to get rid of players he didn't like in exchange for those he did. Patrick and the young forward Darren Turcotte were dealt away, while the Rangers picked up tough-guy fourth-liner Nick Kypreos, signed holdout defenseman Jeff Beukeboom, and acquired Chicago and Team Canada mainstay Steve Larmer.

Messier was having an eventful early season. He became an honorary vice president of the Tomorrow's Children Fund, a charitable organization for children with cancer and serious blood disorders. He would give generously of his time and money to help and comfort sick kids over the coming years.

On the ice, he had a run-in in October with Canadiens defenseman Kevin Haller, which would mark the start of a long run of antagonism between the two. With Messier and Graves breaking up the ice on a two-on-one, Haller wound up with a two-handed chop and slashed Messier's glove. As soon as the play was over, both Rangers went after Haller, though no actual punches were landed. Messier had to leave the game for a while with a badly bruised thumb. Haller eventually got a four-game suspension for the slash. On November 16, the Rangers were in Miami to play the Florida Panthers, coached by Roger Neilson. For whatever reason—most likely Keenan's penchant for humiliation as object lesson—Messier was benched for a long stretch during the game, which New York won, 4–2. Messier laughed about it afterward, noting, "There's more than one way to skin a cat." On the way out of the rink, the Ranger players stopped to chat and shake hands with Neilson. But as Rick Carpiniello noted, Messier did not; he walked past without acknowledging his former coach's presence.

In December, Messier was hurting from a series of nagging injuries to his right wrist and sat out five games; in his stead Graves wore the captain's C. On January 3, 1994, prior to a home game against Florida, Smith again displayed his talent for staging ceremonies, setting up a surprise presentation for Messier in honor of his 800th assist, recently scored, and 1,000th game, played during the horrible previous season. Mary Jean and Alice Dea were on hand for the festivities, which moved Messier to tears. As if inspired, Messier returned on January 8 and notched 10 goals and 11 assists over the next 12 games.

The NHL All-Star Game was held at Madison Square Garden later in January, and all four Rangers in the lineup—Messier, Graves (on a torrid pace as Messier's wing), Leetch, and Richter—starred. Messier had a goal and two assists, but Richter was voted the game's MVP. A decade later, fans at the Garden still would wear the Eastern Conference sweaters of the four Rangers who played in that game.

On January 31, the Rangers got their first hat trick of the season, from Mike Gartner, in a 5–3 victory at home against Pittsburgh. All three goals came on the power play, and for the last one, Messier passed up a chance to fire at an empty net, slipping the puck to Gartner instead. That assist moved Messier past Alex Delvecchio into tenth place among the NHL's all-time scorers.

Gartner stood fourth on the all-time goal-scorers list, with 607 tallies, but as early as training camp, Keenan had wished him gone. The Rangers had already retooled: former Oiler Esa Tikkanen had been added to the lineup late in the previous season, and Darren Langdon, a Newfoundlander who got into a lot of fights—and lost most of them—had been added since New Year's Day. But the lineup was overhauled enough to suit Keenan. He subscribed to the unfair yet widely accepted opinion that Gartner was great in the regular season but wasn't tough enough for the playoffs, when his goalscoring totals dropped off and his teams—both the Washington Capitals of the first half of his career and the Rangers of recent vintage—went nowhere. Keenan relegated Gartner to the third line, yet still Gartner continued to rack up the goals. To his discredit, Keenan went so far as to humiliate Gartner in front of his teammates. One night in Montreal, as Barry Meisel wrote in his book *Losing the Edge*, Keenan shouted at Gartner in the dressing room, asking if he'd ever "gotten the shit kicked out of him by the Montreal Canadiens, and if so, is that why you're playing so scared?" Later, in Dallas, he yelled, "Mike Gartner, what have you done in your life?" and told him he'd "embarrassed" himself. Gartner faced the torrent of abuse and maintained his calm and dignity, but it was clear he was going to be gotten rid of.

The Rangers were first overall in the NHL standings, yet that meant nothing to Keenan; they had finished first a couple of seasons earlier, he said, and what good had that done in the playoffs? He continued to throw purposeful tantrums, once forcing the talented but absentminded Alexei Kovalev, who regularly overstayed his shifts, to take several consecutive shifts without coming off the ice; another time he stood behind the bench and stopped coaching altogether, making the players call their own line changes. Smith and Keenan were by now completely at loggerheads, and their communications with each other had to be passed through third parties. Nevertheless, at the March 21 trade deadline, Smith again acceded to Keenan's demands, and in the interest of winning the Stanley Cup, dealt Gartner away to Toronto. In return, he got Glenn Anderson, the man with whom Messier had combined for more goals than any other. Anderson joined the Rangers' first line alongside Messier and Graves. For Amonte, Smith acquired two earnestly plodding Keenan footsoldiers from the

Blackhawks, Brian Noonan and Stéphane Matteau. He also picked up Craig MacTavish, the last helmetless player in hockey, from Edmonton in exchange for prospect Todd Marchant.

There were now seven ex-Oilers in the Rangers lineup: Messier, Graves, Beukeboom, Lowe, Tikkanen, Anderson, and MacTavish; this truly was the kind of team Messier liked. He now had his lieutenants with him, as he had in Edmonton, and they shared the load of leading the team. As Cal Botterill told Jeff Gordon in Gordon's biography, *Keenan*, "on a day-to-day basis, Kevin [Lowe] was probably more active in a leadership role" than Messier was. But Messier was the captain, and in that capacity he held constant private meetings with Keenan to discuss the state of the team. Despite Keenan's volatility, Messier never criticized or opposed him, even if Messier would sometimes obliquely acknowledge that Keenan could be a problematic man to work under. "Mike's reputation as a power-hungry dictator is well known," he said at one point during the season, "but most of all, he's a great coach." On another occasion, he said: "A coach needs to have a dark side to get results. But if that's the only side you show your players, it gets old pretty quickly. Mike has learned a lot from his past experiences. He's been fantastic." Larmer observed the symbiosis between Messier and Keenan. "In a strange way, they almost think alike," he told Gordon. "They're both highly motivated, almost win-at-any-price guys. I think Mark had a calming effect on Mike and Mike had a lot of respect for Mark. Mike learned a lot from Mark, and vice versa."

From the trade deadline until the end of the season, the Rangers went 8–2–2. Their first game after the deadline took place in Edmonton, and it was fitting that Messier, who had sat out the previous two matches with a bruised thigh, found himself in the middle of two important moments. The first came early in the game, as he prepared to take a faceoff. The Northlands scoreboard flashed the news that in Los Angeles, Wayne Gretzky had just scored his 802nd NHL goal to break Gordie Howe's career record. The crowd started to applaud, and Messier stepped back from the face-off dot to allow a long, full ovation in honor of his friend and Edmonton's eternal hero. The second moment came in the game's fifteenth minute, after an Anderson pass sent Messier and Graves off on a two-on-one break. Before the contest, Messier had promised Graves, who was seeking his 50th goal of the season, that it would be scored that night. Now they were barging in on the Oilers net, Messier with the puck. He held it, held it, held it till the last possible moment, drawing the Edmonton defenseman to him, then laid a perfect saucer pass right on Graves' stick. Graves one-timed a shot past the by-now overcommitted Bill Ranford, and he had his 50th, just as Messier had promised. The Northlands crowd gave the winger a gracious ovation of his own, and he followed with another goal—a team-record 51st that brought all his teammates off the bench to congratulate him—as the Rangers rolled on to a 5–2 victory.

After the game, Graves said of Messier's role in his 50th, "It couldn't have come any other way; he has been such a big influence on my career," and Lowe spoke for the seven ex-Oilers about returning to Edmonton. "It's exciting, but there's no time to get nostalgic out there," he said. "We try to downplay that, trying to rekindle the '80s. We don't look at it that way. We've got a good team we believe in. This is the New York Rangers of 1994."

In Vancouver, the Rangers were winning 5–2 when the Canucks got a power play in the final minute. Canucks coach Pat Quinn put hulking tough guys Tim Hunter, Shaun Antoski, and Gino Odjick on the ice, and predictably, mayhem ensued. As the players wrestled near the benches, Messier yelled at Quinn, "Why the fuck did you have those fuckin' guys on the power play?" As teammates in future seasons, Odjick and Messier would have further, more serious run-ins.

The Rangers were on their way to a second Presidents' Trophy in three years, managing to just pip the Devils for the honor. Compared with the embarrassment and discord of '92–93, the worst season of Messier's career, the good feeling of '93–94, when the Rangers finished first overall with a record of 52–24–8 for 112 points (the team's best mark ever), was all the better. "I can't remember having a season as enjoyable as the one I've had this year," Messier said. His scoring stats—26–58–84 in 76 games—were second best on the team behind the underrated defenseman Sergei Zubov. His plus-minus figure, plus-25, was unusually good for Messier and third best on the roster. And his 76 penalty minutes reflected the fact that at thirty-three, he still played tough but let the others police the ice. As the stats show, Messier was certainly the leader of the club, but he was no longer its best player—he was merely *one of* its best.

The Rangers' first playoff foes were the Islanders, and the matchup figured to be as hate-filled as any past confrontation between the Manhattan and Long Island teams. The "Potvin sucks" chants came loud and long in the first two games, and the Garden crowd also reserved a special serving of bile for stick-swinging goaler Ron Hextall, chanting "Swiss cheese" as he allowed goal after goal. Both games ended 6–0 in favor of the Rangers. The scene shifted to the Nassau Coliseum, where the level of hatred for the Rangers was intense enough that in 1992, a game summary in Long Island *Newsday* for a Rangers game contained the message "Messier sucks" in agate type. Despite the change of venue, the results were no different: the Rangers won 5–1 and 5–2, completing a four-game sweep unprecedented in its one-sidedness—22 goals for New York, 3 for the Isles. Next up was Washington, and it was almost as easy. The Rangers jumped to a three-games-to-none lead before suffering their first postseason loss, then won game five. Messier had six goals in nine games.

The Rangers' opponents in the semifinal were the tough New Jersey Devils. Both teams were better than they had been two years earlier, when New York won in seven games, and this year they had finished 1–2 in the regular season. New Jersey won the first game in two overtime periods, but the Rangers bounced back in game two, as Messier started the game with an unbelievable sequence. Off the opening draw, the puck was dumped into the Jersey end. Devils defenseman and captain Scott Stevens went behind the net to retrieve it, and looked up to find Messier bearing down on him like a runaway train. Stevens, big, strong, and fearless, went flying like a rag doll, his stick cartwheeling through the air. The puck went into the corner, where another big bruiser, Ken Daneyko, took possession, only to be stapled to the boards by Messier. The puck went back behind the net, and Messier got to it ahead of Daneyko, whirled to the front of the net and stuffed it between Martin Brodeur's skates for the goal. Later, Messier stayed on the ice to kill an entire two-man disadvantage, then went out on the next shift for a power play. The Rangers won, 4–0. "You're a little like a fan watching a player like that take over a game," Brian Leetch said.

Game three, played just across the Hudson at the Meadowlands, distilled the essential character of the two teams. The Rangers attacked, the Devils lay in wait to counterattack, and the shot count wound up 50–31 for

New York. The game lasted into a second overtime period, when Matteau scored on a backhander to give the Rangers a two-games-to-one lead. The Devils bounced back to win game four, 3–1, but it was Keenan's irrationality behind the bench that dominated postgame discussion. He sat Leetch after the blueliner took a penalty that led to the first goal. He sat several other players as well, including Messier for a couple of shifts. Always a poor manager of goaltenders—he tended to yank them out of games and put them back in at a moment's whim—Keenan pulled Richter after the Devils made it 2–0. With the Rangers back to within 2–1 over the final 25 minutes of the game, Keenan still refused to put Leetch on the first power-play unit, and in the final minute he didn't call goalie Glenn Healy off the ice for an extra attacker until time had almost expired.

In the dressing room afterward, according to Barry Meisel's account, Keenan yelled at his players, "What the fuck are we doing? Do we want to win? Do you care? Does anybody have anything to say?" When Ed Olczyk, a healthy scratch from the lineup, said it was okay, that the series was even and the next game was to be played in New York, Keenan blew up. "Are you saying I'm not loyal?" he hollered.

Richter and Leetch drove up to Rye with Messier the next day and relayed to him their concerns, as well as those of the other players. Keenan's behavior during the game, if it was just another strategic tantrum, was completely inappropriate and counterproductive at this point in the playoffs, with the whole season on the line; if it was sincere, then his petulance and anger had to be brought under control. As Meisel reported, that same day at practice, Messier, clad only in his underwear, went into Keenan's office and shut the door for what turned out to be a highly emotional forty-five-minute meeting.

Messier told Keenan that the players did not need object lessons at this point; they needed to feel that their coach supported them, was loyal to them, and would always give them their best chance to win. Keenan explained why he had benched Leetch (he thought Leetch's injured shoulder rendered him ineffective, something he neglected to tell Leetch) and pulled Richter (he thought a goalie change would wake the team up). He said the Rangers were Messier's team, not his. Messier explained how mentally and physically exhausting the postseason could be for the players.

Eventually the dialogue turned the corner, and both Keenan and Messier became more optimistic.

Finally, Messier, emotionally exhausted, began to cry. He fell into the arms of Keenan, who embraced him until Messier stopped weeping. Then Messier emerged from the meeting and dressed for practice. His teammates sensed that the situation had been taken care of. The next night, before game five, Keenan apologized to the players. But it didn't help; the Devils dominated and won, 4–1, as Messier's thirteen-game playoff point-scoring streak came to an end. The Rangers were one game from elimination.

The next two days would prove to be the most legendary of Messier's legendary career. At the morning practice in Rye following the game five loss, Messier sensed his teammates' wavering confidence. Afterward, the huge gaggle of reporters following the series gathered around Messier and lobbed him the usual question about his feelings on the upcoming game, expecting the usual vanilla answer about taking it all one game at a time, one shift at a time. Instead, he answered that the Rangers were going to win, period. He did not stick his jaw out and proclaim it; rather, he stated it simply. Still, he repeated it again and again to whomever asked. To Carpiniello of the Gannett Westchester papers, he said, "We're going to go in there and win game six. We've responded all year. We've won games we've had to win. We know we're going to go in there to win game six and bring it back for game seven. We feel we can win it, and we feel we are going to win it." To Frank Brown of the *Daily News* he said: "We're going to go in and win game six. That was the focus this morning, and it's the way we feel right now. . . . We have enough talent and experience to turn the tide. That's exactly what we're going to do in game six." To Laura Price of *Newsday* he said, "We know we have to win, and we feel we will win." To Frank Orr of *The Toronto Star*, he said, "All season, when we've really been tested, we've responded with a big performance. We're certain that will happen again." To Joe Lapointe of *The New York Times*, he said, "We know we have to win it. We can win it. And we are going to win it."

Elsewhere in the Rye dressing room, the mood was subdued, even downcast. Kevin Lowe was about as optimistic as any other player would dare get. Asked how the Rangers were approaching game six, he said they were going to be like ducks: "Cool and calm above water, and paddling like hell below."

When the papers came out the morning of game six, they were full of what they called Messier's "guarantee." "Mark Isn't Worried; Messier Vows Rangers Will Take It to a Seventh Game" was *Newsday*'s headline. "Messier Guarantees a Win; Rangers Confident Facing Game of Their Lives" was that of *The Record* of Bergen County, New Jersey. "Rangers' Messier: We'll Win Game 6" was *USA Today*'s. "Captain Courageous' Bold Prediction: We'll Win Tonight" was splashed across the back page of *The New York Post*.

All the stories contrasted Messier's bold prediction of victory with the expectation of defeat that most observers shared. In his *Times* column, George Vecsey wrote, "The Rangers are quite likely to be blown away by the surging New Jersey Devils tonight, and poor Messier looks 62 years old. Older teams break down in the long march to the Stanley Cup. Is this fair?" That would have been the tenor of all the coverage had Messier not said what he said; seen in this light, his decision to project such an air of confidence in his teammates makes a lot of sense. But Messier's pledge certainly surprised a lot of people—including Gretzky, who found it strange coming from his old teammate, who had always been mindful about not saying anything an opponent could pin up on a bulletin board. "He was a really big believer in that," Gretzky later told Meisel. "I guess he just felt he needed to do something to rally his own teammates, and he didn't care about the opposition or what it would do to them because he needed to rally his own guys." Messier himself was a little surprised at the reaction, recalling later that in making the guarantee to "jump-start" his teammates and "do something to instill our old confidence," he "forgot that every New Yorker, plus every Devil, would be reading that story." As he put it, "When I saw the headline with 'I'm going to guarantee a win,' I wanted to roll back under the covers and call it a day."

That night, the Rangers came out for the big match and played conservatively. Lowe had noted earlier that New York would have to be more like the Devils and take the emphasis off offense and put it on defense—an irony that without a doubt, Neilson would have savored. Still, the Devils jumped to a 1–0 lead in the first period, and early in the second Keenan called a timeout, during which Messier did all the talking. But things got worse. New Jersey scored again, and during a post-whistle scrum behind the net, Daneyko thought he saw resignation on Messier's face. "He thought it was over," he told Carpiniello. "You could see he was frustrated. I saw it in his face."

But Keenan made a strategic move that saved the Rangers' bacon. He pulled the slumping Glenn Anderson off Messier's right wing and replaced him with Alexei Kovalev. The combination clicked. With just under two minutes left in the second period, Messier brought the puck over the blue line, drawing the two defensemen to him, then dropped it to Kovalev, who was standing stationary inside the blue line. Kovalev waited while Messier clogged up the front of the net, and, still wide open, shot. Brodeur never saw it. Now it was 2–1. Soon thereafter, the Rangers went a man down, but Messier and Graves killed off the portion of the penalty that took the game to the second intermission. They killed off the rest of it at the start of the third, a stint that included a patented Messier–Graves two-on-one break that almost worked. In the third minute of the third period, Kovalev repaid his debt to Messier, finding him open with a pass. The centerman's innocent backhander squeezed between Brodeur's leg pad and the post, tying the score at 2–2.

In the thirteenth minute of the third, the teams were at four skaters a side, and New York's quartet was Messier, Kovalev, Leetch, and Zubov. They moved up ice in a beautiful weaving pattern, Kovalev and Leetch dropping it to each other as they crisscrossed, then Kovalev shot from the left wing. Brodeur gave up a rebound, and in one motion Messier beat Bernie Nicholls to the puck and swept it into the net. The Rangers were ahead, 3–2. In the final two minutes, they were killing a penalty against six Devils skaters desperate to draw even. But the puck came to Messier in the high slot in front of Richter. He whirled around and put it on his forehand and, without looking as he moved into the circle, fired it into the air. It came down beyond the Devils blue line and slid, straight and true, into the net 140 feet away. Messier glided over to the bench, where all his teammates stood howling, opened his arms wide, and fell into their embrace. A pure hat trick, all in the third period, for Messier, resulting in a 4–2 win and renewed life for the Rangers.

It was an unbelievable performance, which afterward had Keenan comparing Messier to Howe, Gretzky, and Orr, then correcting himself and calling it "the most impressive performance by any hockey player in the history of this league." His teammates exclaimed in awe; Richter called the performance "one for the ages." Even Messier's foes threw superlatives at the problem of expressing what he had just done: Nicholls called him "the greatest clutch player in the game" and said, "when the chips are down, I want Messier."

The next day's papers were ecstatic in their appreciation for Messier's performance. They added it to the sacred canon of immortal New York sports moments, alongside Babe Ruth's called shot against the Chicago Cubs in the 1932 World Series, Joe Namath's guarantee of a Jets victory over the Baltimore Colts in Super Bowl III, and Willis Reed's surprise appearance and one-legged performance for the Knicks against the Los Angeles Lakers in game seven of the 1970 NBA finals. The sad, strange truth was that almost no one in New York actually saw Messier's heroics; the game was carried only on the SportsChannel cable system, which few in the city had access to. As few as 20,000 New Yorkers watched the game on television.

As great as game six had been, the deciding match would turn out to be, simply, one of the greatest ever played. It was tight-checking and drenched in anxiety, and the jam-packed Garden yelled and gasped and rocked at every moment. Leetch put New York ahead midway through regulation time with an impossible 360-degree twirl in front of Brodeur, followed by a short shot that trickled through Brodeur's pads. The Devils pressed relentlessly over the next thirty minutes, their attacks becoming more desperate as time grew short. In the final minutes, the Rangers iced and smothered the puck repeatedly to try to kill the clock. With eighteen seconds left, they could not clear a face-off from their end. Claude Lemieux passed in front to Valeri Zelepukin, who scored with only seven seconds to go. The Garden crowd suddenly switched off, dead silent. The only sounds, of joyful whoops, came from the Devils players and staff. But the Rangers did not grow despondent. In the dressing room before the first overtime session, Messier added to the general hopeful chatter. "We'll win this game," he said.

The teams played through one overtime and into an excruciating second, the crowd becoming ever more expectant as the agonizing suspense continued. Four minutes in, there was a scramble behind the Devils' net. Stéphane Matteau and Scott Niedermayer struggled for the puck. Matteau emerged with it, straddling the goal line to the left of Brodeur. Slava Fetisov slid to the front of the net to block Matteau, and Brodeur sidled his pad against the post and bent to lay the paddle of his stick along the ice. Matteau shot at Brodeur's pads, and the puck trickled through.

The Garden exploded as it had never exploded before. The radio announcer, Howie Rose, screamed into the microphone, "*Matteau! Matteau! Matteau! Matteau!*" over and over. The Rangers mobbed one another, then shook hands with the downcast Devils, who filed this mandatory suffering away for later use. The Prince of Wales Trophy was brought out for Messier—who had scored eleven points in the series, five more than anyone else on either team—to dutifully pose alongside, but of course the Stanley Cup was the prize on everyone's mind. The crowd began an incessant chant of "We want the Cup," which quickly, even frighteningly, elided into a primal "*We want Cup! We want Cup!*"

The Rangers' run was reaching critical mass, but as June approached it was only one of several stories converging in the most incredible month of sports that New York, or any North American city, has ever experienced. Besides the Rangers' quest to shake their fifty-four-year curse, by the middle of the month their co-tenants, the Knicks, would be in the NBA finals seeking their first title in 24 years and creating a frenzy of their own. Day after day, the teams alternated in dominating the back pages of the tabloids. On top of that, the U.S. was about to host the world's biggest sporting event, soccer's World Cup, with the apocalyptic Ireland–Italy match at Giants Stadium in New Jersey's Meadowlands complex. Off the mainstream sports map, New York also hosted the quadrennial Gay Games, which turned out to be the largest participatory sports event ever held. Thousands of athletes at every level, from beginner to elite, converged on the city. In the middle of all this, the former football star O.J. Simpson fled from the Los Angeles police in the infamous low-speed car chase that the entire country followed live on television. Against this backdrop, the fact that the Yankees were in first place and running away from the pack, which normally would have been *the* sports story, was completely lost. That magic spring, the entire city was swept up in Blueshirt mania, in ways and in places it never had before. At Yankee Stadium, a spontaneous "Let's Go, Rangers" chant was singsonged by more than 40,000. It happened at a Knicks playoff game, too.

Uptown in Washington Heights, Dominican kids who had never expended a moment's thought on hockey walked the steaming late-spring streets in heavy white Rangers jerseys.

Hysteria gripped Vancouver, too. The Canucks, a middling team during the regular season, were headed for the Cup final too, having surged through three playoff rounds, starting with a rebound from a three-games-to-one deficit against Calgary in which all three of Vancouver's comeback wins came in overtime. The Canucks had never won the Cup in their 24 years of existence, nor had any British Columbia team since the Victoria Cougars of 1925 and the Vancouver Millionaires of 1915.

Now the Canucks were facing the Rangers in the opener of the finals. Displaying the brinkmanship they had shown throughout the postseason, they tied the game on Martin Gelinas's tip-in with a minute left, then won in the twentieth minute of overtime, starting a rush after Leetch hit the Vancouver crossbar, and scoring on Greg Adams' shot. Messier closed the door to the dressing room afterward and is reported to have said, "I am 100 percent sure we will beat this team over a seven-game series." He then reeled off tactical points like the need to forecheck and apply pressure to Canucks goalie Kirk McLean. In game two, Richter turned aside a Vancouver flurry at his goalmouth in the dying seconds, allowing the Rangers to tie the series with a 3–1 win. Messier set up the game-winner.

In Vancouver, the Rangers took game three easily, 5–1, prompting Canucks coach Pat Quinn to say, "We're out to hit Mark Messier, and to hit him often," even if it took "25 guys hitting him." In game four, the Rangers fell behind 2–0, with Messier taking a major penalty for boarding Sergio Momesso. According to Meisel, Keenan browbeat the players during the first intermission, accusing them of not caring. Then, as he sometimes did in dressing-room lectures during the regular season, he turned to Messier for confirmation. "Is that not correct, Mark?" he asked rhetorically. This time, though, Messier stared angrily back at Keenan, which brought the coach back to earth instantly. "Oh," Keenan said, "I didn't mean you're not trying." The Rangers rallied for a 4–2 win. They were up three games to one, with a stranglehold on the series.

The teams returned to New York on June 8, with game five to be played the following evening, and the city expected to celebrate. But that day, items suddenly started moving on the newswires, reporting that Keenan wanted to bolt the Rangers after the finals to take the vacant coaching job in Detroit. The timing was unbelievable—and the reports were in fact true. Keenan had become locked in a hostile battle of wills with Neil Smith—neither man was talking to the other—and he was looking either to oust Smith or to get out himself. Keenan's denials of the Red Wings reports were somewhat wan, adding to the surreal atmosphere that surrounded the whole final series.

In game five itself, the Canucks jumped out to a 3–0 lead by the early stages of the third period, yet the Rangers fought back, with Messier tying the score halfway through the final session. But Vancouver bounced back for three more goals of its own, and the series had to go back to British Columbia. There, the Canucks won easily, 4–1, amid scenes of adrenaline-saturated ecstasy in the stands at the Pacific Coliseum. The Stanley Cup frenzy that was inflaming two big cities—on either side of the border, and on opposite coasts—was completely unprecedented.

The Rangers flew back to New York to prepare for game seven. By now practically no player on the club wanted anything to do with Keenan; it was Messier's team, just as Keenan had said at Rye a few weeks before, only neither man would have wanted it to be so literally true. There were two off-days coming up, and Keenan thought the team should spend them in Lake Placid, away from the pressure of the city. He discussed the idea with Messier and Lowe, but in the end Messier thought it wasn't what the team should do. "This is the chance of a lifetime, Mike," Meisel reports him as saying to Keenan. "Let's come back here and do the things we did all year." Messier's word was law: the Rangers faced their destiny in New York.

At their last practice in Rye, Keenan showed the team the same video montage of ticker-tape parades he had played for them at training camp. Reporters asked Messier if he'd make any guarantees as he had against the Devils. He declined, but he did give the most unforgettable single quote of his career. "This is no time for the faint of heart," he said.

At the Garden before the game, Keenan spoke to the players, many of whom by this point despised him, and offered them an old coaching bromide that nevertheless inspired them. "Go out and win it for each other," he said, "and if you do, you will walk together the rest of your lives." Messier later said it was the best dressing-room speech he ever heard.

In the first period, the Rangers drew first blood. Messier came over the Vancouver line and created space by coming hard down the middle. The two Vancouver defensemen backed up, and Messier dropped the puck to Zubov, who waited to shoot, then hit Leetch with an incisive lead pass to the other side. Leetch was sprung—he never played better than he did in '94, with Zubov as his partner—and he fired through the tangle in the slot, past Kirk McLean and into the net. Later in the period, Zubov sent away Kovalev, who centered to Graves, who scored. In the second period, the Canucks clawed their way back into the game as their heart-and-soul captain, Trevor Linden, scored shorthanded to cut the deficit in half. But eight minutes later, a Graves shot rebounded into the crowded Vancouver slot. Sticks thrashed at the puck. Messier, standing at the side of the net, got hold of it and put it into the net. He leapt in the air and danced behind the goal, where he was mobbed by his teammates. The Rangers led, 3–1, after two. Early in the third, Linden scored again, on a power play, his two goals sandwiching Messier's—Linden, Messier, Linden, two gutsy captains giving it everything they had. Now it was 3–2, and later in the third Nathan Lafayette hit the goalpost, off by an inch from what would have been the tying goal. Time ran down, and as they had done against the Devils in game seven of the conference finals, the Rangers iced and froze the puck repeatedly. With 28 seconds left, Messier lost a face-off for the first time that night, to Murray Craven, and after what seemed like an endless struggle, the puck was iced. There were 1.6 seconds left on the clock. One last draw to the right of Richter, and just enough time for a goal. Pavel Bure stepped into the circle to take the face-off for the Canucks, probably to shoot it right off the draw. But Messier did not step into the circle for the Rangers. If anyone on the team could be considered a better face-off man than he, it was Craig MacTavish. At last the puck was dropped, and the bareheaded MacTavish got to it first, sweeping it to the corner, and while Messier cross-checked Bure one last time, Steve Larmer shielded the puck. The game was over.

Fireworks erupted. The building shook. Messier leapt up and down, his mouth open in an impossibly huge smile, his helmet pulled low over his brow, his arms windmilling, his knees pumping in unison all the way up to his chest. The celebration on the ice, as ecstatic as it was, was actually surpassed by the pandemonium in the stands, where fans howled and wept and celebrated with religious fervor. One held aloft an unforgettable sign that read simply, "Now I can die in peace." Helmeted cops ringed the rink and stood amid the tumult; it seemed as though there wasn't a spare square inch anywhere in the Garden. The rapture, the cheering, would not stop, except for thunderous chants that suddenly swept through the building and then stopped just as suddenly, to be replaced by new ones. They chanted "1940" one last, exorcistic time, then followed it with "1994"—although through the thick working-class accent of the city it came out sounding like "NOIN-teen NOINTY-foah." And of course, over and over, "LET'S go, RANGE-uhs!"

The teams shook hands, and the applause for the Canucks was subsumed by the ceaseless racket of celebration. The fans quieted for a moment when Leetch was presented with the Conn Smythe Trophy, then they roared "We want Cup!" again as they awaited the ultimate prize, which sat atop a small table at center ice. NHL commissioner Gary Bettman said something about New York's long wait being over and summoned Messier to "come get the Stanley Cup." Messier grasped the big silver grail and shook it, his mouth open wide with joy. Then he lifted it over his head, and the other players skated over to hold it with him. The first person he passed the Cup to was Lowe, then several other players had their turn with it, then Messier took it back and skated it over to Keenan. It made its way back to Messier, who skated over to the corner glass to show his family. According to Carpiniello, Messier stood there with it, repeating, "I don't fucking believe it!" He brought the Cup to the entryway and stopped so fans could reach over the railings and caress it.

Beneath the stands, the dressing room and all the adjoining rooms were packed solid with celebrants. President Clinton called to talk to Leetch, the first American ever to win the Smythe trophy. "Congratulations, man," Clinton said. "I've been sitting here in the White House watching this, cheering for you, biting my fingernails, screaming and yelling. . . . You didn't choke. You just kept playing. . . . America is proud of you tonight." Leetch hung up, looked around disbelievingly, and asked, "Was that Dana Carvey?" Everywhere you went in the warren of rooms and corridors, people were dousing one another with champagne, high-fiving, and embracing. It was almost impossible to move. Everyone drank from the Cup, including myself, and I can report that as I drank, the bowl was cold to the touch. The partying had just begun.

Messier, the first man ever to captain two separate clubs to the ultimate prize, had done what he was brought to New York to do: banish all the ghosts, all the curses, all the futility that attended the Rangers. He did it with his performance on the ice—he scored 12 goals (including the Cup-clincher) and 18 assists and went plus-14 in 23 playoff games—but more so with his leadership, taking over when Keenan started to disintegrate, applying a deft, intuitive sense of negotiation and balance that held the whole fragile thing together. "This club won a Stanley Cup because of a commitment to each other," Keenan said. "And because Mark Messier is the greatest leader in professional sports today."

Messier talked about a brief conversation he had with Keenan before the game—one that touched on the now-banished curse of the Rangers. "They talk about ghosts and dragons," he said. "I said to Mike, 'You can't be afraid to slay the dragon.' We're going to celebrate this like we've never celebrated anything in our lives."

There was a great deal of revelry in New York that night, all peaceful (in counterintuitive contrast to Vancouver, where disappointed fans caused disturbances and police overreacted; several people were injured and one was killed). The party in Manhattan lasted through the night, and the focal point was an Upper East Side bar, where the crowd spilled onto the sidewalk and swelled into the hundreds, all trying to get in for a drink from the Cup, forcing police to cordon off the entire block. Finally, Tikkanen brought the goblet out into the throng in the street so that the faithful could spend time with it. Sometime before dawn, Messier brought it to Scores, the city's most prominent—if that's the right word—strip joint. Then he took it to his apartment to spend the night. The next day Messier, Leetch, and Richter took it onto the David Letterman show, where the audience went wild as Leetch paraded it up and down the aisles before the taping began. Then Messier took the Cup to the Garden for game four of the NBA finals between the Knicks and Houston Rockets, and at halftime he escorted it to center court, driving the fans into a frenzy. A couple of days later he took it to Yankee Stadium, and the fans went crazy there, too.

On June 17, the Rangers paraded the Stanley Cup up Lower Broadway, through the so-called Canyon of Heroes. Police estimated the turnout at 1.5 million—an exaggeration, as all crowd estimates at outdoor civic gatherings are, but nevertheless a reflection of the surprising extent of the Rangers' following. In the near future, parades for the Yankees would clearly outstrip that held for the Rangers, but this, the first for a New York sports team since the 1986 World Series champion Mets, was still huge. People lined up four and five deep along the entire route, and as they stood and cheered, office workers threw shredded paper out of skyscraper windows. The Cup rolled up the narrow gorge of Broadway on a two-storey-tall platform, accompanied by Messier, Graves, Leetch, Richter, Lowe, and Larmer, all of them beaming in their sunglasses and wearing their home Rangers sweaters despite the bright sun and 89-degree heat. Messier reached up, grabbed a bit of the cascading paper, and tucked it into his belt. At the end of the route lay City Hall, a low Federal-style building dating back to 1811, and on its steps Mayor Rudy Giuliani hosted a ceremony in which he presented everyone on the team with a key to the city. Hundreds attended—all of them invitees or press— while the public at large strained against the fences of City Hall Park to catch a glimpse of the proceedings. The Rangers were Giuliani's second-favorite team, after the Yankees, and he was the first mayor in at least a generation to show his face at Ranger games; even the family dog was named Goalie. Evoking memories of the Yankees' World Series hero of the late 1970s, Reggie Jackson, Giuliani referred to Messier as "Mr. June." Many Rangers spoke, but Messier came last, saying that what was happening "shows that dreams do come true," and, echoing Keenan's words, adding, "We will walk together the rest of our lives." The crowd in the streets would not go away. Twenty-five were treated for heat exhaustion. Scores of homemade, foil-wrapped replicas of the Cup bobbed up and down above the sea of people. Many in the New York media, long unfamiliar with and dismissive of hockey, were astonished at the breadth and depth of the enthusiasm for the Rangers' victory.

This was the crowning moment for Messier, and for hockey as well. The NHL's long-cherished dream, deferred for more than half a century, was a Stanley Cup for the Rangers. The league fathers knew that for hockey to pass the tipping point in the U.S., there would have to be a championship in the media capital. And this one had been tailor-made: the Rangers played two of their four series entirely in the metropolitan area; the final two series were as dramatic as any in the history of the game; and the Rangers were full of charismatic personalities, none more so than Messier. The NHL had moved its offices from Montreal to New York a few years earlier for this very reason: to conquer the American media, and to be in place should the Rangers ever win it all. It was all so perfect—and it had to be. The league's collective-bargaining agreement with the players had expired again, salaries were shooting through the roof, and the owners were crying poverty. The league governors had their hearts set on further expansion, and they had hired Gary Bettman a year earlier to expand the NHL's "TV footprint" in the States, even if that meant traditional Canadian franchises would have to be sacrificed. Money was sought, money was needed, and Bettman was on hand to sell hockey after the basketball model, using strong personalities— like Messier—as the key.

Already Messier had cracked the ice that froze hockey players out of product endorsements and nationwide recognition in the States. In March, he appeared in national TV spots for the Starter jersey company, alongside basketball's Larry Bird and Karl Malone, football coach Don Shula, Lenny Dykstra from baseball, and Florence Griffith-Joyner from track and field. It was a modest advertising achievement, but a breakthrough for the NHL, which was still trying to capitalize on Gretzky's L.A. adventure. The Rangers' Stanley Cup was going to put the finishing touches on the game's entry into every American's consciousness, from San Jose to Anaheim to Dallas to Miami. And from a financial standpoint, this was vitally important. The NHL's shortcomings in the television-revenue department were enormous, as the virtual blackout of game six of the Rangers–Devils series demonstrated amply. Even after ESPN signed on in 1992, contracts were still in place that left local systems in control. And as long as there was no over-the-air network coverage of games in the U.S., hockey would remain more or less invisible.

But now the game was suddenly being touted in the pages of *Sports Illustrated* and even the Style section of *The New York Times*, as new, hip, even sexy. Fashion shoots were being arranged for glossy magazines that hadn't touched hockey since the days of Ron Duguay. (Brendan Shanahan, for instance, would find out he had been traded from the St. Louis Blues to the Hartford Whalers while doing a shoot for *Mademoiselle*.) All the attention generated by the Rangers was creating the ineffable media buzz that, however ridiculous it may seem, does indeed translate into economic power. Basketball was suffering from a kind of hype-related burnout, as Michael Jordan left the game to try his hand at baseball and young stars were becoming notorious for their on- and off-court antics. Baseball had alienated fans after years of skyrocketing salaries, boorish behavior by its players and owners, and constant threats of work stoppages. The opening was there for hockey, and its sudden surge in perceived hipness was reflected by sales in the new arena of home video games, where hockey simulations consistently outstripped those of other sports. And the media were willing to jump into that opening, clutching U.S. greenbacks in both hands. *Sports Illustrated* put hockey on its cover two weeks in a row for the first and only time in its 41-year history—a Messier cover followed by one split between the Stanley Cup final and the NBA finals. In the New York area, that second cover consisted solely of a shot of Richter, the first time ever that *SI* had run a different, targeted cover in a specific area of the country. It was an innovation that would become a staple of the magazine business in years to come. *SI* also printed 200,000 copies of a special 100-page commemorative "Broadway Blues" edition in time for the Cup parade, which sold for $5 a copy—again, the first time the American sports bible had ever lavished such treatment on hockey. The game was hot because it generated money, a fact that would not have been possible without a Rangers victory. And a Rangers victory would not have been possible without Messier.

The Oilers had made the Cup a trophy for the people back in the mid-'80s, squiring the old receptacle to bars and hospitals all over town, and now the Rangers did the same. It became a surprisingly commonplace experience, considering the millions who lived and worked there, to run into Manhattan office workers all starry-eyed, enthusing over how they had just seen the Cup at their local watering hole during lunch hour. Ed Olczyk, Esa Tikkanen, Nick Kypreos, Mike Richter, Brian Leetch, and Mark Messier made it practically ubiquitous. It showed up at Belmont Park racetrack, where Olczyk held it while the Kentucky Derby winner Go for Gin stuck its nose into the bowl as if it were a feedbag. Messier and Leetch took it to Columbia-Presbyterian Hospital and the bedside of a critically ill boy awaiting a heart transplant. Messier placed it on the roof of his limo, and the players stepped back to watch in amazement as the silver chalice cast its spell. Traffic would literally stop as drivers got out of their cars and pedestrians swarmed off the sidewalk to gather round. It was talisman, drinking buddy, religious relic, conversation piece, and, to the vast majority of New Yorkers, the first glimpse into the special passion that lives and breathes inside everyone who loves hockey. A Stanley Cup triumph in Edmonton or Calgary or Montreal or Detroit is great, but no one in those cities needs to be told what the Cup means. A championship in Pittsburgh, Denver, or even New Jersey or Long Island is significant, but only on a local level. But a Stanley Cup triumph crossed with the glamor and power of New York City was something different; it glittered and gleamed and reverberated across the whole United States.

A few days after the Rangers beat the Canucks, the Knicks went on to lose the NBA finals in game seven in Houston. Had they won, there would probably have been an even greater celebration among New Yorkers, and the Rangers' victory would have been upstaged. As it was, the Rangers and hockey ruled the roost during the summer of 1994. Messier had given the sport its long dreamed-of shot at conquering America, and all the riches that would come with it. It would be up to the NHL to make the most of that chance.

PARADISE LOST

In June of 1994, the National Hockey League had achieved a place of prominence in the American sporting universe that it had never known before. But within weeks, all of the goodwill and opportunities that the Rangers' Cup triumph had generated would wither away. Neither the league, nor Mark Messier, would ever again experience another season like 1993–94.

New York's magic season had relied to some degree on exhuming and reanimating Messier's past, as his old teammates from the Edmonton glory years were summoned to realize the Stanley Cup dream. And it worked fantastically well—this once. Messier's teams would try to duplicate the formula over and over in the years to come, but it would never again succeed. Nineteen ninety-four was the apex of his career, but the thing about any apex is that once you reach it, there's nowhere to go but down.

The problems began on the coaching front, where the strife between Mike Keenan and Rangers GM Neil Smith was chronic and irreparable. Soon after the Cup win, they pledged to work together, but fate intervened when the Garden and its various components were sold by Viacom to ITT/Cablevision for more than $1 billion (the Knicks were listed as being worth $150 million of that figure, the Rangers $100 million, a fair reflection of the relative popularity and clout of the respective clubs at the time). The completion of the sale soon after game seven meant that Robert Gutkowski, the urbane and highly competent CEO of the Garden and the main mediator between Smith and Keenan, became a lame duck. Meanwhile, the conditions of the deal dictated that Smith and Keenan both stay in place, so that neither would be able to force the other out. Still, the two rivals were on a collision course, and the inevitable crash took place on July 15, when Keenan and his agent used a questionable loophole to get out of their contract with the Rangers. A bonus check to Keenan, cut by the Rangers for $625,000, arrived one day late—an error the Keenan camp pounced upon, claiming that the coach's deal with the team was now null and void. There was much fulminating on both sides, and the Rangers filed a breach-of-contract lawsuit in civil court, but ultimately the team decided not to dispute Keenan's claim. He clearly wanted out, so he was let go. Later that summer, he was hired by the St. Louis Blues.

The dispute shocked Ranger fans. The big, happy family that had celebrated the Cup just four weeks before was letting that façade slip, revealing a dysfunctional core. Many players were glad to see the back of Keenan. As Leetch put it later in the season, "When we won there was the question of how things could ever get better. I have to say that when Mike left, it was better in a hurry for a lot of players." But another faction—one that included Messier—was sorry to see Keenan go. Keenan had valued him as captain and role model in a way that Neilson had not. Moreover, Messier had had to draw upon all his people skills to act sometimes as buffer, sometimes as filter, between the players and Keenan's sometimes destructive motivational gambits. It had been a thoroughgoing, engaging, and challenging experience for Messier, and above all it had resulted in a Stanley Cup. Messier would have preferred for Keenan to stay for another round.

Instead, Messier would have to deal with yet another coach: Colin Campbell, the fourth of his four-year career in New York. Campbell had been a Rangers assistant coach since before Messier's arrival, and when Neilson was fired and Ron Smith promoted from Binghamton, Campbell took over the farm club. He returned to assist when Keenan took over the Rangers, and he was the natural choice to take charge when Keenan left. He was formally handed the reins on August 9. As even-keeled as Keenan was volatile, Campbell had a long relationship with Messier (they had played together with the Oilers during Edmonton's first NHL season in 1979–80, when Campbell was a journeyman defenseman). The two got along well, and lest there be any misconceptions about how he viewed Messier, Campbell stated explicitly that his captain would take an active role in decisions that would normally be the exclusive preserve of the coaches. "Mark's at the point in his career where he has to have an impact with the coaching staff and the management of the organization," Campbell said. "Some teams have success using the trap, but you can't ask an Adam Graves or a Mark Messier to hang around in the neutral zone and wait for the other team to come at them." In return, Messier offered his stamp of approval while shutting down any chance of the Rangers adopting a Neilsonian defense-first philosophy. "I wouldn't foresee him changing a lot from last year," he said of Campbell, then proceeded to bend his genders "and I say that because of the type of team we have. You don't take a ballerina and turn him into a blacksmith."

For Messier, the coaching change, though regrettable, was a relatively minor issue. His own contract was a much more pressing issue, and here too the good feeling that had prevailed in June gave way to rancor throughout the summer and into the fall. The five-year contract Messier had signed soon after joining the Rangers in 1991 carried an incentive clause that opened the deal to renegotiation should the Rangers win the Cup. At the time, the contract put Messier behind only Gretzky and Lemieux in the salary parade. But by '94–95, his current stipend of $2.65 million placed him well down the list once again, at approximately fifteenth. Soon after the Cup was won, Doug Messier contacted Smith and reminded him that the renegotiation clause had been activated. In early August, the Messiers (besides Doug, Paul Messier and accountant Barry Klarberg also represented Mark in these contract talks) made their first concrete offer: a three-year contract worth $6 million each year. It would be a huge raise if granted, one that would put Messier just behind Gretzky, who was earning about $6.5 million annually. Smith and Gutkowski, who was still involved with the team at this point, countered with $4 million a season—also a big raise, but not quite at the Gretzky–Lemieux level.

The two sides negotiated regularly and cordially into early September, but little progress was made. Training camp was due to open, although no one ever expected Messier to show up; he had missed several in his career, and it had never adversely affected him. (If anything, Messier is a living argument for the notion that a grueling training camp and exhibition season are superfluous when preceding an already-overlong regular-season schedule.) Still, the talks started to break down, and, according to Barry Meisel's *Losing the Edge*, Smith sensed that Doug Messier viewed him as a source of friction. He decided to bow out, leaving Gutkowski the only negotiator on the Garden side. Soon thereafter, Gutkowski made an offer of $5 million a year, and Doug Messier felt that at last the two sides were getting somewhere.

A few days later, however, the ITT/Cablevision team moved Gutkowski out of the president's suite at MSG and replaced him with Dave Checketts, who had been the general manager of the Knicks. Checketts knew as much about hockey as, say, Smith knew about basketball, which is to say, very little. He was certainly aware of all that Messier had done, having seen it from close quarters at the Garden, but hockey and basketball represent entirely different cultures in practically every regard, including the area of player salaries. As if the uncertainty the move revealed weren't enough, the tone of the talks was garbled further when Neil Smith was required to resume an active role in the talks. Doug Messier certainly was not keen on this idea. "What I was told, and I don't know why," he said, "is that this was like starting all over again."

To make matters still worse, negotiations between the NHL and the players' association over a new collective bargaining agreement broke down entirely, and with opening night of the 1994–95 season only a week and a half away, Commissioner Gary Bettman announced that the owners would lock the players out if no agreement was reached. Bettman was playing hardball all the way: the owners wanted to cap players' salaries as basketball and football had done, and they were willing to sacrifice the entire season to get what they wanted. The immediate effect on the Messier negotiations was to add further delay and complication. On October 1, which was to have been opening night, the owners imposed their lockout, and for the second time in three seasons a labor dispute shut down the NHL. By this point, the Rangers and the Messiers were only $500,000 apart, with the Rangers offering very close to $6 million a year. But there could be no resolution until contact resumed between players and owners.

The lockout dragged on through October and into November. Messier had been in Hilton Head since August, speaking often with the press to express his optimism that a deal with the Rangers would get done and pledging to be there for the home opener, when the Stanley Cup banner would be raised to the Garden ceiling. But now that the season was on indefinite hold, talking about his contract became unseemly, so he more or less stopped. At first, he also said very little about labor-management issues, creating the impression that he had softened since 1993, when he had taken a militantly pro-union stance.

By the end of November, however, he found a way to express his solidarity. In the absence of interaction between Bettman and the NHLPA beyond mutual recriminations and surprisingly vitriolic accusations that one side or the other was acting in bad faith, Wayne Gretzky decided that the time was right to realize a long-held dream: to gather an all-star team and conduct a barnstorming goodwill tour of northern Europe. A team of Russian NHLers had just barnstormed through Russia and drawn enthusiastic crowds while winning five out of six. A similar tour would be fun and, thought Gretzky, long an admirer of the European hockey ethos, it would give something tangible back to the countries that had done so much to elevate the game in North America. It would also keep the players in shape in a politically acceptable way during what would otherwise be a prolonged period of inactivity. Ultimately, it would make a statement more vivid than any picket line: this is the hockey that the NHL owners are preventing North American fans from seeing.

The first player Gretzky called in planning his tour, according to Roy MacGregor, who chronicled it in reports for the *Ottawa Citizen* and in his book *The Home Team: Fathers, Sons, and Hockey*, was Messier. They discussed which players would be invited to take part, and they talked about who else would be invited along to help. At Gretzky's suggestion, they decided that the players would invite their fathers. Gretzky's father, Walter, was recovering from a 1991 stroke that, in an especially cruel twist, had robbed him of about fifteen years of memories—a span that coincided with his son's entire glorious professional career. Meanwhile, Messier's father had little to do now that the frustrating negotiations with the Rangers were stalled indefinitely. Walter Gretzky and Doug Messier would be assistant coaches, helping Doug Wilson, the recently retired defenseman who would be the nominal coach, to run the bench. Later, the fathers of Paul Coffey and Marty McSorley were brought along, too.

Gretzky and Messier filled out the playing ranks with an all-star roster that consisted largely of their friends from the old Oilers, including Coffey, McSorley, Grant Fuhr, Charlie Huddy, and Pat Conacher. Steve Larmer would also be on hand, as well as Brett Hull, Steve Yzerman, Sergei Fedorov, Al MacInnis, Kelly Hrudey, Kirk Muller, Rick Tocchet, Russ Courtnall, Tony Granato, and Todd Gill, who replaced Kevin Lowe when the latter defenseman backed out at the last minute. Other players would show up for one or two games once the tour got under way. No French-Canadian players joined the team, even though some were invited (Lemieux, Patrick Roy, Vincent Damphousse, and Luc Robitaille were reportedly asked); this situation touched off a kerfuffle that, if nothing else, highlighted how few of Gretzky and Messier's confidantes are francophones.

The team practiced in Detroit for a few days and lost 4–3 in an exhibition to the Detroit Vipers, an independent team in the International Hockey League, then flew to Helsinki to play against Jokerit. Jari Kurri joined the touring team, now called the Ninety-Nine All-Stars and co-captained by Gretzky and Messier, and played against his old Jokerit side, whose lineup included Teemu Selanne. The All-Stars won, 7–1, with Messier among the goal scorers. But then came a 4–3 overtime loss to Ilves Tampere and an unimpressive 6–3 win over a Norwegian select team in Oslo. The tour was always meant to be something of a lark—the players definitely were enjoying themselves late at night in the sophisticated capitals of Scandinavia, and the reception was enthusiastic everywhere they went—but there was some surprise at how close the games were, especially the one against the Norwegians, in which the All-Stars had to rally to win. Commentators and fans on both sides of the Atlantic started to wonder whether the Ninety-Nine All-Stars, with their 2–2 record as a unit, weren't more of an Over the Hill Gang than a star-studded flying circus. Were the Russian barnstormers really that much better?

The next game, against Djurgarden, was in Stockholm, where the All-Stars were joined by Doug Gilmour. With Messier as ringleader the players got serious, engaging in weight training, pregame naps, even a curfew. The first period was close, but Messier was pumped; he strode off the ice to the dressing room and emitted a yell rendered by MacGregor as "*Yeeeee-hawwwwww!*" Inside, he stood up and gave a concise inspirational message that hushed the room. According to Wilson, all Messier said was "Enough is enough!" That brief pronouncement was enough to electrify his teammates. Messier went on to score two goals as the All-Stars romped, 9–3. A couple of nights later against Vastra Frolunda in Goteborg, Messier threw some big bodychecks and added a late goal in a 5–2 win. MacGregor, reporting in the *Ottawa Citizen*, noted that while Gretzky was the star whose autograph everyone lined up for, and Fedorov was the best player on the ice, Messier was the most important man on the team. His was the iron will that drove the wheels. He had decided that a poor showing by the All-Stars would send a bad message to everyone back in North America, so he pulled up his socks and made everyone follow along. MacGregor opined that the team really should be called Mark Messier and His Teammates.

At this same juncture in the tour, Messier was backing up his on-ice militancy in the press, reviving the players' league concept he had floated during the 1993 stoppage. This time, thanks in large part to the All-Stars tour, the threat was much more plausible. "Seven hundred players in the NHLPA are not going to sit around if we are locked out," he said in Stockholm. "We're going to try to find an alternative in which we can take care of our players in some sort of manner." If the CBA talks failed, he continued, the union would form a league consisting of teams in Canada, the U.S., and Europe. Gretzky mentioned February as a rough date for the league to start play. The two players even outlined how it would work. The players' league would be organized by the NHLPA. There would be twenty teams, each playing a twelve- or sixteen-game schedule that would run to the beginning of April, when playoffs would begin. Twenty corporations would commit $1 million each to get a team; three to five of the corporations would be European and would sponsor sides that would play on the

Continent. Gretzky and Messier suggested that a company like Volvo might put up $5 million for a playoff purse in much the same manner that Avco had done in the old WHA days, and that CTV, ESPN, and Euro Sport would be engaged to televise the games. Union chief Bob Goodenow would be the commissioner, and all NHLPA members would share equally in large percentages of the revenues and franchise fees. "We want to play and we're going to," Messier said. "We're not going to sit around and take this. There are ways to go involving five hundred guys, and eventually everyone, with a new league."

Back on the ice, the All-Stars' seriousness may have been a bit unfair; the teams they were playing were treating the games as friendlies, making sure that everyone on their rosters, including retired stars and untried prospects, got a turn on the ice. The All-Stars were taking the vast majority of the penalties, although that happened whenever a North American team encountered the much stricter, more consistent standard of refereeing found in Europe. Still, the Ninety-Nines were beating legitimate opponents that featured such future NHL stars as Selanne, Miroslav Satan, and Robert Svehla. As if to emphasize Messier's centrality to the team, the All-Stars lost their next outing, in Malmo, by 6–5 in overtime, after Messier had to leave the game in the second period with muscle spasms in his back. In his absence, the Malmo line of Tomas Sandstrom, Raimo Helminen, and the retired Mats Naslund sparked a comeback, Naslund scoring with just 54 seconds left to tie the game. Messier returned for the tour finale in Freiburg, Germany, and scored a brace of goals in an 8–5 victory over a select team made up of German and Swiss players. In the end, the All-Stars went 5–2–0 in their two-week tour of Europe, Messier scored seven goals, and the message was sent to the owners and union that a new league could work. (Upon the All-Stars' return to Toronto, Gretzky told *The Toronto Sun*'s Al Strachan that he had financial backing for a January tour of Japan with more players, enough to split into one team led by himself and another by Messier.)

On a personal level for Messier, the tour was immensely satisfying. Besides the pleasure of playing with his friends, he got to experience Europe in a way similar to that of his brother Paul, who had spent so many years as a pro in the German league and who came along for this ride. What made this trip different from Mark's previous hockey visits to Europe—as part of

Oilers or Rangers training camps, or the one year he played for Canada in the World Championships—was that this was a low-pressure tour that allowed him to savor the sights and sounds of European hockey. Most of the rinks the All-Stars played in were small, with capacities of less than 6,000 and as low as 2,500, and there were usually more places to stand than there were seats. The fans sang and chanted all night long, sometimes prompted by public-address systems, sometimes by drummers and trumpeters in their own midst, sometimes entirely *a capella*, but however they expressed themselves, they were always loud, boisterous, and inspiring. They leapt up and down in unison, waved flags, and held up roadside emergency flares, the terrace culture of a century of European hockey and soccer fandom turning the intimate little rinks into living cauldrons of sight, sound, and smoke. And the applause for the All-Stars was always loud, the welcome always warm. This was European club hockey; there was nothing like it in North America, and it was fun and intoxicating, a foreign experience in the best way.

Most satisfying for Messier was the time he spent with his father. Messier said that sometimes when he came off the ice after a shift it felt strange and different, because he'd see Doug standing behind the bench, a flashback to the days of his childhood. "I sometimes look over at him and think how great this must be for him," he said. Doug was the only one of the touring fathers who took his coaching duties seriously—he had, after all, been an AHL coach as recently as a decade before—and he found his own new insights as he marveled at his son's play. "He's just a horse out there— a horse," he told MacGregor. "I can't explain it, but when the going gets rough, he just seems to become bigger out there."

The tour had been a marvelous respite, but when Messier returned to North America, the same big problems remained to confront him. There was still a complete impasse between players and owners, and a corresponding impasse in his own contract disagreement with the Rangers. The new year came and went, and the entire season stood in danger of cancellation.

Finally, in early January, there was a breakthrough: the owners dropped their demand for a formal salary cap, replacing it with a plan to limit incoming rookies' salaries. Goodenow and Mike Gartner, the president of the NHLPA, called a meeting to be attended by the player reps of each team as well as several other leading players—Messier, Gretzky, Montreal goalie Patrick Roy, and hard-nosed Calgary winger Gary Roberts among them. They rejected the owners' plan, 26–0, but at least the two sides were talking again. Messier flew to New York and drove up to Rye, where some of his teammates had been renting out ice time to stay in shape; this time, Messier had none of the complaints that he had expressed in 1993, and even joined them in a skatearound.

Within three days, an agreement was reached that gave true free agency to players in their early thirties and imposed a cap only on entry-level salaries. In subsequent years, it would become clear that the new contract was a boon to the players, as payrolls would continue to escalate much as they had before the lockout. The owners' shortsightedness did not end there. They inexplicably made almost no provision for revenue-sharing among the clubs, dooming those teams in such smaller cities as Winnipeg, Hartford, and Quebec to extinction.

The belated start to the season was set for January 20, 1995, which gave players a week to get in shape for an abbreviated, 48-game schedule, the shortest for the NHL since 1941–42. The owners had squandered three and half months in taking a gamble they wound up losing anyway. In doing so, they had not only forgone a salary cap, they had also missed their chance to capitalize on the surge in the game's Stateside popularity that the Rangers' Cup triumph had generated.

The timing of the lockout proved especially unfortunate: in October 1994, when the NHL season would normally have been getting under way, a labor dispute in baseball forced the cancellation of that sport's postseason. When the World Series was scratched, fans' ill will toward Major League Baseball's players and owners was enormous—but the NHL was not there to fill the void. The league blundered badly, missing a golden chance that would never present itself again—and worse, earning for itself the same reputation for greed and heedlessness that had tarred the image of the U.S. national pastime. Worse still, the NHL had just signed its first network TV contract in a decade and a half, a five-year, $155 million deal with Fox. The Fox telecasts were slated to begin amid much fanfare in December, but the shutdown sabotaged the one thing Bettman and the owners prized above all others. And while hockey's loyal core fans across Canada and in the U.S.

might not have lamented the loss of the first few weeks of the tedious regular season, by the time December arrived they were homesick for the game and had grown sour toward the squabbling owners and players. In every conceivable aspect, the lockout was a disaster for the NHL.

Meanwhile, Messier had missed out on his own chance at greater fame and wealth, though it's equally true that he had little desire for more of either. He was definitely sought after for product endorsements, as the national deal with Starter demonstrated, and had he chosen to, he probably could have signed with any number of companies after the Cup parade and had his face plastered all over America. But he did nothing more than commission some new wall posters, leaving the business side of the transaction in the hands of his family. The league would have benefited had Messier decided to become a national figure in the U.S., where Gretzky remained the only NHLer ever to gain a high public profile. But Messier valued his privacy and his vacation time too much to pursue endorsements and the obligations that went with them. According to *Forbes* magazine, he would make $1 million in endorsements in 1995, a healthy total but well below the amount earned by most other top-earning athletes. Messier's deals were relatively low-profile: Starter, the sneaker company L.A. Gear, and the videogame company Mariah Entertainment.

The fact was that Messier's professional interests lay almost solely in playing hockey, and now that the lockout was over, he, Doug, Paul, and Barry Klarberg had to reach an agreement with the Rangers so he could play hockey again. When they left off, they were only a few hundred thousand dollars apart, but when the Messiers returned to the negotiating table, they asked again for $6 million for 1994–95, even though the season would now be more than 40 percent shorter. Smith and Checketts objected, and the two sides, each irritated with the other, seemed far apart once again. Messier had already made it clear that deal or no, he would be in uniform when the Rangers opened at the Garden and raised their banner a few nights hence; moreover, he was still under contract to the Rangers, even if he was in the process of renegotiating its terms. He worked out with the club, appearing on *The Late Show with David Letterman*, and putting on a happy public face, making pronouncements of confidence that all differences would be overcome. He was at the team dinner at the St. Regis Hotel in Manhattan when

Smith presented everyone with their Stanley Cup rings ("When you get a ring, it's like having a library of films on your finger," Messier said. "Every time you look at it, a whole new movie comes up.") and when the players got to see the Cup with their names engraved on it. He had no desire to put a damper on the good feelings surrounding the Rangers' Cup defense. But at the same time he was impatient enough with the negotiations to enter them personally, and two hours before the season opener he told Smith and Checketts that he was ready to sit out game two and beyond.

The home opener was another beautifully stage-managed extravaganza of the Neil Smith era. More old Ranger icons were trotted out, as well as some Ranger fans who held season tickets going all the way back to the sainted 1940 season. The boy to whom Messier and Leetch had brought the Cup in hospital, now up and around with a transplanted heart beating strongly in his chest, was also on hand. The house lights were brought down, and a ten-minute video chronicling the Cup campaign was shown on the scoreboard, along with a special Top Ten list provided by Letterman for the occasion. The preliminaries took more than half an hour, and not once was Keenan's image shown or his name uttered. Finally, the Rangers were introduced, one by one. Some from the Stanley Cup team were not present, including Esa Tikkanen, who went to St. Louis in the compensation package worked out when Keenan bolted for the Blues; Craig MacTavish, gone to Philadelphia as a free agent; and Glenn Anderson, off with the Canadian National Team while he held out for a new contract.

Messier was the last to emerge. He stood in the runway, his eyes brimming, and then he skated out, his arms aloft, to a deafening ovation. At the ceremony's climax, the players took their places around the perimeter of the center circle, and with colored lasers illuminating billowing clouds of dry-ice vapor, the Cup itself was lowered from the rafters, a custom introduced by the Oilers during the '80s. Messier picked it up off its platform and handed it off to his teammates, who skated it around the rink in a curiously half-hearted display that was applauded appreciatively, though not thunderously, by the crowd. The game started nearly an hour late, almost an afterthought. "We were kind of reminiscing," Messier said. "You know, thinking about last year, how great it was. And then all of a sudden the lights were on and we had to play." The Rangers lost to the Buffalo Sabres, 2–1. Messier wore a new white helmet for the first time since 1983. His original WinnWell was cracked and dangerous by the end of the '94 Cup run, so he retired it and, because the company was long out of business, found a replacement through an Internet search conducted by his old friend, Edmonton trainer Barrie Stafford.

Messier's contract negotiations continued over the next several days, the Rangers moving with enough urgency to keep Messier from following through on his threat to sit out. In the end, the team retained their right to buy Messier out of the 1996–97 season, but added a $5 million bonus if he led them to the Cup in 1995 or 1996. Messier would earn $4.9 million for the shortened 1994–95 season, $6 million for the next, and another $6 million if the Rangers exercised their option on a third year. Messier was happy at last, and at the press conference announcing the deal, he broke down in tears once again. Meisel rendered his words this way: "The commitment that the Rangers have made to me is pretty overwhelming. I guess I'd like to thank . . . there are a lot of people to thank . . . oh, man. . . . Is it hot in here, or am I just crazy?"

In retrospect, though, the season already lay in ruins. The Rangers were 1–3 by the time Messier signed, their team fractured by the Keenan affair. The NHL had lost its chance at breaking out to a wider audience while at the same time alienating its existing fans. And an undercurrent of bitterness now lay just below the surface in Messier's relationship with the Rangers management. Things had already broken down on three fronts—and there was more trouble on the horizon for Messier.

The 1994–95 season—or more properly, the 1995 season, since no games took place during the latter months of '94—was an anomaly. Only 48 games were played, and teams played only against the clubs in their own conference. It was in many ways an ideal regular-season schedule: every game was important, and no team could afford to dog it even for a single night. Furthermore, every game was a four-pointer; you not only played to get two points, you played to prevent the other team from getting two points. There were no East-versus-West snorers featuring two teams unfamiliar with each other, no endless road jaunts crisscrossing the continent. It was just intense, meaningful hockey, night in and night out—a little like the playoffs.

Since every game was for keeps, teams stressed defense, close checking, and the clogging up of the neutral zone. The conservative play that Neilson had championed now became the gold standard of success. To compound that trend, goaltenders were performing better than at any time in recent memory, using new techniques that had been evolving over the past few seasons: playing in a crouch, keeping the paddles of their sticks along the ice, dispensing with the stand-up style altogether. They had bigger equipment, too, that bloated them to Michelin Man proportions. The statistics proved that goaltenders were finding new success in foiling NHL forwards. In 1987–88, the last time Gretzky won the Cup with the Oilers, NHL goalers had a collective save percentage of .879—in other words, they stopped roughly seven out of eight pucks to come their way. In the Rangers' Cup year of 1993–94, it was up to .895. In the lockout-shortened 1995 season, it burst through the 90-percent barrier, to .901—a gain of twenty-two points in eight seasons. A sea change had taken place, and an era of 1–0 shutouts had begun. NHL offenses mustered an average of 5.9 goals per game in 1995—down substantially from the Oilers' glory years and a far cry even from the 6.4 of 1993–94. This was neither the type of hockey Messier liked nor the type he was good at. And at age thirty-four, Messier, who was bullheaded to begin with, was not inclined to adjust his play to fit the new paradigm. It is unfair to claim that hockey was about to pass Messier by, but it is true that from this point on, he never again experienced the kind of success to which he had been accustomed over the first decade and a half of his career.

Still, for now, he was simply one of the three best players in the game, relieved to be back where he wanted to be—on the ice, leading his team. In February, he gave the most interesting interview of his entire career, a rare one-on-one with the *New York Times* sports columnist Robert Lipsyte, who specialized in an alternative approach to sportswriting, coming at the subject from a more self-consciously sociological viewpoint than other scribes.

In 1991 Lipsyte had decided to embrace a new sport and a new team so that he could more honestly experience the joy and despair of true fandom, correctly believing that most sportswriters had suppressed or lost that impulse. When Messier arrived from Edmonton as designated messiah, Lipsyte decided to become a Ranger fan. He spent the next few years writing about the team, its white, blue-collar fan base, and about Messier, whom he dubbed "Captain Dad." His obsession with Messier and the Rangers reached a crescendo during the 1994 Cup run, and it caught the eye of Mary-Kay, who called and offered Lipsyte that rarest opportunity: a chance to spend a couple of hours alone with her brother.

They met at a restaurant near Rye, and Messier looked back over his Rangers career and offered a glimpse into his beliefs on the joys and burdens of captaincy. "It's an interesting dance between the coach and the captain," he said. "It's never for the captain to say who plays. It's his job to give confidence, to be a nurturer. . . . If Mike Keenan thought it was necessary to act harshly toward a player to bring up his level, it would be my job to restore the player's esteem without telling him the coach was wrong. I would say, 'You're a good kid, now go suck it up, you can show them.'" Messier called the inner game of hockey "a sport of mind games. We play it on ourselves. We drive ourselves to the brink of craziness. Some of us need to be hit every day with a two-by-four to play our best. There are tough guys and fragile artists and lazy boys, that's how people are, it doesn't mean one is better than another." About life under Keenan, he said, "Keenan was easy. Edmonton was the psychological boot camp. Endless seminars on how to find your superconscious, the zone. It sounds like insanity. Except how do you explain those nights when I'm so focused that I fly, never feel my legs, no pain, see everything, score three goals?"

Messier reflected on his first three seasons in New York and said he still got emotional thinking about them. Lipsyte reports that at this point Messier's eyes grew watery. "Right after I got to New York I knew something was very wrong," he said. "I knew we couldn't win the Cup. But we won a lot of games before we lost in the playoffs. But by that next season I had to speak out against Roger Neilson and be willing to take the lumps as a coach-killer, a spoiled athlete, and to take the blame for that season coming apart. I really had no choice. I couldn't just shut up and finish out my career; nice try, Mark. I had to stand up, almost cross that line of what a captain is about. It was my obligation." He said he was glad when Keenan arrived as coach. "I could be the captain again, the top guy, but still one of the guys. And winning. Ahhh." He told Lipsyte of the complete psychological commitment needed to succeed. "You must be willing to be consumed by this game for nine months, twenty-four hours a day, to be totally free to think about it, help a teammate, work harder," he said. "It's tougher on the married players, the ones with children. It's the reason I haven't committed myself to long-term relationships yet. Or to many endorsement contracts. I can't be distracted."

The Rangers were streaky all season long, dipping well below .500 to start, then zooming past that level, then sputtering again and settling in for a battle to retain the last playoff berth. One major issue was Messier's relationship with Petr Nedved, the talented twenty-three-year-old Czech centerman who had defected to Canada in the last days of communist Czechoslovakia, but who had been something of a bust in Vancouver and St. Louis. Still, Neil Smith had coveted him, and he came to New York as part of the Keenan–Tikkanen compensation package worked out by the league. Nedved liked to work the perimeters and stayed away from the heavy traffic in front of the net, a tendency that soon made him the whipping boy of the Garden fans. Campbell benched him and told reporters that he was being advised, taught, and warned to become more willing to fight his way through checks. When word somehow got out that Messier was dissatisfied with Nedved's play, the old rumors of Messier throwing recalcitrant teammates up against the wall were revived. In fact Messier reportedly was never harsh with Nedved; rather, he calmly lectured and cajoled his teammate into wading into traffic more often. By March, Nedved was telling reporters that he was having a difficult time fitting in and finding acceptance with his teammates; he said he felt like an outsider among all the players who'd fought for the Cup the year before. In response, Messier offered lukewarm reassurance. "I think for anybody coming into a dressing room like this, especially when we were so successful last year, you have to earn the respect of the players first and foremost," he said. "That's the bottom line. And I think Petr has worked hard at it."

Nedved was supposed to be the Rangers' number two center, but all the time he spent on the bench meant more ice time for Messier, who wound up leading the team in scoring again, at 14–39–53 in 46 games, ninth best in the league. It would be the sixth and final top ten finish of Messier's career. He registered 40 penalty minutes, five of which came after he thrashed his nemesis Kevin Haller, now with Philadelphia, in a fistfight. He chewed out his teammates in a closed-door meeting ("How much longer are we gonna bullshit ourselves?" he yelled during an intermission at Nassau Coliseum, according to Meisel. "This is not good enough. It's just not."). His late-season scoring streak pushed the slumping Rangers into a push for the final berth. All of this came despite a badly strained back that was being treated with acupuncture.

New York finished the abbreviated schedule with a 22–23–3 record, good for only a .490 winning percentage—177 points worse than their 1993–94 performance. Still, they were in the playoffs, and their first-round opponents were the Quebec Nordiques, a team that had missed the previous six postseasons but emerged in '95 as the best team in the east. The Nordiques had used their long sojourn in the wilderness to stock up on high draft choices, and now they were armed with Joe Sakic, Peter Forsberg, Valeri Kamensky, and other young, gunning speedsters. The team was also in financial trouble, and it was all but certain that they would move to Denver over the summer.

The teams split the first two games at Le Colisée, with Messier scoring his 100th playoff goal in the second match. Back in New York, the Rangers won game three, but game four was marred when referee Andy van Hellemond blew a call, waving off a perfectly legitimate Sakic goal after Alexei Kovalev went down with a seeming injury, even though the Rangers never possessed the puck on the play. The Rangers wound up winning the game by a single goal, a fact that left the Colisée crowd in a sour mood a couple of nights later, during what everyone knew would probably be the last NHL game ever to be played in Quebec. The fans littered the ice on several occasions with papers, cups of soda, and even rolls of coins. The Nords won to extend the series, but afterward Messier was in high dudgeon. "Being Canadian and thinking it's a Canadian game, I think the fans should respect the game more if they want to think it's their game," he said. "To throw coins and pop on the ice at the players and the referee is the most disgusting thing I've seen. It sheds a bad light on the whole game itself and on the people of Quebec."

The Rangers eliminated *les Nordiques* in game six at the Garden, and in the game's final moments the New York fans, emboldened by the remarks of Messier and other Rangers, jeered the Nords and taunted their fans for losing their team to Denver. It was a display far more disgusting than anything that had taken place in Quebec, and was one of the lowest points in the history of Madison Square Garden. New York hockey fans, in their peculiar Eastern Seaboard cocoon, were only dimly aware of what a truly *québécois* team meant to the culture of the game. Sadder still for the people of Quebec City, the franchise would win the Stanley Cup the following year, but as the Colorado Avalanche.

The next round pitted the Rangers against the Philadelphia Flyers. The big story here was supposed to be the battle between the young behemoth Eric Lindros and his idol, Messier. But the series turned out to be completely one-sided, a sweep for Philly. Campbell matched Messier's line against Lindros's Legion of Doom combo—Lindros and the gigantic John LeClair and Mikael Renberg—and the Flyers ran roughshod. Lindros shrugged off Messier time and again, and his line accounted for five goals in the first two games. Worse for Messier, Haller had a great series, with an overtime winner in game two among his four goals. Ron Hextall was in the nets for Philadelphia now, and the Garden crowd, which had gleefully singsonged "We want Hextall" at the end of the Nordiques series, looked on sullenly at his flawless goalkeeping in New York.

The Rangers went gently into that good night, and in the final minute what remained of the Garden crowd arose and gave the outgoing Cup champions a standing ovation. To see Ranger fans so good-natured in defeat after so many years of heaping bile on their team was a jarring sight. Afterward, Messier talked about defeat. "When we see someone else carrying the Cup around it will be that much tougher," he said. "We gave it all we had and it wasn't enough. We got beat. You take your lumps and your licks and go home and come back next season." Meanwhile, across the Hudson, Jacques Lemaire's neutral-zone-trapping New Jersey Devils were putting to use everything they had learned against the Rangers the year before. They rolled on to win the Stanley Cup and accelerated the trend toward defense by succeeding so thoroughly with the kind of game that Messier hated.

In the off-season Messier went to Maui, where he played roller hockey in an abandoned World War II airplane hangar in the middle of a sugarcane field, and to the Gulf Stream off the South Carolina coast, where he went deep-sea fishing. As he was trolling for marlin on the high seas, the Rangers traded away Sergei Zubov, and Nedved was dispatched to Pittsburgh for Luc Robitaille and Ulf Samuelsson. It was a fascinating trade, bringing to the Rangers an all-time great scorer off the left wing and a rugged—read, dirty—defenseman who had been a keystone of the Penguins' two Stanley Cup victories. But both came with baggage. When he was with L.A., Robitaille did not get along with Wayne Gretzky, which precipitated his trade to Pittsburgh. (When Robitaille did not accompany the Ninety-Nine All-Stars to Europe, he said that in order to be on that tour one had to be "*téteux*," a French term for "idiotic.") When Messier arrived at training camp in Burlington, Vermont (he now seemed more inclined to show up for training camp), he was asked whether Robitaille's clashes with Gretzky would be a problem. "I judge players on how they've done against me," Messier answered. "I've known Luc a couple of years off the ice, too, and that didn't enter my mind at all." As for Samuelsson, with whom he had had the near stick-fight a couple of years earlier, Messier said: "We've had a few run-ins over the years. He's a lot like Claude [Lemieux] and Darius [Kasparaitis]; when they're on the ice you have to be aware of it." Messier and Samuelsson, both of whom were win-at-all-costs types on the ice but gregarious away from the rink, got along well in their years together with the Rangers, as could have been predicted from something Messier said about Samuelsson not long after the original incident: "He was just doing his job."

The NHL saw something of a return to a more open game in 1995–96 —the average match would see 6.2 goals, the last time to date that the league average has topped six goals per game. In this modestly free-wheeling environment, Messier would blossom one last time as an offensive star.

In a 4–2 victory on November 6 at the Garden, Messier notched a hat trick, the twenty-first of his NHL career; the third of these goals was his 500th. As for so many of his greatest moments, his mother, father, sister, and grandmother were on hand—they were in New York for a dinner marking the renewal of the Mark Messier "point club" for the Tomorrows Children's Fund—and so was Glen Sather, in town for the general managers' meetings. Still more fittingly, the Rangers' opponents were the Calgary Flames, and it was just as appropriate that Adam Graves passed to set up Messier's wrist shot past Rick Tabaracci for the milestone goal, then was the first to leap into Messier's arms to celebrate. The tributes flowed like wine from his teammates after the game. "It's nights like these when you want to pinch yourself and say, 'I'm a better person and player for him having been around here,'" Richter said. "When he got here, he came with such a great reputation that you began to wonder whether he was more than just a player and a guy. But then he started to do all these things and your suspicions were confirmed: he is more than just a player and a normal person. He's the greatest leader I've ever seen." Neil Smith added, "He's a master of being able to grab the moment," and cited his famous 1994 guarantee against the Devils.

Smith's unqualified praise was noteworthy. The Rangers had until midseason to notify Messier about whether they'd pick up their option for the '96–97 season at $6 million, or exercise their buyout for $1 million and let him become a free agent. If there was any question about how the Rangers felt, it had to have been dispelled a few nights later, prior to a game against Tampa Bay, when Smith arranged for still more pageantry, this time marking Messier's 500th goal in a ceremony that included his family and even his son, Lyon. In the game itself, Messier sparked another comeback, and afterward Colin Campbell said: "We can't continually count on Mark Messier saving us. We spoke before the game that we can't say, 'Mark, do something heroic again.'" Clearly the Rangers needed him, and clearly they appreciated that any success they were experiencing was attributable to his efforts. A couple of games later, six weeks before it was due, the Rangers sent word that they would re-sign Messier for another season.

The Rangers rolled on behind Messier, consistently among the league's top five or six teams. With seven games to go in the season, they played Philadelphia, who were just ahead of them atop what was now called the Northeast Division. As had become customary down through the years at the Spectrum, the game took a backseat to the donnybrooks. In the first period Lindros and the Rangers' Marty McSorley—yet another ex-Oiler wearing Broadway Blue—collided in the Rangers' end during a stoppage. During the requisite pushing, shoving, and posturing that followed, Philly's Karl Dykhuis and New York's Sergio Momesso threw down. On the ensuing face-off, Jeff Beukeboom attacked Shjon Podein, and Messier fought his old Calgary antagonist, Joel Otto, along the boards. Referee Don Koharski wound up ejecting Otto for instigating the fight with Messier, who was so frustrated at being bested by Otto once again that he threw his elbow pad at him. Later, Messier lined up for a face-off and noticed that he had no strength in his side; he had torn cartilage in his oft-injured ribcage.

Messier, who had tallied 47 goals to date, had to miss the final six games of the season. It was pointed out that if he'd played and made it to 50 goals, it would have been the second time in his career that he reached that plateau—fifteen seasons after his first. No one else had ever gone more than four years between 50-goal campaigns. In any case, New York finished with a record of 41–27–14, fifth overall in the NHL. Messier led the team in scoring at 47–52–99. It was a fine performance, if perhaps not quite worthy of the Hart Trophy nomination he received. But his reputation, longevity, and ability to come back at age thirty-five and continue to lead indomitably were all enough to properly impress the sportswriters who voted on the honor. In the end, Mario Lemieux outpolled him.

The Rangers' captain was playing like the vintage Messier, a fact that had its ugly side. The bigger, tougher, dirtier Rangers (who had added the fistically inclined Shane Churla to the assortment of yobs already on the roster) took more penalties and were shorthanded more often than any other team in the league, and Messier chipped in a hefty 122 penalty minutes, the third-highest total of his career. His play was as low-down as anyone's on the roster. In mid-March, as the Oilers were en route to a 4–1 victory over the Rangers at the Garden, Messier cross-checked mild-mannered winger David Roberts in the face, fracturing his cheekbone, breaking his nose in four places, damaging his eye socket, and damaging nerves in his cheek. Messier received a roughing minor for his efforts and said afterward, "We're all responsible for our sticks, but this was unintentional." League disciplinarian Brian Burke fined him $1,000, saying that Messier got Roberts with his glove, not his stick. Dave Molinari of the *Pittsburgh Post-Gazette* calculated that at Messier's salary, he earned the amount of his fine during his first 49.2 seconds in the penalty box. Roberts' comment on the matter: "I've had so many X-rays, I'm glowing."

A few days after that incident, the Penguins whomped the Rangers, 8–2, at the Garden. Nedved, who was playing outstanding hockey for the Penguins, was on his way to a five-point night. This was more than Messier could stand, and midway through the game he speared Nedved in the stomach, dropping him to the ice. Later in the game, Messier two-handed him in the back, raising a huge welt. Messier told reporters, "I went for his hands or stick. I was killing a penalty." But Carpiniello heard him say afterward, with evident distaste, that Nedved was "fuckin' laying there like a fuckin' lapdog." Now that Nedved was on another team, Messier was openly contemptuous of him.

A few days later, at the Nassau Coliseum, Messier decked the smooth Islanders defenseman Kenny Jonsson with an open-ice elbow that left him with a concussion. There were echoes of the elbow Messier had thrown to knock Islanders rearguard Tomas Jonsson out of the Cup finals almost a decade and a half before. "We were coming from behind the net," the Isles' Darius Kasparaitis said, "and Messier elbowed [Jonsson] right in the face. He always does that. When you go to hit him, he sticks his elbow up. The ref should give more than a two-minute penalty. If I do this to Messier, I'm going to have maybe a game misconduct. Kenny's our main player. He could have helped us a lot." Messier said, "I didn't even know it was Kenny Jonsson until I went in the penalty box. It was just a normal play. I didn't even know what happened. I just hit him in the jaw." It was actually the cheek, but no matter. Such was the respect and admiration for Messier that even Mike Milbury, the Islanders' coach, praised it as a "good, stiff elbow" and "a classic Messier move—you get the other team's key guy with an elbow to the head."

Also on Messier's resume this season was a fight with the hard-rock Red Wings defenseman Vladimir Konstantinov that followed an interlude in which he repeatedly pushed Konstantinov's head into the ice; then there was a game against Ottawa in which he elbowed defenseman Frantisek Musil in the face and opened a cut in Kerry Huffman's face with a high stick.

What it says about North American hockey that so many observers admired this aspect of Messier's game is a basis for debate, but many forecasters figured the rugged Rangers, led by the rugged Messier, were contenders for the Stanley Cup. They opened against Montreal, and after dropping the first two games at home—with Messier going minus-5—it looked as if they would bow out quickly. But in Montreal, where New York had not won since Messier's first game as a Ranger back in 1991, the Blueshirts rebounded. Messier assisted on both goals in a 2–1 win in game three and scored another in a 4–3 win that tied the series. The Rangers received a lucky talisman from Susan Sarandon, who along with her husband, Tim Robbins, were friends of Messier's and frequent attendees at the Garden. She offered Messier her Oscar for *Dead Man Walking* to keep in the team's dressing room for good luck. It seemed to work. Jari Kurri, yet another ex-Oiler recycled and brought in at Messier's behest, had a goal in the Rangers' 3–2 win in game five. Before the sixth game, Habs coach Mario Tremblay took a page out of Messier's book by guaranteeing a victory, but it didn't work: a 5–3 victory gave New York four wins in a row and a trip to the quarterfinals against Pittsburgh.

Colin Campbell didn't exactly help his team's cause when he said before the series that the Penguins were "soft players" and "crybabies." After a game one loss, Messier set the tone for game two by splattering ex-teammate Sergei Zubov against the end glass just 30 seconds into the first period; later, he scored the game-breaking goal that evened the count and paved the way for the Rangers' victory. In game three at the Garden, Campbell double- and triple-shifted Messier, but the Lemieux–Jagr–Nedved line was too potent, and the Pens won narrowly. In the next game Messier threw elbows all over the place, but it did not deter Jagr, the main target of Messier's wrath, or the rest of the Penguins, who won easily. Unlike Neilson in '92, Campbell was putting Messier on the ice against Lemieux's line. But it wasn't helping. Back in Pittsburgh, the Pens closed out the series by a 7–3 score that featured hat tricks from Jagr and Lemieux. The Rangers, all bulked up to outmuscle Philly and New Jersey, all answering Messier's call to toughness, had instead been undone by the overwhelming speed and finesse of the Penguins, which they had mistaken for weakness. In the dressing room afterward, Messier seemed at a loss for why it had all gone so wrong, so quickly.

Former Oilers had been instrumental in winning the Cup for the Rangers in 1994, other former Oilers had been brought in since, and even if the later imports didn't work out as well as the first crop, the Rangers were still a very good team that seemed just a couple of steps away from recapturing glory. Why not, then, pursue the ultimate former Oiler?

Neil Smith had already tried; with Messier's encouragement, he bid for Wayne Gretzky's services when it was made clear early in the '95–96 season that Gretzky wanted to leave the rebuilding Kings. But Number 99 was instead dealt to St. Louis, where he teamed with Brett Hull and pushed the Blues through one playoff round and nearly through a second. But Mike Keenan hadn't changed; he managed to alienate even Gretzky, blaming him for a loss after one of the postseason games. That resulted in Blues' management withdrawing their lucrative offer to retain Gretzky after the season. The Great One bolted as soon as he was eligible, on Canada Day.

Three weeks later, he signed with New York and the chance to play nightly with his old pal Messier. So eager was he that he took a pay cut, down to $4 million a year. The Vancouver Canucks had made an offer that was actually a little better, but they pressured Gretzky to make an immediate decision. When they woke him with a late-night phone call demanding a yes-or-no answer, Gretzky chose the Rangers. "What tipped the scales was to play with Mark," he said, omitting the part about the Canucks at the Garden press conference heralding his arrival, "and with a team focused on winning a championship." Checketts relayed to reporters something he had told to Gretzky's agent Mike Barnett: "I said to Barnett, 'You can't send him to Vancouver, not to finish his career.' He doesn't deserve to go to a place where you never hear what he's doing or see him." The statement was astounding in the way it betrayed New York's self-centeredness and myopic view of where the real centers of the hockey world actually lie.

At the Rangers' news conference for Gretzky, Messier spoke about persuading his friend. "The last five years of my life have been the most incredible five years," Messier said. "Those are some of the things I tried to get across to Wayne when the decision-making was getting close to him coming here. But make no mistake about it. We're here for one thing, and that's to win the Stanley Cup."

All the reports that followed the announcement, and indeed those filed throughout the season, focused on Gretzky's status as second banana in New York. Would his ego accept that billing? Would Messier feel as though his territory was being encroached upon? These were, of course, ridiculous questions, usually asked by American reporters unfamiliar with the players' work together over the years in Edmonton, at the Canada Cup, and as recently as the Ninety-Nine All-Stars tour. The subject was broached with Messier at the news conference, and he answered, "It's so natural for us, it isn't even an issue. Our styles complement each other." Gretzky was asked, too, whether he could stand being 1B to Messier's 1A. "Mark and I have been best friends since we were eighteen years old," he said. "I don't care if I'm 3B."

In August, the two were reunited on yet another Team Canada, this one in the World Cup of Hockey, the successor tournament to the Canada Cup. (Alan Eagleson, the mastermind behind the Canada Cup. had been dethroned and brought to trial for his mismanagement of the NHLPA pension fund and for personal use of revenues from the tournaments. Under the new CBA, the World Cup was created to restock the coffers of the players' pension fund.) This time there were to be no embarrassing cuts, no players breaking their teammates' arms to show they can make the grade—all twenty-six Canadians invited would be on the final roster. Mike Keenan, the coach of the last two victorious editions of Team Canada, was not chosen this time; instead, Sather, the GM, asked Scotty Bowman to run the bench. But after Bowman helped select the team he dropped out as coach, and Sather decided to take over that duty as well, even though it had been quite some time since he'd stood behind a bench. Gretzky was captain, Messier and Paul Coffey the co-captains.

The team was a bit older than before; it seemed that Canada was no longer producing quite so many young players of note. Mario Lemieux and Al MacInnis were unavailable because of injury. Ray Bourque stayed home to spend time with his family, despite phone calls from Sather, Gretzky, and Messier pleading with him to change his mind. Still, Canada had Lindros, Graves, Steve Yzerman, Brendan Shanahan, Trevor Linden, Theoren Fleury, Scott Stevens, Rob Blake, Eric Desjardins, Scott Niedermayer, and several other players of enough skill to make the Canadians favorites to lift a fourth straight world title—not least because Gretzky and Messier, the stars of '84, '87, and '91, were still forces to be reckoned with. "What is at stake is supremacy in hockey, and it's belonged to us for a number of years," Messier said on the eve of the opener. "Canada's forte is playing with emotion and its physical play."

Canada's first game, in Vancouver, was against Russia, and despite the passage of five years since the end of the Soviet Union, there was still plenty of old-style aggro between the two sides. Messier wowed everyone with two thread-needle passes that set up goals by Desjardins and Shanahan. Canada

had a 4–3 lead in the final minutes when Sergei Nemchinov put the puck
in the net—only to have the goal waved off because Russia had too many
men on the ice. It was the team's second tally to be called back. Gretzky
scored on the ensuing two-man advantage to make the final score 5–3.

The next outing was against the United States in Philadelphia. A huge
brawl started just twenty seconds into the game; four players received majors
for fighting and two of them earned game misconducts. Gretzky and Messier
scored to make it 2–1 for the northerners after one, but the Amerks roared
back to win, 5–3, behind a pair by Brett Hull, born and raised in Ontario
and British Columbia but playing for the U.S., the country that first offered
him a spot on its national team. It was the first time the USA had ever
beaten Canada in these competitions—its record against Canada now stood
at 1–7–1. The Americans had turned a corner.

Canada, meanwhile, struggled to get past Slovakia, 3–2, in a game in
which Shanahan went berserk, NHL-style, and slashed and slew-footed
Slovaks all over the ice. They sleepwalked past Germany, 4–1, to reach the
semifinals against Sweden. At various times Messier played on a line with
Shanahan and small, scrappy Pat Verbeek, then with Lindros and Graves,
then on something dubbed the "Take No Prisoners" Line with Lindros and
Shanahan. The Canadians were 3–1–0, but unimpressively so—their usual
modus operandi in the early stages of these top-tier international tournaments. Messier had a goal and three assists, but he was ineffective in the
semifinal in Philadelphia, when Sweden scored two unanswered goals in the
third to send the game into overtime—Canada needed a goal from Fleury in
the second overtime to advance.

Both Gretzky and Messier were hurting, Gretzky with a strained back
and Messier with a pulled groin, but they played the whole way. Christie
Blatchford, writing in *The Toronto Sun*, described the scene in the corridor
after the Sweden game: "'He's Mark Messier,' Sather snapped. 'Nobody else
could have done that.' Someone from the training staff walked past him as
he said it and shook his head in awe at the old boys. 'They can still do it,
can't they?' Sather said. The man answered, 'They still do it because they're
the greatest players in the game.'"

Messier also was suffering from an increasingly severe case of the flu. In
the overtime against Sweden he became dizzy and later said he had trouble

seeing out of his right eye. The symptoms persisted in the later stages of the first game of the best-of-three final, in Philadelphia against the U.S., but you couldn't tell from watching him. Messier had a great game, setting up a goal by Claude Lemieux that helped the Canadians to a lead that stood at 3–2 with just nine seconds left. Messier stepped in to take a draw against Joel Otto in the Canada end, but Kevin Collins, an excellent veteran linesman who on this night had uncharacteristically blown a number of calls, threw him out of the face-off circle. Graves took Messier's place and lost the draw. A shot went to the Canadian net and lay in the crease, unseen by goalie Curtis Joseph. Desjardins tried to sweep the puck under Joseph's pads but wound up putting it into his own net instead. The error should have been demoralizing for the Canadians, but they dominated the overtime period and won on Yzerman's goal—on a play that was definitely offside, Collins having missed the call.

Messier was on the sidelines when the finals shifted to Montreal for game two. The stomach flu had left him dehydrated with congested head and lungs and sent him to bed for forty-eight hours. Many wondered how Canada would fare without its inspirational leader; they remarked on how, when players put on their country's sweater, old animosities were put on hold. Messier was identified as the ideal in this regard. After all, he had made it a point when with Edmonton never to talk to Calgary Flames players, but after Fleury's goal beat the Swedes, he and Messier embraced, forehead to forehead, howling in celebration. Without the camaraderie Messier seemed to bring to the Canadian team, could they beat the U.S.?

The answer probably would have been yes had Richter not been brilliant in the American nets. He stopped 35 of 37 shots and preserved a thin one-goal lead in the last minutes before a pair of empty-netters made the score a more flattering 5–2 for the Amerks. Hulking Keith Primeau played in Messier's place and was ineffective. "We definitely felt the loss of Mark; there's no question he's the emotional leader of this team," Sather pointed out afterward. "You don't replace Mark," Gretzky said. "Get us some IV tomorrow, willya?"

Before the deciding game at the Molson Centre, all the Canadian players, coaches, commentators, and fans spoke about the vaunted Canadian heart, and as if to embody that quality, Messier announced that he would play, no matter what. But Canadians acted as though simply evoking their "heart" would be proof against whatever the Americans threw at them. Any neutral observer could see how naïve this belief was, not only because of its gorm-lessness, but also because the Canadians and Americans played exactly the same style, one that depended on hard hitting and hard skating. It was not as if the final was a clash of philosophies, as Team Canada's previous apoca-lyptic finales against the Soviets, Swedes, or Czechoslovaks had been.

Richter was superb again from the start of the rubber match, nursing a 1–0 lead until six seconds remained in the second period, when Lindros scored on a two-man advantage with Canada's 34th shot. With seven min-utes to go in the third period Adam Foote gave Canada a 2–1 lead that seemed to follow the expected script for the heart-and-soul Canucks. But Hull, who played the tourney's final games under taunts of "Traitor! Traitor!" from the partisan Montreal crowd, tipped in a shot with 3:18 to go and tied the score. Canada argued that Hull had held his stick too high, but replays were inconclusive and the goal stood. Just 43 seconds later, Tony Amonte scored, and incredibly, the USA led—but only after another delay for a replay, which again affirmed the goal. The crowd was silent, shocked into disbelief.

The Canadians were desperate to equalize. With less than 50 seconds left and an extra attacker on the ice, Messier found Gretzky open behind Richter—but his pass hopped over Gretzky's stick. Seven seconds later, Derian Hatcher scored into Canada's empty net. Then Adam Deadmarsh scored into the empty net to make it 5–2.

The Americans were world champions. They'd won in Canada, playing Canada's game, using a Canadian style, and they'd even shown more "Canadian" heart. It was truly a shocking victory for the U.S.—and the sad thing was that although all of Canada mourned, almost no one south of the border even noticed.

Messier finished the tournament with a goal and four assists in seven games, and a minus-5 rating that looked worse than it was because of the empty-netters. Considering his bad groin and respiratory infection, he'd played well. But as was so often true with Messier, it was the intangibles he provided that made him so special. The U.S. coach, Ron Wilson, acknowl-edged this in a telling way. "I kept hearing that we weren't tough," he said after the game. "I heard a lot of whispers that we didn't have what it takes. I heard people talk about how Mark Messier was going to come riding in on his horse to save the Canadians. Well, we showed how tough we were tonight."

Messier said all the correct, gracious things after the game. But a week later he said something very strange. In Las Vegas for the Rangers' preseason opener, the New York press corps, which had not been present for the World Cup, asked him about the tournament and what it was like to play against his Rangers teammates. "Leetchie and Richter were the two best players for the U.S.," he said. "To go out and take Leetchie's head off to slow him down, I found that very difficult. I didn't enjoy it that much. And because of that, I don't know if I'll play in another one. And because of the Olympics [NHL players were to take part in the Winter Games in Nagano, Japan in 1998], I don't know if we need another Canada Cup or World Cup again."

Messier described his pride at how well Leetch and Richter were playing for the Americans. "That's where the whole conflict came in," he said. "I found myself being distracted about it. And I didn't like the feeling, to be totally honest. I just wasn't about to go out and try to hurt Brian in that tournament. It just didn't make much sense to me. When push came to shove, I found it very difficult to play that type of hockey when I knew, two weeks from then, I was going to go back to playing with those guys for the thing we really grow up learning to play for." What he was saying, though not in so many words, was that playing for the Stanley Cup had turned out to be more important to him than playing for his country.

Back in 1984, he said, when there were no Russians in the NHL, it was easier to play international events with "a take-no-prisoners attitude," as he put it. But now it was a different story. Gretzky saw the change in Messier, too. "He's a power player," Gretzky said. "Mark's biggest strength is he really dislikes opponents. I know it was killing him because he didn't want to hurt Brian Leetch. To be effective, we had to eliminate him. One reason why we lost was because we didn't." None of what Messier or Gretzky was saying was being offered as self-criticism; rather, it was meant to show how close-knit and focused on the single goal of the Stanley Cup the Rangers were. But it was a jarring admission. How could Messier, who knew everything there was to know about competitiveness and fire and winning, hold back when his nation's hopes were riding on his shoulders? And why was it imperative that he *slaughter* Leetch in order to neutralize him? Would not a simple body-check have been sufficient?

"It wasn't easy to focus on the intricacies of the game—intimidation—and to be willing to do what you had to do to win," Messier said. But why not? Or better still, why was intimidation so important? It was at the root of Messier's game, as it was of Canada's. So was emotion. But for Messier, emotions became clouded when he was wearing the maple leaf, not the word "Rangers," on his chest. Bob Goodenow, whose union benefited from the World Cup, did not think that excessive chumminess among the players mitigated the tournament in any way. "It's not a problem, because I don't think there are any more than four or five guys whose trademark game is intimidation like Mark's," he said, although he allowed that "I can see Mark's difficulty because of the unique type of player he is."

Elite-level players in various sports all around the world, when playing for their countries, often compete against their club teammates in international matches. For them, it's simply not a problem, whether they embrace warmly before and after the match or not. Some of those sports can be violent, like rugby, water polo, or, sometimes, soccer. Hockey is a violent game, too, but teammates have faced off against each other in international competitions for generations. Yet in 1996, Messier found that he was troubled by such confrontation, and no matter how bravely he played through illness and injury, the man who had helped lead Canada to three world titles held back when a fourth was on the line. It was the first time doubt had ever entered his warrior psyche.

He did not know it, but history would prove that at this very moment, Mark Messier ceased to be an effective leader.

THE LAST FINE TIME

For Messier, the 1996–97 season beckoned with the sheen of an incipient golden age. He was reunited with Wayne Gretzky, and the promise of fun and success and acclaim was palpable. It marked the debut of Messier as shtickmeister, as he teamed up with his old friend for a couple of promo spots for the Fox network's hockey coverage. In one, the two of them played chess, Gretzky representing the cerebral, creative approach to hockey by painstakingly moving a pawn, Messier embodying the brute-force approach by knocking the board and the pieces all over the floor. The second was a spot-on spoof of the opening to *The Odd Couple*, with Gretzky in the role of the fastidious Felix Unger and Messier as the slovenly Oscar Madison; standing in front of an Upper West Side apartment house, Gretzky disposes of the apple core Messier has dropped in the gutter.

The national media, for what would turn out to be the last time, was paying attention to the Rangers. Gretzky appeared on the Letterman show, and Messier strolled out, Bob Hope-style, for a cameo appearance.

(Characteristically, Messier commandeered the interview as well, as Gretzky conceded the chair of honor next to the host without even having to be asked.) They shared the cover of *Sports Illustrated*. They were profiled in *The New York Times Magazine*. It was the feel-good sports story of the year.

Gretzky's regular-season home debut as a Ranger was given the by now obligatory smoke-and-lasers treatment. Amid the billowing vapors of dry ice, the Garden crowd gave Gretzky a big ovation, but they gave Messier a still bigger one. The Rangers then played the Florida Panthers, the Cup finalists the previous year by virtue of their unstinting devotion to the neutral-zone trap, and lost, 5–2. Gretzky did little of note, but Messier smashed the Panthers' Mike Hough into the boards from behind, leaving him dazed and confused and flat on the ice for about a minute. Messier was ejected with a boarding major and wound up with a two-game suspension.

The Rangers struggled through the first portion of their schedule, but Messier bailed the team out repeatedly. On a western road trip that many thought would go disastrously enough to cost Colin Campbell his coaching job, he came through with nine goals in six games, notching, for instance, all the Rangers' tallies in a 3–1 win over Phoenix and two in a 5–2 upset at Colorado. And he had the flu while he did this.

Beginning with the early part of the schedule and escalating as the season went on, writers began speculating that a clash of egos was developing between the two superstars. These rumors gained momentum as the season went on. The supporting evidence for this contention was sketchy, but supposedly added up to a persuasive argument. There was the time Messier missed a few games to injury and Gretzky skated out suddenly wearing the captain's C on his sweater, even though he had not previously been one of the alternate captains. They were not seen out on the town together very much, and sometimes they stood at opposite ends of the room when they were at the same function. Still, no one could produce any hard evidence of strife. When Frank Brown of the *Daily News* visited the penthouse apartment Gretzky, his wife, Janet, and their three kids shared on East 57th Street, Gretzky told him what his six-year-old son Ty said after his first day with his new rec-league team: "I said to Ty, 'What number have you got?' He said, 'I got the best number.' I said, 'What number did you get—99?' He said, 'No, 11.'"

But if anyone in New York knew how little substance was behind the rumors that Messier's friendship with his old teammate and captain had waned, it was Sultan Captan, who spent hours with the two nearly every day.

Captan is perhaps an unlikely arbiter in hockey matters. He is a shaven-headed man of medium height and fairly trim build who grew up in Lebanon and Liberia, went to college in California, and then settled in New York, where he worked as a vendor and eventually owned a jewelry store.

But one night early in 1994 he was at a bar on the East Side of Manhattan when he met Mike Richter, who had been told that rubbing Captan's bald pate would bring good luck. Captan didn't follow hockey, so he didn't know who Richter was, but they got along well during their fifteen-minute conversation, which included a quick rub of Captan's head. The Rangers went on a tear for the rest of the season, culminating in their ecstatic Stanley Cup victory.

In a different bar at the start of the next season, Captan met defenseman Brian Leetch, who had heard from Richter about the bald man whose head had brought luck to the Rangers. Leetch told Captan to come back to the bar in a couple of nights because Richter would be there. So he did, and the Rangers, who had just returned from a road game in Montreal, were all assembled in the bar. Leetch brought Richter over to Captan, and they renewed their acquaintance. Captan could see the other Rangers looking at him and talking to one another. "That's the guy," they were saying; Captan's reputation had preceded him. He met the other players, and they all got along well. At one point he went over to introduce himself to Mark Messier, but Messier mistook him for a fan and gave him, in Captan's words, "the cold shoulder." But the next couple of times Captan ran into the Rangers, Messier saw that Captan was friendly with many of his own friends. Over the course of the next few months, Captan started hanging out with the Rangers, everyone who played on the '94–95 team, including Mark Messier.

From then on, whenever Captan encountered Messier at Manhattan bars, they got along famously. Soon the two had an arrangement by which Captan became part of Messier's entourage, helping Messier and his family arrange things, hanging out, entertaining, and carrying out the occasional task or errand—as Captan puts it, an "unpaid escort"—and in exchange Messier picked up the tab. The Messier entourage hit Manhattan nightspots, like the China Club, Ferrier, and Au Bar, and over the next couple of years he and Messier became very close, "like brothers," Captan says. "It was very intimate. He relied on me. I'd have breakfast at his house. We had a very close relationship, and I got to know him very well. He's sharp, focused, stubborn, and curious, like a cat—always interested in new experiences."

Messier found a new friend in early December. The Rangers served as escorts for a group of runway models at a charity event held at Wollman Rink, the outdoor arena set picturesquely in the southeast corner of Central Park. The group, called D.I.S.H.E.S., was staging the event to benefit research into pediatric AIDS. But even though it was taking place on the ice, there was only one model there who could skate: Frederique van der Wal, one of the lead lingerie models for Victoria's Secret, who was better known professionally simply by her first name. Smart, leggy, athletic, Dutch, and, it bears repeating, leggy, her fame and fees were such that she qualified as a supermodel. Frederique remembers saying to Messier, as they stood on the rink in their skates, "'Since I used to play ice hockey on our pond as a kid, I'll take you one-on-one.' Can you imagine? Well, I passed him, and he was in shock." They started going out, and soon the city's gossip columns were noting Messier's presence in the front row at lingerie shows and the couple's presence at various clubs, restaurants, and openings around town.

By now Messier had long shed all vestiges of rubehood. He was still every inch a rugged hockey player, but he was also sophisticated and worldly. When he first arrived in New York, his dress sometimes veered dangerously close to a quasi-pimp look, but by now it was sharp, flash, and fashion-forward. He favored Kangol caps that referenced the black street style of the early '70s, jackets that cleverly crossed the Nehru cut with a kind of leisure-suit effect, and the latest in cool sunglasses. He had his fans among women and gay men, and with the rise of the Internet throughout the '90s, Messier's attractiveness became an oft-discussed topic that proliferated through chat groups and on homemade Web sites. Some thought him ugly, but more lusted after him, and a few fairly explicit fantasies found their way into the mix. By the '96–97 season, Messier's bald head was often the focus of discussions of his sex appeal.

People in Canada had been having those discussions for quite some time; it's just that previously, before the ubiquity of the Internet made them privy to everyone, they existed only as an undercurrent. Messier's allegedly prodigious sexual appetite served as the basis for story after story, passed around, growing, mutating, like an urban legend. What is curious is how these stories, or versions of them, are known to so many in Canada—and to so few in the United States and especially New York, where, after all, Messier has spent so many years. It may have something to do with the stature that hockey players hold in Canada, where they stand atop the pyramid of sports celebrity, yet at the same time are familiar to everyone, because practically every Canadian seems to have some personal connection to a hockey star. In the States, geography and the sheer size of the population combine to make athletes remote figures; most individual Americans do *not* know a big-league jock, and there is little speculation on the personal life of any athlete—even Michael Jordan.

In Edmonton, the young, charismatic, party-hearty Oilers were the topic of much speculation and admiration, from all quarters. One such admirer is Darrin Hagen, a drag actor, playwright, television host, and author of *The Edmonton Queen*, a memoir of his days as one of the city's most fabulous personages in the 1980s. During the Oilers' glory days, Hagen was working as bartender and head drag queen at Flashback, a bar in the downtown warehouse district. "It was a drag version of Studio 54," Hagen says, "or as close to Studio 54 as you could get on the Prairies. If you wanted to do anything special in Edmonton, you did it there. It was not just a gay bar or a drag bar, but a swinger place, a meat market. Anyway, one time, Mark Messier and his brother were in, way after hours. One of my drag daughters, Ora Fice—she's no longer with us, so I can tell this story—was behind the bar, serving illegally. She was making Paralyzers, only they were her own version, with both vodka and tequila. She called it an Oralyzer. So I'm working there and all of a sudden my drag offspring comes in and says, 'Oh my god, I got Mark Messier and his brother so bombed tonight!'"

What Hagen describes seems pretty tame by today's standards, but in Edmonton in the mid-'80s, there was still a huge divide between the straight world and the "demimonde" that Flashback represented. That Messier felt at ease enough to go there to drink after hours may have been taken by some as a sign of wild and bizarre tendencies, but it more likely speaks to a natural curiosity about and comfort level with all different kinds of people and places.

Because their rise to prominence happened to coincide with the rise of the first proudly out gay generation, the '80s Oilers drew a lot of comment in certain circles; they were the first sports dynasty Canadian gay men could openly ogle. "I can't tell you how 'the gay community' felt about the Oilers, because every one of us is different," Hagen says. "I can only speak for myself. I had a friend, Daryl, a huge Oilers fan. He wasn't butch; he was a queen, in fact. But he loved the Oilers and he loved Wayne Gretzky. When Gretzky got married to Janet Jones, Daryl sat in my living room and cried. He was going to marry Wayne Gretzky, but now his dream was ended. I don't find Wayne Gretzky attractive. Mark Messier has his moments, though. He has a weird, scary kind of intensity—it can be very sexy. And he's got that big daddy thing going, with the receding hairline. And I love his laugh."

Captan was to hear this laugh often. Late in 1996, Messier decided that he wanted to have his own car and driver, and he asked Captan if he wanted the job. "When Mark asked me, he leveled with me right off," says Captan. "He said to me, 'Sultie, I want you to work for me, but you've got to understand, it's going to be every day, seven days a week. Sometimes you won't be able to hang out with us. Whenever I need you, you've got to be there. You'd be working for me, but you might be driving me, my family, my friends. Wherever I go when I'm here in New York, you've got to go, too. It'll be hard. Do you think you could handle that?' I told him that I gave my word that I'd be fully committed, and that was that—I was hired. First thing I did was go out and buy an Armani suit, because he was always dressed sharp, and I wanted to show him that I was going to do this job all the way."

Captan's job was to drive Messier's Lincoln Town Car—a simple black sedan indistinguishable from thousands of other Town Cars plying the streets of New York. Before Messier hired Captan, he and his party often got around in a chauffeured stretch limousine, a dead giveaway that whoever inside was very rich, very important, or simply willing to blow some money to look very rich or important. But when Wayne Gretzky arrived in New York in the fall of 1996, Messier wanted something more private, someplace where he and Gretzky could be alone together, without the distraction of others inside and without attracting the attention of those outside. Unlike a stretch limo, a black Town Car could have anyone inside—maybe a VIP being chauffeured around town, but more likely an office worker getting an expense-account ride home after a late night battling a deadline or, say, a young woman taking a gypsy cab from a part of town where regular taxis don't stop for street hails.

Captan lived on the East Side and kept the car in a garage on East 90th Street, close to his home. On mornings when the Rangers were in town and there was a practice at the team's facility in Rye, he'd get up and get the car around 6:30, take it to be washed, pick up Gretzky, and take the quick crosstown drive through Central Park to Messier's apartment on West 75th Street. By 8:30 they'd pick up Messier's West Side neighbor Brian Leetch, and then get onto the West Side Highway for the forty-five-minute drive north to suburban Rye. Sometimes Messier would drive, in which case Captan would sit in the back seat with Gretzky, and sometimes Captan would not make the trip up to Rye at all, leaving the three players to make the drive themselves. Sometimes Captan would pick up Messier from practice or from the airport in White Plains, where the team's private jet was based, and would have no idea where they were headed next. "It was often a mystery with Mark, where we were going," Captan says. "It might be a benefit meeting, or to shoot a commercial or to get examined by a doctor. If he didn't want people to know about something, he knew how to keep it a secret."

If there was a home game, Captan would get over to Messier's house, his boss always waiting to be picked up at the stroke of four, and then drive him the forty blocks to the Garden. At the game, he'd wait in the family lounge, where he was known as Messier's guy, and have to field numerous requests for meetings with the great man and answer questions about which place Messier had chosen for the night's postgame revels. Later, after Messier had announced to Captan what the destination would be and who should be informed, they would go to the various nightspots, where Captan would wait dutifully, often into the wee hours, never taking a drink himself because he was driving, after all. This was the routine, although Captan did not see it as one; rather, he viewed it as a chance to observe and experience at close quarters the life of a revered athlete in New York. From his spot in the driver's seat or just down the bar, he was an integral part of Messier's life for some three years. They were so close, and so frequently seen in each other's company, Captan says, that people would think the two bald men were related.

Messier got a kick out of that, and would sometimes refer to himself and Sultan as "Captain and Captan."

"I have never met anyone as focused as Mark," Captan says. "When he sets his mind to something, that thing is going to happen. I saw that all the time in social situations. He was always arranging things, taking players aside, rookies, young guys, and making sure they were invited out, made sure they got where they were supposed to go. Mark was always coming up to me and saying, 'Sultie, give him a ride home,' or 'Be certain to get him over to this bar or that bar by midnight, because we're all meeting there,' things like that. And pretty soon everyone on the team figured they had to be nice to me, because I was the boss's hand. I was his guy, and he made the call about where everyone was going to go, where the party was going to be. And Mark definitely was the party. When he goes into a room, he lights it up. It's like the party has started."

More often than anyplace else, the party was at an Upper East Side establishment called the Auction House. It is a smallish place divided neatly into two rooms with a bar in each. There is a policy in force that no one under the age of twenty-five can enter, which perhaps accounts for the faintly sophisticated, debauched air about the place, and although it's a far cry from what might be called bohemian, it does tend to draw an attractive crowd. It was where the Rangers wound up taking the Cup during their epic all-night party on June 14, 1994. The nights in 1996–97 were less eventful, obviously, but there was still a penumbra around the Rangers and especially Messier, the afterglow of that Stanley Cup victory. Captan would pull up in front of the Auction House with Messier and whoever else was with him, and then run interference so that Messier could set himself up in his accustomed spot in the room closer to Second Avenue, at the corner of the bar near the back wall, close to the small men's and women's rooms. Captan would then position himself a few steps farther back, against the wall at the bartender's entrance, so that he could get a view of the whole room. "He wanted to be able to see everything that was going on, and so did I, because you never knew how people were going to act when they saw him. One time there was a woman who was obviously drunk, and she kept calling over at Mark, but he paid her no attention. But I was watching, and finally she picks up a glass candle holder and thrusts it right at his face. I was standing behind her and quickly got hold of her hand, took the candle away, and put it down. Mark looks at me, shocked, like, 'Whoa!' He was a bit shaken up, then he says to me, 'Sultie, you're *fast*! That was awesome!'

"But that kind of thing didn't happen very much. People would want to talk to him or shake his hand, and I'd have to get between him and them if he was trying to get somewhere. One time, I saw someone in a crowd at the China Club trying to get to him, so I got in front of Mark and shoved the guy a little bit, and it turned out to be Bruce Willis. He joked about it with me later. Something about bald guys sticking together. But no one ever came up to Mark to challenge him to a fight or anything. People treated him with respect, or they were sort of in awe of him." Indeed, throughout Messier's nearly decade-long, two-part tenure in New York, he has never once been involved in an "incident," despite being out on the town with frequent regularity. Yet in that same period, several Knicks, Giants, Yankees, and Mets stars have endured various extracurricular tabloid controversies, ranging from Lawrence Taylor's run-ins with the law over his cocaine habit that stretched into the early '90s, through a series of fistfights involving various Knicks at the China Club in the middle of the decade, all the way up to David Wells' argument and fight with a Yankees fan in 2002.

Still, Messier did not avoid this kind of notoriety by confining his New York nightlife to visits to the Metropolitan Opera. "After a game," Sultan says, "if there was a break in the schedule, he'd usually go out. He was very responsible about it—if there was a game coming up in the next day or two, or if he needed rest, he'd go right home after dinner and that was that. But if there was no game for a couple of days, he'd be out till two, three, four in the morning, and wherever he was, there was always something going on. And yes, there were always women around. He liked good-looking women. One night at the Auction House, I remember there was a beautiful woman, very petite. I had never seen Mark dance, but this night he started dancing with her, and it was unbelievable. He was twirling her around, flipping her upside down—it was amazing. He's a fantastic dancer. No matter who was around, he behaved the same way, and his family would often come out with him to the Auction House. Generally, his mom would be the first to go home, then maybe Mary-Kay and her husband, but often Doug and Paul would stay out with him. They'd all be having a great time, but Mark would do whatever he wanted no matter who was around."

Messier does have a reputation as a relentless carouser, but he has also been involved in more exclusive relationships. During some of the time Messier employed Captan, he was involved with Frederique, the statuesque lingerie model from the Netherlands, who at five-foot-eleven was only a couple of inches shorter than Messier himself. "The two of them, when they were going out, really did act like a couple. They'd go to the movies together on a Sunday afternoon or go to dinner a lot by themselves. They'd try all kinds of different restaurants—Italian, Japanese, French, Chinese—all over town. She lived in the West Village and she knew all the places downtown, so they'd go there. They would go to premieres and events, and their picture was always in the [New York] *Post* on Page Six, and people always wanted them to come out—I remember once Eddie Murphy trying to go to some party with them—but they'd usually say they couldn't, then they'd go off and have a quiet dinner somewhere themselves."

Captan started working for Messier in December 1996, during the one season in New York when Messier played alongside Wayne Gretzky. The belief in New York is that the close friendship between the two deteriorated during their season together, that the two had some kind of falling out over an inability to reconcile who was expected to be the leader of the team. But Captan saw nothing like that. "At parties, they'd generally be on different sides of the room, but that was because they had their own families around them, and then Wayne would go home kind of early because he had little kids at home and he was very involved with them. There was no rift between Mark and Wayne. In fact, at those parties, even though they were in different parts of the room, they'd sometimes exchange a glance, and there was a lot there—you could tell there was a very, very strong bond between the two of them.

"I know there was a very strong bond, because in that Town Car it was just Mark, Wayne, and me. Whenever they got back from a road trip their plane would land at White Plains airport, and I'd pick them up and drive them into town. That's a good hour they'd be in the car together, talking the whole way. They would talk about things, almost always about hockey—who on the Rangers they could believe in, who they needed [to acquire]. And every time, Wayne would tell Mark to tell me that I shouldn't say anything I heard to anyone. Mark knew I could be trusted, but because Wayne wasn't sure, Mark would reassure him by saying to me, 'Sultie, what Wayne and I were saying, that stays here. Don't tell the guys,' which meant the other players or anyone else, so I didn't even tell Mark's family. Mark and Wayne would discuss strategy, what to do against certain players on other teams, where to shoot on goalies, what had happened in the last game. They were always talking about their legs. 'My legs were heavy tonight,' Mark would say, or 'I didn't have my legs,' or 'My legs felt good.' Always 'the legs.' As the season went on, their talk became more intense. Eventually it became about preparing for the playoffs, then it became the playoffs themselves, and it got even more intense. By now I had learned a lot about hockey and how to look for all the subtle things that go on, and I began to see—the things they'd talked about in the car, they'd happen right on the ice! Wayne and Mark, they'd make it happen in the game itself.

"It's funny—as strong as their bond was, as close as they were, they are really very, very different types of people. Mark is very punctual—the most punctual person I've ever met. When he says he's going to be somewhere at five o'clock, he's there *at* five, and he's never a minute late. And he expected the same from me and from everyone else, too. He's very serious about that. Wayne, on the other hand, is a much looser type of person. The nicest, most gracious guy in the world, too, and pretty often he'd be a bit late. So we'd be late to get to Mark's, and later Mark would make eye contact with me, and I understood that to mean, 'Why were you late?' I'd glance over at Wayne, and Mark would understand. Later, he'd tell me, 'Listen, it doesn't matter if Wayne is a big star, try to get him here on time. Call him from the car if you have to. Don't let him make us late.' But the thing about Wayne is that he's so down-to-earth, just a regular guy, very polite. He'd always go out of his way to thank me for driving him. It was always a pleasure dealing with him.

"The time that was most amazing with those two was during the playoffs in '97. Every night those two were in the car together, talking about what they were going to do in the next game. And it was top secret. It was incredible, and in that first round against Florida, Gretzky was unstoppable, and he'd score exactly the way they'd discussed it. Then against New Jersey they'd talk about how they'd beat [Devils goalie Martin] Brodeur, and sure enough they beat him that way. And because I had a bond with Mark, I bonded with Wayne, too. It felt like family."

Captan also got to know Messier's actual family very well over the nearly three years of his time with Mark. He and Doug got along well, he says; Captan would ask Doug to explain hockey to him, Doug would oblige, and Captan would return the favor by telling Doug all about the city. Doug was big and bluff and liked a good time, while his wife, Mary Jean, was quiet and retiring in public. "But once she got behind closed doors," Captan remembers, "she had some very strong opinions, and she expressed them strongly too. She is one tough lady." Messier's sister Mary-Kay was very involved in her brother's business affairs, and Paul was too, although to a lesser extent. Mark's younger sister, Jennifer, whom Captan recalls as being "a very nice young woman," was the least involved in the family enterprise that revolved around Mark. But the remarkable thing about Messier is the strength of the bonds of family, and how those bonds were replicated among friendships and other relationships. What Captan observed was the creation and maintaining of similar ties by Messier with his hockey-playing peers, with friends, with girlfriends, and even with members of his retinue. Each relationship seemed to carry about it an aura of specialness, one that required a sense of loyalty above and beyond that which would exist in most friendships. You are either inside this circle of Messier's trust or you are not, and those who are on the inside are very respectful of their status.

In mid-December Messier missed four games with a hyperextended left elbow. He returned for a game against Kevin Haller, now with Hartford, and although he didn't square off with him, Gretzky did—a brief, flailing flurry in which the Great One earned a rare roughing penalty. The Rangers won the game, 5–2, and went over .500 for the first time. Gretzky had a goal and an assist and took over the league lead in the scoring race.

Gretzky did not hold onto that lead, but he did play very well the rest of the season and finished fifth overall in scoring. Messier's injuries accumulated and slowed him down as the schedule progressed, but he too had a creditable campaign. They were both now 36 years old, yet still believed in their abilities. "Sometimes I feel like I could play for another ten years," Messier said. The Rangers kept their heads just above the .500 mark, a modest regular-season performance that left them 38–34–10 and in third place in their division. Messier finished the season with 84 points (36 goals and

48 assists) in 71 games. Along the way he reached the 1,500-point plateau, only the fifth player in league history to get there.

But as much as he was enjoying life off the ice, he seemed to play much of the season's second half in a foul mood. In a game in Calgary, he dropped the gloves and pummeled the smallish, relatively well-behaved Todd Hlushko after Hlushko supposedly elbowed Leetch and caught Alexei Kovalev with a late hit. At other junctures he got into a fight with his fearsome former teammate, Marty McSorley; he initiated a feud with referee Don Van Massenhoven over an alleged missed call that may have led to a referees' vendetta against the Rangers; and he pulled a snit with management over personnel moves, further souring the atmosphere around the team. Sometimes Messier seemed to be acting in much the same way he had when he was publicly at odds with Roger Neilson.

Messier's petulance had at its base two causes: first, he was worn down and carrying a frightening load of injuries to his wrist, elbow, ribs, and thigh, on top of lingering effects of the virus that struck him during the Canada Cup. More to the point, though, was the new contract dispute developing between him and his father on the one side, and Neil Smith and the Garden on the other. The '96–97 season was the last on Messier's contract, and he grew surlier as springtime approached. Inevitably, there'd have to be a new negotiation. If it was anything like the previous one, it was sure to be highly unpleasant, with the Rangers looking to cut the pay of their aging captain, and Messier seeking a monetary expression of the respect he thought he deserved.

The Rangers started their postseason in Miami against the Florida Panthers, the team they had opened their season against, and who had gotten to the Cup final in '96. It would be a test of styles, the attack-minded but creaky Rangers against the epitome of a mediocre team made strong through the cynical ploy of the trap. Most people thought Florida would win easily, and even Messier sounded sardonic when asked whether he was confident in the Rangers' chances. "Yeah, absolutely," he said. "With the shaky season we've had, we remain pretty confident."

The teams traded 3–0 shutouts to start the series, and the Rangers were losing, 3–2, in the dying seconds of game three in New York. With an extra attacker on the ice, Messier and Gretzky wreaked havoc in the Florida zone until they worked the puck to Luc Robitaille, who tied it with 18 seconds left. Tikkanen, reacquired in a late-season trade, won it in overtime. After that Gretzky took over, scoring a pure hat trick in a 3–2 victory in the fourth game. Then it was Messier's turn. In the series-clinching 3–2 repeat win, he scored twice, doled out several rugged body checks, and set up Tikkanen for another overtime winner. The ex-Oilers had done it again.

In the quarterfinals, the Rangers faced their foes from across the Hudson, the New Jersey Devils, another archetype of the trap. The Rangers had by now taken to using the trap themselves; they were sending one passive forechecker into the attacking zone, and his job was to force the flow over to the side of the boards in the neutral zone, where the other forwards waited to clog things up some more and hope for a turnover. No one was exempt from Colin Campbell's plan, not even Messier—even though it was exactly the kind of tactic that Messier got Neilson fired for trying to use a few years before. New York lost the first game, then won the next four in a row, relatively easily. (The tone for the Rangers' victory was allegedly set in game two, when Messier cross-checked Gretzky's shadow, Doug Gilmour, in the face and got away unpenalized.)

The Rangers were through to the semifinals, and Gretzky's performance was captivating everyone; he was scoring goals like younger self. After the Rangers lost the first game of the semifinal round against Philadelphia, Campbell put together a line of Messier, Gretzky, and Tikkanen and freed them to attack without concerning themselves with the trap. They accounted for four goals in game two—three of them by Gretzky, one by Messier—in a 5–4 victory that evened the series.

That turned out to be the last hurrah for the two old friends. The next game was dominated by the Flyers' huge dreadnought, Eric Lindros, and Lindros scored the game-winner with six seconds left in the next contest to give the Flyers a 2–1 lead in the series. Suddenly, articles heralded the twilight of the Rangers captain, such as the *Times*' "Messier's Era Wanes as Lindros's Waxes," which pointed out that Messier had scored 32 goals in the first 50 games and just 7 since then. The end came in Philadelphia in game five, a 4–2 loss in which Messier logged a lot of ice time. In the handshake line afterward, he told Lindros to simply "Go get it," then retired to the dressing room. He had gone 3–9–12 in 15 playoff games—not bad, but not great either, and a number of commentators were suggesting that he was washed up.

Campbell noted that circumstances forced him to keep Messier on the ice for many more shifts than Campbell wanted. "You just can't do it at his age," Campbell said. "It's not an excuse. It's a statement." The implication seemed to be that the other Rangers were underperforming, and therefore Campbell had to double-shift his captain. But in the middle of the following season Campbell was fired, and afterward he said that he had tried to reduce Messier's ice time but that Messier would not accept a reduced role. Campbell's statement after the Flyers series, therefore, sounds less like an indictment of his other players and more like a complaint about Messier himself.

One of the things Gretzky was asked after the game was what he knew about Messier's unsettled contract situation. "I know Mark wants to stay in New York," he said. "I believe it's going to be worked out. I hope it gets resolved quickly. I'm really positive it'll get done."

Messier and his family prepared to go to their compound in Hilton Head, as always, while Captan would remain in New York to look after Messier's apartment over the off-season, a task he had also carried out the previous couple of years. At the Rangers' farewell dinner for the season, Captan remembers talking to backup goalie Glenn Healy, who predicted that Messier—whose contract was about to expire—would re-sign with New York within three days. "I remember I was sitting next to Esa Tikkanen," Captan says, "and I had to get up. When I got back, [Rangers GM] Neil Smith was sitting next to Esa, talking to him, and when he saw I was back he finished what he was saying quickly and left. So I sat down again and Esa says to me, 'Sultie, if Mark isn't back here next year, you can come work for me and I'll pay you twice as much as Mark did.' I thought it was a funny thing to say, but I didn't pay any attention to it, because why wouldn't they bring Mark back? They'd be crazy not to—they were coming off a great play-off run and with Gretzky on the team, they were going to make another run at the Cup."

But Tikkanen must have known something. There was an unbridgeable divide between Messier and Smith. Neither side approached the other with an offer during the season, and once the playoffs were under way, Doug

Messier refused to negotiate until after the free-agency window opened on July 1. Once that date passed and the contract impasse became public, it slowly dawned on Ranger fans that Messier might leave New York. The corporate owners of the Garden had directed Smith to offer a one-year $4 million contract, putting Messier on the same pay scale as Gretzky, but on a short term that the Mark and Doug considered an affront. Meanwhile, the Garden signed Patrick Ewing of the Knicks, who was about to become a free agent, to a $68 million contract. Days passed, then weeks. Messier was holed up in his Hilton Head retreat, but he was telling reporters how slighted he felt by what he thought was the Rangers' deliberate insult.

Into the breach rode telecommunications tycoon John McCaw, owner of the Vancouver Canucks. He okayed a trip to Hilton Head by Canucks GM Pat Quinn and corporate executive John Chapple, who courted the Messiers. Mark sought advice from his friends, and at least one, Kevin Lowe, advised him to go to the Canucks because in New York "things were going a bit sideways for a few years," while in Vancouver "they were really dying to have an icon to look up to." McCaw then sent a jet and flew Mark, Doug, and Paul to the West Coast. He took them deep-sea fishing aboard his yacht off San Francisco Bay and offered a three-year contract at $6 million per year.

Doug called the Rangers to hear their latest offer, as McCaw wanted a quick answer from Messier, much as he had when he alienated Gretzky during the abortive attempt to sign the Great One a year earlier. This time, McCaw was dealing with someone eager to finish the deal quickly. So when Doug was told that the Rangers' latest offer was for a series of $5 million contracts, renewable at the club's discretion, Mark made his decision. He phoned Gretzky to let him know that, sadly, their reunion was coming to an early end.

Over the years, Captan became close friends with many of the players, but the nature of pro hockey and especially the Rangers being what it is, there was a lot of turnover. "Russ Courtnall, Nick Kypreos, Eric Cairns, Nik Sundstrom—when those guys left the team, I was very upset, because they were such close friends. It's very hard to see your friend get traded; it happens so much that after a while you feel like you're making friends with a product. It hurts a lot—it's like getting close to these guys is a bad emotional investment." Eventually Messier moved on, too, although it caught Captan completely by surprise.

Sultan was sorry to see Messier leave, but he was hardly surprised. "Mark thought that the team disrespected him," he said, "And there's nothing more important to him than respect and trust. When John McCaw took the effort to send a boat out to Mark and take him fishing and court him, that must have impressed him. After he left for Vancouver, I didn't work for him anymore. I stopped going to games, and even though some players invited me out to dinner or asked where I'd gone, I never came back, because I thought if Neil Smith screwed my boss, then screw Neil Smith— I'm not going to do anything to help the Rangers."

Captan has seen Messier only a couple of time since he stopped working for him in 1997. They were friendly encounters, but both have men have moved on in their respective lives. Nevertheless, Captan remembers his time with Messier as an exciting and fascinating one. He has a series of snapshots of the team's 1995 Halloween party at a bar near the Museum of Natural History, not far from Messier's house. There are several photos of a large crowd, everyone in costume, facing a stage where someone is performing. Messier is in the center, dressed as the late Vegas–period Elvis; sitting next to him is Janet Jones, dressed as Dorothy from *Wizard of Oz*; and below and in front of her, Wayne Gretzky, dressed as the Tin Man. Adam Graves is there too, dressed as a Jayne Mansfield-esque blonde bombshell; Paul Messier, in an Indian chief's crimson headdress; Bruce Driver as Captain Picard from *Star Trek: The Next Generation*, and a couple of dozen other men and women, including Sultan Captan, dressed in a getup that makes him look like some kind of red blood cell. He's got a wide smile, as does most everyone else in the picture, but the one with the widest smile of all is Mark Messier.

When Messier's move to the Canucks was announced, the recriminations flew fast and thick. Ranger fans were shocked, then livid. Dave Checketts got into a shouting match with a sports talk radio host. "We didn't think he was worth $20 million for the next three years," Checketts protested. "Would we have paid him $7 million for one year? Yes! How's that? But he wouldn't take it." Leetch said that Messier would have stayed in New York had the team made more of an effort to keep him. "He began to get a little bit upset," Leetch said of the long period of silence that followed the Rangers' initial offer. "He went from thinking something was going to be done, to getting upset, to accepting a different offer and going to a different team. It was very difficult. It hurt him a lot to have to go through this." It hurt Leetch too. He was playing golf with the former Ranger and current Canuck Brian Noonan in Massachusetts when they got word of Messier's defection. Noonan was elated. Leetch was depressed. Gretzky was despondent as well. "If I'd known he would leave," he later said, "I would never have signed here."

The press conference was held in Vancouver, and for the official portion of it Messier did all the expected things. He smiled for the cameras, donned a Canucks sweater (a new design that Vancouverites derisively called the Free Willy jersey because of the orca on the crest), and raised both arms high in a pantomime gesture of victory. There was much for Messier to look forward to in Vancouver. It was a beautiful, cosmopolitan city in the Pacific Northwest that he had loved as a child. Back in the '80s, when every trip into town was a sure two points, he and his fast-lane Oilers teammates hit the Vancouver nightspots with reckless abandon, as he would have put it at the time.

But that was then and this was now, and after the press conference, as he talked to the New York reporters on hand, he seemed haggard and sad. "When you give everything you've got for six years," Messier said, "and to be accepted the way I was, and to win the Stanley Cup and the way the organization treated me—it was a big decision to move. But I just knew in my heart that something wasn't right. . . . I can't sit there and try to explain it. I can't. Because those are things that weighed on me. I think Wayne understands. He was in the same position in '88 when he left Edmonton. You just know when it's not right. And I just knew there was something wrong. I couldn't put my finger on it. And to this day, I don't know what it was."

But, in fact, he did. Once again for Messier, gesture was bound up in money, which in turn translated into a question of respect. It had been true in his departure from Edmonton, in the difficulties over the renegotiation of his contract after the Rangers' Stanley Cup win, and now again as he left New York for Vancouver. The Rangers had been his team, but that was in the past. The Canucks would be his team now.

THE TWO CAPTAIN CANUCKS

The Canucks were a wreck. They had a long, dreary history of mediocrity—by the time Messier arrived they had endured yet another sub-.500 season, the twenty-second in their twenty-seven years of existence—and were in complete managerial disarray. John McCaw had just bought out the franchise's founders, the Griffiths family, and the club's new building, GM Place, was awash in a tide of red ink. The coach, Tom Renney, and general manager, Pat Quinn, were being overseen by an ever-shifting management team of business executives. The only relief in recent times had come in the miracle run to the '94 final, which Messier and the Rangers cruelly ended by the margin of a single goal.

Messier was going to fix all this. At his introductory press conference, while the beat writers from New York were probing him with questions about his emotional well-being in the aftermath of his traumatic breakup with the Rangers, the Vancouver writers had other concerns. They asked him if he was being brought to the Canucks to be team captain. "Everybody knows Trevor Linden is the captain of Vancouver and that he's done a tremendous job being captain," Messier said. "There is no reason to change that."

Linden was the longtime captain of the Canucks and tremendously popular with Vancouver fans for the honest effort he unfailingly gave as a two-way player, all-around battler, and not least for his extensive work for children's charities. His nickname was "Captain Canuck." He had worn the Canucks' C since 1991–92, and it seemed unthinkable for anyone to take over the job as long as he was around. But Messier was a different story. Even as Linden drove down to Vancouver from the mountain resort of Whistler on the day the Messier signing was announced, the question was being raised. "I turned on the radio in my car," he said later, "and it was the first thing I heard: Would Messier be captain?"

That was the situation Linden was trying to defuse when the Canucks went to Tokyo to play the Mighty Ducks of Anaheim for the first two games of the '97–98 season, part of an NHL push to raise interest for the 1998 Winter Olympics in Nagano. For several weeks, he had considered relinquishing the captaincy to avert speculation of a potential clash with Messier. He sought the advice of his teammates, who told him to do what he thought right. He asked Messier, who told him the same thing. When the team arrived in Tokyo, even the Japanese journalists bombarded him with questions about whether he'd give up the position.

Finally, before a morning practice prior to the first game, Linden stood up in the dressing room and in a voice choked with emotion, told his teammates that he wanted to turn over the captaincy to Messier. It was a characteristically selfless gesture, even flamboyantly selfless, if there can be such a thing, from Linden. Equally characteristically, Messier accepted it.

"It was just something I had to do," Linden told Gary Mason of the *Vancouver Sun* years later. "If I remained the captain, bringing in a player with his history and his leadership qualities, if things did go wrong I was going to be second-guessed the whole time. So my only option was to say, 'Mark, listen, I think this is the way it should be,' and Mark accepted it, so we moved on. Obviously, he felt that was the way it should be. I think he felt being captain would maximize his presence on the team. He's a great leader, and if he was going to be the best he could be, he felt that was something he needed, which is fine. I don't fault him for that."

To Vancouver fans, the transfer of the captaincy seemed amicable. But many were already leery of Messier, who was automatically suspect, given his many years as a Canuck-killer with Edmonton and New York. But there was also the matter of the Canucks' history. It was obscure for most hockey fans across North America, but in Vancouver, club tradition was a treasured matter. Players like Orland Kurtenbach, Rosie Paiement, Dunc Wilson, Andre Boudrias, Gary Lupul, Petri Skriko, Stan Smyl, and Harold Snepsts, little known elsewhere, were the fans' favorite Canucks of all time. One of the key figures in team annals was winger Wayne Maki, who had died of brain cancer in 1974. Maki wore the number 11 sweater for Vancouver, and after his death as a gesture of respect the club never issued the number to another player. But when Messier signed with the Canucks, a clause in his contract stipulated that he would wear number 11.

Maki's widow still lived in North Vancouver and was surprised and heartbroken when, watching the news on the night of Messier's press conference, she saw Messier wearing her husband's number. "Wayne's mother phoned me from Sault Ste. Marie," she said, "and she was really upset, too. I always felt the number was retired, and nobody from the Canucks phoned me to ask our permission." She called Pat Quinn, and when Quinn finally called back he told her she should be honored that Messier had the number now. "I told him 'I'm not honored,'" she said. "Messier can wear number 111 if he wants. I guess this is the way it's going to be, but I'm just hurt the way it happened." Maki's son said pointedly that the Canucks did not have the family's blessing to give Messier Maki's number. Messier said he was embarrassed by the situation but was told by Quinn that everything was being taken care of. Later, Toronto newspapers criticized the Canucks for being "callous" and Messier for being "classless."

The Canucks split the two opening games in Tokyo, then returned home and tied the Maple Leafs. The fourth game of the season would be an emotional one for Messier: against the Rangers at GM Place. His old team arrived in Vancouver and found the city blanketed with Messier's image on billboards heralding the Canucks' new era, on newspaper boxes, in TV ads hawking Lay's potato chips. Although some Rangers did not view the game as a monumental event—the Canucks and Rangers had already met in the preseason, and Messier and Ulf Samuelsson got into a post-whistle shoving match—others felt differently. Some of his closest friends on the Rangers sounded despondent about having to go up against him. "I'm not really looking forward to it," Leetch said. Adam Graves said wistfully, "Other than my father, there is no one I respect more than Mark Messier." But when Messier was asked whether he felt any special emotions facing his ex-teammates, he said only that the game would serve as a good "measuring stick" for gauging the Canucks' progress and that facing Wayne Gretzky was "not that big a deal anymore."

Gretzky, on the other hand, was more frankly emotional, and he expressed himself in surprisingly beautiful words. "I could say it's just another game, but that's not true either," he said. "It's hard for guys to play against friends. You think that feeling of togetherness will last forever. But in life, things that you think will go a long time are cut shorter than you think. There are a lot of emotions that go with it, a lot of feelings. Memories and friendships are never going to close. One door shuts, but one door's always going to be open."

Once the game started, Colin Campbell, still the Rangers coach, yanked Gretzky's line whenever Messier's line took the ice. Messier struck first, scoring on a tap-in off a nifty Pavel Bure feed. But then Gretzky—flush with a new three-year $17.5 million contract with the Rangers, which was conspicuously greater than what they had offered Messier—took over the contest. He scored three times, the last a breathtaking solo effort in which he circled the cage and flipped it over a sprawled defenseman and flailing goalie into the open net. The Vancouver fans gave Gretzky a standing ovation. The Rangers won, 6–3, with Gretzky conjuring his 50th and final career hat trick, as well as his 66th five-point game, his first in three and a half years.

Afterward, the Canucks' dressing-room door was closed for a long time for a players-only talk given by Messier. In another context, Leetch recalled that when Messier first came to New York, he blended in for a couple of months before finally speaking up as a team leader. Now with the Canucks, he was delivering a lecture after only the fourth game. When he emerged from the dressing room, he evinced a curiously egocentric view of what he had to do in Vancouver and what he had once done elsewhere. "I have deep responsibilities to this team, and hopefully I can do the things I was able to do in Edmonton and New York," he said. "It took a long time in Edmonton and it took a long time in New York. This is like when I went from Edmonton to New York."

Meanwhile, Canucks coach Tom Renney was asked whether some of Messier's signature cross-ice passes, which had been intercepted and led to a number of scoring chances in the Canucks' first four games, were a problem. "High-risk passes usually mean low percentage success in the end," Renney said. "We want to play a low-risk game. We have a number of guys trying to make the ninety-foot home run passes, so that's not just a problem Mark Messier had." It sounded innocent at the time, but as anyone familiar with Roger Neilson's tenure at the helm of the Rangers could have told, it was tantamount to Renney reading out his own resignation letter.

The loss to New York marked the start of a ten-game losing streak for the Canucks. If Messier had made a poor first impression on Vancouver fans, with this streak he lost them altogether, and he never really won them back. Meanwhile, reporters raised the inevitable question about how long the coach could hang on. As Kerry Banks points out in his biography *Pavel Bure: The Riddle of the Russian Rocket*, Messier sounded more like an administrator than a hockey player during this period. "I came to Vancouver with an open mind," Messier said as Renney dangled in the wind. "I am trying to learn what the problems are and what deficiencies we have. I'll evaluate that and take the steps necessary to turn the team around." Soon thereafter, Pat Quinn was fired as GM, and very shortly after that Renney was given his pink slip too.

The Canucks did not have to look hard for a new coach. Mike Keenan's tenure in St. Louis had ended in disaster; he had torn the team up, alienating players and fans, and leaving a shambles in his wake. Now he lobbied for the Canucks' coaching position, and Messier let management know that he was the right man for the job. Keenan was hired on November 13. The Canucks' record was 4–13–2.

Keenan promptly announced his alliance with Messier in the expectation that they could duplicate the kind of magic they had worked together in New York. "Mark is one of the finest leaders in pro sports," he said. "His presence alone means a lot to me. When you have a great star in the locker room like Mark, he knows the ingredients of winning, and that's hard to find." Messier confirmed that he would be working hand-in-glove with Keenan. "Coaches in one room, players in the other—that went out with the hula hoop," he said.

Everyone knew what was coming: conflict and chaos meant to harden the Canucks into an alert, Spartan cadre of invincible warriors, but which could just as easily hurl the team into an abyss of hate, resentment, and failure. Keenan immediately put some spin on what was about to happen. "My reputation as a taskmaster is good copy," he said. "But I don't think, in particular, it is a reflection of my ability. I think Mark Messier said it best. Of the 550 players I've coached in the league, probably 500 would play for me again. And those 50 who wouldn't probably don't have what it takes to win."

Messier, noting that Keenan was "what this club needs," prepared everyone as well. "Mental toughness is something most teams that aren't successful lack, and I think that's one area our team has to improve dramatically," he said. "Winning demands that. Winning sometimes can be very brutal. Winning is not all flowers and fun and games. Winning, sometimes, is sheer hell."

Less than two weeks after Keenan was hired, the Canucks flew into New York for what was sure to be an epic night of emotion: Messier's first game in Madison Square Garden since leaving the Rangers. It was Messier's first time back since the season started; Mary-Kay was now living in his apartment on West 75th Street, and his relationship with Frederique had ended around the time he left for Vancouver. Things were different for Messier now, and when the Canucks practiced the day before the game at the Garden, the memories came flooding back. "I left a piece of my soul here," he said. "When you spend some time in New York, certainly under the circumstances that I was able to, it becomes a part of you. These are the positive things. You move on. You make changes, and sometimes changes are good. You do the best." There was, he said, "no animosity, no hard feelings. Disappointed might be a better word for it. I'm happy in Vancouver." He sounded like he had merely come to an accommodation with his feelings. "There's never too many storybook endings. It's unfortunate. Things change, move forward. What we're all trying to do now is move forward."

But the Rangers had planned a long look back. They could have done a thing or two to recognize Messier's return, and left it at that. But instead they went all out. It was an immensely classy move, and what they did made the night unforgettable.

It all started with the pregame warmups, when Messier circled with the Canucks at one end of the ice. Hundreds of fans moved down low to watch, many of them wearing number 11 Rangers sweaters, some holding signs that bore such sentiments as "Management's Mess-take," "Welcome home, Mess," "Messier: gone but not forgotten," "11—forever our captain," and "He came. He saw. He won. Thanks, Mess."

A quarter-hour later both teams returned for the national anthems and the opening faceoff, but before the draw the Garden went dark, the only light emanating from the giant scoreboard video screens at center ice, where a retrospective film of Messier's Rangers career was played. It was scored to Carole King's "Now and Forever," and it showed every high point, starting with his first night at the Garden. It ended with the famous image of Messier holding the Stanley Cup, which drew an enormous ovation from the crowd. Messier watched it while standing in front of the Canucks' bench, leaning against the boards, tears in his eyes. After a full two minutes, the ovation still had not subsided. Both teams stood and tapped their sticks on the ice or against the boards, joining in the applause. Messier glided slowly to the center circle, still weeping enough to make referee Don Koharski ask whether he was all right. He said yes, the puck was dropped, he played on, and he was still crying. Afterward he said he couldn't see through the first shift. "I didn't think I had any tears left after this summer," he said.

Late in the second period the score stood at 1–0 for the Canucks. The teams were skating four-on-four when Leetch, the new Rangers captain, got off the ice late on a line change. That left an opening for Messier, who broke in on Richter and beat him between his skates. Messier glided behind the net as he had done so many times as a Ranger, both arms in the air, smiling his huge smile. Half the crowd cheered Messier, the other half booed the Rangers. Late in the game, Messier laid a wicked two-hander on Samuelsson's thumb, prompting the deadpan Swede to say later, "I was proud of him." The Canucks won, 4–2. There was a storybook ending for Messier after all, at least on this night.

Less than a week after that memorable evening in New York, the Canadian Olympic team was to be announced on national television in Canada. There had been plenty of speculation in the press about who would be on the team, which after winning three international tournaments in a row (all at home) was still reeling from losing to the Americans in the '96 World Cup (also at home). The Olympic tournament would feature full professionals for the first time, and it would also mark the first time a full international tournament was played on neutral ice. Practically every speculative lineup offered in newspapers and sports broadcasts across the country included Messier. Given what the Moose had done for Team Canada over the years, he seemed a lock for inclusion. Messier said on several occasions that he hoped to play on the Olympic team, and a week before the selection, Gretzky said emphatically, "Without question, Mess should be on the team. With the type of intense atmosphere and the kind of pressure that is going to be involved, there is no doubt in my mind he belongs. How could Canada send a team over there without him?"

As it turned out, the defeat in '96 had far-reaching repercussions. Sather was invited back to the national team but only as part of the management committee. He was associated too closely with the collapse against the U.S., criticized for hiring, then losing Scotty Bowman as coach at that tournament, then for being too soft on the players when he ran the practices. Considering the success Sather had with the '84, '87, and '91 Canada Cup teams, the decision to dilute his power in '98 seems somewhat rash. He declined the offer and was replaced as national team GM by Bobby Clarke, manager of the Philadelphia Flyers. When Sather was running the national team, he had used his favorite Edmonton players as the core: Gretzky, Messier, Coffey, Anderson, Fuhr. But now Clarke was in charge; his assistants were Bob Gainey of the Dallas Stars and Pierre Gauthier of the Ottawa Senators, and the coach was Marc Crawford of the Colorado Avalanche. None of them owed any allegiances to Messier or had much of a connection to him at all.

So it was that on the day before the telecast, Messier received a call from Clarke, who told him that he had not been chosen for Team Canada's 23-man roster. It was a courtesy call, a heads up for the storm that was sure to break the next evening when the national team roster was announced. Messier, Clarke said later, "handled it with class and dignity, as you'd expect. He knew how hard it was to select a team, and he wished us good luck."

Millions of Canadians tuned in the next evening and heard Clarke read down the names of the select, in alphabetical order, before an audience at the Corel Centre in Ottawa. In goal, Martin Brodeur, Curtis Joseph, and Patrick

Roy; on defense, Rob Blake, Ray Bourque, Eric Desjardins, Adam Foote, Al MacInnis, Chris Pronger, and Scott Stevens; at forward, Rod Brind'Amour, Shayne Corson, Theo Fleury, Wayne Gretzky, Paul Kariya, Trevor Linden, Eric Lindros, Joe Nieuwendyk—there was an audible gasp when Messier's name did not follow Lindros's—Keith Primeau, Joe Sakic, Brendan Shanahan, Steve Yzerman, and Rob Zamuner. Gretzky was not even an assistant captain; Yzerman and Sakic were. The captain was Lindros.

Messier was gracious about not making the team. "Disappointed is probably the best word," he said when asked how he felt. "The most important thing is that we all focus on the players that are privileged enough to play for the country and really put a positive spin on it for Canada, press included." That night he went out and scored the winning goal for the Canucks in a 4–2 victory in Toronto.

The shock that so many Canadian fans felt was immediately expressed by television and radio commentators and in the next day's papers. Why had Clarke given the captaincy to Lindros, a fantastic player, but one who had always seemed too young, too immature, and too emotionally fragile to wear the Flyers' C, never mind that of Team Canada? Was Messier left off the team because Lindros would never have been able to be the captain, and may not have even wanted to, with Messier in the dressing room? Was the whole thing a ploy to mold Lindros into the Flyers captain Clarke always wanted him to be? Why was Messier missing while players like Primeau and Linden, who had disappointed the last time out for Canada, were picked? Why was Bourque there, even though he had often turned down invitations and pleas to play for Canada? Why Shayne Corson? And who on earth was Rob Zamuner? Clarke never gave any reason for his selections other than that he thought he'd put together the best possible combination to compete at the Olympics.

There were certainly plausible reasons to exclude Messier from the lineup. His play in the latter stages of the '96–97 season was not particularly stellar, and his conduct in the contract talks with the Rangers might have been interpreted as potentially disruptive on a team sequestered in the close quarters of the Olympics. There was also a glut of talented centers to choose from, and Messier would, after all, be thirty-seven when the Olympic tournament started in February. Finally, as Clarke told Red Fisher just before the selections were announced, like other "great players in their late 30s" Messier "cheated" a lot; that is, he tended not to come all the way back to his own zone on the backcheck. Still, those reasons could easily have been overriden by Messier's fine record as a Team Canada player and his excellent one as a Team Canada leader.

But there was another reason why Clarke may have seen Messier as no longer fit for the national team. It was rarely mentioned but perhaps critical: the distaste Messier had expressed for playing hard against his Ranger friends on the U.S. national team in '96. How could someone represent Canada with all his heart when he said he couldn't play full out against certain opponents?

No matter what kept Messier out of the Olympics, most Canadians were appalled at his exclusion. There was a remarkable groundswell of protest against the selection process and support for Messier. On the forum at the CBC Web site and elsewhere across the Internet, hundreds of "My Canada includes Messier" messages were posted. The slogan was printed on T-shirts and bumper stickers, in the hope that Clarke would come to his senses and say he'd replace the first player injured with Messier. But he never did. Messier's international career was over, ended by the man whose picture hung in his boyhood room in St. Albert.

Meanwhile, back in Vancouver, the sheer hell that Messier promised upon Keenan's hiring was exactly what the Canucks got. Linden strained his groin during a practice on Keenan's first week on the job and was publicly excoriated by his new coach for being out of shape. Three weeks later, and about a week after the Olympic team announcement, the Canucks came to St. Louis for Keenan's first game at the Kiel Center since being fired by the Blues.

The reception he received was thunderously negative. The St. Louis fans booed him incessantly and chanted "Keenan sucks." It also happened to be Linden's first game back, and during the first intermission, with the Canucks behind, Linden was telling the fourth-liners that they were playing well. According to Gary Mason, Keenan walked into the dressing room at that point and started hollering at Linden in his classic style. "Sit down, you fucking idiot!" he shouted. "Shut the fuck up! Just shut the fuck up! Who are you? Who are you anyway? What have you ever done?" It went on for a couple of minutes, and Messier said nothing. His job, as it had been in New York, was to let Keenan do his bad-cop ranting and later step in with his own good-cop words of comfort and encouragement.

The Canucks lost, 5–1, and fell into a tailspin. Keenan continued to lay into Linden, telling reporters that the ex-captain was giving only "50 percent" and had to step up his game "unless he is not the player everybody in the country, including Team Canada, thinks he is." It was the usual Keenan routine of humiliating a well-respected, accomplished player whom he found unworthy. But unlike in New York, there were players willing to speak out against this tactic. Gino Odjick, a hulking winger who had pierced the 300-penalty-minute barrier a mind-boggling three times, spoke out forcefully against what Keenan had done. "There is no use slandering Trevor or embarrassing a guy who has devoted his heart and soul to the team," he told Iain MacIntyre of the Vancouver *Sun*. "In the eight years I've been here, there's no player I respect more than Trevor Linden." Jyrki Lumme also spoke on the record against Keenan's treatment of Linden, and several other Canucks, speaking anonymously, agreed. Canuck players challenged Keenan behind the scenes constantly. Once, Odjick hinted darkly to Keenan that a fistfight would not end well for him. Another Canucks golem, Donald Brashear, actually challenged Keenan to a fight on the bench during a game. In Philadelphia and Chicago, Keenan wore out his welcome after a couple of seasons; in New York and St. Louis it took one season; in Vancouver, he was unwelcome almost from the moment he walked through the door.

Linden endured emotional agony during his short time under the misrule of Keenan. He prayed and wept and found himself eager to leave Vancouver, a city he loved. Messier's only public statements on the matter were in support of his coach. "Unless we're willing to change the behavior that's been here a long time, things aren't going to change in the standings," Messier said. "Players have to make the commitment and change necessary to win."

The whole situation was devolving into a public debacle. Messier found the Vancouver hockey media not nearly as pliant as their counterparts in New York. There were fewer outlets in Vancouver, and hockey coverage was given a much higher profile—and because the public as a whole cared so much more about the game than did New Yorkers, those fewer media voices had much heavier clout. The New York journalists were excellent, but none had a citywide following like that of, say, Gary Mason or Tony Gallagher or Elliot Pap or Iain MacIntyre, and there were no commentators with the authority of Harry Neale or Don Cherry. In New York, the media had been and always would be worshipful toward Messier. In Vancouver, the media was more like it had been in Edmonton—fair but skeptical and, at times, adversarial. The same went for the fans in Vancouver. They were hardly overawed by Messier, as the New York fans had been.

Messier was troubled by all the leaks to the press from Canucks players, which he felt violated the basic nothing-leaves-the-dressing-room tenet he knew from his childhood in Portland. But when he went to Gary Mason in early January to complain about the leaks, many of which had appeared in Mason's column, he sounded downright Nixonian. "That is completely unacceptable, it's completely gutless," Messier said. "And everybody in the dressing room should have been fucking pissed off about it because that destroys anything we've been trying to build and tears it down. Then we're starting from ground zero.

"We're not in a goddamn soap opera here, we're in an organization that's trying to get itself back on its feet and try and do the things you need to win. I was so fucking disgusted that I had to sit down for two days and finally let go. It was a complete betrayal of your teammates."

Elsewhere in the interview, he struck a more spiritual tone, even quoting a Buddhist verse. "I can't teach my students; I can only help them explore themselves," he said. "To show them what it's like to be on a championship team and to feel how good and what a great feeling it is to completely commit yourself and be completely selfless and do whatever it takes to win instead of worrying about the end result."

But as ethereal as that sounded, he insisted that the Canucks needed to be "restructured" because "a lot of the players have been used to doing their own thing for so long without any regard for the team concept." When Mason mentioned that Messier was seen at a Vancouver Grizzlies basketball game with Keenan and John McCaw, which confirmed the view of many that Messier was a de facto general manager, he scoffed: "That's so ridiculous. My allegiance has always been toward the players and to protect them from the coaching staff, press, outside people, whatever it is. It just makes me sick to my stomach. Trust in the team is the most important thing your teammates can have with each other. And if I'm the captain of this team, the players have to trust me that no matter what happens I'm in their corner. I have nothing to do with player personnel on this team or who's going where or who's doing what. The players have to know I'm on their side and in their corner. The players have to be able to look each other in the eye and know you're going to war with each other."

Messier surely didn't mean by that last sentence that the Canucks would be fighting one another, but that's what was happening. And soon thereafter, Keenan's whipping boys started getting dealt away.

A couple of temporary respites provided relief from the anguish that was the Canucks' season. The first was the NHL All-Star Game, played in mid-January at GM Place. Messier, specially added to the North American team by Gary Bettman, and Gretzky were on the same side, playing against the World team. Everyone knew that it would probably be the last time the two would ever play together. North America was leading, 7–5, early in the third period when Messier took a clever Gretzky pass and roofed a backhander over Nikolai Khabibulin's glove. It proved to be the winner in an 8–7 result. "It felt like it was yesterday," Messier said. "There's just magic sometimes. The years we spent together in Edmonton, the style we played, I don't think that ever really goes away. We seemed to be in tune, right from the get-go." Messier had just turned thirty-seven that day.

Two weeks later the league took a break for the Nagano Olympics, where Clarke's Team Canada played well early on but was stymied in the semifinals by the Czech Republic, whose goalie, the great Dominik Hasek, stopped all five Canada shooters in the penalty-shot contest that decided the game after overtime failed to break a 1–1 tie. Gretzky was not among the shooters, and Canada seemed to miss the leadership and fire that Messier used to provide. To make matters worse, they lost to Finland in the third-place game and came home without a medal. Messier followed the tournament on TV in the Vancouver area, New York, and Hilton Head. "I watched all the games," he said. "I was up late most of the time, just out of pure interest and a love of the game. But knowing you're watching it, instead of being there trying to make something happen, is pretty disappointing."

The New York part of Messier's Olympic break was necessitated by a hearing in Manhattan Family Court over his financial support of his son, Lyon, now a 10-year-old who loved playing hockey and soccer and who still lived in Virginia with his mother, Leslie Young. The original ten-year agreement called for Messier to make child support payments of $1,500 US per month, which at one point Messier voluntarily increased to $3,000, while also picking up school and medical expenses. The issue later became contentious, and under court order in the fall of 1997 the payments jumped to $5,000. Now the original agreement had expired, and Young was seeking an increase to $10,000. There was potential for real friction, but on the second day of negotiations the two parties and their lawyers emerged with a new ten-year accord that seemed to satisfy everyone. "We're happy we were able to come to an agreement," Messier said. "I love my son very much. I have taken responsibility for him from the time that he was born." Young's statement was remarkable, considering how difficult disputes like these can be. "I'm glad Mark loves him," she said outside the courthouse, with tears in her eyes. "Lyon loves his dad very much. He idolizes his father. He looks like him. He skates like him, too."

After the NHL schedule resumed, the Keenanite purge in Vancouver started anew. One trade sent enforcer Enrico Ciccone packing to Tampa Bay. He had offended Keenan by telling the French-language press in Montreal that the situation in Vancouver was a nightmare. The coach got wind of it and confronted Ciccone in the dressing room, which led to a blowup in which Ciccone was told he was finished with the team. "One guy stood up and defended me," Ciccone said later, referring to Brad May. "I'll remember that the rest of my life, the courage that took. He's a guy who should have the C." Clearly Ciccone didn't think much of the conduct of the man actually wearing the Canucks' C.

Linden himself was finally purged, in a trade to the Islanders. Not long after, Odjick was sent there too. From Long Island, Odjick spoke more freely about what he thought of Messier. "He didn't break a sweat for the first ten games and just waited for Tom Renney and Pat Quinn to be fired," he told Tony Gallagher of the Vancouver *Province*. "They signed him to help us, but all he wanted was most of us out of there so he could bring in his own people. He talks to ownership all the time, and he's responsible for Keenan being here and he's part of most of the trades. He sits in with management for four hours every time there's a trade. Everyone is brought in to play for Mark.

"Look what happened with Trevor in St. Louis when Keenan gave him shit," Odjick continued. "Did he come over to him and say, 'Look Trev, we're with you?' He didn't say a word. How can you be captain like that? How can the team be together that way? He's not with the players. He's the one who controls everything."

None of this did the Canucks any good in the standings. They finished the season 25–43–14, dead last in the Western Conference and far worse than the season before. Messier played much of the year between the two Russian speedsters Pavel Bure and Alexander Mogilny, but they were disgruntled over contract issues, and Messier was hobbled by the usual array of injuries he refused to sit down for, continuing to log his customary twenty to twenty-five minutes a game. Such behavior no longer seemed courageous; it seemed selfish. In the first half of the season Messier went plus-10; in the second half, minus-20. His scoring dropped off drastically too, and he finished 22–38–60 over the full 82 games.

The season was a total disaster. It was literally hard to believe how many missteps Messier had taken, starting with the hard-hearted gaffe over Wayne Maki's number, all the way through to his disastrous backing of Mike Keenan, and all the bad things that happened in between.

The last thing Messier needed after a year of almost ceaseless conflict was to see his name and photograph in a huge *Sports Illustrated* exposé about athletes fathering children out of wedlock. Even though Messier's relationship to Lyon was loving and his conduct towards Leslie Young was on the whole honorable, as had been demonstrated at the court hearing in New York, he nevertheless found himself included in *SI*'s rogues' gallery of pro jocks who'd fathered multiple children with multiple women or skipped out on child support obligations. Although he was mentioned only in passing in the May 4 article, his picture was included, and among many it left a mistaken impression about Messier's behavior toward his son.

Messier found what refuge he could from this lost season with the Canucks at his home just over the British Columbia border in Semiahmoo, a resort near Blaine, Washington. Several Canucks lived in the area, where taxes were considerably lower than in Canada. His condo was set alongside a country-club golf course designed by Arnold Palmer, and it was a forty-five-minute drive to Vancouver when traffic was cooperating. Messier also kept a pied à terre in Yaletown, a trendy Vancouver loft district, which he used when the commute was impractical. He also got involved in Canuck Place, a Vancouver children's hospice, and devoted himself to raising funds for and visiting sick kids there as he had with the Rangers. Being on the West Coast also enabled him to see more of his Uncle Victor, Doug's brother and a student of Zen Buddhism, who had lived in Hawaii and taught education, a bit of a latter-day hippie. It was he who passed along books on Buddhism to Mark, and it seemed as though some of it was rubbing off.

Over the summer the Canucks hired Brian Burke to take over as general manager for the '98–99 season. The club had lost a reported $36 million (Cdn) in Messier's first season, and now McCaw shut off the flow of cash and hired a smart no-nonsense type who was both a hockey guy and smart with money. Burke, a bullnecked, scowling, Harvard-educated American who had been a general manager in Hartford and later NHL vice president in charge of discipline, seemed a good choice. The team pursued no new free-agent signings and started to dump salary, all of which made Messier's massive $6 million per annum look that much worse in comparison.

Burke was asked about the players who said Messier took part in personnel decisions, an observation shared publicly by none other than ex-GM Pat Quinn. Was it a problem if Messier had a hand in making deals? "It doesn't matter," Burke said, "because he doesn't now. All Mark Messier is going to be for me is a player, and he's a great player. We need Mark to play better than he did last year, and I think he can. I'm going to simplify his life. All he has to do now is play. I do not involve players in personnel decisions. I think it's deadly."

Burke was tough and gruff and more than a match for Keenan. Unlike Neil Smith, who would put up with any outrage Keenan could concoct as long as the Stanley Cup lay within reach, Burke saw no Cup on the horizon and thus no use for Keenan's shenanigans. Now Keenan was the one dangling in the wind. Messier's power play was fizzling out.

The Canucks' chances were further compromised when Bure announced that he was sitting out the season until he was either traded or became a free agent. The new era of frugality in Vancouver apparently had nothing to do with it; Bure had asked for a trade during the previous season, the most recent in a series of money disputes with the team. He said he had nothing against the city or the fans, and it seemed as though Keenan was not a problem for him. He said only that he wanted to move for "personal reasons," which he never specified. That led to plenty of speculation as to what those reasons were. Bure was known to associate with influential figures in the Russian *mafiya* in Moscow and in North America, and he had had a couple of somewhat stormy relationships with girlfriends. He was also upset with the Canucks for much the same reason Messier had been upset with the Oilers and Rangers: he felt he had been disrespected by the club during past salary talks and in instances when he'd played injured only to have his effort questioned.

But in the absence of a stated reason for Bure's desire to leave, a story involving Messier arose that, like others about him, acquired the status of urban legend. According to this tale, Bure and Messier had had a falling out during a sexual situation—some versions have the situation involving a woman, others do not—one that so outraged Bure that he supposedly went to management the next day and demanded a trade. It was the kind of story that has the I-absolutely-swear-it's-true, I-have-a-good-friend-who-heard-it-from-someone-on-the-Canucks air of authority—except that there seems to be no evidence for it. Beside the fact that Bure had many potential reasons for leaving the Canucks and had been threatening to do so since before Messier got to Vancouver, Bure and Messier wound up together again on the Rangers in less than three years, in which case either Bure's outrage dramatically cooled or, more likely, there was never any outrage in the first place. Kerry Banks, author of the Bure biography, dismisses the story out of hand, as does Gary Mason. It is another example of the peculiar hold Messier's private life has on the popular imagination.

When Bure sat down, the season was already in dire jeopardy. Keenan wanted Burke to trade him away so the Canucks could get some offensive help, but Burke didn't pull the trigger through the whole first half of the season, even after several players went down with injuries. On November 25, in Toronto, Keenan showed Burke up by pulling his goalie during power plays early in the third period because, as he said afterward, the Canucks were short on players. Burke still didn't deal Bure. Bure's place on the line with Messier and Mogilny was taken by the big, promising, but as yet unproductive winger Todd Bertuzzi. Messier was leading the team in scoring, including the 600th goal of his career in a late-October win over Florida.

Three days before Christmas, while scoring a goal in Calgary, Messier crashed face-first into the crossbar, then fell backwards and struck his head on the ice. He was helped off with a concussion. After that, Messier missed his first game as a Canuck. "You feel like you're in a big space and it's very hollow," Messier said the next day, sounding like his bell was still ringing. "I can't remember what I remember. But I didn't put my milk in the oven after breakfast this morning so I think I'll be okay." He only missed the one game, though, and was rushed back into the talent-strapped lineup, where he was double-shifted by Keenan for games in San Jose and Edmonton, sometimes playing on a line with the slowly improving young Swede Markus Naslund. Messier seemed disoriented, giving the puck away to his old team, the Oilers, on more than one occasion. He claimed a couple of days later that he had shaken off the effects of the concussion. "That's a big King Kong off my shoulders," he said, but in the first week of 1999 he admitted he'd come back too soon. Keenan said that Messier "looked very tired." He was slumping now, and so were the Canucks.

On January 17, Burke finally traded Bure to Florida, and one of the players who came in return was defenseman Ed Jovanoski. Just two games later, at the start of the All-Star break, he fired Keenan. His place was taken by the former Quebec and Colorado coach Marc Crawford, who had won a Stanley Cup in 1996, had a better record than Keenan, and did not torture his players, staff, or supervisors. Messier's man was gone, replaced by the coach who had been in on the decision to leave him off Team Canada. Crawford was a month younger than Messier.

Messier said nothing about the firing for a couple of days—he was in Hilton Head during the All-Star break—but when he returned to Vancouver he admitted, "I would be lying if I said I wasn't disappointed, but I've been disappointed before." He continued, "The bottom line is I feel I have a responsibility here in Vancouver to my teammates, the people in the organization and to the city. I'm not going to waver off my convictions over what I set out to do here, and I've just got to move forward. Brian Burke was hired to be the president and general manager and he has the liberty to do what he feels is best for the hockey team. It's not for me to question.

"I want to be a part of the solution to this franchise and get it back competing for the Stanley Cup. I don't have any interest in playing anywhere else. I've made a commitment to Mr. McCaw and to Vancouver to try and do that—and that's the way I feel. People can speculate all they want, but I have never said anything otherwise to anybody else ever, and that is honestly the way I feel. I'm looking forward to whatever challenges lie ahead."

Messier's statement sounded legalistic and half-hearted. He soldiered on over the next month, then strained the ligaments in his left knee. At the time he was second on the team in scoring. His place at center was taken by Bertuzzi, who blossomed in the job, the first real indication that he would realize his huge potential.

Messier returned near the end of March and played the final few games. On the last night of the season he picked up an assist, the 1,050th of his career, and moved past Gordie Howe into fourth place on the all-time NHL helpers list. But Vancouver lost anyway, 5–4, to Calgary. The Canucks finished 23–47–12, again dead last in the West and again out of the playoffs, the first time in his career that Messier had missed the postseason twice in a row. He finished the campaign having played in only 59 games, going 13–35–48 and minus-12. At least the season wasn't a total loss. He dated Tyra Banks, another statuesque Victoria's Secret model. Later he said that they were never intimate and that the relationship didn't last because they were both too busy with their careers. (He did, however, say those things to Howard Stern, so skepticism may be warranted.)

In New York, the last game of the season was going to be the last game of Wayne Gretzky's brilliant career. Speculation over the Great One's retirement had been mounting over the final few weeks of the schedule, and his stops in Calgary and Ottawa generated spontaneous standing ovations from the crowds there. Finally, he decided that the season closer, against Pittsburgh on April 18 at Madison Square Garden, would be the end. Before he announced it publicly, Messier was among the first people he called to tell the news.

Messier was there on the big day, introduced during the pre-game ceremonies at center ice as "the best Gretzky ever played with." When Messier walked out in a sleek jacket and slacks, and blue-tinted sunglasses in case he started crying, the crowd erupted in the longest ovation anyone aside from Gretzky received that afternoon. Afterward, Messier talked about the bond he shared with Gretzky, how it made them "next to being brothers," and how the friendship they shared with all their old friends from the Oilers "will be there forever."

Number 99 had retired in 1999, just as Peter Pocklington had wanted way back on the night at Northlands Coliseum when Gretzky signed that contract at center ice and Messier looked on from across the rink, wearing the uniform of the Cincinnati Stingers. Now Messier was alone, the last man skating from the WHA, the last man standing from the original core of stars at Edmonton. The calendar would soon turn over to 2000, yet Messier had no intention of stopping.

With Gretzky's departure, Messier's oldest, dearest friend was gone from the ice, and the game lost not only its greatest player, but also its greatest ambassador, its greatest advertisement, and its greatest personality. The NHL was without those qualities now, and it lost them at a time when its stewardship of the game was deteriorating into disaster. Rule-tinkering clogged the flow of the game, already deeply compromised by the trap, huge goalie equipment, and institutionalized lax refereeing, with needless stop-pages for video replays of goals, which were often called back for niggling infractions. The 1999 Stanley Cup final would end in fiasco, as Dallas's Brett Hull scored a clearly illegal goal in the third overtime of game six in Buffalo, and Commissioner Bettman rushed onto the ice to award the Cup in what looked like a sop to American TV, whose broadcast had gone way over its allotted time. Worse, the league's skewed economics and the weakness of the Canadian dollar had Canadian clubs teetering on the brink of bankruptcy and dumping high-salaried players. Vancouver, hardly a "small market" in real terms yet made into one by the circumstances prevailing in the NHL, was one such example; the Canucks could pay Messier a lot of money, but only if they cut salary elsewhere. The upshot of all this was that as Messier's game declined, the overall state of the game was declining too.

If his body could no longer do quite what it used to, his mind was as sharp as ever. At one point in the later stages of his career in Vancouver, Messier spoke at some length with Dr. Saul L. Miller, a sports psychologist who worked with the Canucks and various other hockey, baseball, and football teams. Messier contributed a jacket blurb for Miller's 2001 book, *The Complete Player: The Psychology of Winning Hockey*, as well as extensive quotes in the text itself. What Miller found was that Messier's own mode of individual preparation and the building of team spirit was not merely intuitive, but was in fact a well-thought-out philosophy based on current motivational and popular psychological theory. Over the years Messier gave tantalizing hints that he had read widely on the subject; once he mentioned *Leadership Secrets of Attila the Hun* as worthwhile to read, and on another occasion, when *New York Times* columnist Robert Lipsyte suggested he write a book about winning, Messier answered that the book had already been written, *The Winner Within*, by New York Knicks coach Pat Riley.

In his conversations with Miller, Messier spoke in a way that seemed to fuse certain simple Buddhist principles with motivational techniques like "self-talk," in which one tries to control the many thoughts that normally course through one's mind unheeded, and direct them in a positive, forceful direction. This melding of the Eastern with the Western for success in sports, business, and life in general was an approach made popular around the same time by Phil Jackson, coach of the NBA Chicago Bulls, in his book *Sacred Hoops*, which Messier also admired. For the hockey player, Messier stressed the need for mental and physical conditioning, because being "weak and tired" can make one feel "vulnerable and less confident." Before a game, he said, it is important for a team to spend time as a group "to bring their energy together." He said, "I like to see everybody in the room with the music off an hour before game time," not necessarily to talk strategy but simply because "that time together is special" and helps them "come together as a team." As a result, the individual is subsumed beneath the greater power of the whole. "You have to sacrifice yourself for the good of the team, no matter what role you play on the team—whether you're playing thirty minutes or two minutes a game."

Messier stressed the value of "the expectation of success," the feeling "that you can and will be successful" that in turn leads to actual success. "Getting the right amount of rest, eating right, and having positive self-talk are all important parts of preparation," he told Miller. "A lot of players don't know anything about self-talk. They don't realize that saying negative things about themselves, even when they are not playing, can lead to more negative play."

Miller found working with Messier an interesting experience, because Messier was conscious of these techniques and had actually used them "in the wars." A couple of years after his dialogues with Messier, Miller was able to look back with some insight on Messier's tenure in Vancouver and how it differed from his time in New York.

"When Mark was in New York the first time, he had a group of players around him such as Leetch and Richter and Graves and Larmer and Lowe, who were all mature, confident players," Miller says. "It was like a cadre, and he was in a sense the leader of the pack. When he came to Vancouver, he didn't have that support cast. And he was at a point in his career where his strength really was his intelligence, his ability to read the game. He was an effective leader and a reasonably effective player, and he could have been much more effective if he had the people around him who would have responded to his leadership. But that didn't exist, and it didn't happen.

"What's interesting here," Miller continues, "was that some of the people who had definite leadership abilities, people like Naslund and Jovanoski, people who have since evolved into being team leaders, were younger. Mark was such a dominant persona that they kind of lay back and deferred to his leadership. So there was a gap, instead of people stepping up to fill in the gap. It was interesting that after he left and Naslund took over as the captain of the Canucks, other players started coming out in a more supportive role. I think that was the thing in New York and why he was so successful: there were other players who were confident, effective and mature enough that they were his buds and his lieutenants and his co-players. Mark had a different role here from a leadership point of view. The gap was enormous. They needed a couple of people to fill in the gap.

"Mark is a gregarious guy. But it was often noted here that he was out alone, by himself. He has a persona that really represents energy and star status—charisma—and a younger player can perhaps be intimidated about moving into that aura. And I think that's what happened."

Even though Messier was often an embattled figure in Vancouver, derided by fans as playing only for the money, for being a catalyst for the disastrous Year of Keenan, and for failing to lead the Canucks to the playoffs, much less the Stanley Cup, he still projected a sense of leadership. "It's interesting if you actually watch how Mark carries himself on the ice," Miller says. "It's with his head up. There are players who play with their heads down—they're straight-ahead guys, maybe they're a little more myopic. From a physical perspective, Mark's a heads-up guy. Psychophysically, he carries himself like a man who sees what's going on and is able to communicate what he wants. It's verbal, but it's more than verbal."

The observation that Messier spent relatively little social time in the company of his teammates was a telling one. None of the friendships he formed in Vancouver carry the famous closeness of those he forged in Edmonton and New York. Perhaps that's part of why Messier's third season in Vancouver had such an aura of disappointment about it. He was again beset by a series of injuries and missed a number of games, but he was still an integral part of the team, and his absence hurt the Canucks' pale offense. Halfway through the season, Brian Burke pointed out that the Canucks were averaging 2.9 goals per game with Messier in the lineup and 2.26 without him.

Messier was added to the North America lineup for the 2000 All-Star Game in Toronto, the fourteenth of his career. San Jose's Ray Whitney, a former Oilers stickboy and son of the Edmonton practice goalie back in the days of the baby Oilers, scored on a second-period breakaway on an assist from Messier, his thirteenth, a figure equaled only by Ray Bourque. "To get a goal with Mark Messier getting an assist on it," Whitney enthused, "well, after growing up watching him play, how good is that?" Messier was also reminded of past days, specifically his first All-Star game, when he flew his family to Washington. "My family was here just like they were 20-some years ago, and I think they are just as excited," he said. "Now I have some nieces and nephews here to celebrate it."

Messier also mentioned that he "wouldn't be surprised" if Vancouver dealt him away at the trade deadline. It was getting to be time to go.

By now Messier was going out with Kim Clark, an aspiring actress whom he met while she was working as a hostess at an upscale restaurant in Yaletown. Their relationship became serious, and she eventually moved in with him.

The Canucks improved over the previous two seasons, but their 30–37–15 record was good enough only for 10th place in the West. They were out of the playoffs again. Messier's stats were pretty thin. He was third on the team in scoring, with only 17–37–54 in 66 games. He logged a mild-mannered 30 penalty minutes, but by far the most damning statistic was his minus-15 mark, easily the worst on the team. Yet at the same time the Canucks' record with him in the lineup was 27–27–11, and without him 3–10–4. There was an argument to make either way, but Messier's mind was made up—he wanted out.

Messier asked Burke for the right to negotiate with other teams before the July 1 free agency window, and it was granted. Messier started talking with Glen Sather, Messier's old mentor and, since the dismissal of Neil Smith at the end of the season, the new general manager of the New York Rangers. So much of Messier's career since Edmonton was built on trying to replicate the formulas that had worked in the past. Sather and New York represented a double dose of that nostrum. Messier would return to the Rangers. In Vancouver, few mourned his departure.

There are a couple of jokes about Messier—you can find them on the Internet—that aptly distill the difference between how people think of him in Vancouver and how people think of him in New York.

The Vancouver joke goes like this:

> Mark Messier was shocked when he saw a Canuck teammate at the hospital after being badly beaten. He had two black eyes, a broken nose and jaw, four teeth knocked out, and a broken arm. "What happened!?" Messier asked.
>
> "Well," the teammate answered, "do you know that real cute groupie chick that always hangs out at the rink? I was in bed with her the other day when her husband came home and caught us."
>
> "Oh yeah, I know her," Messier replied. "That's a real bummer. Oh well, it could have been worse."
>
> "Look at me!" the teammate said. "How could it be worse?"
>
> "Messier replied, "It could have been *me*."

The New York joke goes like this:

> One day, Mario Lemieux, Wayne Gretzky, and Mark
> Messier stand before God at his throne.
>
> God asks Lemieux, "Mario, what did people think of you?"
>
> Lemieux answers, "The people in Pittsburgh loved me!"
>
> God asks Gretzky, "Wayne, what did people think of you?"
>
> Gretzky answers, "The people of North America loved
> me so much they called me The Great One!"
>
> Then God asks Messier, "Mark, what did people think
> of you?"
>
> And Messier answers, "Well, the people in New York
> loved me, and frankly, they think you're sitting in MY seat!"

In the summer of 2000, Messier understandably chose to return to
New York.

BACK TO NEW YORK

On July 1, 2000, Messier came back to New York, and the Rangers, now more than ever, were Edmonton East. The new coach was the phlegmatic Ron Low, who had been a road roommate of Messier's in Messier's rookie year, and Low's staff included assistant coaches Walt Kyle and Ted Green and scout Harry Howell. That meant that exactly twenty members of the Oilers' 1984–90 dynasty had been hired by the Rangers over the years. The strategem had worked once, in 1994, and the Rangers kept trying it again and again and again.

Messier's press conference at Madison Square Garden took place the next day and was one of the best-attended in club history. As always, the Garden orchestrated the event well. Brian Leetch, one of Messier's best friends and the man who took over the Rangers captaincy after Messier departed, was chosen to make the introduction. "I have the utmost respect for Mark," he said, "as much as for anyone I've ever met, on or off the ice." Then he directed Messier to come up to the podium and "put on the jersey that looks best on you." Messier duly stepped up, took the sweater, unfolded it, and discovered that, stitched to the front of it, was the captain's C. He put it on and promptly broke down in tears. At one point he had to pause for forty-five seconds to compose himself, interrupted only by one admission: "Oh man, this is ridiculous." Finally he gathered himself sufficiently to speak.

"The people close to me know how much I think of Brian," Messier said. "For him to turn the captaincy over to me, and for me to accept it, is a real honor." Leetch quipped that he turned over the C because "I was concerned that Mark might become a problem in the locker room if we didn't make that move." It was a joke, and a funny one, although Trevor Linden or Gino Odjick, had they been in the audience that day, might not have been laughing.

Garden president Dave Checketts, who had publicly excoriated the departing Messier in 1997, now stepped forward as a large glass tank filled with dirt was brought onto the stage, along with two shovels. Checketts picked up a small axe, threw it into the tank, and then he and Messier shoveled more dirt atop the ax—literally burying the hatchet. That was the picture that made all the papers the next day. "Mark Messier has become synonymous with New York like few other modern-day athletes with any city," Checketts said. "He carried a championship on his shoulders. He has arguably meant more to the Rangers sweater than anyone who has ever worn it. I know I speak for Rangers fans everywhere—most of whom I've heard from over the last three years—when I say that it's an honor Number 11, Mark Messier, has returned to New York and to the Rangers."

Checketts cited the reception Rangers fans had given Messier when he appeared at the Wayne Gretzky farewell in 1999 as the fateful moment when he knew he must bring Messier back to the city. "The fans' appreciation for Mark," Checketts said, "I actually said it to a number of people that night, that this is the way it ought to end for *him*. That night I decided we were going to get him back here, one way or another." Checketts went on to say that, looking ahead, if Messier wanted a job with the Rangers after he retired as a player, he would have one, and that no other Ranger would ever wear number 11. He was almost obsequious, and reporters asked why, in light of all the hoo-hah, Checketts had let Messier go in the first place. "We all make mistakes," he offered as a *mea culpa*.

Now it was Messier's turn to answer questions, and he was out to change the elegiac tone, at least in one respect. "I'm not here to retire," he said. "I'm here to win, to do the things I've done in the past. New York is going to be proud of this team again."

Afterward he spoke to reporters, continuing on the theme Checketts had inadvertently raised when he spoke of Messier's eventual retirement. "I still feel like I can make a difference," Messier said. "It's a challenge. I'm not twenty-five anymore. I can't walk through walls and not feel a thing like I did then. Sometimes I spend more time between games resting than I used to. But I still think I know what it takes to get players around me to tick."

For much of August, Messier stayed at his compound at Hilton Head, building a log cabin modeled after his family's cabin on Mount Hood, where he had spent his childhood summers. There was no television, just as it had been in the idyllic Oregon days, but there was enough room to accommodate more than twenty people, should he ever want to invite all his teammates down. He left his apartment in Vancouver's Yaletown district and moved back to the Upper West Side of Manhattan, taking a new apartment on West 85th Street just off Central Park, while his sister Mary-Kay kept his old place on West 75th. Back in the city, on one of his first nights out, he reportedly went to Shun Lee, a venerably glitzy Chinese restaurant in his neighborhood, and opened a fortune cookie that read, "Friends long absent are coming back to you." He is said to have passed it around the table, asking, "See that? See that?"

In early September, the Rangers convened in Burlington, Vermont, for training camp, where Sather, whom Messier called "a master motivator," impressed upon the players that it was a privilege to wear the Rangers sweater and that problems within the team should stay within the team, rather than be aired through the press. "It was pretty emotional," Messier said, "a real rallying cry, and I think everyone was ready to go to war right after that." Messier said that he spoke to the team, too, although all he would say about it was "I didn't cry, so that was good. I'm making progress."

Messier clearly relished being back in Sather's company. Guy Lawson, who was thirty-seven at the time and a writer who had grown up playing a fairly high level of hockey in various Canadian cities in the east and on the prairies, was at Burlington with the team's consent as a player to write an article for *GQ*. He spent a week in the Rangers dressing room, at practices, and even in scrimmages as just one of the prospects. "One of the things about Messier I remember," Lawson recalled a couple of years later, "was how often you'd see him and Sather talking to each other in the halls, conferring, just the two of them." Lawson also remembered the extent to which everything having to do with the players, on and off the ice, seemed to revolve around Messier. "It was almost like there was an expectation, both on Mark's part and on the part of the other guys, that things had to be sort of approved by Mark. The guy is a great player, or maybe it's a little more accurate to say he *was* a great player, and he had earned the deference everyone showed him. But I also sometimes wondered whether all that deference really was good for the team."

The *GQ* article itself, which appeared in the February 2001 issue of the magazine and was intended as a *Paper Lion*–type first-person account of a part-timer's brush with big-league hockey, made only brief mention of Lawson's interaction with Messier. ("In the hallway, on my way to the ice bath in the trainer's room, Messier stopped me. 'What are you going to write in this article of yours?' he asked. 'I don't know,' I said. 'You'll probably write that you were just killing it out there,' he said and laughed. "Streaking down the wing with Messier," he said. "Give and go all the way." 'I won't write that,' I said. 'Go ahead,' he said. 'I don't care.'") At one point, Lawson was skating in a scrimmage with Messier and Theo Fleury and overcame his awe long enough to park himself in the slot. He remembered Messier's advice in the dressing room—to go to the front of the net, keep his stick on the ice, and wait for the pass Messier would send him—and sure enough, Messier did indeed put it on his stick from behind the net. Flustered, Lawson returned the puck to Messier, whose shot was stopped. But two years later, Lawson remembered it a bit differently: "There was no way he could get the puck to me. It bounced off someone else and came to me. I'm sure once Messier could've made that pass perfectly, but I don't think he could do it anymore."

However valid Lawson's later assessment of Messier's skills may be, and there is much evidence to support his assertion, it's also true that not just anyone can bounce the puck off someone, perhaps a bit clumsily, and have it end up in the right place. Luck, as the epigrammatic baseball executive Branch Rickey once said, is the residue of design. That was demonstrated during the Rangers' home opener on October 11 against Montreal. In the first minute of the third period, with the Rangers ahead 1–0, Messier broke in around defenseman Eric Weinrich and took a snap shot, which was turned aside by Jeff Hackett as Weinrich broke his stick over Messier's arms. Messier went behind the net, picked up the loose puck, and tried to center it to Adam Graves. But the puck hit Weinrich, who was fumbling with a stick handed to him by a teammate, and bounced past Hackett and into the net. Messier threw up his hands and, laughing, gazed heavenward. He'd scored his first goal as a Ranger since 1997, and it turned out to be the winner in a 3–1 triumph. Messier, closing in on forty, could still score, even if the beautiful goals weren't coming quite so often.

The goal was a fitting exclamation point to the usual grand spectacle that the Rangers produce for opening nights. Coming on the heels of the season opener, a 2–1 win in Atlanta against one of the NHL's growing number of irrelevant teams in irrelevant cities, the pregame ceremony lasted half an hour and was meant to mark the team's seventy-fifth anniversary. In an echo of Messier's arrival in 1991, a parade of Blueshirt stars from the past was brought out onto the ice, starting with Clint Smith, the last surviving member of the 1940 Cup winners. He was followed by Emile Francis, Rod Gilbert, Eddie Giacomin, Jean Ratelle, Andy Bathgate, Gump Worsley, Chuck Rayner, Vic Hadfield, Brad Park, Ron Greschner, Dave Maloney, Steve Vickers, and Walt Tkaczuk, as well as former coach Mike Keenan, who to everyone's surprise received a big ovation. Then the current players were introduced, Messier emerging last to the strains of Beethoven's "Ode to Joy" and a thunderous welcome from the fans who turned out with banners and signs hailing the return of the Messiah, number 11 sweaters that had never been mothballed through the three years of exile, and an overall sense of genuine juiced expectation not seen since Messier had last worn the uniform. The cheering would not stop, and Messier started to tear up yet again. He then skated over to Clint Smith and presented him with a gold shield, a symbolic vouchsafing of the Ranger covenant from the Cup winners of 1994 to those of 1940.

The emotion still seemed to affect the captain after the opening face-off. "I thought he was very nervous at first," said Low. "He handled the puck a couple of times and it was bouncing off his stick. That's not like Mark at all. For him to be nervous says an awful lot about the way he plays the game, and the emotion he brings." Messier agreed. "I was a little nervous," he said. "I couldn't believe it. I've played in a lot of big games. I don't know if I was putting too much pressure on myself, or to do too much too early, but I felt better as the game went on." At that point, with the Rangers having won their first two games, the latter a pageantry-filled home opener, it wouldn't have occurred to anyone that perhaps too much emphasis was now being placed on the emotionality of Messier's game rather than on its actual effectiveness in terms of goals for and goals against, pluses and minuses.

Three weeks after the opener, the Rangers were hovering around .500, a pattern they would follow for most of the season. After losses to the bumbling Chicago Blackhawks and to the Philadelphia Flyers, Low separated Messier from his historic linemate, admirer, and protector, Adam Graves. During the off-season, Graves' father had died only four months after being diagnosed with cancer, and Graves was badly shaken by the loss. Now his game appeared to be suffering, and from there it would only get worse for him.

A few nights later against Pittsburgh, Messier played his 1,488th game, one more than Gretzky and good for sixth on the all-time list, and commemorated the milestone by getting into a punch-up with universal antagonist Darius Kasparaitis. That made Messier one of the oldest men in NHL history ever to fight on the ice, although it wouldn't be the last time. Meanwhile, he was scoring at a healthy clip, enough to elicit from Low the sentiment that Messier had been one of the six best centers in the NHL the previous year, with Vancouver, and that he hadn't lost a step this season. A few weeks later, Low would point to Messier's fight with Kasparaitis as a turning point; the Rangers won six of eight following the fracas and, Low said, "Up until that point we wouldn't touch a soul." Messier also demonstrated his full team-leadership repertoire, that first month, treating the team to an impromptu dinner in Ottawa and unilaterally switching the club's travel arrangements for a game in Washington from train to plane.

At the end of October a profile of Messier appeared in *ESPN Magazine*. Written by Tom Friend, the article referred to Messier's dressing up in drag at team parties. Friend quoted Messier's Uncle Victor, who said: "I've seen Mark with a G-string on and a blond wig, driving his boat. He doesn't mind getting dressed up as a woman. Mark doesn't have a lot of boundaries. It's just humor, fun, whim. It's childlike, and it's freeing for the other people around him."

It was the first reference in print to what a lot of people around hockey and in Canada already had seen or heard about Messier, and, for that matter, about many other hockey players who liked to party hard and goof off in any number of ways. But among Rangers fans, cut off as they are from the hockey mainstream, the whole thing came as a huge shock. Internet message boards lit up with expressions of bewilderment, distaste, and condemnation. Their stalwart hero liked to dress up . . . as a *woman?*! Never mind that the New York mayor, Rudy Giuliani, did exactly the same thing to perform at the annual political roast by the New York press corps. For Rangers fans it was all too much, but Messier took it in stride and soon the controversy died down.

In mid-November, the Rangers prepared for a trip to Vancouver, Messier's first game back in British Columbia and one for which he was certain to get a hostile reception. "We never had the chance to complete the task at hand in Vancouver," Messier said, giving the most comprehensive analysis for public consumption of what he felt went on during his tenure there. "In Edmonton and New York we went the whole distance and won in both places, which makes the feeling more complete. It was a different set of circumstances in Vancouver in my three years there. At the same time, I was proud the way the team came together and played well that third year after a tough couple of years there.

"We played well last year," he said, speaking at a time when the Canucks had a strong record and at least one current Vancouver player, Ed Jovanoski, had publicly credited Messier with helping instill a winning attitude, "and I think we got a little taste of success and how hard you had to work to get success. I think last year filtered over into this year. You could see it start to turn the corner last year. I take a lot of satisfaction out of it, particularly," he quipped, "since they're not in our conference."

In the Vancouver papers, biting indictments of the Messier "experiment" were offered up by columnist Gary Mason and talk-radio commentator Dan Russell, reflecting the prevailing feeling that Messier came to Vancouver, made a lot of money, captained a losing team, and touched off massive dressing-room turmoil. But to Iain McIntyre of the *Vancouver Sun*, who took Messier's side in the kerfuffle, Messier gave an unusually long interview in which he viewed the Vancouver era as a saga of personal growth. "I don't look at it like lost years," he said. "I look at it like being a great learning experience for me, one I'll hold with me the rest of my career. Every work stop you have, you leave a piece of yourself there because you give everything. I learned about myself because it was an experience I'd never been through before. It's easy to be this or be that when you're winning and things are going well. But can you be the same kind of person, the same kind of leader, when things aren't going well?

"Winning is a large part of it," he continued, explaining what he saw as the need for change. "The team in Vancouver was a pretty tight-knit team. They had some success, had gone to the Stanley Cup final, they were together a long time, they had a good relationship with their coach, Pat Quinn, they were entrenched in the community, doing a lot of good things. The only thing that wasn't happening was they weren't winning. So when I came in there and all that was broken up, I was largely viewed as the guy who was breaking up a good thing, so to speak. But it would have been happening whether I was there or not because the bottom line is winning, and changes are going to be made. That, along with the fact that we struggled the first two years, a lot of very popular players were moved, and only last year could you see any real headway.

"There were a lot of things said and written. You have to be consistent in your approach and attitude when all hell is breaking loose around you and you're the one people are looking to. It's important to remain calm and maintain your professionalism."

McIntyre praised Messier's commitment to the Canucks, whom, he pointed out, Messier could have left when his friend Mike Keenan was fired as coach, or when Brian Burke came in as general manager and started tightening the payroll, or when the Canucks made it clear they would exercise their buyout clause in Messier's contract and as it was subsequently revealed, ask him to cut his salary in half. But, McIntyre wrote, Messier stuck around and would even have stayed with the Canucks were it not for "personal reasons."

"I wouldn't have had any problem coming back," Messier said. "But I made a decision more on the personal level than anything. My family has always been a big part of my career, and my brothers and sisters all have kids old enough to come and see games. Vancouver was a long trip.

"I really enjoyed my time in Vancouver. The first two years were very difficult. The third year was a fun year. We had a great time together as players. The latter part of the year we really kicked some ass. The players in Vancouver really care for each other; that's what has to happen for a team to be a contending team. If that's something that came to fruition, something left over with the players here, that obviously is very satisfying for me. You can help people along the way and lead by example. But in the end, it's important that they make a commitment to being part of a team and find a way to help themselves. And that's basically what the players did last year."

It sounded like spin-doctoring, but it was at least plausible. Still, not many people were buying when the Rangers blew into Vancouver's GM Place on November 17. Fans gathered at the players' entrance hours before game time to await the arrival of the Rangers' team bus, and a large media contingent from across Canada showed up to chronicle the contest. When the Rangers hit the ice, Messier was booed lustily, and the boos continued to rain down every time he touched the puck. Fans brought plenty of signs, including one that read, "Messier is a great player . . . for me to poop on," and another, unfurled behind the net: "Younger, Faster, Better . . . No More Mess, Eh?"

The Canucks scored three times in eight minutes in the second period, and the final score, 4–3, flattered the Rangers. Messier hardly sparkled; he was credited with an assist on New York's final goal, but he also allowed Daniel Sedin to get past him and score a shorthanded marker. Low, as if to minimize the abuse his old roommate would have to endure, limited him to 15 minutes, 12 seconds of ice time, the least action he had seen during the season up to that point.

Afterward, Messier and his teammates dismissed the booing as simply the efforts of local fans to find a focus to support the Canucks, a far-fetched explanation but one that kept reporters' questions from becoming too probing. "For me," Messier said, "it was an environment that's hostile, and when you go on the road those are fun games to play." Eventually, he couldn't resist getting in something of a passive-aggressive dig at the Canucks fans: "I'm happy they're cheering for the home team. It's been a tough few years over there, and it's nice to see the boys getting some support." Leetch, asked about the fans' unfriendly treatment of Messier, stood up for his friend. "They obviously didn't have a good understanding of what they had here in Vancouver," he said.

Over on the Canucks' side, good feeling reigned. "It was a good atmosphere in the building and I'm sure it had to do with Mess's return," said Markus Naslund, whom the departing Messier had anointed with the captaincy at the end of the previous season. "I think it's a new era now." Matt Cooke said the victory was like "cutting the cord," especially because there "was some doubt about not re-signing Mark." And Andrew Cassels, who took over as Vancouver's number one center after Messier left, said: "I don't think a lot of guys were looking at it as the Canucks versus Mess. We all had a great time when Mess was here. Everyone has a lot of respect for him. But we were concentrating on getting two points, not trying to beat Mark so we could say, 'Look at us now.'" But however much some Vancouver players tried to pass the whole thing off as not such a big deal, the team's owner, John McCaw, made no pretense that it was anything but, making a rare dressing-room appearance after the game to congratulate his players.

What went unreported at the time, however, was that the man so widely reviled in Vancouver had actually performed an act of grace, typical both in its consideration and in the utter lack of fanfare with which he carried it out. At GM Place three hours before the game, Messier met individually with each member of the Vancouver medical and training staff, including the stickboys, to thank them for their help over the three years of his tenure in Vancouver. Messier presented each with a number 11 Canucks sweater, set aside by previous arrangement with Canucks equipment manager Pat O'Neill and autographed with a personal message.

A couple of weeks later in New Jersey, the Rangers met the Devils, a team they hadn't beaten in nineteen games during the three years of Messier's absence. The Rangers lost this one, too, 5–2, although the game was tied 1–1 when Messier had to leave after a puck hit his knee and deadened his leg. "We broke down," Low said after the game. "When we lose someone like Mark, we've got to have more resolve." Before he left, Messier cross-checked Devils center and Rangers bête noire Bobby Holik repeatedly in the back. Messier was playing fearsomely, and the question of international play arose again. With Wayne Gretzky newly named general manager of the 2002 Canadian Olympic Team, to be assisted by the new Oilers GM—and former defenseman—Kevin Lowe, the inevitable had to be asked of Messier: Would you play for Canada again? That question was asked by *The Globe and Mail*, and Messier replied: "I've told Wayne and Kevin not to feel obligated because of what we went through in the past. There are going to be some tough decisions. Nobody's ever going to be totally happy with the selections."

By the time of his fortieth birthday on January 17, however, Messier was slumping, and his plus/minus rating had become an embarrassment. It was not a good time for reflection, but as always he took questions and made a legitimate effort to answer them. In the end he provided a glimpse of his Zen-like approach to the divide between aging physically and maintaining a youthful outlook. "It's no different today than last year or the year before," he said. I really don't hold any significance to it. When I came to New York when I was thirty, I was supposedly at the end of my career. I had heard about the concerns. I had hurt my knee the year before. At the same time, I was kind of thinking to myself, 'Jeez, I'm only thirty years old and I feel fine.' But if you let that seep into your consciousness, I think that could be a determining factor where guys *do* reach the end.

"I was kind of laughing to myself when I first came to New York. I just felt that I had all this experience and I was still a young man that had a lot left. But the only thing you can do is go out and prove it."

By the end of the month, Messier was in the midst of the second-worst slump of his career, seventeen games without a goal, and Low had broken up his line, separating Messier from the perpetually injured Valery Kamensky and the dejected Adam Graves, who had been hit by a second terrible loss—this time, an infant son. Now Messier was skating with various combinations of the challenged wingers Jeff Toms, Brad Smyth, and Michal Grosek, who were doing no worse than Messier but who could do nothing to lift him from his slump. The Rangers found themselves in ninth place in the Eastern Conference, six points out of the playoffs. For the first time in his career, Messier was not killing penalties, nor was he being put out as the extra attacker when the Rangers had to pull the goalie. Sather told reporters that he had had dinner with Messier to ask him whether he shouldn't take a rest, but that Messier had said he was fine. "Mark's no different from anybody else," he said. "He needs positive reinforcement." After a 7–2 loss at the Garden to Atlanta—7–2, to Atlanta!—Messier seemed to give up. "You never hope to get this bad, and you never really think it's going to get this bad. But we are what we are, we stand where we stand. No denying it or hiding it or trying to make excuses for where we're at. It's pretty evident." In the first game back from the All-Star break, against the Sabres and Dominik Hasek, whom the Rangers always found especially unbeatable, Messier's miscues were so frequent that the Garden crowd actually cheered sarcastically when he succeeded in carrying the puck out of his own zone. He did finally score, though, ending his scoring drought at nineteen games, but Buffalo won anyway, 6–3, and put the Rangers in still a deeper hole. Things had gotten so desperate, Carpiniello wrote, that one day around this time Low went to the office hot-beverage machine, looked at the buttons for coffee, tea, and chocolate milk, and asked, "Any arsenic?"

Carpiniello also reported that it was around this point that a Ranger who chose to remain anonymous told him that he and several others believed Sather was the real coach of the team, not Low, and that Messier was a "selective leader." The player, Carpiniello reports, said that Messier had not spoken to him all season. Carpiniello also decided to ask Messier whether he would definitely be back for the 2001–02 season, and got an uncharacteristically angry response.

> "Why are you asking me that?"
>
> When it was explained that it was an inevitable question that had to be asked, Messier wasn't buying it.
>
> "You must have some ulterior motive for asking me that," he said. "What's your point?"
>
> Honestly, he was told, there is no motive. But if he has decided definitely to come back, or not to come back, either way it's a story—a much bigger story if he's calling it quits. He is forty. At some point, he will stop playing. The question didn't infer that he was finished, or that he should retire, or that there was a reason why he shouldn't come back for at least one more season.
>
> Still, Messier wasn't convinced.
>
> "I'm shocked you asked me that," he said.
>
> When he finally calmed down, he said, "You know me long enough to know that if I make a decision, everybody will find out about it at the same time."

At the end of February, with Richter already done for the season because of a knee injury, Theo Fleury, who stood fourth in the league scoring race, announced that he was entering a drug rehabilitation program and would miss the rest of the campaign. His old problems with cocaine and alcohol had flared up again in what Messier called a relapse. "Everybody was aware of this situation," he said, "and Theo himself made everyone aware of what he was going through, but it's just something that nobody could really control, other than the person himself. That's the unfortunate part. We all feel, perhaps, we could have prevented it or done more or seen something that was leading to it, but in the end you really can't, and it's something he has to deal with himself. When it's in a group situation like this, we can give him support and things he needs, but it's just a terrible disease and I really hope he gets himself straightened out."

Without Fleury, the Rangers were doomed, and by the first week of March, Messier conceded that "we're not in the playoff hunt." The season wound down, the mathematical end finally coming in a 6–0 home-ice loss to Detroit, marking the once-indomitable Messier's fourth consecutive season out of the playoffs. On March 31, he got into a second fight, jumping New Jersey's Jason Arnott and bloodying him after Arnott started pounding on diminutive Ranger Mike Mottau. Messier, 40, and Arnott, 27, were both thrown out of the game. Arnott afterward announced, "I thought it was a cheap shot, whether it was Mark Messier or anybody else." As far as anyone could tell, in all of NHL history only Allan Stanley (42) and Tim Horton (44) were more grizzled when they received fighting majors, and Horton didn't actually fight, he just bearhugged his foes so that no punches could be thrown.

In the end, Messier wound up playing the full schedule, 82 games, for only the second time in his career. He scored a healthy 24 goals and 43 assists, but he went minus-25, one of the worst figures in the league. With numbers like those, he no longer deserved to be a number one center. After the season, Sather admitted to reporters that he should have persuaded Messier to sit out some games and take a rest, but, he said, "I'm not sure how you do that. We asked him if he wanted some time off this year and he didn't. He sure isn't going to volunteer." Were it another player, such reluctance to give up ice time might be viewed as selfishness, but no such charge would ever be leveled at Messier. Still, the deference accorded Messier that Guy Lawson saw at training camp, the sense that everything revolved around him and that he so thoroughly inhabited that central role, had worked both for better and for worse in Messier's first season back. The reason the Vancouver fans booed him, despite his very real commitment to the Canucks, despite all he had taught the younger players about the desire to win, despite his exemplary thoughtfulness toward the support staff, was that with him as captain, they lost; indeed, they never even made the playoffs. Canucks fans were judging Messier by the same harsh, unforgiving standards by which he himself judges success and failure: winning. And by those standards, although Messier never acknowledged it, he had failed in Vancouver. Now, if those standards were to be applied again to his first season back in New York, he had failed once more. The Rangers had missed the playoffs and played poorly in doing so, and despite the goodwill engendered among fans and organization by their captain's return, the team was still in the disarray from which he and Sather were supposed to rescue it.

On May 15, five weeks after the Rangers packed their bags and took off for the summer, Dave Checketts, the Garden president, abruptly resigned. The Rangers' poor showing was the least of his recent troubles: the basketball Knicks, a bigger moneymaker despite a bigger payroll, had also missed the playoffs; the MSG cable network was about to lose its most lucrative property, the rights to televise Yankee baseball; and moreover, *The New York Times Magazine* had reported on anti-Semitic remarks made by Knicks guard Charlie Ward, to which Checketts was very slow to react. There was also the issue of Checketts's boss, Jim Dolan, wanting to become the public face of the Garden. Confronted by all this, Checketts, the basketball man from Utah who had played such an important role in Messier's career in New York, was gone.

   With or without Checketts, something clearly had to be done to make the Rangers competitive. One thing Madison Square Garden has never been shy about is spending a fortune and running up a big payroll. The organization had also been quite willing to take a shot on a superstar who made his name elsewhere and may or may not be over the hill. Messier,

Lowe, Glenn Anderson, Steve Larmer, and Graves (traded away to San Jose after his nightmare season, despite his previous nine years of excellent play and remarkably selfless charity work) are examples of this strategy succeeding, albeit from a very narrow slice of Ranger history. Far more often, the gambits have not paid off, and even in cases where the acquired superstar still put in some fine years, Rangers fans considered the move a bust: namely, Doug Harvey, Phil Esposito, Ken Hodge, Marcel Dionne, Guy Lafleur, Pat Lafontaine—and even, ultimately, Wayne Gretzky. Now the Rangers were going to roll the dice again. They tried and failed to pick up Jaromir Jagr and Joe Sakic, and Sather was excoriated on the sports radio call-in shows for blowing the deals. So Sather moved on, and wound up signing Eric Lindros.

Lindros had been out of hockey since the 2000 playoffs, when he was knocked unconscious by a frightful Scott Stevens hit in open ice. It was the sixth concussion of the then twenty-seven-year-old's career and the third in less than a year. He sat out the 2000–01 season because he was at war with Bobby Clarke, the vindictive Philadelphia GM who repeatedly bad-mouthed Lindros publicly after he and his family questioned the motives of a Flyers medical staff that, among other things, wanted him to take a potentially lethal airplane trip while Lindros was complaining of what turned out to be a punctured lung.

He was undoubtedly a great player, who scored at a fantastic clip and whose plus-minus marks were always good to excellent. The problem with Lindros, the thing that kept him from attaining greatness, was the expectation that the North American hockey establishment placed on him from the very beginning of his professional career. Everyone always expected Lindros to be another Mark Messier.

Lindros was made captain of the Flyers at age twenty, a role for which it was screamingly obvious that he was not ready and perhaps never would be, and he was made captain—perhaps at Messier's expense—of the '98 Olympic team that failed so completely at Nagano. Lindros was a great player, but not a leader like his idol, Messier, and no one seemed prepared to recognize that there is no shame in being simply a great player. Nevertheless, he was the one the Flyers looked to for leadership, spring after disappointing spring, and instead of grabbing the situation by the throat in a Messier-like manner, he seemed to turn inward and mope listlessly. Worse, he seemed to feel obligated to play like the "power forward" he was supposed to be. His juggernaut of a body would steamroll everyone in its path, just like Messier's, but over the long haul it couldn't withstand the physical toll like Messier's could. Lindros usually played only three out of every four games; after a while, he could actually be called physically brittle. Yet he played on in the very same way, claiming he couldn't change his game, and nobody pointed out to him that Steve Yzerman, Sergei Fedorov, Stan Mikita, and Red Kelly had successfully changed *theirs*. The concussions finally forced Lindros to stop altogether.

But now he was back, with doctors' neuropsychological clearances and—after Clarke torpedoed a pair of attempted deals with Lindros's first choice, the Toronto Maple Leafs—a stated desire to play alongside Messier. It was a gamble: if Lindros stayed healthy, the Rangers got a standout number one center to succeed Messier, and maybe their next captain, once he'd been tutored by the greatest leader ever. But on the other hand, one knock on the head would render the whole thing a disaster, to say nothing of the potentially catastrophic consequences it might have on the permanent health of Lindros himself. Most Ranger fans believed that the latter was far more likely than the former, and they blasted the deal on talk radio.

The atmosphere at the August 20 press conference the Rangers called to introduce Lindros was actually more somber than festive. Lindros tried to put a bright face on it, but with little success: "I'm ecstatic about being here right now," he said. "This is a real special day for me. I know what I can do. I know what I can accomplish. I know how healthy I feel. We'll just leave it at that." And when asked about the response from Rangers fans, he said: "I understand that people are skeptical because of my concussion history, so we're just going to have to win them over. I know when I'm healthy, I can play this game. And I will be healthy."

The Rangers, naturally, enthused over Lindros's power-forward attributes. Sather noted that Lindros "has 9 percent body fat, weighs 245 pounds, and is in tremendous shape." Messier, on hand to underline the significance of Lindros's arrival, called him "the prototype New York hockey player—he's a tough player, he plays hard every night, he plays physical. I just see it as a great match for New York. I don't look at it as being a tough decision when you can add a player like Eric Lindros to a team." And, Messier pointed out, with himself still captain, the burden of leadership would be off Lindros's shoulders for the time being. "I think," he said, "he was put in that position maybe a little too early in Philadelphia."

Ron Low saw another benefit. "It makes it easier now to ask Mark to take a day off, although you'll likely get the same answer from him: No." Meanwhile, at the Flyers' corresponding press conference called to introduce the players Philadelphia had picked up in the Lindros deal (highly regarded prospects Pavel Brendl and Jamie Lundmark), Clarke was still swept up in a vortex of hatred toward Lindros. "He hurt this organization," Clarke said. "I could care less about him."

As for the Rangers, there were plenty of indications that in their zeal to make a blockbuster deal, they may have misunderstood what they were getting in Lindros. In the days preceding the transaction, Sather seemed to be under the impression that the hulking centerman had suffered only two concussions, not six, or so he indicated in discussing Lindros with reporters. After the trade, Lindros appeared in his first competitive scrimmage, at the Canadian Olympic team's orientation camp. He impressed onlookers with his size and imposing strength, but some noted that he was still in the habit of crossing the neutral zone with his head down, which had been his undoing when Scott Stevens knocked him unconscious sixteen months before. A player at the camp told *New York Times* reporter Jason Diamos that Lindros might be better off playing on the wing, where he'd be less vulnerable to open-ice body checks. But when asked about working to keep his head up, Lindros, Diamos reported, "bristled." Later, Sather said "that's something he'll have to learn to be a little more aware about. My feeling is that it's a natural instinct. He's been cutting through the center ice his whole career, and when he was younger, people got out of the way because he is so big and strong. But he's certainly not too old to get rid of that habit."

Carl Lindros—who, like Doug Messier, acted as his son's agent—looked to Mark Messier to provide an example for Eric. "Mark's changed his approach," Lindros *père* said. "He organizes his energy. You don't necessarily have to destroy somebody to end up with the puck." Thus began Lindros's tutelage with Messier. About to turn forty-one and with one year left on his contract, he was no longer being held up as the perfect exemplar of ferocity and reckless dash, but rather as a Zen master at conserving his vitality, at husbanding effort until the right moment. No one said it, but it seemed to be in the back of everyone's mind: that the final act of Messier's playing career would be devoted to bringing about the maturation of Lindros as a leader. Accordingly, Messier put Lindros up in a room in his apartment on West 85th Street. It was September 2001 in New York.

AT GROUND ZERO

A couple of months before the Rangers signed Eric Lindros, Glen Sather and the staff decided to move training camp from Burlington to Manhattan to reconnect the team with its fans, something that several other NHL teams had done with some success. Two sites in Manhattan were considered: Chelsea Piers, a large, privately owned recreational complex that stretched along the Hudson River for several blocks in the West 20s, and Madison Square Garden on West 32nd Street between Seventh and Eighth avenues. Chelsea Piers encompassed several cavernous quays where, in the era of the great transatlantic passenger liners, the ships of the Cunard Line would tie up. It was at one of these piers that the *Titanic* was supposed to dock at the end of its maiden voyage, but where the *Carpathia*, carrying many survivors of the *Titanic* disaster, docked instead. But as big as the Chelsea Piers complex was, its twin rinks and dressing room facilities were simply not large enough to accommodate the more than seventy players, plus all the coaches, trainers, and support staff an NHL training camp entails. Moreover, the players would have to stay at, and undergo medical examination at, the Marriott Hotel in the World Financial Center, two miles farther downtown. The Rangers decided that Chelsea Piers was too logistically complicated and went instead with the Garden, where hotels were located right across the street. Opening day for training camp was set for September 11.

"We were doing training camp for the first time at the Garden," said John Rosasco, the Rangers' public relations director. "We had a ton of stuff planned, a lot of interactive activities. The rotunda was set up with a slap-shot booth, that sort of stuff. Everyone was feeling really good about it." The Garden sits atop Penn Station, one of the city's two main commuter rail stations. Every weekday morning, tens of thousands of commuters arrive at Penn Station from Brooklyn, Queens, New Jersey, and Long Island, and tens of thousands more enter the station via the city's subway system. "The 11th was our testing day," Rosasco said, "and we would've been on the ice on the 12th. So I came in, and we had Penn Station all set up—we had a giveaway contest to let people know that camp was going on all week at the Garden. So the morning of the 11th, 7 a.m., we're in Penn Station and everyone's coming to work, and we're giving out T-shirts. We had someone from the TV network down there hosting everything and interviewing the guys. I came upstairs around 8." Rosasco made his way to the lobby of the Garden's 3,000-seat theater and found the players' medical testing already under way. "We probably had thirty guys there at the time," Rosasco said. "At that point it was all the kids, the youngest guys, who you bring into camp the earliest."

Rosasco left around 8:45 with Darren Blake, the Rangers' travel coordinator. They had to get a quick ride uptown to Messier's place on 85th Street between Columbus Avenue and Central Park West, where they would pick up Eric Lindros, then head back down a few blocks to the ABC television studio at 66th and Columbus, where *Live with Regis and Kelly* was being broadcast. Lindros was scheduled to be a guest on the show, a huge coup for the Rangers and for the NHL; *Live* had a national audience of five million, tops in its time slot.

"As we were walking out of the Garden," Rosasco said, "we got a phone call from our bus driver that a plane had just hit the World Trade Center. We didn't know anything at that point. We put on the radio when we got in the car, and they were saying that it was a small plane." That first plane struck the north tower of the trade center at 8:46 a.m.; the south tower was struck at 9:04. "While we were driving uptown the second plane hit, and that's when we knew it was terrorism." At the same time, at their apartments on the Upper West Side a bit west of Messier's, Mike Richter and Brian Leetch had been getting ready to head down to the Garden. "I was with Leetchie," Richter said, "and when we heard about the second plane, we had no idea if we were under attack altogether, or what. We figured it was just as smart to stay put."

Rosasco and Blake made it uptown quickly. "When we got to Mark's place ten minutes later, he said, 'You'd better come upstairs and look at this.' So we went into the little room Eric had at Mark's and watched the TV. And I said, 'All right, let's go down'—at this point we still weren't sure of the severity of it—and we went to ABC. They have a television in the lobby, and as we walked in, the audience was coming out. They had just dismissed the audience and said the show was canceled. And as we're standing there watching the TV in the lobby, that's when the Pentagon was hit."

Rosasco, Blake, and Lindros were doing what most New Yorkers did in the first few minutes after the planes hit on September 11. Unsure of exactly what was happening and incapable of conceiving that anything worse could happen—let alone something of the unimaginable magnitude of what was about to take place—they continued to go about their business. But they did so tentatively and always looking downtown, toward the smoke pouring from the twin towers or, if the towers couldn't be seen—as was the case in the area where Messier lives and the ABC studios are located—to television screens where the same inescapable, incomprehensible scenes were being shown. They went to work, to school, to dentist appointments, to the corner bodega, or to television appearances. But only now, as television replays showed again and again the image of a second plane, a full-size passenger jet, slamming into the south tower; as reports came in of an attack on the Pentagon and of a jet going down in western Pennsylvania; and with more reports coming in of planes missing and unaccounted for, the nature and scope of the terrorist attacks was becoming horrifyingly clear. Everything in New York came to a stop, as it did everywhere across the continent and around the world.

From ABC, Rosasco, Blake, and Lindros went back uptown to Messier's apartment, and by the time they arrived sometime after 10 a.m.

the impossible had happened: the south tower had already collapsed. Upstairs on television, they were watching as, at 10:28, the north tower fell, too. Now the focus shifted, as it did for most everyone else in the city who was not in the immediate area of the collapsed towers: how to keep everyone safe. Rosasco and Blake wondered aloud about what should be done about the players and the Rangers personnel at the Garden. Messier pointed out that if terrorists were singling out New York targets to hit, Madison Square Garden was "probably on their list." Rosasco and Blake decided to return to the Garden while Messier and Lindros stayed at Messier's apartment.

"When we got back, everyone was still at the Garden," Rosasco said. "The testing was still kind of going on, but everyone was watching TV, trying to figure it all out. Donny Maloney [an assistant GM] was there, and he was concerned because his brother-in-law was working at Cantor Fitzgerald [the investment bank offices were on the 100th through 105th floors of the north tower]. We were only starting to grasp the severity of everything. We stopped the testing, and Glen gathered everyone together and told them to go back to their hotels and return the next day, Wednesday, at 8 a.m." The players dispersed to their hotels, all of which were near the Garden—where, even though it was roughly three miles uptown from the trade center site, the huge cloud of smoke and debris was now plainly visible, as it would be for weeks.

Any notion of conducting training camp at the Garden had been rendered completely unworkable, even if anyone had been in any mood to practice hockey. Its large interior spaces were being set aside for an anticipated influx of people displaced from apartments near Ground Zero, as the smoking mountain of rubble and twisted steel that was the trade center was now called. (Those residents never wound up at the Garden; they were instead accommodated at the homes of families and friends and at various hotels throughout the city.) Furthermore, below the Garden, Penn Station needed to be kept clear; rail traffic into Manhattan was suspended in the immediate aftermath of the attack, and it would be a couple of days before rail service was restored. When it was, Amtrak trains would bring New Yorkers home from all across North America, where they had been stranded by the grounding of passenger jets.

Meanwhile, Chelsea Piers, from which Ground Zero was a straight two-mile drive down West Street, had been transformed into a gigantic staging area for supplies for the rescue effort. Ambulances from all over the eastern United States and Canada poured into New York to transport the hundreds of injured who, sadly, never materialized, yet they sat at the piers alongside their idling EMS vehicles in a ten-block-long queue, hoping to help in whatever way they could. Volunteers stacked the supplies that flooded in from private citizens, stores, and corporations, turning the piers into vast warehouses of food and equipment. A report would circulate via the news media or through the Internet grapevine that, say, granola bars were needed, and within hours hundreds of boxes of granola bars would arrive, brought in by truck from stores or in carloads or even by hand by everyday people. The same held true for goggles, work gloves, food for rescue dogs, toothbrushes, bottled water. Trucks and police launches from Ground Zero would pull in, calling for crates of work boots, flashlights, raincoats, coffee machines; these were loaded on immediately, and the trucks or boats would head back downtown again, sometimes with a few volunteers who had talked their way on board.

Down at Ground Zero itself, the debris pile swarmed with police, fire-fighters, ironworkers, and volunteers, scrambling over the wreckage, search-ing in vain for signs of life. Around the edges of the vast pile of what had been the largest office complex in the world, volunteers passed out hard hats, respirators (the most important item, and the only one, it seemed, that there was never enough of), whatever was needed. The Marriott, where the Ranger prospects would have been staying, was abandoned and caked with the thick, choking dust that covered everything downtown all the way east to Chinatown and the Brooklyn Bridge. Exhausted rescue workers collapsed on floors and beds in the hotel to get a couple of hours' sleep before return-ing to the debris pile.

In the face of so much death and destruction, absolutely everything seemed utterly trivial. Yet in the initial confusion and disbelief the Rangers planned to continue camp at the Garden. Late on the morning of the 11th, Glen Sather told *The New York Times* that the start of the first practice would be moved back from 9 a.m. to 1 p.m. "But all this is secondary to what's going on," Sather said, adding that camp "means nothing. It is devastating, what has happened today." But by the afternoon, plans were revised. The team felt a responsibility to get their players and personnel somewhere that seemed safer. And, as Mayor Rudolph Giuliani was already telling New Yorkers, it was important to continue living their lives and doing their work as best they could under the circumstances. The best alternative for the Rangers, Sather and his staff decided, was to move camp to Rye, New York, where a rink was available and hotel rooms were secured. While getting through police checkpoints into New York by car or bus was virtually impossible, getting *out* was relatively easy. Buses were rounded up, and on the evening of the 12th the players from out of town were taken to Rye, joined by Messier and Lindros, who drove up on their own. They had a team dinner that night and hit the ice the next day, the 13th, for a camp now scheduled to run two days instead of the original four. The mood was understandably subdued.

A large media contingent showed up at Rye, eager for something different from the pervasive mood of horror, outrage, and grief. It was Lindros's first appearance in a Rangers uniform, and immediately it became obvious that if one of the things that defines leadership on a hockey team is finding the right words for expressing the right sentiment, Lindros needed some work. "It's just fun to get back on the ice," he said, making him perhaps the first public figure to use the word "fun" since September 11, "but there is a lot happening outside of hockey that really puts things in perspective as far as sports goes. It's tough to focus on hockey right now. And I don't think it's all sunk in." Messier's first public words since the attacks were more measured: "Life must go on and go on the way it did in the past. The best therapy is to get back to your normal routine, whatever you do. There is obviously a tremendous amount of mourning going on and that probably will never go away. But you have to fight back and continue to live the way we've chosen to live in a free world."

Also on the 13th, newspapers carried the names of the first of the known dead, among them Garnet "Ace" Bailey, the director of pro scouting for the Los Angeles Kings, and Mark Bavis, also a scout for the team; they were both aboard United Airlines Flight 175, which crashed into the south tower. Several Rangers knew the men. Bailey, who played eleven seasons in the NHL and won two Stanley Cups with the Boston Bruins in 1970 and '72, finished his career with the Oilers in 1978, when they were still in the WHA, was Wayne Gretzky's first Oiler roommate, and was an Oiler scout who had so much to do with devising strategy during the team's Cup runs. He was fifty-four. Bavis played for Boston University and was drafted by the Rangers in 1989, though he didn't play in the NHL. He was thirty-one. Others, too, were missing and feared lost, never to be found. Maloney's brother-in-law, Tom Palazzo, was one, as was a friend of Leetch's, John Murray.

That evening, Messier spoke again to reporters. "Living in the city, it could have been any one of us at any given time," he said. "I have friends that were in the buildings. I'm sure that everyone in New York has been affected directly or indirectly, so we're certainly no exception. I look at the unbelievable leadership we've gotten from Mayor Giuliani and Governor [George] Pataki, the work done by all of the professional people involved in the rescue operations, and the unity that's come out of this in the city and across the country, and it's amazing.

"It's important," he continued, "that we don't allow this to affect how we've chosen to live in our country. We need to establish that we won't allow our freedom to be taken away from us. I think the best way to fight back is to continue with life the way we've chosen to live it in America, Canada, and the free world."

Messier was easing back into a leadership role, but in a remarkable way for which he is not often given credit. His words were eloquent, certainly, but also very close to what most politicians and public officials were saying in the first days after the attacks. That is what's remarkable. Consider first that Messier is an athlete, and then think about the number of athletes who could have spoken so thoughtfully about so difficult a subject. Surely a jock shouldn't be faulted for not expressing himself well verbally; his talent, training, and occupation are all about the way he expresses himself physically. Occasionally a particularly well-spoken athlete emerges, but one with Messier's sense of what to say and how best to say it is rare indeed. Among all the athletes quoted after the terrorist attacks, no one was as consistently eloquent as Messier.

The next day, Friday the 14th, was the second and final day of camp. It happened also to have been designated a national day of mourning by President George W. Bush. As the players came onto the ice for practice, Messier accordingly called them together and led the team in a prayer.

Afterward, he told reporters, "We've got to get back to normal living, as tough as it is. It may be the best thing for everybody." And in answer to a question about what the Rangers could do, if anything, to help with the recovery, he said, "In the end, we will. It's so early on right now. The best we can do is stay out of the way and let the people down there do what they can to find people alive." The realization, too, that the players could have come much closer to harm than they wound up doing was also beginning to sink in. "We could just as easily have been skating at Chelsea Piers, staying at the Marriott right down at the World Trade Center. But that's life. You try to figure out why sometimes and try to help out the ones who aren't so fortunate."

Two days later, Messier found his first chance to help out. He and some of the other Rangers mentioned to team staff that they would like to go to Ground Zero to do what they could. The NHL's security director, Dennis Ryan, was a former city police chief. He was friendly with New York City Police Commissioner Bernard Kerik from the days when Ryan was in the NYPD and had hired Kerik onto the force. Ryan called Kerik and arranged for a small group from the Rangers to tour the trade center site, stopping first at police headquarters. "It was Mark, Eric, Mike Richter, Glen Sather, and myself," Rosasco said. "Nobody knew we were going down there. We had to walk through these checkpoints to get into police headquarters. One area was set aside for the press. Mark didn't want to walk through there because he didn't want anyone to see him. And the cop who was with us said, 'Don't worry, you'll be okay, it's only international press here.' So as soon as we turn the corner we hear this guy: 'Mark! Mark! I'm from the *Edmonton Journal*!' And it wasn't five minutes later that I started getting calls from people who knew we were there."

Richter remembers going to police headquarters. "I was wearing flip-flops, so they gave me heavy boots and all of us put on hardhats. At the time in police headquarters they had an area where all the families of missing police officers stayed, awaiting word on their loved ones. But they were all New Yorkers, so they were pretty glad to see us there, but it was very sobering to walk through there. Then we went down to Ground Zero itself—the north end of the site, right where the Century 21 store is—and since this was only five days after the attack, the firemen were still out in full force, and there were still volunteers everywhere. When we got down there we said hello to some of the people who seemed to recognize us, and we signed a few autographs, and a few people even had pictures taken with us. But for the most part it was pretty wrenching. We were pretty close. We could see the pockets in the wreckage where rescue workers were still climbing down, searching for survivors. I remember seeing that Burger King that had 'Temporary Police Headquarters' spray-painted on it."

Rosasco recalled the mood at Ground Zero, and his own reaction to being there. "I think the whole city at that point was still stunned. There was still no way to truly comprehend everything, and yet at the same time there was so much grief, but also hopefulness about digging out and searching for people. Some of the rescue workers would see us, and they'd actually ask, 'How are we going to do this year?', 'How's the team stack up?' I think the best part of what we did was to provide a diversion to the people who were down there, to get them thinking about something else. And that's really what it was all about for us, to say thanks to those people for what they were doing."

But even down at Ground Zero, Messier's magnetism was inescapable. "Obviously, he's a hell of a player," Richter said. "But he's got kind of an aura about him. He's a very special person. I've seen him in so many situations where he doesn't just get by, he thrives. That was a difficult situation to go into, with the loss of life that was obviously present, and Mark was having people look to him for answers. It's amazing. I guess he comes with the precedent of being such a great leader that people expect him to lead in many, many contexts, and he does. He really does. He knows what to say." Later, Messier was asked about the visit, but he refused to say anything about it.

The next day, only six days after the attacks, the Rangers, sans Messier, took their chartered jet from the White Plains airport in suburban Westchester to Detroit for their exhibition opener. Theirs was one of the few planes in the air, and as they climbed over New York they could plainly see the smoking ruins of the trade center. "Looking down at that," Manny Malhotra said, "reminds you of what happened, how many people died, as if you needed a reminder." At Joe Louis Arena in Detroit, the Rangers and Red Wings joined hands at center ice, then played an understandably uneventful game.

Two days later, on September 20, the Rangers were set to meet the New Jersey Devils in the home exhibition opener, the first scheduled public event of any kind to be held in New York since the attacks. Messier would not play in this game, either, but he was present at the Garden and spoke to reporters. He still seemed shaken by the new sense of insecurity that had befallen so many Americans, especially in New York. "It's so unnerving," he said, "how exposed we are. I don't even like to talk about it." Messier nevertheless continued to talk about it, although in his defense, he was hardly the only one in the city expressing these concerns. "Obviously, we'll be more protected from now on, but there have been events with masses of people for a long time. There were 25,000 people in the World Trade Center, a lot of whom got out, but there are 80,000 at a football game. This has been an awakening for everybody. I think the way we do things will have to change. But to say we'll never feel confident again—never is a long time. It's important that we fight to establish freedom again in our everyday lives. Sure, it's going to be a while until things are as they were, and they may never be exactly the same. But the goal for all of us is to be able to walk around, not in fear."

The game itself provided New York with the first taste of what post–September 11 gatherings would be like. Everyone entering the building had to pass through metal detectors, and all bags were searched. The idea was not simply to increase security, but also to give everyone present the clear idea that they were somewhere where precautions had been taken to prevent any kind of repeat of the unthinkable events of the week before. The crowd for an exhibition game at the Garden would have been sparse under normal circumstances, but on this night there were no more than 2,000 people dotting the building's 18,200 seats. Along the boards, the advertising had been removed and replaced by a single message: "Our thoughts and prayers are with the families of all injured and lost, New York's finest and bravest, all volunteers and rescue workers." Painted on the ice were the words "United we stand." Rangers play-by-play announcer Sam Rosen and color commentator John Davidson opened the telecast by pointing out that "we know that many of the firefighters and the policemen that were involved in this tragedy were sports fans, and we honor them and their memories." The Rangers and Devils came out to light applause, then lined up along the boards and watched overhead video screens, where scenes from the recovery effort were shown, accompanied by Lee Greenwood's maudlin patriotic ode "I'm Proud to Be an American." Such was the depth of grief that even that song seemed moving. The teams next skated out to stand mingled along the red line for a moment of silence that was very silent indeed. Anthem singer John Amirante then performed an a cappella version of "God Bless America," his voice catching at the end. On the red line, Lindros, making his first-ever appearance in a Rangers uniform, seemed as if he was about to cry. Then the hockey game began, and it seemed especially pointless.

The attacks made almost every activity seem pointless, except those that somehow related to helping, commemorating, or expressing gratitude. People stopped in at all the city's firehouses, so many of which had lost personnel, to thank firefighters for their efforts and their sacrifice. Immediately, the firehouses were plastered with floral tributes, handwritten posters, memorial candles, and various other expressions of thanks from neighbors and from all over the world; these would still be in place a full year after the attacks. Messier stopped by the firehouse closest to his home, Engine Company 74 on West 83rd Street, which lost one fireman in the disaster. "A few days after 9/11 he stopped by," Firefighter Tom Brown remembered. "He was just walking past the firehouse by himself. It seemed like he was a bit timid to walk up and actually say hello at first. Then somebody recognized him and said hello, and he came in. We brought him in the back to the kitchen, where he met everybody.

"It was a big thing; everyone was really excited. One of the officers had a son who was here. We asked him, 'You know who that is?' He didn't really know at first, but then he realized who it was, and he was kind of in shock. Mark was great to the boy, answering all his questions. After a while we started asking him for autographs, giving him papers and things to sign. He was ready to sign them, but then he stopped and said, 'Wait a minute,' put the pen down, and said, 'I'll be back tomorrow.' And we were saying, 'Sure you will.' But he came right back the next day with a whole bunch of photos, and he signed them all. A lot of the kids were around. He was awesome."

Messier later told Sather about his visit. "He put on the full fireman's regalia," according to Sather. "The hat, the big tank, the jacket. He wanted to see how tough it would be to carry the stuff up the stairs in the World Trade Center. He said it was heavy, about ninety pounds." Sather remained impressed by Messier's charisma. "I've never seen anybody quite like that," he said. "He walks in the door and those guys are just all over him. He's as much in awe over those guys as they are over him, and it's genuine as hell."

The Rangers opened the season in Carolina, a 4–3 loss in which Messier, who had sat out all five exhibition games, was held off the scoresheet. But the match served as mere prelude to the Rangers' home opener against the Buffalo Sabres on October 7.

The Garden did what it does better than any other NHL organization, with the possible exception of the Montreal Canadiens: create an emotionally appropriate commemorative ceremony—a difficult enough task under normal circumstances, but infinitely more so this night. The tone was set at the start when Al Trautwig, an MSG Network announcer serving as host of the on-ice ceremonies, began by telling the crowd in the darkened arena, "Tonight, more than at any time in our lives, we are proud to be New Yorkers." In contrast to the exhibition opener on September 20, the mood in the rink on this night was more expansive, and the fans reacted to Trautwig's opening with loud applause. The applause grew louder when he introduced the NYPD and FDNY hockey teams. The policemen wore their white sweaters with the Police Benevolent Association crest on their chests, while the firemen were clad in red sweaters featuring a big, flaming *F*, à la Calgary's flaming C. They lined up on the ice outside the Zamboni entrance at the Eighth Avenue end of the rink, all of them wearing baseball caps bearing their department's initials—except for one fireman, who wore a fire helmet to which a photo of a fallen fire officer had been attached. The applause only grew louder and turned briefly into a chant of "USA, USA." The cops and firemen banged their sticks on the ice, then waved them in the air to salute the crowd.

Next, the Rangers were introduced, one by one, with the usual spotlight-and-dry-ice treatment, as they skated through the lines formed by the police and fire department teams. In place of the usual "RANGERS" legend, the front of each player's jersey was inscribed with "NEW YORK" in block letters. There was polite applause for Lindros, mixed in with a few boos—not the warmest reception, but then again nothing like the eerie silence that greeted Dave Karpa, or Barrett Heisten, who laughed at his own anonymity. For their part, the cops and firemen reserved their heartiest welcome for Bryan Berard, the defenseman who had nearly lost an eye while playing for

Toronto a year and a half before, and who was now making his comeback to the league. As always, Messier was saved for last. The only player not wearing a helmet, he skated out to the biggest ovation of the evening.

As Trautwig announced the names of the Rangers who were not dressed for the game, the fireman wearing the fire helmet skated over to Messier, who smiled, and then put the helmet on Messier's head as the crowd roared its approval. This is the picture that would appear the next day in sports sections all over the continent: Messier grinning, the big hat perched way up high on his head, the fire officer's memorial photograph tucked into the front of the helmet.

The firefighter who gave Messier the helmet was named Larry McGee, and he worked at Engine Company 66 in the Bronx. He was one of the FDNY team's two captains, a position he had held on the team for seventeen years. A good player, he was Iona College's all-time leading scorer and made the final thirty at the camp for the 1984 U.S. Olympic Team. The officer whose picture he carried was Ray Downey, the FDNY's chief of operations, the highest-ranking fireman killed on September 11. Downey was the world's most highly decorated fireman; he had gone to Oklahoma City to coordinate the recovery from the 1995 terror bombing there, and he was also the founder of the fire department hockey team, its only current or former member lost in the trade center catastrophe.

"I was working that day, and I had a picture of Ray Downey in my locker," McGee remembered. "I thought that night at the Garden that maybe they would introduce us, do a ceremony, the song, a moment of silence, whatever. I thought, 'Wow, if they're going to introduce me out there as Larry McGee, captain of the fire department hockey team, they're probably going to zoom in on each of us on MSG. This is going to be pretty cool, all these people will be watching us, so I'm going to put Ray Downey's picture on my helmet, still missing, the captain of the first fire department team, the most decorated guy to be lost, the number one–trained fire officer in the world.' So I brought the helmet down with me, because that's kind of our trademark, you know?

"I assumed we'd all be wearing our helmets, but when we got there I couldn't believe that I was the only guy. So I kept it in my bag to see how it was going to go. They started handing out baseball caps to us. Now, some of our guys get so uptight with things like this—they get so concerned that someone is going to do something wrong that's going to make everyone look bad. I don't know—running naked through the Rangers locker room, that'd be wrong, but this? So I knew if I told them that I wanted to wear the helmet, they would've all said, 'No way.' So I kept it in my bag until the moment we were going out on the ice. The only other guy who knew I had it was the other captain of the team, Joe Byrne, and when he saw me pull it out he goes, 'What the hell are you doing?' But then I showed everyone the picture, and then they were all saying, 'Ya gotta wear it!'

"So we go out on the ice, and I'm standing there at the end of the runway next to Joe Byrne. Messier comes out, and I say, 'Joe, I'm going to give Messier my hat. He has to wear it—how can he say no?' Joe's looking at me and he's saying, 'Are you fucking nuts? They're going to kill you. Someone's going to chase you across the ice—they don't know what you're going to do.' But I say, 'Come on, they know who we are.' So we're kicking it around like this in a matter of seconds, and I'm like, 'If I don't do it now, it's over.' So I just said, 'I'm outta here.'

"I started skating across, but it was pitch black at that end of the ice. I just took my time and made sure I didn't trip and make a fool out of anybody. But the crowd could see me coming, and they got louder and louder, and the next thing you know I'm at Mark.

"He looks at me, and he's smirking—and I'm thinking, 'I just skated all the way over here, there's no way I'm just going to hand my hat to him and skate away.' So Mark looks at me and says, 'They don't know you're doing this, do they?' And I laugh and go, 'No.' That's why he was smirking. He goes, 'I love it! It's great!' So Lindros is next to him, and they were looking at each other, laughing. So then I said to him, 'Mark, the guy on my hat is Ray Downey. He's the first captain of the Fire Department hockey team. He was lost at the trade center. And you would do us an honor if you could wear the helmet for a few minutes. I'm sure you've got stuff to do, make speeches and stuff like that.' And he was great. He says, 'I'll do whatever I can. I'll wear it as long as I can.' I laughed and said, 'It's probably not going to fit on your head.' He's got that frickin' huge head. It looked weird, sitting on top of his head. If I would've known that was going to take place, I would've taken the biggest helmet we had."

As Messier stood on the Rangers' blue line wearing McGee's fire helmet, with Ray Downey's picture stuck on the front, the Buffalo Sabres were introduced as "fellow New Yorkers," and they skated out en masse. Predictably, the crowd booed, but slowly the jeers morphed into applause as the fans realized that the Sabres, instead of their usual bison-head crest, had "NEW YORK" emblazoned down their chests, just like the Rangers. It was the perfect gesture, and Messier had a role in its conception. "It was Mess who wanted to create two special jerseys for that night," Rosasco said. "There wasn't enough time for CCM to make 'em, and I'm pretty sure it was Mark Piazza on our staff who said, 'Why don't we put "New York" on both?' But it was Mess's idea to have special jerseys to wear."

Now John Davidson took the microphone. "Tonight," he said, "not only are we celebrating the return of Rangers hockey, we are celebrating the return of New York City, the city we're all privileged to call home. Rangers hockey has been a part of this city for seventy-six years, and since the very beginning the men and women who have followed the team are the same people who held jobs in the World Trade Center, the same men and women who rushed down to the towers and who worked twenty-four-hour shifts in the days that followed and are still there today. We as an organization have always been proud of our fans, but as New Yorkers we have never been as inspired and humbled by your show of strength as we have in the last few weeks."

A video was shown on the scoreboard, and instead of the overt patriotism of the music chosen for the first exhibition game, Bruce Springsteen's "Land of Hope and Dreams" provided the backdrop for scenes of the recovery effort, candlelight memorial services, and the ruins of the trade center. With all hope lost of finding survivors now that three weeks had elapsed since the attacks, the focus had shifted from one of shock and overwhelming grief to one more characterized by a feeling of dull, constant pain and respect for those lost, and the video was refreshingly light on expressions of jingoism. This was all the more notable because a few hours before the Rangers took the ice, the United States announced the start of its bombing campaign in Afghanistan against Al Qaeda and the Taliban-led government. Although there was overwhelming support for the bombing across the country, in New York the sentiment tended to be more nuanced, as many felt uneasy at the prospect of hitting civilians—which was, after all, more or less what their own city had experienced. The well-spoken Richter was one of those who had already expressed his ambivalence. "This is no cowboy movie, something to be glib about," he told Johnette Howard of *Newsday*. "It just scares me. There's a lot of rage you feel when somebody takes this liberty within your own country. Okay, acknowledge that it's there. At the same time, do something constructive about it. Maybe there are solutions to problems that don't involve bombing other innocent people."

Davidson next introduced five men from Ground Zero, all of whom wore the uniforms of their respective trades: a Port Authority police officer who had been trapped for four hours before being rescued; a union ironworker removing debris at the site; a heavy-equipment operator from a different union; a fireman from Ladder Company 24, down the street from the Garden; and a New York City policeman whose arm was injured when the first tower came down. Messier skated over to them, presenting them with a framed, signed sweater, then called them to stand around the sweater for a photo. Then he put McGee's fire helmet back on, but thought better of it, and skated over to the microphone at center ice.

The crowd started to cheer, and Messier acknowledged them by holding the fire helmet aloft once again, turning to face each corner of the rink. The cheers mounted. Finally he leaned over the mike and, speaking without notes or a script to refer to, said this: "On behalf of the players and the entire Rangers organization, we'd like to express our deepest sympathies to the families and friends that were lost, but we'd also like to express our deep appreciation for all the firefighters, the police department, the rescue workers and all the volunteers who helped out so heroically. We as a group, and as an organization, I can't tell you how proud we are to represent this city and all of you. And we'd like to dedicate this season—from the top of the organization, from Mr. Dolan and the management and Mr. Sather, all the players, to the training staff and all the training room attendants—we'd like to dedicate this season to all of you, and all the heroes. Thank you."

With that, Messier returned to the blue line and took his place next to Lindros, who gave him a little pat and said, "Nice job." Messier nodded almost imperceptibly, and then, when a moment of silence was announced, he checked to see that Downey's photograph was still fixed to the front of

McGee's fire helmet before placing it back on his head. A children's chorus sang "God Bless America," a city policewoman sang the national anthem, and the ceremonies were over. Everything about the ceremonies struck the perfect chord, but in retrospect it is Messier who stands out as the most memorable figure.

"That speech was 100 percent Mark," Rosasco says. "He's as good as anyone I've ever seen at capturing the moment and saying the appropriate thing. He's incredible about that. He does it himself, and it's not like he sits down and writes something out. He thinks about it, obviously—I didn't spring it on him before the game. We talk about it ahead of time; we plan out the whole ceremony. I don't know how to put into words what it is about Mark, but it's an intangible quality that not very many people have."

For McGee, Messier's qualities are tangible, which is why he was drawn to him. "Why Mark? Me being a hockey fan, and Mark's one of the legends of hockey, and not only that, he's the leader of the Rangers, and he's one of the symbols of the strength of New York, if you want to look at it that way. That's what Ray Downey was like for us on the hockey team. He was always around, always a perfect gentleman. Here he was the highest-decorated guy, I'd walk by him at seminars and he'd always stop and say, 'Hiya, Larry, how's it going?' Never gave you the brush-off. Kind of like what you'd expect from Mark, not knowing him that well. That similar strength, but also the compassion to let you know, 'Hey, how's it going, I'm here, we'll get through this.'

"I don't think the reaction would have been the same if it had been Leetch or Richter without a helmet, great as they are. It's just that magnetism, that right moment, that mix that made it work. It wouldn't have had that same impact on people who saw it, like my family. 'Wow,' they said. 'It was Messier.'"

Another thing that made the idea of Messier resonate so deeply in the aftermath of September 11 was the class connection the Rangers have with the white, working-class men, generally from the outer boroughs, who make up practically the entire fire department, a big majority of the ironworkers and construction workers who cleared Ground Zero, and a good portion of the city and Port Authority police departments as well as the financial managers and traders who worked at the trade center. Of the five rescue personnel introduced on the Garden ice at the opener, all were men and four were white (the fifth was Asian). The city's football, baseball, and basketball teams are predominantly black and Latino, as they are everywhere in America, but the Rangers, of course, are not, and the city's hockey fans, generally, are not.

Messier was only one of scores of celebrities whose fame got them into Ground Zero in the days following the attacks; many of them actually stayed on site as volunteers alongside the many regular citizens who managed to get down to the site to help out. And the presence of no celebrity at Ground Zero, including Messier, ever came close to overshadowing those lost or the recovery workers. But in terms of New York's sports teams, only Yankees manager Joe Torre matched Messier in terms of resonance with the firefighters, ironworkers, and construction workers who were the most visible recovery workers on the debris pile—a surprising phenomenon, given hockey's low status and modest following in the metropolitan area. The Yankees, Mets, Giants, and Jets were all playing at the time of the attacks, yet despite the magnitude of those teams' stars, and the success especially of the Yankees (who in October made another enthralling—and at this particular time, uplifting—World Series run, only to lose on the last pitch of game seven), no sports star meant more than Messier.

White, working-class men from Brooklyn, Queens, Staten Island, Long Island, and New Jersey, the demographic group hardest hit by the attacks, are the Rangers' main support, and it is they more than any other New Yorkers who know and understand what Messier means. A different disaster with different victims would have meant different touchstones. But considering the nature of the World Trade Center catastrophe, it is understandable that Messier became a touchstone, just as it is understandable that the most emotionally resonant music that was created in the year following the disaster came from Bruce Springsteen.

The Rangers beat the Sabres on opening night, 5–4, on an overtime goal by Brian Leetch. Later, the sweaters worn by both teams were auctioned off to benefit the Twin Towers Fund, raising a total of $215,000; at $20,010, Messier's commanded the highest price. Ten days later, he attended the Concert for New York at Radio City Music Hall—his face beaming in the audience while Springsteen, Neil Young, Paul McCartney, Alicia Keys, Sting, and Jewel performed, his recorded voice greeting some of those who called in to donate. He was one of more than a dozen Canadian celebrities who appeared in ads for the Canada Loves New York campaign, an effort that brought thousands of Canadians to the city in a show of support that passed virtually unnoticed in the city itself, but which generated millions of dollars for New York merchants still reeling from the loss of business that followed the attacks.

In late October, ESPN.com conducted an Internet poll asking who were "the most beloved athletes in New York history." Messier finished fourth, behind only Babe Ruth, Don Mattingly, and Mickey Mantle—making him the top-ranked non-Yankee and non-baseballer—and ahead of Lou Gehrig, Patrick Ewing, Joe Namath, Joe DiMaggio, Lawrence Taylor, Thurman Munson, and a host of other icons such as Willie Mays, Derek Jeter, Yogi Berra, Reggie Jackson, Phil Simms, Willis Reed, Jackie Robinson, and Tom Seaver. The only other hockey player to get more than a tiny smattering of votes was former Rangers goalie Ed Giacomin.

Messier had become more than just one of the city's most respected athletes ever, he was a symbol for the city itself. The 2001–02 season was getting under way, and as it proceeded the pain and grief of the attacks would lift, but slowly, slowly. Eventually, it became possible to think about hockey again.

THE MESSIAH IN WINTER

I n New York, it took an entire year for the grief of September 11 to begin to lift. Playing hockey helped, but as he passed his forty-first birthday, Messier just couldn't play like he used to anymore.

Of all the injury-riddled seasons of his long career, 2001–02 was his worst. The primary culprit was an injury to his left shoulder, where he had developed bone spurs and chronic pain in the rotator cuff. In Toronto he underwent ultrasound treatment—legal in Canada but not in the United States—but it did not work quickly enough. Finally, on March 1, having already missed twenty games, he entered St. Vincent's Hospital in the West Village and underwent the first surgery of his career.

The Rangers had started the season strong, and as late as December 29 they held first place in the Eastern Conference. But then Messier and Eric Lindros went down (Lindros sustained a mild concussion, then two knee injuries and a foot injury). By the day of Messier's surgery the Rangers were tied for the eighth and final playoff spot. Messier's statistics were modest—7–16–23 in 41 games, which would wind up being good enough only for thirteenth place on the team in scoring—but it was hoped that if the Rangers made the playoffs for the first time in five years, he would be ready to play. His one bright spot had come on December 15. Though he was barely able to skate because of back spasms, Messier scored a goal in a 4–2 win over Buffalo at the Garden. It was the 1,800th point of his career. Only Wayne Gretzky and Gordie Howe had scored as many.

That day, the selections for the 2002 Canadian Olympic team were announced. Theo Fleury, back from his recovery program for alcohol addiction, was one of those chosen, and, in fact, the Rangers had nine players for various national teams in their lineup. But by now no one expected Messier to be selected, even though Wayne Gretzky was running Team Canada with help from Kevin Lowe. In February, Messier watched the Olympic tournament on television and saw Canada beat the U.S. in Salt Lake City for the gold medal, recapturing the world title it had lost when he had trouble facing his American friends in the 1996 World Cup, and which it failed to recapture when he was left off the Olympic team in 1998. Everyone agreed that after the speed and passion of the Olympics, the watered-down, slogging version of the game played in the NHL was a disappointment.

Sather pushed hard to get the Rangers to the postseason. He and Messier visited the Rangers' farm club in Hartford and evaluated the talent there—Messier playing the role of shadow assistant GM in a way he never openly played it in Vancouver—but there was not much help to be had in the AHL. It would have to come from elsewhere. Sather, the former advocate of small-market teams, fiscal frugality, and building from within, had been handed a blank check by James Dolan and told to go out and sign whomever he wanted, price be damned. At the trade deadline, he grabbed Pavel Bure from Florida. Bure, Messier's old Canucks teammate, still had the soft hands of a sniper, but his injured knees were questionable. Nevertheless, he scored 11 goals in 10 games as a Ranger, and the brittle Lindros returned to finish with 36 markers.

But despite a late spurt, the Rangers missed the playoffs again, and so did Messier, hitting the golf course early for his fifth straight year. The press and Ranger fans saw the team's $70 million payroll, the second highest in the game, as the embodiment of mismanagement by team executives. They believed the players were spoiled, pampered, and lazy, although Messier was exempt from this judgment.

What was galling was that hockey's highest payroll belonged to the Detroit Red Wings, who won the Stanley Cup in 2002. They even had the one player who was older than Messier: Igor Larionov, the man Messier helped shut down in the '87 Canada Cup. Larionov played superbly in a limited role in the Wings' Cup run. Chris Chelios, only one year younger than Messier, was terrific, logging a lot of ice time on defense. The performance of these two oldsters showed that in the NHL of the new millennium, age need not be an issue. That meant that Messier was not necessarily an anomaly for continuing to play—but it also meant that he could be expected to play better.

Messier's linemates came and went, his teammates came and went, his coaches came and went. Only Messier, Leetch, and Richter were constants. Old friends and rivals appeared and reappeared in the revolving door powered by the Rangers' constant dealing. Darius Kasparaitis became a Ranger. So did Kirk McLean, Vladimir Malakhov, Tom Poti, Sandy McCarthy, Radek Dvorak, and dozens of others. Ron Low was relieved of his coaching duties at the end of the '01–02 season, and Sather replaced him with Bryan Trottier, the smoldering centerman who defined Messier-like qualities with the Islanders before Messier helped dethrone that dynasty and replace it with his own.

But before Sather hired Trottier, it was later revealed, he offered the head-coaching job to Messier. "He did ask me last year if I was going to play," Messier said in January 2003, referring to a conversation he had with Sather in the summer of 2002, "and if I didn't, would I be interested in coaching the team. I said I didn't know if I was going to play. And he said, 'Well, if you don't play, would you be interested in coaching?'

"Glen has been asking me to do that for a long time, but I'm a player right now and I don't want to coach," Messier continued. "I have a lot of respect for the coaching fraternity. I don't think coaching is easy. I don't pretend that I could come in here and coach without any experience whatsoever. I know what a good coach means to a team. I saw what Marc Crawford's done in Vancouver. I saw what Mike Keenan did here. I saw what a good coach can do for a team. So I'm under no illusion that because I've played the game and been involved and won before that that automatically translates into being a coach."

At training camp in Burlington, Vermont, in September 2002, there was Messier again, ready to start his twenty-fifth professional season, loving every moment of being a hockey player. Doug and Victor watched from the stands at the university rink as he led his team in an intrasquad scrimmage, Doug silent and watchful, Victor yelling and jumping with anxiety, as if it were a playoff game seven. Afterward, Mark appeared below the stands, clad only in a towel wrapped round his waist, calling up to his uncle. "Come on!" he shouted. "We can get in a quick workout before we go!" Victor called back, "Okay!" and bounded down the steps, disappearing into the weight room. Up in the seats high above one of the goals, Glen Sather explained that Messier wanted to play not only the coming season, but the 2003–04 season as well.

The Rangers went nowhere in '02–03. They seemed rudderless under the direction of Trottier, whose demeanor was quiet and patient, but who shuffled lines around so often it seemed to confuse the players. Players started leaking their dissatisfaction to reporters.

On the eve of his forty-second birthday, Messier seemed to announce that he was stepping back a bit from the duties of the captaincy so that others, notably Lindros and first-year Ranger Bobby Holik, known for his verbosity from his years with the Devils, could step to the fore. "I think at some point—and taking a page from Phil Jackson's book—sometimes it's good to take a step back and force other people to assume a bigger role and take more responsibility," Messier said. "Sometimes, for the success of the team, you need to do certain things at certain times. And I thought it was a good thing to let things work out this year and let other people take, hopefully, a stronger presence."

It was a bland statement on the face of it, but it took the skills of a kremlinologist to read between the lines. Messier was very craftily letting the press and the players know that as far as he was concerned, whatever was said about Trottier was fair game. And with that statement Messier also gave himself full deniability—if Trottier was going to be let go, it wouldn't be because of anything Messier said. It was another deft political maneuver by the consummate dressing-room politician. "It's not that I'm taking a step back in my leadership role," Messier said. "I'm just trying to get more people involved. The more people who feel responsible for winning and losing, the better off the team will be for it." Two weeks later, Trottier was fired.

By now Messier had finally accepted a role as third-line center, behind Lindros and Petr Nedved. Under both Trottier and Sather, who finished out the year as coach, his ice time was down to 18 minutes a game, but he still took a lot of shifts on the power play and killing penalties. He scored only 18 goals and 22 assists for 40 points in 78 games, sixth best on the team. His minus-2 mark was about average, but it had been six straight years since he'd finished the season with a plus. And because the Rangers finished in ninth place, five points out of the final postseason berth, it was also six straight years since he had played springtime hockey. Mark Messier, once the greatest leader in team sports, had failed to captain his team to the playoffs for more than half a decade.

Still, Messier had the respect, gratitude, and deference of New York fans and the New York media, and almost no one openly suggested that he should hang up his skates for good. When politely asked on breakup day whether he would be back for the next season, he gave the same response he annually gave on breakup day: he would decide over the summer.

Meanwhile, Messier lived the life of a New Yorker, or at least the life of a New Yorker earning more than $5 million a year. His carousing days long over, he continued to live with Kim Clark, his companion from Vancouver. They went out to restaurants and shows, saw friends, vacationed in Hilton Head, where by now Messier had a whole complex of seaside homes and cottages. The hockey world continued to move and change without him and without the Rangers. The Mighty Ducks of Anaheim reached the seventh game of the Stanley Cup final, led in part by their inspirational oldsters Steve Thomas, 39, and Adam Oates, 40. They were beaten by the Rangers' trans-Hudson rivals, the Devils, captained by Scott Stevens, whom Messier had obliterated with a body check in that unforgettable semifinal in 1994, and backstopped by Martin Brodeur, whom Messier had beaten for two of his three goals in that magical game six, nine years ago. Messier's friend from his teenage days back in Edmonton, Ken Daneyko, now 40 years old, lifted the Cup one last time before hanging up his skates for good after twenty seasons in New Jersey.

Messier had been around a long, long time. In 2003, he found himself playing against Niklas Hagman of the Florida Panthers, the son of Matti Hagman, one of his original Edmonton linemates. But then, Messier's career had always been full of synchronicities, from when he was a boy of 17 taking a face-off against Gordie Howe, whose records he would eventually challenge, to taking the place of Wayne Gretzky as a centerman on the roster of the Indianapolis Racers, to winning his last Stanley Cup alongside the old friends with whom he'd won his first. He finished the '02–03 season as the third leading scorer in NHL history, just six points shy of Howe's 1,850. He had scored against 155 different goaltenders since 1979 (he victimized Richard Brodeur 20 times, more than anyone else) and had set up goals for 148 teammates. He assisted on tallies by his free-spirited linemate Glenn Anderson an astounding 167 times; his greatest admirer, Adam Graves, 98 times; his best friend Gretzky, 68 times; the high-flying Finn, Jari Kurri, 59 times; the refugee from Pittsburgh, Craig Simpson, 45 times; the object of Mike Keenan's wrath, Tony Amonte, 41 times; and his dearest friend in New York, Brian Leetch, 40 times. On and on the list goes, all the way to the last man he set up near the end of the '02–03 campaign, a hard-working Slovak named Ronald Petrovicky—1,168 assists in all.

The July 1 free agency deadline passed without Messier signing a contract extension with the Rangers. They dealt his rights to the San Jose Sharks, but it was merely a paper transaction, a maneuver that preserved the Rangers' chances of re-signing their eternal captain. The weeks passed without Messier giving any word, even to his close friends, on whether he'd be back for another season that would take him past his 43rd birthday. It felt a little bit like holdouts past, although now the picture was clouded by Messier's age, by the fiscal uncertainty caused by the labor strife expected to accompany the expiration of the NHL-NHLPA collective bargaining agreement after the '03–04 season, and by the possibility, however remote, that he might not finish his career in New York. It would feel strange indeed to see Messier, his neck ever so slightly wrinkled now but his skull still bald and hard as a bullet, his gaze still as alert and sharp as a pair of lasers, his laugh still as big and infectious as when he was a tot in that Christmastime home movie, in a uniform other than that of the Rangers—unless it was the uniform of the Oilers. And indeed, at the end of July, Doug Messier said he had recently golfed with his son's old friends, Edmonton GM Kevin Lowe and coach Craig MacTavish. "Kevin," Doug reported, "said he'd love to have Mark, it being the 25th year of the Oiler franchise and Mark's 25th year, and he can move past Gordie Howe in points. Not that Mark's ever been interested in records. It's Stanley Cups with him."

In August, Messier's son, Lyon, now a six-foot-tall Junior B defence-man in Tecumseh, Ontario, able to do 52 pushups in one minute, visited Hilton Head. In September, Messier finally signed on for another year. He would break Howe's record as a Ranger.

But for all the big games, big goals, big hits, and Stanley Cups, people who know Messier well keep coming back to one thing, the generosity of his spirit. He remains as close as ever to everyone in his close-knit family, and he continues to share everything with them, including late-night clubbing, exotic vacations, and living the good life in general. The same family that allowed him so much freedom so soon, that granted him the latitude to quit school in grade 12 and to live more or less unsupervised and get into some close scrapes as a young man, allowed him ultimately to grow into a worldly, experienced man who had traveled well and widely, and who contributed so much to the communities in which he lived. He and his family, one of his friends has said, are true Westerners, remarkably generous, open, expansive people, always glad to include others in their lives. These qualities—not as evident to those on the outside but so consistently and emphatically talked about by those on the inside—are what make so many people so loyal to Messier.

As hard as it is to imagine him in a uniform other than that of the Broadway Blues or the Oil, it's even harder to imagine Messier never wearing a uniform again. But that day will come, as it did for his old friend Gretzky—even if he clearly doesn't want it to. Way back in Edmonton, before the fame and the championships, he said that the man he'd really like to be would be Mick Jagger. And as coincidence would have it, the Rolling Stones played Madison Square Garden in 2003. There, prancing about and singing with the vigor and ease of a man thirty-five years his junior, was Jagger, running the show and bringing the crowd to a frenzy over more than two hours of high-energy performance, an ageless wonder, still having a blast at the center of it all. If Messier could have his way, you have to think, it would be that way for him, too, for years and years to come. "To be a rock 'n' roll star and drive the fans crazy," he once said, a long-haired, teenage prodigy, grinning in a frigid Alberta winter. "Would that be a rush or what?"

BIBLIOGRAPHY & ACKNOWLEDGMENTS

A twenty-five-year pro career is roughly twice as long as that of your average hockey great, which means chronicling it comprehensively takes roughly twice the research and twice the thought. Since I am incapable of even half the thought required for most simple tasks, it's a good thing I got four times more help than most writers get.

I found that last calculation difficult enough, and I'm still not sure it's right. But it only proves my point, which is that between my own shortcomings and the volume of events I tried to cover, I find I am deeply indebted to the efforts of many people. First among those are the newspaper beat reporters and columnists who follow hockey teams day in, day out, for close to ten months of the year. Their job is incredibly difficult, yet we take what they do for granted, forgetting how thoroughly they keep us informed of what's going on with our favorite teams on a daily basis. But now, anyone armed with the power of the computer and a Nexis password will gain a renewed sense of appreciation for the Domesday Book of exhaustive detail they have assembled over the decades. In telling Messier's story I have tried to name these writers within the text whenever appropriate. Mostly they are from the papers in Edmonton, New York, and Vancouver, but there are many others, too, who wrote for papers in other cities or for wire services, but who added so much of value to the Messier record. I have tried to credit them as well, but alas, their accounts of goals scored on the ice or of things said in the dressing room sometimes blend into the background, as they do when we read their work, uncredited, in the papers or on the Web.

If daily newspapers provide the first draft of history, magazines provide the second draft. Every magazine article I quote from is duly noted and the author credited in the text. Here, though, I give special props to *Sports Illustrated*, *Maclean's*, *ESPN the Magazine*, and most especially to the good old *Hockey News*.

Many books proved indispensable. Here too I have tried to credit quotes and observations gleaned from books previously published, although sometimes that task was complicated when I found that the quote or observation had actually originated somewhere else, usually in a newspaper or magazine article. In any case, each book was immensely helpful in its own way, as were a handful of videos. I relied on some more than others. First there is the biography of Messier written by Rick Carpiniello, which goes by different titles in the U.S. and Canada. The American version is called *Messier: Hockey's Dragonslayer* (McGregor, 1999), the Canadian version *Messier: Steel on Ice* (Stoddart, 1999). It is an excellent book that briefly but nicely summarizes Messier's early years with the Oilers, then zeroes in with a highly detailed, closely observed account of Messier's first stint with the Rangers. It is briskly written and packed with anecdotes and fly-on-the-wall observations that only a longtime beat guy like Carpiniello could have compiled. All in all, it's a must-read for any Ranger fan. The other Messier bio that anyone interested in the subject must have is the video/DVD *Mark Messier: Leader, Champion, Legend*, produced and written by Darryl Lepik (USA Home Entertainment, 2000). It contains all the highlights of Messier's career (and has even more features in its DVD form, which is how I saw it) and a number of valuable interviews with Messier and his family. It is as yet the only authorized account of Messier's career. There's some spin at work in it, so you lose a little bit there, but you gain a lot by hearing directly from the man himself.

In following Messier's early pro career, *Champions: The Making of the Edmonton Oilers*, by Kevin Lowe with Stan and Shirley Fischler (Prentice-Hall Canada, 1988) is an excellent guide, filled with plenty of anecdotes and smart observations. Not quite as pithy as Lowe's book but still chock-full of great stuff about the Oilers are *Gretzky: An Autobiography*, by Wayne Gretzky and Rick Reilly (HarperCollins, 1990), *Looking Out for Number One*, by Dave Semenko with Larry Tucker (Stoddart, 1989), and the lyrical *The Game of Our Lives*, the classic by Peter Gzowski (McClelland & Stewart, 1982). For more background on how closely intertwined the roots of the Messier family are with those of the game in the West, see *Alberta on Ice: The History of Hockey in Alberta Since 1893*, edited by Gary W. Zeman (Westweb Press, 1986). To examine how Peter Pocklington's financial ups and downs affected the Oilers' on-ice fortunes, see *The Glory Barons: The Saga of the Edmonton Oilers*, by Douglas Hunter (Viking, 1999). A must-see video for any Oilers or Messier fan is *The Boys on the Bus: A Teammate's View of a Year with the Edmonton Oilers*, directed by Bob McKeown

(McKeown/McGee Films, 1987). The teammate in the title is the narrator, Lowe, who was quite busy in those days chronicling the Oilers from the inside. Another video, harder to find and not nearly as good, called *The Boys Are Back*, directed by Bob McKeown and Michael Boland (McKeown/McGee Films, 1988), has fascinating footage of Gretzky's return to Edmonton for his first game as a Los Angeles King.

There is a long tradition of operatically titled books depicting the utter horror that is the existence of the New York Rangers, and a couple of them provide a terrific account of Messier's arrival and ascendancy with the team. First there is *Broadway Blues: The Rangers' 12-Month Tour of Hockey Hell*, by Frank Brown (Sagamore, 1993), an account of the '92–93 season. It has about it, as season chronicles usually do, a bit of the beat guy's notebook dump. But Brown is a fine reporter and passionate Ranger fan (and now the NHL's chief flack) who is there for the big Messier-Roger Neilson blowup. Then there is *Losing the Edge: The Rise and Fall of the Stanley Cup Champion Rangers* (Simon & Schuster, 1995), Barry Meisel's superb story of the club's season to remember and the one immediately following. Meisel got stuff no one else got, and this book is required reading not just for Ranger fans, but for all hockey fans, period. For a day-by-day review of Messier's return to New York in 2000–01, scan Carpiniello's *Nightmare on 33rd Street: A Long Season With the New York Rangers* (Albion Press, 2001). It's not nearly as engrossing as his excellent first book, but it's interesting to note the disillusionment Carpiniello seems to feel towards Messier the second time around.

For a good summary of Mike Keenan's Stanley Cup year with the Rangers as well as his sojourn with Messier in Vancouver, see Jeff Gordon's *Keenan: The High Times and Misadventures of Hockey's Most Controversial Coach* (Stoddart, 2000). Another good source for Messier's stay with the Canucks is Kerry Banks's engaging and insightful *Pavel Bure: The Riddle of the Russian Rocket* (Greystone, 1999). For getting inside Messier's head while he was in Vancouver, there are some fascinating passages in *The Complete Player: The Psychology of Winning Hockey*, by Dr. Saul L. Miller (Stoddart, 2001).

Messier's international career comes under far less scrutiny than his NHL play, but there are a couple of useful sources. For an inside look at Messier during the European tour organized by Gretzky during the 1994–95 NHL lockout, read Roy MacGregor's moving *The Home Team: Fathers, Sons, and Hockey* (Viking, 1995). And for a nifty overview of Messier's Canada Cup and World Cup exploits, see *The World Cup of Hockey: A History of Hockey's Greatest Tournament*, by Joe Pelletier and Patrick Houda (Warwick, 2003).

Other books provided valuable background, stories, and statistical analysis: *Why Is the Stanley Cup Still in Mario Lemieux's Swimming Pool?* by Kevin Allen (Triumph, 2001); *99: My Life in Pictures*, by Wayne Gretzky with John Davidson (Dan Diamond & Associates, 1999); *Fire on Ice*, by Eric Lindros with Randy Starkman (HarperCollins, 1992); *Jagr: An Autobiography*, by Jaromir Jagr and Jan Smid (68 Productions, 1997); *Mario*, by Lawrence Martin (Lester, 1993); *Boss: The Mike Bossy Story*, by Mike Bossy and Barry Meisel (McGraw-Hill, 1988); *The New York Islanders: Countdown to a Dynasty*, by Barry Wilner (Human Kinetics, 1984); *The Top 100 NHL Players of All Time*, edited by Steve Dryden (McClelland & Stewart, 1998); *Pride and Passion: 25 Years of the New York Islanders*, by Stan Fischler and Chris Botta (New York Islanders Hockey Club, 1996); *Breakaway '87–88*, by Stan and Shirley Fischler with Vic Morren (Totem, 1987); *Bad Boys 2* (McGraw-Hill Ryerson, 1994) and *Hockey Stars Speak* (Warwick, 1996), both by Stan Fischler; and *My 26 Stanley Cups: Memories of a Hockey Life*, by Dick Irvin (McClelland & Stewart, 2001). A couple of other books provided itching and a rash: *The Death of Hockey* (MacMillan Canada, 1998) and *The Hockey Compendium* (McClelland & Stewart, 2001), both by Karl-Eric Reif and myself. Finally, these dependable statistical standards are vital for any work about contemporary hockey: *The National Hockey League Official Guide and Record Book* (published annually); *Total Hockey: The Official Encyclopedia of the National Hockey League* and *Total Stanley Cup* (both Dan Diamond & Associates).

For their help in the actual writing of this book, I owe thanks to many people, beginning with my wonderful agent, David Johnston. At Doubleday Canada, where everyone was always patient, understanding, professional, and, I'll say it again, patient, I especially thank Brad Martin, Maya Mavjee, Nick Massey-Garrison, Christine Innes, Scott Richardson, Suzanne Brandreth, Valerie Applebee, and Carla Kean, and, at Triumph Books, Mitch Rogantz. Lloyd Davis did a great job, editing smoothly and skillfully.

Strange but true: two women, both named Meg Taylor, were hugely helpful. Meg Taylor of Toronto edited the early stages of the book. Beyond her generous supportiveness, she graciously played host to me at her home in the Beaches neighborhood one beautiful summer evening after two straight dusty days of driving all the way from Edmonton. Meg Taylor of New York was my companion for that transcontinental drive, hitting all the high points on the Messier grand tour from New York to Portland, Oregon, to Vancouver to Edmonton and home again. She also conducted several interviews for this book, did research, tracked people down, and spilled inside info, much of which she has picked up over the years in her work for various publications and Web sites. I was lucky to have Meg's smarts to call on.

People went out of their way to help in many ways and many places. In Portland, thanks to Carol McMenamin and Sandy Macomber at *The Oregonian*. In Vancouver, Bob Mackin, Kerry Banks, Gary Mason, and Peter Sheldon kindly offered valuable advice, and Catherine Urquart of Global TV took time out from a busy day to find an old videotape. A special thank you to the Shepherds of New Westminster, Chris and Michelle and their upstanding daughters Montana, Mikayla, and Christa, for their warm hospitality and entrée to Salmonbellies lacrosse. In Edmonton, thanks to Dominique Ritter, Rick "The Stick" Elaschuk, and especially Jim Matheson and Debbie Dittrick of *The Edmonton Journal*, and to Murray Greig, knowledgable dinner companion and former WHL goon. Particularly selfless in their help was the great group of guys at the Society for International Hockey Research, including Martin Harris, John Kreiser, Stu McMurray, and Ernie Fitzsimmons. My gratitude also goes out to Matt Hays of Montreal, to Benny Ercolani of the National Hockey League in Toronto, to Ann Elizabeth and Eddie Burke of the Uniformed Firefighters Association in New York and William Kammerer of the FDNY hockey team, to the public relations staff of the New York Rangers, and in Jersey City, to listener-supported WFMU for keeping me company through another book.

Big thanks to Stu Hackel, new father and brilliant hockey mind, for allowing me full access to his voluminous library and for offering all the right advice. A shout-out, too, to the hockey mavens in New York who helped out, starting with the Hockey Maven himself, Stan Fischler, as well as Joe Lapointe, Guy Lawson, Hal Fischer, Rick Carpiniello, Bob Lipsyte, Tom Mariam, and Alyce Appleman Mariam. At my day gig at *The New York*

Times Magazine, thanks to all, especially Rob Hoerburger, for tolerating the mounds of hockey books stacked everywhere. Thanks to my uncle, Manny Winopol, for putting me up and for putting up with me, and to his fellow Torontonian, the brilliant, ever-inspiring Dave Bidini. My biggest thanks go to Karl-Eric Reif, my old friend and longtime writing partner, who not only spent hours in the basement of his home outside Buffalo wading through crumbling copies of *The Hockey News* in search of Messier tidbits, but then slogged through the entire manuscript and provided, as always, the perfect arcane references and barbed burlesque to liven up my wooden prose. He's the best writer I've ever had the honor to work with.

Finally, I owe everything to my father, Irwin Klein, my mother, Frances Winopol Klein, and my sister, Phyllis Prussin, and her family. I can never thank them enough for their help, their generosity, and their love. Meanwhile, my kids, Asher and Grace, owe me big time. Still, every day they make me proud to be their father. And, as ever, a kiss to Danya Reich, the smartest, funniest, most beautiful rec-league basketball player in the world. As they say, much respect to the ballers.

CREDITS

Every effort has been made to contact copyright holders; in the event of an inadvertent omission or error, please notify the publisher.

Messier: Hockey's Dragonslayer by Rick Carpiniello. Copyright © Rick Carpiniello, 1999. Used by permission, McGregor Publishing.
From *The Game of Our Lives* by Peter Gzowski. Used by permission, McClelland & Stewart Ltd. *The Canadian Publisher*.
From *The Glory Barons* by Douglas Hunter. Copyright © Douglas Hunter, 1999. Reprinted by permission of Penguin Group (Canada).
From *The Home Team* by Roy McGregor. Copyright © Roy McGregor, 1995. Reprinted by permission of Penguin Group (Canada).
The Complete Player: The Psychology of Winning Hockey by Saul Miller. Copyright © Saul Miller, 2001. Used by permission of the author.
Gretzky: An Autobiography by Wayne Gretzky with Rick Reilly © 1990 Wayne Gretzky.
Looking Out for Number One by Dave Semenko. Copyright © Dave Semenko, 1990. Used by permission of the author.

INDEX